Praise for *Global Crossings*

"This compelling book is a must read for anyone on the vital yet contentious issue of immigration. *Global Crossings* puts a personal face on the issue, superbly arguing that restrictions on the basis of accident of birthplace have no economic or social justification, and in the hands of government are a dangerous infringement on individual liberty and human well-being."
— **Daniel L. McFadden**, Nobel Laureate in Economic Sciences;
    E. Morris Cox Professor of Economics, University of California, Berkeley

"*Global Crossings: Immigration, Civilization, and America* is a much needed antidote to the hysterical drivel that dominates the debate over immigration reform. The book demonstrates how important it is to adapt our immigration policy to the needs of our economy and to welcome those who will make a genuine contribution to our future prosperity. America's success as an immigrant nation is in danger from those who would close our borders out of fear and ignorance. *Global Crossings* dispels both."
— **Linda L. Chavez**, former Director, U.S. Commission on Civil Rights

"*Global Crossings* dispels the myths over the crucial yet divisive issue of immigration. As a nation of immigrants, America has been enriched economically and culturally from these new arrivals, and Vargas Llosa shows why our future will depend on continuing to advance a welcoming immigration policy."
— **Stephen Moore**, former Senior Economist, U.S. Congress Joint
    Economic Committee; Founding President, Club for Growth; author,
    Who's the Fairest of Them All? The Truth about Opportunity, Taxes, and
    Wealth in America

"Why do people migrate? What motivates people to go from one country to another? Alvaro Vargas Llosa responds to these vital questions in his new book *Global Crossings: Immigration, Civilization, and America*. He leads us on a valuable tour of immigration throughout the world and then focuses on aspects of the history of immigration in the U.S. The book highlights the role of immigrants in the development of nations, throwing overboard the myth that immigrants cost more than they provide or take away the jobs of citizens.

Vargas Llosa encourages an 'open mind' which supports national policies that assimilate the cultural richness of immigrant groups and also fights against the criminalization of migration."

    —**Vicente Fox**, former President, Republic of Mexico

"Using facts, history, logic and his own personal experiences, Alvaro Vargas Llosa vividly demonstrates why immigration is almost always economically, culturally and morally beneficial. *Global Crossings* is an essential and highly readable, even riveting, tour de force."

    —**Richard K. Vedder**, Distinguished Professor of Economics,
    Ohio University

"Vargas Llosa's brilliant, scholarly book *Global Crossings* brings down the temperature of the immigration debate. In prose filled with analysis and stories, statistics and history, he shows that 'Hispanic' immigrants are nothing new—not 'barbarians' but future Americans. Theologically speaking, faith is a backward-looking identity, where you come from. Hope is the forward-looking project of your life, the answer to *Quo vadis*? Which way for America? For their benefit in every way, Americans need to be hopeful citizens of the world, as they have been. Vargas Llosa sees America in terms of hope, not faith, a 'credo,' as he puts it, of progress, not a catechism of nationalism. Long may *Global Crossings* flourish. I lift my lamp beside the Golden Door."

    —**Deirdre N. McCloskey**, Distinguished Professor of Economics, History,
    and English, University of Illinois at Chicago

"At a time when there is much hyperbole and hysteria about immigrants and immigration policy, Alvaro Vargas Llosa's path-breaking book *Global Crossings* delivers much needed level-headed insights into the nature of migration and the ramifications for the United States as a nation. Immigration is an immutable part of the American story and Vargas Llosa's contributions to the conversation are important, not just for exploring socioeconomic dynamics, but for providing a window into the personal experiences that are often lost in the larger debate."

    —**Mario H. Lopez**, President, Hispanic Leadership Fund

Global Crossings

Global Crossings

IMMIGRATION, CIVILIZATION, AND AMERICA

ALVARO VARGAS LLOSA

The INDEPENDENT INSTITUTE

Oakland, California

The Independent Institute 100 Swan Way, Oakland, CA 94621-1428
Telephone: 510-632-1366 Fax: 510-568-6040 Email: info@independent.org
Website: www.independent.org

Library of Congress Cataloging-in-Publication Data available

ISBN: 978-1-59813-133-8

Cover Design: Keith Criss
Cover Photo: Pali Rao/E+/Getty Images
Interior Design and Composition by Leigh McLellan Design

Contents

Acknowledgments

I WISH TO THANK Gabriel Gasave for his invaluable help in researching this book and his thoughtful comments on the successive versions that I came up with before I put the book into final form. Gabriel's passion for the topic of immigration was a constant source of inspiration for me.

I could not have written this book without the support of the Independent Institute, to which I have been attached for more than a decade now. I wish to express my gratitude to David and Mary Theroux in particular for believing in this project from the very beginning.

Several people had access to the manuscript and provided very valuable guidance and suggestions. Alexander Tabarrok, who patiently endured a reading of the very long first version as well as the following ones, steered me, among other things, towards a better selection of the dominant themes and a more functional structure. Roy M. Carlisle made useful suggestions regarding the need to separate some of the material relating to immigration in the United States from segments that deal with other countries. Finally, William Ratliff shared with me insightful observations regarding the cultural aspects of immigration and persuaded me to expand the focus on areas that could strengthen the essential argument.

Needless to say, none of the people mentioned above is in any way responsible for the content of the book.

Prologue
From Altar To Arizona

MY COMPANION AND I had driven about halfway along a secret dirt trail that connects Altar, a small town in Mexico's Sonora Desert, to Sásabe, a little known border crossing into Arizona's Altar Valley, when a burst of wind enveloped our car in thick dust and forced me to apply the brakes and bring the vehicle to a screeching halt. A big noise that sounded like a gigantic bird flapping its wings shook us out of the surprise. Something wasn't quite right.

"For almost 90 miles, you will hear nothing and see nothing but desert flora and fauna, and an occasional van carrying migrants," the priest who had obtained permission for us to use the trail from the local smugglers had said. "Eventually, you will reach an old brickyard, about ten miles from the legal border crossing. There the migrants take a detour to the left or to the right in order to get around the little border checkpoint located at the end of the village that sits near the area where the trail ends."

Suddenly, through the dust that had settled on the windscreen we saw a chopper landing awkwardly about twenty yards in front of us. Apparently the landscape had something more to offer than just nopal cactuses, biznagas, boojum trees, scorpions, black widows and coralillo snakes. "An Army helicopter," I thought, looking at the inscriptionless, military-green aircraft blocking our way.

Three men dressed in civilian clothes jumped out, clutching machine guns. They ran towards us keeping a good distance from one another, their bodies moving as if performing choreography. I opened the window and heard one of them yell at me in Spanish, "Where are you going?" I was about to explain that I was driving back to the United States after traveling for a week along the U.S.-Mexican border in connection with a book project. But before I could finish the sentence, the man, escorted by the other two, ran back to the chopper. They climbed aboard, and in no time the chopper was in the air; The visitors were out of our way.

My cell phone did not get reception at the moment, so I was unable to call the priest immediately to let him know about the government's visit. Twenty minutes later, a call finally came through from Altar. I explained to the priest what had happened.

"That was not the Army," he said. "It was Beltrán Leyva's people checking on you. Because the car is not a migrants' van, they wanted to make certain you were really you and not some rival gang member. The people who authorized you to use the trail on my recommendation probably passed on the message to higher-ups."

"Does that mean that they don't trust your word?" I asked, recovering from the shock of the encounter. "If that's the case, the superstition that killing a priest brings bad luck may not be enough insurance for you." No sooner had I uttered these words than I felt stupid for inadvertently offering a bit of humor at this inappropriate time.

"I think I am safe, but they like to check things," he replied.

Little did I know that December morning in 2009, that two days later Arturo Beltrán Leyva, the head of one of Mexico's most notorious drug cartels, active and feared in eleven Mexican states, would be hunted down and killed by the Mexican Marines after a two-hour battle in Cuernavaca, just south of Mexico City, and that a couple of weeks later his brother Carlos would be captured.

The trail led indeed to where the priest had indicated. A few miles before the trail's end, we came upon an apparently abandoned brickyard, from which two tiny detours led straight into Arizona some fifteen minutes away. We took the detour to the left, which crossed desert land punctuated by an innocuous-looking fence apparently set up to prevent cars, not people, from squeezing through. Beyond the brickyard, the detour trail leads to a hill—the *sierrita* they call it—and into a Papago reservation, an Indian tribe that prefers to call itself Tohono O'odham and whose main territory, in southeastern Arizona, stretches from Tucson to Ajo, and houses a few thousand members.

For a long time, the Papago tribesmen, a smaller number of whom live on the Mexican side, were free to come and go across the border, something they did frequently to take part in ritual ceremonies and other forms of exchange. In the mid-1990s, as tough restrictions in other parts of the U.S.-Mexican border drove illegal migration to the Sonora Desert, the flow of Papago tribesmen was abruptly interrupted. However, significant numbers of migrants continue to sneak in through this vast, labyrinthine desert. "We even get help from some Tohono O'odham people on the other side," I had been told repeatedly by some smugglers in Altar in the days prior to my venture along the trail to Sásabe, when I explored the town of Altar, whose life revolves entirely around clandestine migration.

After reaching the clandestine entry point into the United States, I went back to the brickyard and took the detour to the right this time, which led to the legal and little-used border crossing. The images of the days I had spent in Altar would accompany me for a long time.

• • •

In recent years, Altar has become a major staging point for illegal crossings. A sophisticated operation sends migrants into southeastern Arizona—not just into the Tohono O'odham Indian Reservation, but also into other parts of the so-called Tucson Sector, including the Sásabe Corridor. This corridor, including areas just east of the crossing, stretches north from the small border checkpoint at the village that bears the same name, across thousands of acres of wetlands, groves, and cottonwoods known as the Buenos Aires National Wildlife Reserve. Most of the routes, as I discovered on my way to Sásabe, are controlled by drug cartels.

It takes eight hours to drive from Ciudad Juárez, El Paso's twin city south of the Rio Grande, to Altar, across the Chihuahua and the Sonora deserts (it would take an hour or so less if it were not for the constant army checkpoints along the road). Altar has only one paved artery—the road connecting it to other cities. Near the road's start in Altar, the visitor is struck by the sight of the Nuestra Señora de Guadalupe parish behind which, facing the sacristy, is the plaza, the small square that holds the town together.

On the Sunday afternoon when I arrive in Altar, a priest is presiding over a funeral service for a man killed two years earlier by a drug gang member and whose body has just been discovered by the family. The overflowing crowd includes some young tough-looking locals, wearing sombreros and leather boots, cell phones in hand, pencils behind the right ear, eyes observing it all, especially entry and exit points to and from Altar. I will encounter these *polleros* (literally "chicken herders") time and again during the coming evening and the following morning as they guard the plaza, working for the smuggling rings that control the Altar operation.

Parked next to both curbs along the side streets are identical white vans with numbers marked on the windows. Those are the vehicles—*las bens,* they call them—that at some point will head for the secret trail to Sásabe carrying ten, twelve migrants each, mostly Mexican but also Central American and occasionally South American. The migrants will have spent the night in one of dozens of run-down guesthouses scattered around Altar and closely monitored by the top guys, such as the one functioning at the back end of Lupita's grocery store, where an aspiring border crosser can stay for 40 pesos (and a bit more if he or she wants to lie on something more comfortable than the floor and rest the head on some form of pillow) before embarking on the final leg of the adventure. That adventure may have started thousands of miles south of there, say in Oaxaca, in Mexico's southern area, where an *enganchador* working for one of the same smuggling rings that dominate Altar will have made contact and explained the deal. The operation will have almost certainly included a journey, strategically planned so as to elude population centers, on one of the chilly cargo trains—overflowing with other migrants and besieged by corrupt policemen and highwaymen—that connect Lechería, in Central Mexico, with various northern destinations.

Everywhere one looks, the signs of "the business" are here. Most of the stores sell knapsacks, first-aid kits and various utensils that will come in handy for the migrants on their way to Arizona. Other shops serve them breakfast on the morning of the crossing, while the migrants give each other courage and wait tensely for the *pollero* to signal that the van is ready. Then they will head towards the secret trail, where the guards at the entrance—employees of the drug lord who controls this route—will make sure that the vehicle number and the number of passengers matches the information previously given to them. Beside the gate leading into the desert trail, which stands opposite a gas station belonging to Pemex, the Mexican oil giant, a car carrying two or three *mascaritas* (literally "the little masked ones") make doubly sure nothing out of the ordinary happens (in all certainty the *mascaritas* are the ones who passed the information about my crossing under the priest's protection over to the higher-ups, triggering the verification process—chopper and all). The travel and border crossing costs 400 pesos per person, but another 50 pesos is usually charged for "extras," tacked on without the migrants' choice—part of the larger package that involves the safe delivery to the destination point.

When the migrants begin the final leg of the journey, they have been well briefed on the drill. They know that the problem will not be getting into the United States, but rather, staying alive during the three or four nights it will take them to trek across the Arizona desert toward Tucson. They are aware of the dangers, which include pumas and other mountain lions, and *bajadores*, as they call the highwaymen who are now also part of the American side of the landscape—not to mention the worst enemies of all—the U.S. Border Patrol Union Local 2544 that incessantly monitors the Tucson Sector border, as well as the Minutemen group of local ranchers who, adopting the legendary name belonging to a militia from the times of the Revolutionary War, search for immigrants from their pickup trucks and SUVs, automatic rifles and pistols in hand.

Part of the information given these migrants before they set out comes from the Casa del Migrante, a non-governmental organization run by the Catholic Church that has offices in various border cities and provides lodging to people aspiring to make it to the other side (increasingly, also to deportees expelled en masse from the United States). The Catholic Church is the only entity not directly linked to the human smuggling business allowed to operate by the gangs that control Altar and other parts of the Sonora Desert—hence my relatively safe passage. The local priest, who belongs to the Sonora diocese, maintains a working relationship with the gangs. He does not interfere too much, and he helps the migrants—for instance by giving them abundant information about the perils involved in the crossing. The briefing includes a video and samples of the kind of hostile flora and fauna the migrants will encounter on the way to the other side. "My job is to try to scare them," he tells me, "a bit like those Zen monks who do all kinds of nasty things to aspiring monks to make sure they know exactly what they are getting into in the hope that some will be put off."

This attempt to dissuade the migrants from leaving home and venturing into the unknown can be traced to the work of the founder of the Scalabrinian Fathers, the religious society founded by Giovanni Battista Scalabrini in Italy in the late nineteenth century. Scalabrini was a bishop who devoted much of his life to trying to dissuade Italian migrants from going to America and helping those who chose to leave so that they would not face horrendous hardship on the other side of the Atlantic. Although the Casa del Migrante in Mexico is run by the Dominican order today, it was founded by the Scalabrinian Fathers and continues to offer warnings, counsel, and help to migrants.

To those determined to make it across the border, the late Father Scalabrini is a powerful protective force—competing for their affection with Saint Toribio Romo, the "patron saint" of Mexicans trying to sneak into the United States who constitutes a fascinating symbol of the way in which migration and religion have become intertwined in a country where the Institutional Revolutionary Party persecuted and marginalized the Catholic Church for decades.

In the late 1920s, Father Toribio Romo was killed by soldiers in Jalisco—he was a victim of the Cristero War, as the persecution against the Catholic Church at the time is known. He was canonized together with the other victims of the Cristero War, but his name did not become a social force until the 1970s, when it mysteriously kept coming up in the tales of migrants. They reported having been helped by a priest, Toribio Romo, who had rescued them from the perils of the journey and helped them across the Río Grande. Some even claimed they had been caught by the border patrols and then set free by the same Toribio Romo. They did not speak of a ghost—a protective soul—but of an actual flesh-and-bone being assisting and guiding them. The reports, laden with details that rendered them credible to larger groups of people, continued to come from towns all across the country. The priest soon became a legend. Today Romo is known as the "patron saint" of migrants—which is why—as I witnessed during my journey along the Mexican side of the border—his picture, together with that of Father Scalabrini, hangs on the walls of all the Casas del Migrante in the various frontier towns of Mexico.

Part of the job of Altar's priest—a young, pretty hip-looking guy who frequently lapses into slang and has lunch at a different house every day both for reasons of security and of public relations—is to preserve a kind of oral tradition of the travails of the migrants. He knows the ropes—he has photographs of himself at various crossing points—and he has explored the dark depths of "the business" in order to understand its modus operandi, which allows him to speak to the smugglers as if he were one of their own. He also happens to come from the same town, Caborca, twenty-five minutes away from Altar, where many of the local kingpins of organized crime originate. Luckily for him, the drug lords who control the migrant routes don't use those same routes to smuggle their "goods," which would make the trails used by migrants all the more dangerous. Although the Beltrán Leyva gang controls the migrant trail to Sásabe, it does not send drug shipments through there. It prefers to use another trail that branches off from the road between Altar and Caborca. which seemed deserted when I visited it one night—though it must have been closely monitored—its eerie silence giving me and my companion a false sense of solitude.

"I keep record of gruesome stories of death and survival," the priest tells me one night while he offers me homemade tequila that he usually shares with his visitors but which he himself does not drink while on duty, so to speak. "The worst story was told to me by migrants who were caught and sent back. They spoke about a corpse they had seen in the middle of the desert embracing a tall cactus, the skin ripped by the spines. After days without food or water, he had apparently had hallucinations and died grasping a cactus that he had mistaken for another person."

Migrants who are caught in the Tucson Sector are not sent back to the Sonora desert locations where they came from. In order to make their new attempts to enter the United States more costly and time-consuming, the authorities send them back through other border crossings, in far away places. But inevitably many of the undesirables come back. "I would say that right now about 40 percent of the people who come through here on their way to the United States, are people attempting to cross for the second or third time" the owner of one of the guesthouses told me. That explains why many of the landlords who see the migrants off bid them farewell with *hasta luego* ("see you later") rather than *adiós* (goodbye).

The locals remember the time when Altar's life was not dominated by the migration business. A couple of decades ago, it lived off agriculture—they still cultivate some grapes and asparagus—and livestock. "Workers, particularly agricultural workers, went back and forth pretty much freely," remembers the owner of a guesthouse. "They knew the times of the year when their labor was needed on the other side and the ones when it was not, and the supply adjusted itself quite nicely to the demand. You never saw a sudden upsurge of crossings or major changes in the flow of people. Altar and other towns of the Sonora Desert area were used to seasonal variations in their population, and nobody cared or thought too much about migration because the vast majority of it was not permanent and because the dangers involved today were not much of an issue."

In two decades, Altar went from an agricultural economy to one entirely based on the flow of illegal migrants.[1] Tragically, the town got caught up, as usually happens in the underground world, with other forms of organized crime to whose power it has had to submit at least partially—which explains why migrant routes such as the one leading out of Altar are under the control of the drug business.

• • •

Drug mafias are not a new phenomenon in Mexico by any means. But it was President Felipe Calderón who, by launching his attack against them in December of 2006, forced a realignment of the cartels that caused an unintended impact on migration by turning the northern Mexican states into a war zone.

Until the government crackdown, initiated with the deployment of 27,000 soldiers in a few key states such as Michoacán, Sinaloa, and Baja California (the number of soldiers would double in subsequent months and years), the various drug cartels operated in relatively low-key fashion in their respective turfs. Occasional turf battles did arise, but they did not constitute an issue of national debate on a permanent basis. The Gulf cartel was dominant in the eastern region of the country; the Sinaloa cartel took care of a good chunk of the western and northwestern part; Los Zetas, an offshoot of the Gulf cartel, operated in Nueva Laredo, next to the border with Texas; La Familia, made up of former members of Los Zetas, had its stronghold in the central state of Michoacán; the Beltrán Leyva cartel, then an ally of Sinaloa in the north, was gradually penetrating some of the territory of the Gulf cartel, which had been somewhat weakened by the capture of its leaders a few years earlier; The Tijuana cartel, which had split off from the Sinaloa cartel years earlier, operated across from San Diego; And some relatively smaller but significant groups, such as the Juárez cartel, generally gyrated in the orbit of the main ones.

The realignment of cartel forces that followed the government's crackdown on drug mafia in 2006 unleashed a war among the drug mafia that, in late 2011, seems to have no end in sight.[2]

One of the first victims of the war was Ciudad Juárez, the mythical border town that was undergoing a period of bonanza thanks to heavy foreign investment and the emergence of a *maquila* industry that saw numerous assembly plants establish themselves there. Under pressure from both the government's attack and the effort by La Familia to push north in response to the military's assault on its bastion of Michoacán in central Mexico, the Sinaloa cartel invaded the space until then mostly occupied by its former ally, the Juárez cartel. The effect was devastating on a city in which drugs had hitherto been mostly an underground affair that had not gravely affected the peace and the everyday life of the city. Long known as a springboard for both legal and illegal migration, Juárez saw its life traumatically disrupted.

Other migrant centers and routes were directly affected too. The Beltrán Leyva drug group had been firmly allied with the Sinaloa cartel, but when the Sinaloa people started to push north, the Beltrán Leyva immediately saw a threat to themselves, which led them to break ranks with Sinaloa and enter into a partnership with the Gulf cartel. Meanwhile, La Familia, under pressure from the government in central Mexico, also expanded to the north, where it became a menace to the Beltrán Leyva organization, which controlled the Sonora Desert area. By all indications, the reason why a helicopter belonging to the Beltrán Leyvas suddenly landed a few meters in front of my car during my passage through the secret trail to Sásabe was precisely the need to confirm that I was not an agent of La Familia or any other rival group, and that I really fitted the description relayed by the *mascaritas* who had seen me enter the trail in Altar.

The migrants, already vulnerable to the exploits of those who control the human smuggling that results from the illegality of the border crossings, are now also the victims of a ferocious drug war, as I saw all the way from Juárez to the Sonora Desert. In August, 2010, the world was horrified when it learned that 72 migrants—including citizens of countries as far away as Brazil—had been massacred by Los Zetas cartel for refusing to be recruited. The sole survivor, an Ecuadorian migrant, escaped with a gun wound and reached a military checkpoint, where he was able to tell the tale of how the group had been kidnapped, sent to a ranch in Tamaupilas, beaten up in an effort to persuade them to enlist with Los Zetas, and then killed in cold blood.[3]

By virtue of the war between the government and the cartels, and among the cartels themselves, the *coyotes* (another term for *pollero,* a human smuggler) are now loosely linked to one group or the other out of a need for protection, while the migration routes are much more tightly and aggressively controlled.

The war has had what Altar's priest calls a "cockroach effect" on the drug trade, forcing it to jump from one place to the other without disappearing, dislocating the structures that were in place by which each group respected the other's turf and the drug lords largely did not interfere with the migration rings.

Nowadays, migrants are caught in the maze of competing and interlocking forms of underground activity, having to pay up to $3,000 for help to cross the border. They oftentimes find themselves in the receiving end of "express kidnappings" by smugglers who hold them hostage to force the families of the victims to pay up front the money they would otherwise not have paid until they received proof that the migrant had crossed to the other side. Central American migrants newly arrived from El Salvador, Honduras or Guatemala on their way to the promised land are brutally abused from time to time; some are simply taken to a location in the Mexican desert and left to their own devices believing that they are already in the United States. According to a study conducted by the National Human Rights Commission, between September of 2008 and February of 2009—that is, in a period of just six months—9,600 kidnappings were documented.[4] The victims—mostly poor Mexicans and Central Americans abducted from trains heading north—paid a total of $25 million to their captors.

• • •

I've wanted to write a book about immigration for a long time. As a migrant myself, I understand the urge to move and start afresh; as a student of migration, I see that movement, relocation, and transplantation are among the oldest and least understood human conducts. Migration has been happening, in varying forms, for millennia but it still elicits primal fear and mistrust, and not just on the part of the "receiving" society: Communities from which people migrate often disapprove of the migrants' decision and consider it treacherous. The re-awakening of the old debate about migration in the new millennium, with intense emotion particularly in the United States and Europe, moved me to finally put pen to paper. I hope this book will help readers cut through the jungle of myth, falsehood, and misrepresentation that dominates the debate in the United States and elsewhere, and clarify the causes and consequences of something that has been happening forever, for very similar reasons and with very similar results.

I spent time visiting the border between the United States and Mexico because I wanted to have a better sense of how and why millions of people continue to risk their lives, and oftentimes lose it, in the pursuit of a chance to establish themselves in a foreign land. Over the last few decades, I have been in contact with many migrants, legal and illegal, getting to know some of them quite closely. I have visited different border regions impacted by migration; each time I was stirred by the human drama. But my visit to the Chihuahua and the Sonora deserts stands in my mind as especially revealing and shocking. Others, including a trip to the northern coast of Africa, where millions defy the elements and the law in their desperation to reach Europe, also shaped my perceptions of the theme the following pages discuss.

No book attempting to explain and clarify the issue of migration would be complete without conveying a sense of what it is like to experience life at the border. But, although I hope the personal tales I have sprinkled throughout the text will help to ground the debate on firmer terrain, this is not a book of reportage. It is a contribution to the discussion on immigration from the vantage point of someone who believes that persuasion—the changing of mindsets through argument and reason—are at least as important as capturing the imagination of readers through storytelling.

Four major themes run through the book, and each of these themes corresponds to a grouping of chapters.

The first theme, comprising Chapters 1–6, describes the immigrant experience, connecting the present to the past, and America to the rest of the world; these chapters explore who migrants are and why they move.

These chapters combine to make the point that there is nothing unique or exceptional about immigration today. Migrants' conduct today is not eccentric compared to that of migrants in the past. The patterns of contemporary migration do not differ fundamentally from those of other epochs—a significant fact in the context of a discussion in which critics of immigration point to major differences between current immigration and the type of immigration that made possible the rise of the United States.

These chapters also point out that the motives of migrants are not substantially different from the motives of natives in the countries to which they migrate. Nor are migrants' motives always dominated by the socioeconomic condition of their countries of origin. Although this is a major factor, migrants' motives are various, as are most people's. Contemporary immigrants, furthermore, do not differ essentially from those of other epochs—a very significant fact in the context of a discussion in which critics of immigration point to grave differences between current immigration and the type of immigration behind the rise of the United States.

The second theme, comprising Chapters 7–10, looks at immigrants from the point of view of culture. These chapters assess to what degree foreigners are different, whether natives can adapt to them, how immigrants assimilate into the new society, and whether there are "good" and "bad" aliens; these chapters dissect the cultural arguments used against immigration. In assessing whether critics are justified in pointing to a major cultural shift, I discuss whether current immigrants differ widely from those of yesteryear. In doing so, I look at aspects as wide-ranging as religion, education, the entrepreneurial drive and attitudes to the social environment. The malleability of culture is a major theme in these chapters. Extreme examples, such as the kind of Islamic radicalism that has taken root in small but significant parts of European societies, are also explored.

I do not seek to minimize the cultural argument regarding immigration. It is true that some immigrant groups do bring with them cultural traits germane to societies that have not thrived on the same kind of attitudes toward work—or the same relationships between effort and reward; between risk and achievement—that are prevalent in prosperous countries. However, several factors point to assimilation patterns that replicate those of the past.

Coming from a country with a long history of underachievement, partially owing to cultural as well as institutional traits, I am aware of the importance of culture in bringing about liberal democracy, the rule of law, and prosperity.

I have also admired and written in these chapters about the cultural conditions that have fueled Asia's rise in recent decades, while other parts of the world were still unable to shed their old habits. But as I see Mexico, my country of origin—as well as many other countries in the Western Hemisphere—gradually break free of their old shackles in this new phase of globalization, I am reminded of how adaptable and ever-changing culture can be. Many immigration critics in the United States understandably worry, in the light of Mexico's socioeconomic and political underachievement during the twentieth century, that the continuous influx of Mexicans might reinforce domestic trends in this country that already point to a deviation from the "good old values" that made America wealthy and stable. In these chapters, I point out that Mexico is moving on from its own past, and—more importantly—there is a disconnect between the achievement of Mexicans back home and Mexicans in the United States, whose assimilation is much greater over time than many people realize.

The third theme, economy, is discussed in Chapters 11–13. These chapters take on the charges leveled at immigration regarding jobs, wages, and the welfare state, comparing the impact of low-skilled immigrants with that of high-skilled workers and drawing parallels—as I do in other parts of this book—between the present and the past. These chapters explore how the market has continued to operate even in the face of major legal obstacles, and how recessions and times of prosperity have influenced—more significantly than government efforts—the number of immigrants coming into the United States and other countries.

These chapters gauge the effect of immigrants on the economy as a whole, and on certain industries in particular, and weighs the burden immigration imposes on social services, including the welfare system and public education.

In these chapters, I conclude that immigration's contribution to the economy far outweighs its cost. In making this conclusion, I take into account the impact both of low-skilled and high-skilled immigrants on the various native socioeconomic groups. I heed the arguments put forward by critics with the utmost respect, and I acknowledge, where need be, the negative impact immigrants have on certain pockets of native society. But I conclude that those effects are temporary and much smaller than generally believed.

The remaining Chapters 14–19 make a call to open minds. They argue that the erosion of national boundaries—and even the idea of the nation state—is already underway. This erosion will make immigration a defining force in the arena of competitive globalization; those countries that learn to embrace it will be better prepared for the emerging world. These chapters propose a bold pro-immigration agenda for the United States and other countries.

Notes

1. Some people take offense at the use of expressions such as "illegal migrants" or "illegal immigrants" with the argument that human beings cannot be considered illegal. I believe the opposite. If a person is considered to be illegally in a country and the state acts against him or her accordingly, it is crucial that language reflect the truth—i.e., the painful implications for a human being of becoming "illegal."

2. According to former Mexican Foreign Minister Jorge G. Castañeda, some 15,000 people had been killed by April 2009. An article of his on this very subject titled "Mexico's War of Choice" was distributed by Project Syndicate in 2009, http://www.project -syndicate.org/commentary/castaneda27/English

3. "Zetas fusilaron indocumentados por negarse a ser sicarios," *Univision Noticias,* August 26, 2010, http://noticias.univision.com/mexico/noticias/article/2010-08-26/zetas -fusilaron-indocumentados

4. The report, titled "Informe Especial de la Comisión Nacional de los Derechos Humanos Sobre los Casos de Secuestros en Contra de Migrantes," is available online. http://www.cndh.org.mx/INFORMES/Especiales/infEspSecMigra.pdf

PART I

The Immigrant Experience

1

The "Takeover"

THERE WAS A time when the word "immigration" was synonymous, in many minds, with the United States. That association was made not only by Americans, who referred to themselves proudly as a nation of immigrants, but just as importantly, by people everywhere for whom the United States was a confluence of migratory flows from the four corners of the Earth. The United States stood in the imagination of millions as a country of countries, a sum total of human diversity.

In recent years, however, the pitched political battle over immigration in the United States has blurred this perception. Opponents and critics of recent immigration have repeatedly argued that the history of the United States is not one of successive waves of immigrants of different nationalities and cultural backgrounds who continually shaped and reshaped the country, but one of early dominance by people of Anglo-Saxon origin followed by intermittent additions that did not significantly alter or influence the so-called national identity established by the dominant colonizers.[1]

According to this argument, the very substantial Hispanic immigration of the last four decades constitutes not a confirmation of the country's history, but a challenge—even a menace—to the Anglo-Saxon cultural legacy. Not everyone who opposes migration offers this line of argument, but some form of it is never far from the bitter exchanges sparked off by the issue of "aliens"—as foreigners are known in the language of legalistic bureaucracy—a word that also describes extraterrestrial beings. As is usually the case in heated political confrontations, the passionate exchanges over immigration have tended to lead people away from nuance and towards dogmatic simplification; the effect has been to blur the rich, evolving history of immigration that is the history of the United States.

As a result of such simplification, American history has, in effect, been parceled out into three distinct chunks: (1) a vague but centuries-old period of English or northern European immigration, (2) a shorter period in which additional immigrant waves fit quite nicely into society's prevailing mold, and (3) a recent flood of "barbarians" constituting an unprecedented, transformative experience capable of diluting and eventually eliminating the rich legacy of immigration. Thus many people have turned away from the notion that the United States is indeed a country of immigrants and have come to believe—or speak and act as if they believed—that the history of America is essentially split into an age of English colonization followed by a long period of consolidation in which immigrants were not really immigrants but, rather, kin of one form or another; and then, in the latter part of the twentieth century, a Hispanic invasion (accompanied, to a much lesser extent, by an Asian one.) Strident immigration critics further claim that this division is an American issue, rather than one shared by many other countries, including much poorer ones.

No, U.S. immigration history is *not* divided into a White Anglo-Saxon Protestant (WASP) era and a darker, culturally unprecedented recent invasion. Nor can one speak of modern-day immigration as a sudden spurt or a uniquely American "problem."

Any discussion about immigration in the United States, or anywhere else, needs to begin with a close look at the country's history. Viewed over centuries, U.S. history presents an ample migratory spectrum with a constantly evolving cultural and institutional pattern whose roots cannot be traced to a single source. The successive waves of immigrants constitute a multitudinous history of "naturalization"—that is, of foreigners of very diverse backgrounds assimilating into the host society, either directly or through their children and grandchildren. The process is ongoing.

Thus, in recent years, an Arabic-speaking descendant of Lebanese immigrants, General John Abizaid, was able to head the United States Central Command, which oversees military operations in a vast area hinging on the Middle East. Similarly, a grandson of Mexican immigrants, Lieutenant General Ricardo Sánchez, was able to serve as V Corps commander of the coalition forces in

Iraq between 2003 and 2004. And, a third example, Major General Antonio Taguba, born in the Philippines and the son of Filipino parents, became deputy commanding general for support of the Third United States Army at the Central Command, based in Kuwait; in 2004, he was assigned to write the politically sensitive report on the abuses committed by United States personnel at the Abu Ghraib prison in Iraq.[2] Thus the United States military, an institution perceived as the quintessential symbol of patriotism, put on the shoulders of a Filipino immigrant the responsibility of holding it to the highest moral standards of civilization.

Without question, the early European presence in the newly colonized territory that comprised part of today's eastern United States established a sort of matrix from which sprang much of the country's history, culturally and institutionally. The European colonizers in the North American continent were predominantly English and, to a lesser extent, Scottish. They and the English and Scottish immigrants who followed dominated the seventeenth and eighteenth centuries, after which there was a pause in migrant inflows into the American colonies because of the Napoleonic wars. It was not until the nineteenth century that immigration became much more diversified.[3]

The early embrace of immigration is stirringly contained in the Declaration of Independence, where one of the charges against King George III was precisely that he had impeded the open door policy espoused by the leaders of that enlightened movement: "He has endeavored to prevent the population of these states; for that purpose obstructing the Laws for Naturalization of Foreigners; refusing to pass others to encourage their migrations hither . . . ."

After the American Revolution, immigration to the United States remained low until the 1830s. During that period, no more than a quarter of a million people migrated to this country.[4] After the so-called First Great Lull, the flow picked up and remained very high for most of the nineteenth century and into the first part of the twentieth century. Between the mid-1800s and 1932, one of the greatest migrations of modern times took place: 52 million Europeans, a mass larger than the current population of South Africa, moved overseas, the bulk of them to the United States (before restrictions were imposed in the early 1920s).[5] By 1870, one in every three people working in manufacturing and mechanical industries in the United States were natives of foreign lands;

given the constant arrival of newcomers, the proportion did not change in the following fifty years.[6]

It would be a mistake to assume that those the waves of migrants between the mid-1800s and 1932 were homogeneous waves of migrants. Eighty percent of the foreigners who settled in the United States between the 1830s and the 1880s came from countries dotting western and northern Europe,[7] and they settled in different locations across America. The Germans, who constituted the key group between the 1860s and the 1880s, famously opted for the Midwest. The northeast attracted the English, the Scots, the Welsh, and, to a lesser extent, the Irish. The Scandinavians headed west across the plains, while the French Canadians worked in the mill towns of New England.[8] After that, immigrants continued to pour into the United States, but they came predominantly from southern, central, or eastern Europe, which were at much lower stages of economic and political development than the areas where previous U.S. migrants had originated, with starkly different cultures.

Appalling economic conditions sent millions of Irish men and women to America in the nineteenth century—bringing into America's immigrant mix a religious, political, and cultural tradition that was profoundly at variance with that of Germans and other northern Europeans. Even though there was a religious motive of sorts in the Irish migration of the 1820s—Catholics suffered discrimination at the hand of the Protestants who had forced Ireland's union with Britain, subsequent waves in the mid-1840s flocked to the United States after the failure of the potato crops, on which millions of peasants depended for their livelihood.[9] By 1880, more than 3.5 million Irish migrants had come to the United States.

The Italians were also from a very different background than the English and the Scots—who were the original colonizers and immigrants—and, of course, than the Germans. There was also a stark contrast between migrants from Italy's two main regions, the north and south, making it senseless to speak of a homogenous Italian migration. In 1850, there were no more than 4,000 Italians in America; by 1930, 5 million had migrated to America.[10] Two million of them returned to their home country.[11]

Another compelling addition to the Protean demographic mix was the Jews.[12] If we overlook the thousands of Ashkenazi Jews from Germany, overwhelmingly secular, who arrived in the early part of the nineteenth century, the great wave of Jewish settlers came after 1880. Between then and World War I, more than 2 million Jews moved to the United States, mostly of central and eastern European background. Four-fifths of them came from various localities in Czarist Russia, including the Pale of Settlement. A large majority of those very poor Yiddish-speaking Jews settled in New York.[13]

At the turn of the twentieth century, the mixture of migrants flocking to the United States could not have been more complex and heterogeneous: Italians, Russians, subjects of the Austria-Hungarian empire, Irish, Brits, Germans, Swedes, and others. The kaleidoscope of nationalities and resulting tensions reduce to nonsense the notion that America's migratory history is essentially divided into a long-standing WASP era and a recent brown Hispanic period. Immigration was never a smooth process; it was a traumatic experience for both the receiving society and for the newly arrived.

The perception that the United States from its early days was a land of immigrants inspired romantic ideas—perhaps inconveniently from the vantage point of immigration critics today. Writers and politicians spoke of a fusion of different peoples, a crucible of nations, a melting pot in which all cultures could dissolve into a larger, integrated whole.[14] The immigration ethos is spectacularly symbolized in the Statue of Liberty, donated by France to commemorate America's centennial.[15] But, as we will see later, things were anything but smooth.

The Hispanics

The statement earlier in this chapter that U.S. immigration history is not divided into an original WASP era and a recent period marked by a culturally threatening influx of low-skilled immigrants does not underestimate the enormous impact of modern-day immigration in the United States. In the new millennium, the foreign-born population, in large part due to Hispanics, is larger, in relative terms, than at any time since the 1930s.[16] By the end of the first decade of this century, almost 12 million of the U.S. foreign-born population were undocumented, a majority of them between the ages of 25 and 34.[17]

The 2010 Census indicates that the portion of the U.S. population of Hispanic origin increased from 13 to 16 percent between 2000 and 2010.[18] If the rate of growth of the Hispanic population continues, by 2050 some 100 million people in the United States, counting those born in the country, will claim Hispanic heritage.[19]

These figures have given rise to numerous sensationalist studies and news reports bombarding the public with the notion that Hispanics are taking over the country, and that American whites will soon be a minority. Those reports—true only if one divides the population into so-called white Anglos[20] and everybody else—are only part of the story, and not one with which everybody agrees. The large non-white Anglo population, for example, is not an organic block of people who think of themselves as the coming majority.[21] Immigrants form a very diverse group of people that includes whites, as well as many shades of skin pigmentation.

The current controversial climate surrounding immigration, amplified by sensationalist media stories, has made many Americans lose sight of the fact that there have been other times in the history of the United States when the population of foreign origin constituted a similarly large proportion of the total population. The censuses taken between 1860 and 1920 found that between 13 and 15 percent of the population was foreign-born. Within that period of more than half a century, there were times when the flow of newcomers was in relative terms greater than in recent years.

From 1901 to 1913, an average of 1 million foreigners—about 2.5 percent of the domestic population—came into the country every single year![22] By contrast, recent annual immigration at its peak has not amounted to more than 0.5 percent of the national census. More generally, in the two centuries between 1820 and 2000 the average proportion of the foreign-born population has hovered around 10 percent of the total, a statistic that belies the notion that an unprecedented foreign invasion has recently taken place.[23]

Until I arrived in the United States, I had never thought of myself as Hispanic. I had been disdained in Peru, my country of birth, for being of Spanish origin—even though my Peruvian ancestry can be traced back at least three centuries—by those who thought that there are two classes of Peruvians—indigenous and Spanish—and that the second class of Peruvians constitutes the enemy. I had also been looked down on, during my stay at a British boarding school in my youthful years, by British kids for whom I was a dark-haired dago because of my looks and my tongue-twisting Spanish name. Because some

Pakistani and, to a lesser extent, Chinese, kids were also treated with the same contempt, I found myself making common cause with these other non-natives from time to time—and therefore feeling like a perfect Asian.

But I had never thought of myself as belonging to any particular ethnic or racial group until I began to be labeled, with millions of others, as a "Hispanic"—the fascinating term used in the United States to refer to persons who come from, or descend from, the Spanish-speaking Americas. It has never been clear to me whether a citizen from Spain is also a Hispanic. The word "Hispanic," derived from "Hispania"—the Latin name given by the Romans to the Iberian Peninsula (on which Spain is situated)—would seem to fit a Spanish citizen like a glove. What makes my Hispanic condition particularly ironic is that the name *Llosa* comes from Catalonia, a region of Spain whose more determined nationalists do not even accept that they belong to a Spanish nation.

The only constant in my various experiences with labels relating to my Spanish ancestry is the fact that such labels were never aimed at lifting my spirits. I first discovered this when I was thirteen. In 1992, I acquired Spanish citizenship and thereby became a citizen of both Peru and Spain. As the years went by, I sometimes had trouble explaining this to some people, particularly in Peru, who did not understand how a person can have more than one nationality. The fact that many thousands of other Peruvians also hold dual citizenship did not seem to cross some people's minds.

I moved to America in 2001, although I had spent short periods of time here for professional reasons earlier in my life. My arrival in the United States confronted me with a puzzling dilemma. I could reconcile my two nationalities, Peruvian and Spanish, to the term "Hispanic"—since it referred to Latin Americans of Spanish origin. But still I wondered: Why are Hispanics, a racially diverse group, labeled as such in lists and databases that seem to classify people by race—the much-debated racial profiling? And why are Hispanics labeled at all in a classification that leaves out so many other ancestries? If the term refers to people from countries that were former colonies of Spain, why are Filipinos not included? And if the term describes essentially Latin Americans, why are Brazilians and speakers of the Portuguese language left out?

I don't have answers to these questions, but one thing is clear: The widespread use of the term "Hispanic" in the United States is definitely related to the arrival of millions of Spanish-speaking Mexicans, Central Americans, South

Americans, and people from the Caribbean in the United States during the last few decades. As of 2010, the U.S. Census (which started to use the Hispanic classification in 1980) counted 50,477,594 Hispanics, that is, 16.3 percent of the total population of the United States.[24]

These figures convey an active force impacting almost every aspect of American life, including its economy, social fabric, cultural life, and politics. Gruma, a company owned by the Maseca group—the world's leading producer of corn flour and tortillas—arrived in the United States in 1976.[25] Three decades later, the Mexican company started to advertise its products in English on national television networks in order to reach millions of Mexican-Americans or Americans influenced by Mexican tastes and inclined to incorporate tortillas into their fast-food diet across the country. Today, tomato salsa, a presence in Anglo barbecues and birthday parties, has overtaken ketchup as the main processed tomato product in the United States.[26]

For much of the twentieth century, the only meaning of the word "bimbo" in the United States, derived from the Italian for "kid," referred to an unintelligent bombshell of a woman. In recent decades, another dimension has been added to the word. Bimbo, the company owned by the Servitje family—the world's largest bakery—arrived here from Mexico in the mid-1980s. Today, the sales of Bimbo bakeries in this country represent a quarter of its total revenue, a proportion that continues to grow. The success attests not only to the way in which Hispanic, and specifically Mexican, businesses have made headway in the world's most competitive market but also—and more importantly from the standpoint of immigration—to the impact that the number of people of Hispanic origin is having on the everyday life of Americans.[27]

Television is another example of the "Hispanization" that America has experienced. In 1961, Emilio Azcárraga, the late Mexican magnate, bought KUAL-TV in San Antonio, the beginning of what would become a media empire. Several developments and changes in ownership later, Univision, a company that has also become a top player in radio and music, now reaches 99 percent of Hispanic households.[28]

Many Americans had the impression that a multitudinous Mexican presence suddenly made itself felt across the nation. No longer confined to certain states or occupations, Mexicans, and Hispanics in general, were becoming part of the everyday lives of Americans who encountered them regularly in all sorts of situations. Whether Americans wanted it or not, and whether they were acutely aware of it or not, the infusion of people who looked different and spoke differently amounted to much more than a foreign appendage to mainstream American society.

Hispanic immigration is more than just Mexican immigration, but Mexicans comprise an unquestionably dominant nationality. The number of Mexicans in America grew from approximately 20 million to more than 31 million between 2000 and 2010. They represent one-third of foreign-born residents and two-thirds of all Hispanics living in the United States.[29] Many Americans might be surprised to know, however, that as a proportion of the entire American population, this increase has not been extremely large. In 1920, there were 486,000 Mexicans established north of the Rio Grande—one-half of 1 percent of the population of the host country. By 2005, when the number surpassed the 11-million mark, they accounted for 3.8 percent of the population of the United States.[30]

The profile of migrants moving north has suffered some variations, the most important one being the number of women migrants. By the middle of the first decade of the twenty-first century, there were at least 5 million Mexican women in the country, on average six years younger than men and slightly more educated. Aside from the usual low-skilled migration of Mexicans settling across the Rio Grande, there was a younger component made up of middle-or-high school students from cities.[31]

Central Americans also migrated to the United States in large swaths, although to many Americans these immigrants may have looked Mexican. The upsurge was particularly pronounced in the 1980s, the period when Central America was engulfed in internal wars. Initially, these migrants settled in California, where there were already large concentrations of Central Americans, but by the year 2000, less than half of all Salvadorans and Guatemalans in America were in California. They had spread out to cities such as Houston, Dallas, New York, Miami, and Chicago.[32] Their grocery stores, festivals, media outlets, money transfer schemes, and supply of labor were all highly visible in many different cities.

All the while, people from Caribbean countries continued to enrich the mix.[33] Nor were South Americans immune to the *nordomanía*, a term coined by

Table 1.1. Hispanic or Latino Origin Population by Type: 2000 and 2010
(For information on confidentiality protection, nonsampling error,
and definitions, see www.census.gov/prod/cen2010/doc/sf/.pdf)

Origin and type	2000 Number	2000 Percent of Total	2010 Number	2010 Percent of Total	Change, 2000 to 2010[1] Number	Percent
Hispanic or Latino Origin						
Total	281,421,906	100.0	308,745,538	100.0	27,323,632	9.7
Hispanic or Latino	35,305,818	12.5	50,477,594	16.3	15,171,776	43.0
Not Hispanic or Latino	246,116,088	87.5	258,267,944	83.7	12,151,856	4.9
Hispanic or Latino by type						
Total	35,305,818	100.0	50,477,594	100.0	15,171,776	43.0
Mexican	20,640,711	58.5	31,798,258	63.0	11,157,547	54.1
Puerto Rican	3,406,178	9.6	4,623,716	9.2	1,217,538	35.7
Cuban	1,241,685	3.5	1,785,547	3.5	543,862	43.8
Other Hispanic or Latino	10,017,244	28.4	12,270,073	24.3	2,252,829	22.5
Dominican (Dominican Republic)	764,945	2.2	1,414,703	2.8	649,758	84.9
Central American (excludes Mexican)	1,686,937	4.8	3,998,280	7.9	2,311,343	137.0
Costa Rican	68,588	0.2	126,418	0.3	57,830	84.3
Guatemalan	372,487	1.1	1,044,209	2.1	671,722	180.3
Honduran	217,569	0.6	633,401	1.3	415,832	191.1
Nicaraguan	177,684	0.5	348,202	0.7	170,518	96.0
Panamanian	91,723	0.3	165,456	0.3	73,733	80.4
Salvadoran	655,165	1.9	1,648,968	3.3	993,803	151.7
Other Central American[2]	103,721	0.3	31,626	0.1	−72,095	−9.5
South American	1,353,562	3.8	2,769,434	5.5	1,415,872	104.6
Argentinean	100,864	0.3	224,952	0.4	124,088	123.0
Bolivian	42,068	0.1	99,210	0.2	57,142	135.8
Chilean	68,849	0.2	126,810	0.3	57,961	84.2
Colombian	470,684	1.3	908,734	1.8	438,050	93.1
Ecuadorian	260,559	0.7	564,631	1.1	304,072	116.7
Paraguayan	8,769	—	20,023	—	11,254	128.3

Origin and type	2000 Number	2000 Percent of Total	2010 Number	2010 Percent of Total	Change, 2000 to 2010[1] Number	Change, 2000 to 2010[1] Percent
Peruvian	233,926	0.7	531,358	1.1	297,432	127.1
Uruguayan	18,804	0.1	56,884	0.1	38,080	202.5
Venezuelan	91,507	0.3	215,023	0.4	123,516	135.0
Other South American[3]	57,532	0.2	21,809	—	−35,723	−62.1
Spaniard	100,135	0.3	635,253	1.3	535,118	534.4
All other Hispanic or Latin[4]	6,111,665	17.3	3,452,403	6.8	−2,659,262	−43.5

– Percentage rounds to 0.0.

[1]The observed changes in Hispanic origin counts between Census 2000 and the 2010 Census could be attributed to a number of factors. Demographic change since 2000, which includes births and deaths in a geographic area, and migration in and out of a geographic area, will have an impact on the resulting 2010 Census counts. Some changes in the Hispanic origin question's wording and format since Census 2000 could have influenced reporting patterns in the 2010 Census. Additionally, changes to the Hispanic origin edit and coding procedures could have impacted the 2010 counts. These factors should especially be considered when observing changes for detailed Hispanic groups.

[2]This category includes people who reported Central American Indian groups, "Canal Zone," and "Central American."

[3]This category includes people who reported South American Indian groups and "South American."

[4]This category includes people who reported "Hispanic" or "Latino" and other general terms.

Sources: U.S. Census Bureau, *Census 2000 Summary File 1* and *2010 Census Summary File 1.*

José Enrique Rodó, a famous Uruguayan author, to describe the Latin American obsession with U.S. materialism at the turn of the twentieth century. The fifth-largest group of people of foreign origin in the United States coming from the Western Hemisphere were Colombians. This community traces its immigrant roots in the United States to the 1940s, the decade known as *La Violencia* in Columbia, during which many thousands of people were killed in a civil war between liberals and conservatives.[34] Today, four South American communities—Colombians, Ecuadorans, Peruvians, and Brazilians—are among the top fifteen immigrant nationalities in this country.

However, although these nationalities were added to the immigrant mix and gave the impression of a Hispanic "takeover," they did not advance the proportion of foreigners significantly beyond historical precedent in America. Rather, they constituted a new phase in a centuries-old pattern of U.S. immigration.

Table 1.2. Ten Places With the Highest Number and Percentage of Hispanics or Latinos: 2010

(For information on confidentiality protection, nonsampling error, and definitions, see www.census.gov/prod/cen2010/doc/sfl.pdf)

Place	Total population	Hispanic or Latino population	
		Rank	Number
Number			
New York, NY	8,175,133	1	2,336,076
Los Angeles, CA	3,792,621	2	1,838,822
Houston, TX	2,099,451	3	919,668
San Antonio, TX	1,327,407	4	838,952
Chicago, IL	2,695,598	5	778,862
Phoenix, AZ	1,445,632	6	589,877
El Paso, TX	649,121	7	523,721
Dallas, TX	1,197,816	8	507,309
San Diego, CA	1,307,402	9	376,020
San Jose, CA	945,942	10	313,636

Place[1]	Total population	Rank	Percent of total population
Percent			
East Los Angeles, CA[2]	126,496	1	97.1
Laredo, TX	236,091	2	95.6
Hialeah, FL	224,669	3	94.7
Brownsville, TX	175,023	4	93.2
McAllen, TX	129,877	5	84.6
El Paso, TX	649,121	6	80.7
Santa Ana, CA	324,528	7	78.2
Salinas, CA	150,441	8	75.0
Oxnard, CA	197,899	9	73.5
Downey, CA	111,772	10	70.7

[1]Places of 100,000 or more total population. The 2010 Census showed 282 places in the United States with 100,000 or more population. They included 273 incorporated places (including 5 consolidated cities) and 9 census designated places that were not legally incorporated.

[2]East Los Angeles, CA, is a census designated place and is not legally incorporated.

Source: U.S. Census Bureau, *2010 Census Summary File 1.*

Figure 1.1. Legal Permanent Immigration Flows and Total Population of Mexican and Central American Immigrants in the United States, 1900s–2000s

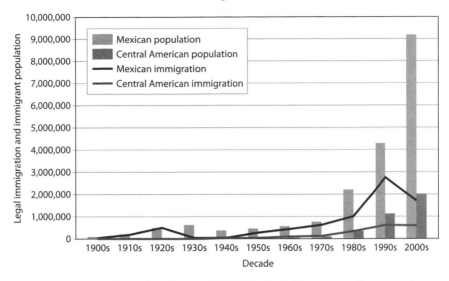

Source: Department of Homeland Security (DHS) *Yearbook of Immigration Statistics,* various years (Washington, D.C.: DHS), and U.S. Census Bureau, U.S. Census, various years.

Notes

1. One of the leading intellectual voices making that argument was the late Samuel P. Huntington in his book *Who Are We?* He argued that the first wave of settlers defined the identity of the nation—an identity that subsequent waves did not alter—leading him to conclude that "Anglo-Protestant culture has been central to American identity for three centuries. . . . In the late twentieth century, however, the salience and substance of this culture was challenged by a new wave of immigrants from Latin America and Asia. . . ." Samuel P. Huntington, *Who Are We?* (New York: Simon & Schuster, 2004), xvi.

2. Roger Waldinger, "Transforming Foreigners Into Americans," in *The New Americans: A Guide to Immigration Since 1965,* eds. Mary C. Waters and Reed Ueda (Cambridge, Mass.: Harvard University Press, 2007), 143.

3. In the seventeenth and eighteenth centuries, the Northeast, the middle Atlantic, the South, and the Mountain South received different groups of newcomers. Between 1629 and 1641, some 21,000 East Anglian Puritans settled in Massachusetts; between 1642 and 1675, about 45,000 gentry and indentured servants traveled from the south and west of England to Virginia; roughly 23,000 north Midland Quakers settled in Delaware between 1675 and 1725, and, in the long period between 1717 and 1775, as many as 250,000 Border English and Scots, as well as Ulster Protestants, established themselves along the Appalachians. See Peter Brimelow, *Alien Nation: Common Sense About*

America's Immigration Disaster (New York: Random House, 1995), 38. A comprehensive study of the four waves of early colonization and immigration in the United States can be found in David Hackett Fisher, *Albion's Seed: Four British Folkways in America* (New York: Oxford University Press, 1989).

4. Philip Q. Young, *Post-1965 Immigrants to the United States: Structural Determinants* (Westport, Conn., Praeger Publishers, 1995), 10.

5. During that time, the peak years of immigration in America were 1851–1854, 1866–1873, 1881–1883, and 1905–1924, after which significant restrictions were imposed. See Reed Ueda, "Immigration In Global Historical Perspective," in Waters and Ueda, *The New Americans,* 15.

6. John Higham, *Strangers in the Land: Patterns of American Nativism 1860–1925* (New Brunswick, N.J.: Rutgers University Press, 1955), 16.

7. Philip Q. Young, *Post-1965 Immigrants to the United States: Structural Determinants* (Westport, Conn.: Praeger Publishers, 1995), 10.

8. Higham, *Strangers in the Land,* 15.

9. Peter Brimelow, *Alien Nation: Common Sense About America's Immigration Disaster"* (New York: Random House, 1995), xii.

10. Anna Maria Martellone, "Italian Mass Emigration to the United States," *Perspectives in American History* 1 (1984): 389–392.

11. See also Samuel L. Baily, "The Italians and the Development of Organized Labor in Argentina, Brazil, and the United States," *Journal of Social History* (Winter 1969): 70, 129.

12. Thomas Sowell, *Migrations and Cultures* (New York: Basic Books, 1996), 282.

13. The Jews were not an entirely new presence in America—perhaps the earliest community in the Thirteen Colonies, Sephardic Jews of Portuguese and Spanish ancestry, came from Brazil in 1654. See Moses Rischin, *The Promised City: New York's Jews, 1870–1914* (Cambridge, Mass., Harvard University Press, 1967), 33.

14. The first to speak of a "new race" of people from different nations seems to have been the famous French immigrant J. Hector St. John de Crèvecoeur. In 1782, in his *Letters From an American Farmer*, almost a quarter of a century after his arrival, he referred to people from all nations "melting into a new race." The letters are widely available on the Internet. See http://xroads.virginia.edu/~hyper/crev/letter03.html [section 55] A century later, Frederick Jackson Turner gave new life to the same idea in his *Frontier Thesis*, published in 1893, where he marveled at the way in which immigrants became Americanized, liberated, and morphed into a mixed race in the Middle West. The next and definitive moment in the idea of the melting pot mentioned by scholars is the best-known one—British-born Jewish author Israel Zandwill's play *The Melting Pot*, which premiered in Washington in 1908. The impact of Zandwill's play is such that most people who are familiar with the "melting pot" expression probably derived it from the influence of the play on the imagination of Americans without them knowing it. It portrayed America as "God's crucible, the great melting pot where all the races of Europe are melting and re-forming." See Nancy L. Green, *Repenser Les Migrations* (Paris: Presses Universitaires de France, 2002), 55. Also see Georgie Anne Geyer, *Americans No More* (New York: The Atlantic Press, 1996), 101.

15. For a long time, the Statue of Liberty was the first sight of the United States seen by travelers who crossed the ocean—a representation conveying the association of liberty and migration. The inscription on the pedestal—the final lines of a sonnet by Emma Lazarus, an American poet whose parents were Portuguese Sephardic Jews—and written as a contribution to a fund-raising campaign for the statue, said it all: "Give me your tired, your poor, / Your huddled masses yearning to breathe free,/ The wretched refuse of your teeming shore, /Send these the homeless, the tempest-tossed to me,/ I lift my lamp beside the golden door." The inscription is widely available on the Internet. http://www.statueliberty.net/statue-of-liberty-poem.html

16. Jonathan Bowles and Tara Colton, "A World of Opportunity," *Center For An Urban Future*, February, 2007, http://www.nycfuture.org

17. The estimate belongs to the Office of Immigration Statistics Policy Directorate and can be seen *www.dhs.gov/xlibrary/assets/statistics/.../ois_ill_pe_2011.pdf*. Sixty-nine percent were Mexican, 11 percent Asian, another 11 percent Central American, 7 percent South American, 4 percent Caribbean, and less than 2 percent Middle Eastern.

18. Sharon R. Ennis, Merarys Ríos-Vargas, and Nora G. Albert, *The Hispanic Population 2010*, U.S. Census Bureau, May 2011, http://www.census.gov/prod/cen2010/briefs/c2010br-04.pdf

19. Nearly half of the illegal Hispanics living in the United States entered the country legally—45 percent used visas, and between one-quarter and one-half million had a border crossing card, a document that allows short visits to the border regions. Pew Hispanic Center, *Modes of Entry for the Unauthorized Migrant Population,* May 2006. http://pewhispanic.org/factsheets/factsheet.php?FactsheetID=19

20. Although the term "white Anglo" is highly debatable and quite imprecise, I will use it for the sake of discussion given its widely extended use to refer to native-born Americans of European descent.

21. In 1982, the Center for Immigration Research and Education published a study by two demographers based on mathematical calculations showing that within the following 70 years, a minority of the U.S. population would be white. On April 9, 1990, *Time* magazine had a cover story saying the same thing. Even the U.S. Census Bureau published a study a couple of years later substantiating the same assertion. See Samuel T. Francis, *America Extinguished: Mass Immigration and the Disintegration of American Culture* (Monterey, Va.: Americans for Immigration Control, 2002).

22. Giovanni Peri, "America's Stake in Immigration: Why Almost Everybody Wins," *The Milken Institute Review* (Third Quarter 2007).

23. Huntington, *Who Are We?*, 46.

24. U.S. Census Bureau, *The Hispanic Population: 2010—Census Briefs,* May 2011, http://www.census.gov/prod/cen2010/briefs/c2010br-04.pdf

In 1976, the Congress of the United States passed the only law in its history that mandated the collection and analysis of data for a specific ethnic group: "Americans of Spanish origin or descent." This group was defined as "Americans who identify themselves as being of Spanish-speaking background and trace their origin or descent from Mexico, Puerto Rico, Cuba, Central America and South America, and other Spanish-speaking countries."

25. The group's official website can be accessed at http://www.gruma.com/vEsp/

26. Jorge Castañeda, *Ex Mex: From Migrants to Immigrants* (New York: The New Press, 2007), 23.

27. Castañeda, *Ex Mex,* 24.

28. See, for instance, the study on Hispanics in Pew Research Center, *The State of the New Media: An Annual Report on American Journalism, 2009,* Project for Excellence in Journalism, Washington, D.C., 2009, http://www.stateofthemedia.org/2009/index .htm

29. Ennis, Ríos-Vargas, and Albert, *The Hispanic Population 2010,* http://www.census .gov/prod/cen2010/briefs/c2010br-04.pdf

30. Castañeda, *Ex Mex,* 6.

31. The data is taken from the NATLHIST database provided by the Mexican Migration Project developed by the Office of Population Research at Princeton University and the Research Department of Social Movements at the University of Guadalajara and the Office. http://www.stateofthemedia.org/2009/index.htm

32. Between 1980 and 1990, the El Salvador-born population officially increased five times to 472,393, while the number of Guatemalans and Nicaraguans tripled to 227,998 and 171,004, respectively. The number of Hondurans almost tripled. The real numbers, behind the official releases, were almost certainly much higher. See Norma Stoltz Chinchilla and Nora Hamilton, "Central America," and Xiao-huang Yin, "China: People's Republic of China," in *The New American,* eds. Waters and Ueda, 328–332, 413.

33. One such community was that of the Dominicans. Almost 1 million people who claimed that ancestry were in the country at the turn of the millennium, just under 70 percent of whom were foreign-born. See Peggy Levitt, "Dominican Republic," in *The New Americans,* eds. Waters and Ueda, 402. Another Caribbean community that was very numerous and also had old roots in the country were the Cubans—they numbered more than 1.3 million. Like the Central Americans, they had spread to the four corners of America. Significantly, 37 percent of all Puerto Ricans, who by virtue of the Commonwealth can legally move to the mainland, were living here. See Lisandro Pérez, "Cuba," in *The New Americans,* eds. Waters and Ueda, 386.

34. About 45 percent of them had arrived in the previous decade, and 30 percent lived in Miami. While Colombians huddled mostly in Florida, New York, and New Jersey, the Peruvians—hundreds of thousands of them—made their presence equally felt in parts of California. See Luis Eduardo Guarnizo and Marilyn Espitia, "Colombia," in *The New American,* eds. Waters and Ueda, 375–376.

2

Not Just Here, Not Just Now

MODERN-DAY IMMIGRATION IS by no means a uniquely American issue, nor is it much larger, relatively speaking, than in other historical periods. Apart from being statistically similar to that of other periods that saw very different types of newcomers, modern-day immigration is by no means a uniquely American issue. Americans who are annoyed by the presence of foreigners often lose sight of the global dimension of immigration. By some credible estimates, by the beginning of this millennium, 30 million people were smuggling themselves into various countries every year.[1]

Between the 1960s and the mid-1990s, 20 million immigrants had settled in Western Europe.[2] In subsequent years, Europeans were just as shocked by the pressure on their borders as Americans were about their border with Mexico. The newspapers were filled with stories of Africans reaching Tangier or Ceuta on the north coast of Africa in order to cross over into mainland Europe; and the French fumed about Pakistanis, Chinese, Egyptians, Indians, and Africans attempting to get into France from Ventimiglia, a city in northern Italy seven kilometers from the Franco-Italian border; just as Italians were scandalized by North Africans trying to make it to Lampesuda, a city in the Italian Pelagie Islands in the Mediterranean some 180 kilometers from the coast of Libya; and the British were increasingly wary of foreigners trying to cross over from Calais.[3] The mix of nationalities in Calais, the northern French city that serves as a springboard for migrants headed for Britain, was such that at one point, people from forty different nations camped there as refugees.[4]

The proportion of legal to illegal immigrants in the European countries that host large foreign-born communities varies quite starkly, but in many cases it is not hugely different from that of the United States. At the turn of the millennium, around 10 percent of the French and Swiss populations were foreign (i.e., from outside the European Union [EU]), as were 9 percent of the Austrian and the Belgian populations, 6 percent of the Swedish population, and 4 percent of the British population.[5] Even countries that had traditionally been exporters rather than importers of migrants, such as Spain, began to experience major incoming flows. Almería, in southern Spain, traditionally a source of emigrants who went to work in greenhouses in the French Midi, suddenly saw itself facing the arrival of Moroccans wanting to do the same kind of work. Valencia, in the east, a major city that had hitherto known almost negligible Latin American or North African immigration, became a principal destination for new settlers. It is estimated that 12 percent of Spain's population is foreign.[6]

Statistics are meaningless until one comes into contact with the stories behind each one of the millions of people who inform them. At the end of 2009, in the southern city of Málaga, I had the chance to meet and talk extensively with numerous foreigners who entered Spain illegally—all of them with chilling personal stories—who were temporarily hosted by CEAR,[7] a Spanish organization that helps immigrants obtain asylum.

Alassane, a sociologist from Mauritania, was a victim of what he characterizes as the "genocide" perpetrated by the Mauritanian government of Maouya Ould Sida Ahmed, who was intent on the forced "Arabization" of the black population. Alassane is a tall, slender man with a goatee beard and a thin moustache, whose eyes still carry the pain he suffered as he saw his family raped and massacred for something they had not even chosen—being part of black Mauritania.

"My mother," he says, speaking slowly and deliberately, "was a mixture of Berber and Arab, my father a black African. In my country, blacks had an education and positions of responsibility in government; my father was one of them. But they had no power. So when those who had power decided to engage in ethnic cleansing, they used the excuse that blacks were from Senegal. They assaulted my house, they tortured most of us and I saw something horrific of which I don't want to talk, but . . . but . . . but I saw them humiliate my family's bodies. I was saved by a group of soldiers who took compassion and expelled me to Senegal. Ethnic cleansing saved my life . . . ."

Alassane returned to Mauritania a decade later. The government had changed. "I wanted to work in the human rights field; after seeing what I had seen, what else would I want to do with my life? I was thrown in jail. My wife was nine months pregnant when I was arrested in 2003, and she had a miscarriage. My father died of a heart attack caused by the tortures he endured. In 2007, they came for me again, this time to kill me. I escaped through my neighbor's house, a woman who knew the truth. I fled to Senegal by crossing the southern border with papers given to me by a friend in the police department. I had a visa to Spain because of my work for Spanish human rights groups. I flew later to the Canary Islands, and here I am."

Solange is a small, round woman from the Ivory Coast, officially the Republic of Cote d'Ivoire, a country in West Africa. She told me her story in delicately-constructed French with a disconcerting, yet moving, matter-of-fact attitude towards her unspeakable suffering—and a poise that perhaps only someone who has been to hell and made it back can master. She was caught up in the war that tore her country apart between 2002 and 2004, when ethnic conflicts that had been smoldering for years exploded. Northern rebels representing people of foreign descent who had been a part of the Ivory Coast for a long time wanted equal political rights. The government and other factions saw them as aliens.

Solange was working in Abidjan, but her family was in a rural area outside Oumé, a small city in the south. "My father, who supported the opposition but had never been involved in any meaningful way, was accused by the rebels of carrying weapons and not wanting to share them with the armed rebellion. He had to flee. He went to Tafierie, a rural part, where I saw weapons for the first time in my life. My mother disappeared; we never saw her again. My brother and my husband were taken because the armed guys said that they might be militarily useful to the rebels. They took me to the jungle and put me in a house with other women. They took turns to have sex with me and, after the initial shock, when I realized I would not die of this humiliation, I figured that the only way to survive was to let them do. I became pregnant but lost my child the day one of them forced himself on me and I struggled. The women guards stood there, watching."

Then, a miracle happened. One of the guards, a man from Cameroon, asked her to come out of the house for a walk. He told her that he knew her husband

and wanted to help her. "He took me to the border with Mali. There I was able to find my husband, who was married to someone else, thinking that I had been killed. I worked as a servant in the house where he was staying. After a year and a half, I crossed to Algeria, and from there to Morocco, where I survived selling fruit. "

After Solange fell ill, she found a way to get to Melilla, one of the two Spanish enclaves in North Africa. She got in using a method that has proven quite successful for many an aspiring migrant. "I was smuggled into Melilla under the engine of a car that was dissembled especially for this. I had a hard time breathing and I think my heart stopped when the car suddenly came to a halt. But I heard there was a change of driver and a Spanish guy took the wheel. Once I was free in Melilla, I wandered aimlessly until I lost consciousness. Apparently, I was picked up by some Nigerians. I was so ill that the local hospital could not treat me, so they brought me here to Málaga. All I remember is that I saw a black man entering through the door, the first black skin I had seen in awhile, and yelled to myself, 'Thank God!'"

As she tells me how safe she felt at the sight of a black man after the ordeal she had gone through and the fear that had invaded her when she found herself alone and helpless in a strange new land, she squeezes her own skin in one arm, smiling.

Solange's story, like Alassane's, has been corroborated by numerous organizations, including CEAR. But what has not been corroborated is what must have gone through their minds, and the minds of the many others who spoke to me in a modest little room in the guest house where they were kept, one winter afternoon in Málaga, when they realized that they would need to spend years trying to persuade cold, cynical bureaucrats of the truth that is engraved on their psyche and yet inspires indifference or skepticism in countries that fear and resent the foreign "invaders."

There was Rachida, an Algerian woman who found out she was married to a terrorist and escaped with her son to Ceuta, an autonomous city of Spain and an enclave on he north coast of Africa. She told me about her past as a victim of gender abuse with the tone of someone so sure of her own tale that she no longer seemed to care if I believed her.

Moments later, I listened to Djamila, another Algerian who arrived in the enclave of Melilla with nothing but the vague notion that North Africa and

Spain, hell and paradise, converge mysteriously in that enclave. A few days before I spoke to Djamila, her son had arrived in Spain on a raft looking for a place under the sun of Western abundance.

Europe, where immigration also stirs many passions, is by no means the only destination other than the United States for people who leave their turf. There are many others. In the Western Hemisphere, Canada, a country with a long tradition of immigration, made it a policy to attract foreigners from the times of Prime Minister Pierre Trudeau in the 1970s. By the end of the century, a robust 17 percent of Canada's population had been born outside of the country. In certain key cities, such as Toronto, the proportion was much bigger.[8] Further south, it is estimated that 40 percent of the foreigners living in Sao Paulo, Brazil's megalopolis, are there illegally. They have come from Bolivia, Paraguay, Bolivia, and, to a much lesser extent, Chile. The small state of Rondonia has seen the number of Bolivians crossing in through bordering cities such as Guarajá-Mirim and Costa Marques go up dramatically.[9]

In Asia—the continent that has the greatest number of migrants both incoming and outgoing—a torrent of women have left their places of origin. Between the 1970s and the new century, the proportion of women among emigrants rose from 17 percent to 65 percent in Sri Lanka, from 15 percent to 69 percent in the Philippines, and from 41 percent to 76 percent in Indonesia.[10]

The area of the world in which the proportion of immigrants is highest is by far is the cluster of Arab states situated around the Persian Gulf. One-third of their population is made up of foreigners. At the turn of the millennium, some 10 million workers of expatriate origin, mostly Arabs and Asians, lived in that region; such workers constituted about half of Saudi Arabia's labor force. The Egyptians are the largest expatriate minority in the Gulf region, followed by the Yemenis, the Sudanians, the Syrians, and the Lebanese.[11]

In the last three decades, an interesting change has taken place in the Persian Gulf. Asians, mostly from the Indian subcontinent, have replaced large parts of the Arab immigrant workforce, in great part due to the development policies of the Gulf states. In some activities, such as domestic service, the Asians have already overtaken the Arabs.[12]

Just as we saw in the case of the United States, massive migration in the rest of the world is not a contemporary social phenomenon. It is a tradition with ancient roots. What appears to many contemporary citizens to be a recent and

Figure 2.1. Modern World Migration Flows

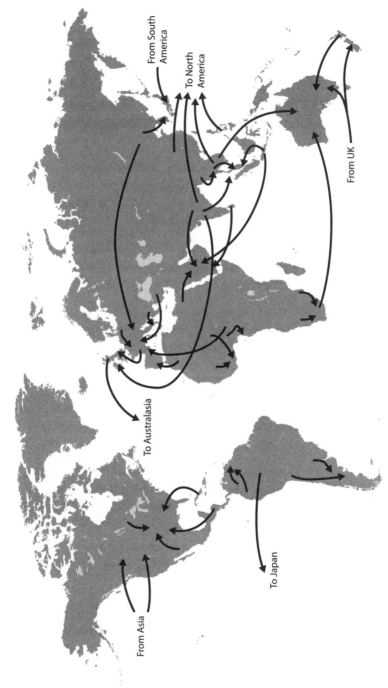

Figure 2.2. A History of Major World Migration Flows

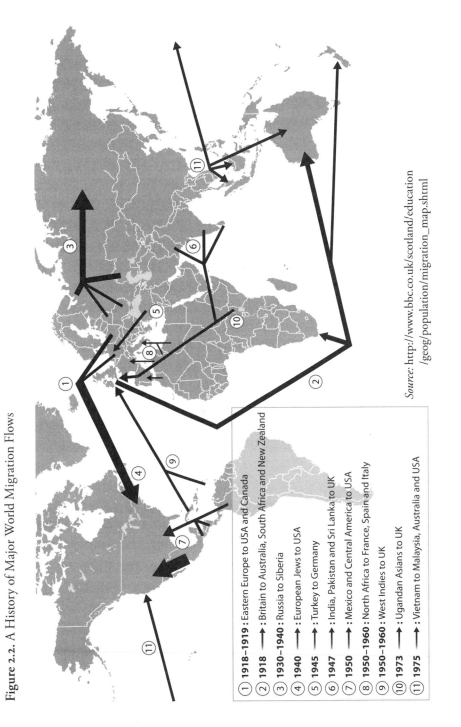

Source: http://www.bbc.co.uk/scotland/education /geog/population/migration_map.shtml

1 **1918–1919 :** Eastern Europe to USA and Canada
2 **1918 →:** Britain to Australia, South Africa and New Zealand
3 **1930–1940 :** Russia to Siberia
4 **1940 →:** European Jews to USA
5 **1945 →:** Turkey to Germany
6 **1947 →:** India, Pakistan and Sri Lanka to UK
7 **1950 →:** Mexico and Central America to USA
8 **1950–1960 :** North Africa to France, Spain and Italy
9 **1950–1960 :** West Indies to UK
10 **1973 →:** Ugandan Asians to UK
11 **1975 →:** Vietnam to Malaysia, Australia and USA

Figure 2.3. Average Annual Number of Migrants, 2002–2005

More coming in
More leaving

Circles are proportional
to the number of people.

1 million
250,000

Source: The New York Times

overwhelming menace, is in fact a very ancient "threat." All regions of the globe have experienced migration either as the origin or the destiny of the movement of people, and many have seen both ends of the stick even in the modern era. Between the early nineteenth and the early twentieth centuries, some 150 million people from Europe, Asia, Africa and the Middle East crossed borders for good. In fact, there was so much migration, that "sending" countries were at a loss to stem the outpour, which they feared for socioeconomic reasons, and "receiving" nations pressed to keep the gates open. This was precisely the dynamic among participants in a world congress on immigration held in Paris in 1889.[13]

The Irish diaspora of the second half of the nineteenth century meant that 72 percent of its citizens emigrated! China is a more contemporary case. By the mid-1990s, there were 33 million Chinese living outside of China, a population greater than that of Peru.[14] Lebanon probably has the world's highest number of expatriates relative to the number of nationals residing in the country. Over the years, some 14 million Lebanese left their birthplace to go to Latin America, North America, Africa, Australia, and Arab destinations.[15]

Migration was always, and continues to be, the stuff of history. It is universal and it is permanent. And the reasons why people move, as we will see in the next chapter, are not as simple as we tend to think.

Notes

1. "The Last Frontier," *The Economist*, June 24, 2000, 63.

2. Hans Magnus Enzensberger, *Civil War* (London: Granta Books, 1994), 112.

3. Manuel Ruben N'Dongo, *Regard sur l'Immigration Africaine en Europe: Les Dictatures Africains, Causes et Effects de l'Immigration* (Paris: Editions des Écrivains, 1999), 72.

4. Maxime Tandonnet, *Le Grand Bazar ou l'Europe Face à l'Immigration* (Paris: l'Harmattan, 2001), 35–36.

5. *Trends in International Migration: Continuous Reporting System on Immigration, 2000 edition* (Paris: OECD, 2001.) Also see Bullent Kaya, *The Changing Face of Europe—Population Flows in the 20th Century*, (Strasbourg: Council of Europe Publishing, 2002), 41.

6. "Feria y fiesta de la inmigración," *El País* (business section), November 29, 2009.

7. CEAR is the Spanish acronym for *Comisión Española de Ayuda al Refugiado* (Spanish Commission of Assistance for Refugees).

8. *Trends in International Migration* Also see Georgie Anne Geyer, *Americans No More* (New York: The Atlantic Press, 1996), 315.

9. "Immigration Law: Sanctions and Enforcement in Selected Foreign Countries," *Report for Congress*, The Law Library of Congress, April 2006, http://www.libertyparkusa

fd.org/lp/Hamilton/Insourcing%20Jobs%5CUS%20House%20of%20Representative%5CImmigration%20Law%20Sanctions%20and%20Enforcementin%20Selected%20Foreign%20Countries.pdf

10. The number of Asian migrants is not spread equally among countries by any means. Bangladesh, Pakistan, and India have sent many fewer women migrants, in relative terms, than the countries cited earlier. Some attribute the reason for fewer migrants to religion, particularly Islam and Hinduism, a claim that some scholars dispute. They point to the fact that among the places of origin of women migrants, there are some—such as Indonesia or the island of Mindanao in the Philippines—that are predominantly Muslim. Also, the rate of female participation in the work force in India is similar to that of Filipino women. See Nana Oishi, *Women in Motion: Globalization, State Policies, and Labor Migration in Asia*, (Stanford, Calif.: Stanford University Press, 2005), 7.

11. Nasra M. Sha, "Arab Migration Patterns in the Gulf," in *Arab Migration in a Globalized World* (Geneva: International Organization for Migration, League of Arab States, 2004), 91.

12. Sha, "Arab Migration Patterns in the Gulf," 100.

13. It was called "Congrès Internationale de l'Intervention des Pouvoirs Publics dans l'Emigration et l'Immigration." See Nancy L. Green, *Repenser Les Migrations* (Paris: Presses Universitaires de France, 2002), 82.

14. *The Republic of China: Overseas Chinese Affairs Statistics* (Taipei: Overseas Chinese Affairs Commission, 1994), 8.

15. Riad al Khouri, "Arab Migration Patterns: The Mashreq," in *Arab Migration in a Globalized World* (Geneva: International Organization for Migration, League of Arab States, 2004), 27.

3

Why They Move

A MISCONCEPTION HOLDS that, by and large, the people who leave their place of origin to set up camp somewhere else are the poorest, least-skilled citizens of the societies that "send" workers abroad. According to this line of thought, sheer economic desperation and its twin sentiment, lust for others' wealth, are the principal motivating factors behind the massive movement from one place to another. In the imagination of many people in the countries that receive newcomers, the word "immigrant" has come to be almost synonymous with undesirable, scruffy-looking, insalubrious reject—someone who, unable to make something of his or her life back home, wants to dispossess the more fortunate middle-classes in the wealthier nations of what is theirs.

That is not how things work. Every year, from 1955 until 1986, about half a million Germans emigrated from their country, even though it was one of the world's richest countries. Germany—the most prosperous nation in Europe, the industrial engine of the old world, and the planet's number-one exporter of goods—was a country of emigrants until nearly the end of the twentieth century—long after the devastation of the war had been dealt with.[1] In fact, Germans, who are very proud of their heritage and can be notoriously unwelcoming of high numbers of immigrants, had been emigrating for centuries. They began to emigrate to the Baltic and to Russia in the eighteenth century (they even moved to Riga, which was under Russian control since 1721, and in due time became known for its advanced technology).[2]

There are a number of relatively prosperous cities, countries, and regions today that export citizens at a much greater rate than poorer, neighboring areas. One such case is Governador Valadares, a well-to-do city in the Brazilian state of Minas Gerais. It is known as a commercial and industrial hub and is associated in the mind of many people with its famous gems. Governador Valadares and the surrounding locations of Minas, a mining powerhouse, are the source of more emigrants to the United States than any other state in Brazil, including states in the northeast, the poorest region. Minas emigrants even have a name—*brazukas*. Close to one-half of the half-million Brazilians living in the United States are from the state of Minas.[3] This is consistent with migration patterns in other Latin American countries. The poorest Salvadorans have tended overwhelmingly to migrate within their own national borders, while those who were relatively better off were the ones who left for the United States.

Theories of immigration did not take shape until the 1970s. The "theory of development" maintains that the underdevelopment of "sending" societies is the key factor in migration to richer nations, a wider assertion that would serve to explain the movement of people generally. This school was led by Richard R. Hofstetter[4] but was espoused by many others, including Richard Lamm and Gary Imhoff.[5] A variation of this idea was put forward with significant acceptance by Elizabeth McLean Petras;[6] her emphasis was on overpopulation as the driving force behind migration.

Both generalizations are suspect in the face of solid evidence regarding the migration of people from developed countries to other developed countries; the presence of migratory flows from sparsely populated countries; as well as the absence of significance movements out of some nations with high population density. In relative terms, South Korea, whose impressive economic growth rates have been a matter of common knowledge for several decades, has been one of the biggest sources of migrants to the United States. Many African countries whose populations were rapidly growing sent very few immigrants to the United States between 1956 and 1990. One of these was Gabon, where the population grew by 4.4 percent annually in the first part of the 1980s. Nevertheless, Gabon sent an average of only four migrants per year to America between 1982 and 1986. China, the most populated country in the world, did not initiate its significant migration to the United States in contemporary times until 1978, when Deng Xiaoping's free-market reforms began.

It is true that, generally speaking, migration from underdeveloped or developing societies has been greater than from fully developed ones. In the 1970s and 1980s, the average annual number of immigrants who originated in relatively poor nations was almost four times greater than those who left more developed countries. However, there was little migration from the poorest nations. If we assume the notion that rich countries are at the "center" of the world economy, the tendency is for semi-peripheral countries, rather than peripheral ones, to be the predominant origin of foreign settlers in the leading parts of the globe. Equally interesting is the fact that rich countries have continued in modern times to export sizeable portions of their populations. The United Kingdom, Canada, Italy, and Germany are among the top twenty source countries of migration to the United States since 1965, the year in which the Immigration and Nationality Act was passed in the United States partly aimed at redressing the composition of immigrant communities, judged too skewed towards Europe.[7]

Researchers who have studied migration in Asia report that migrants do not necessarily move from poor countries to rich ones, and that unemployment is not necessarily the determining factor in the decision to leave behind one's native land. For example, few women have left Bangladesh, one of the poorest places on earth. And in Pakistan, where the unemployment rate for women is twice that of men, women only constitute 0.2 percent of the total number of people who leave.[8]

In her extensive field research on Asian women migrants, Nana Oishi discovered that money was only one of many reasons why people left their place of origin or permanent residence to start afresh elsewhere. Other determining motives had to do with adventure, being a dutiful daughter, a distressed condition, helping the family, and fleeing from local troubles.[9]

Contrary to widespread perception, migratory flows frequently change direction and have always done so. Clearly, for many people from less prosperous societies, the superior living conditions of wealthier shores are a potent allure. But because wealth has been a flux rather than an immovable condition, and prosperity has shifted from region to region and country to country, migration dictated by the search for better conditions has constantly changed direction too. This will continue to be the case. A few generations from now, in this era of upward mobility in which countries considered very poor until recently are now leaping to prosperity, many of the "sending" countries will have become "receiving" ones. Strictly speaking, many countries are already both "senders" and "receivers." The Dominican Republic attracts Haitians but also exports Dominicans to the United States.

No doubt, Americans easily recognize and understand the ancient European roots of their society. But how many know that Europe was a net exporter of migrants until as recently as the 1980s! How many *Europeans* of the younger generations are aware of this reality? And how many Frenchmen, Germans, or Britons realize that between World War II and the 1980s, the number of Europeans who left their places of origin was considerably greater than the number of immigrants who moved to a European country?

It is easier to understand the changing, evolving nature of migratory flows if we think about them within the confines of a single country, region, or continent. Until well into the 1970s, Spain, Portugal, Greece, and even Italy were exporting people who, dissatisfied with their living conditions, looked for an improvement further north in Europe. Today, all four countries receive many immigrants, to the dismay of large portions of the host populations.

Spain, a fully developed country considered one of the dream stories of economic prosperity in the second half of the twentieth century, used to send migrants to two continents—Africa and Latin America—that subsequently became sources of migrants keen to settle in the Iberian peninsula. Many Spaniards know that in the middle of the twentieth century their country exported citizens to richer European nations; but even fewer know that, between 1887 and the 1960s, Latin America was the main destination for Spanish emigrants. In that period, the Spanish- and Portuguese-speaking countries of the Western Hemisphere received between 60 and 75 percent of all Spanish emigrants seeking a chance to move ahead in life.

It is ironic that in the 1940s, North Africa—whose citizens are the least welcome by a majority of Spaniards today— was one of the preferred destinations for those who left their native Spain. In that decade, Oran and its surrounding areas in Algeria, as well as the north of Morocco, received between 35 and 41 percent of the migrant Spanish workforce. It was only after economic growth in the industrialized countries of Western Europe escalated in the 1960s that Spanish emigrants changed direction, flocking instead to Germany, Switzerland, and France (the guest-worker programs set up at the time inspired the famous aphorism by Swiss writer Max Frisch: "We asked for workers, and got people"[10]).

Some theoreticians have preferred to give less weight to economics as the main reason for continuous migration to a particular territory, and focus instead on social networks established by previous waves of immigrants as the key motivating factor. Illsoo Kim,[11] J.S. MacDonald, and L.D. MacDonald, for instance, have reflected on the crucial role of family reunification and occupational preferences.[12] Relatives, friends, organizations, and various types of middle people have a significant "pull" on those who move from "sending" to "receiving" nations. The "social network" theory wrongly ignores the motivational aspect of emigration, which is also influenced by the conditions back home and by the physical and human capital needed in order to migrate. Although there are aspects to this theory that seem to be backed by factual evidence, it leaves out too many other determining elements out and is contradicted by other significant facts. The connection between migration and the political causes of underdevelopment and instability does not, in and of itself, generate any kind of rightful claim on more stable, richer societies. But a better understanding of this nexus should at least help to change the parameters of the discussion because it indicates that most migrants are not a "different" kind of human being or hostile invaders, but are instead ordinary folks reacting in the way citizens of richer nations would react in similar circumstances. It also points to the not-insignificant part that Western support for policies behind the underdevelopment of poorer societies has played with regard to the condition of some "sending" countries.

African intellectuals have reflected on the responsibility of the leaders of that continent's independence movement in the tragedy that, from the 1960s onwards, generated conditions of violence, economic misery, and existential despair triggering mass migratory outflows. It would be inaccurate to say that tribalism began after decolonization because Africans had always been proud to belong to clans and tribes. But African leaders during the 1960s, as well as their heirs, exacerbated tribal and clan loyalties for political reasons. Many of those leaders had the cynical support of Western democracies; first, because the United States and particularly Europe did not want to be seen as opposing independent governments; and, second, because Western democracies thought that close ties with authoritarian and corrupt regimes of Africa would guarantee the Western countries a stake in resource-rich African economies. Central Africa's Jean-Bédel Bokassa, Guinea's Ahmed Sékou Touré, Uganda's Idi Amin Dada, and others had political entourages made up of their own clans that made sure power was concentrated in the tribe—or in a very small part of the tribe—while other groups and clans were subjected to discrimination and horrific repression.

The twisted use of tribal loyalties and connections to justify dictatorships, the plundering of national resources, and general violence kept Africa poor, with notable exceptions, for most of the twentieth century. Between 1975 and the end of the century, per capita economic growth in sub-Saharan Africa averaged a dismal –1 percent.[13] That has led Manuel Ruben N'Dongo to conclude that "tribalism is the essence and the poison of African peoples."[14] After independence, African leaders, many of whom cloaked their naked power plays under Marxist ideology—a perfect alibi at the time—used their ethnic and linguistic singularity stemming from a complex and troublesome geography to impose themselves on their countries, and forced millions to flee. The creation of clan-based armies made things worse. Ethnic cleaning and ethnic massacres happened almost everywhere across the continent: in Angola, in Sudan, in Congo Brazaville, in Sierra Leone, in former Zaire, in Guinea-Bissau, in Liberia, in Equatorial Guinea.[15] In such a context, Western support and foreign aid aimed at stemming immigration could not possibly work. Corrupt, despotic politicians used the legitimacy brought about by the active support of Western guilty consciences to reinforce their rule.

Because of the concentration of power in the cities, millions of Africans migrated from the countryside to urban areas, where they found no opportunities. Realizing they could not go back to their tribes given the prevailing conditions, they opted for emigration. "The African person in his or her tribe of origin," says N'Dongo, "has the same dream than the French who exiled themselves in order to populate America in the nineteenth century, with the only difference that the African person migrates to a country stuffed with unemployed people."[16]

Robert Mugabe's odious regime in Zimbabwe is a good example of the calamity that African tyrants have brought on their people, creating the conditions for emigration. The Zimbabwean masses fleeing desperately towards neighboring South Africa in recent years have acted in a way that is easy to understand for anyone vaguely familiar with conditions in that country. Joseph Conrad could have been describing Mugabe's regime when the character Marlow, in *Heart of Darkness*, described an ivory company as "reckless without hardihood, greedy without audacity, and cruel without courage."[17]

The story behind Latin American migration is also one of homegrown authoritarianism and economic incompetence, often with support from leading democracies. If this story were better understood in richer nations, it might throw a more benign light on emigrants and enlighten those who see immigrants as hostile invaders. What Mexican governments did with that country's agriculture, for instance, explains why millions of peasants migrated to the cities and why they—or their children—eventually moved to the United States.

A couple of years ago, during the shoot of a documentary series for *National Geographic,* I had the chance to encounter Emiliano Zapata, a laborer who is the grandson and namesake of the legendary leader who was part of the Mexican Revolution, and the hero of many a movie. Their story allows one to get a clearer sense of how the migration of Mexicans originated a few decades ago, and why.

The state of Morelos is where Zapata's revolution—one of the various armed struggles that made up the multifaceted Mexican Revolution—started almost a century ago, before it spread all across the south of Mexico. Zapata (Emiliano's grandfather) was a mestizo whose lifelong mission was the return of land to indigenous people who had been dispossessed by Europeans. The Institutional Revolutionary Party, or PRI, which was a by-product of the revolution and governed Mexico for almost the entire twentieth century, styled itself "Zapatista" and staked its legitimacy in great part on a massive land reform. Today, Zapata's grandson Emiliano, who lives in misery, explained to me why the legacy of the revolution is an unmitigated failure with respect to peasants in the countryside.

"The land was given to the people, all right," Emiliano told me. "Under the *ejido* system, a plot of land was handed to peasant villages and communities, and each one appointed a commissar to preside over it. Then the politicians bribed or co-opted the appointees and politicized the whole thing. The local party bosses would get the commissars to inflate the price of public works in their villages and towns, splitting the excess money with them. The commissars would also ensure that the *ejidatarios* gave political support to the party."

Emiliano was raised in Cuautla. He grew up listening to stories of his grandfather's exploits told by his father, Nicolas, and he dreamed of owning some land. "All I could get hold of," he remembered, "were a few cows. I had to sell them because the government started to produce and sell milk at subsidized prices, and ruined me."

He tried to obtain credit to buy land. After all, everywhere he went he came across speeches by the president or the state and local authorities claiming to be Zapatistas and promising to help redeem the Mexican peasants. "But the credit was reserved for the cronies and families of the politicians. I wrote letters to the authorities—and not once did they grant me a interview."

Today, he lives in poverty under a tin roof in Anenecuilco, where his grandfather was born. His wife sells tortillas—the best I have tried in Mexico—and he gets up at 5 a.m. every day to go and clear the land on somebody else's property with a chain saw.

What has been the consequence of a century of collectivization of the land? In the 1990s, when trade policies became more liberal, Mexico's rural population found itself caught up in an extremely inefficient system that was undercapitalized, making it very difficult for Mexican peasants to compete with the outside world. When the government finally allowed the villagers to sell the *ejidos*, something they had been prevented from doing since 1917, many of them put their land on the market and left for Mexico's cities. When the urban areas did not offer improved conditions, they migrated to the United States. "If my grandfather came back," pondered Emiliano, "he would die of sadness."

Mexico's official history has always maintained that Zapata fought for a socialist revolution. He did not. Zapata was many things—a womanizer, a drinker, an occasional bandit. Some of his ideas were muddled, but he was no socialist. As the son of small-property owners—they lived in an adobe house whose ruins I visited in Anenecuilco—Zapata genuinely wanted his people to own their land. He mistrusted the state: He even refused to sit in the presidential chair when, in 1914, he and Pancho Villa entered Mexico City, seemingly on the verge of total victory in their revolution.

There is an ironic little coda to the story of the grandson, the landless Zapatista: A few years ago, some of his children tried to enter the United States in search of a better future—but this is a topic Emiliano was reluctant to discuss. There has been some improvement in Latin America in the last decade. If the trend continues, it is not inconceivable that in the not-so-distant future, as the economic environment improves, migratory flows will be significantly reduced. But the poverty that still prevails is the result of many decades of the kind of political economy that Zapata's case exemplifies.

As mentioned before, because conditions change, migratory flows linked to underdevelopment also change. But in many cases, connections between "sending" and "receiving" countries go back a long time. The fact that certain nationals have a disproportionate presence among today's immigrants in certain countries can be traced back to heavy involvement by these countries in the places of origin of those migrants. Oftentimes, the historical involvement by a "receiving" country in a "sending" country was brutal; sometimes it was subtle.

Blowback

In the nineteenth century, during the so-called Meiji Restoration, Japan underwent a radical transformation. That transformation can be characterized as a Westernization of the general outlook of Japanese society and many Japanese institutions. The cultural change was led by a government deeply grateful to the United States for the help in ending Japan's isolation earlier in the century. Among other manifestations of this gratitude, and of the general embrace of the values and symbols of the West, were government-issued textbooks that held up Abraham Lincoln and Benjamin Franklin as models. English was introduced in Japanese schools.[18] When Americans think of Japanese immigrants, they don't tend to consider those ancient connections. To the extent that any historical elements are brought to the conversation, they point to World War II.

Economic involvement by the United States in Cuba was a major factor in establishing a Cuban presence in North America in the early nineteenth century. Cubans, then under Spanish control, had helped the Thirteen Colonies struggle for independence against England; part of the funding had come from commercial exchanges between the Americans and Cuba. Those exchanges grew when the United States emerged as an independent nation. Florida's Key West became almost an extension of Cuba's cigar industry. As early as the 1830s, factories with Cuban owners or workers were rolling tobacco leaves imported from the island. The cigars were exported to New York and from there distributed to other states. By the 1870s, Cubans in New York were the largest Latin American community east of the Mississippi. These business groups were also politically active. They became a source of defiance against the Spanish colonial administration. Preeminent among Cubans actively stirring trouble for Spain in New York was José Martí, the precursor of Cuba's independence, who had also worked as a laborer in the cigar factories of South Florida.[19] Similarly, in New Orleans, a community of Cubans emerged in the early nineteenth century due to the intense commerce between that port city and Havana. Cuba was a major sugar producer, and New Orleans was a key player in extracting and refining the product of the sugar-cane stalk.[20]

After the Cuban Revolution, thousands of Cubans fled to the United States. They were continuing a long tradition dating back to the economic connections between the United States and Cuba. Washington's opposition to the dictatorial regime established by Fidel Castro was a key element in generating and sustaining the flow of Cubans to South Florida. The first waves of Cuban exiles were also warmly welcomed by the United States.

Likewise, Filipino immigration in the United States— the third-largest foreign-born group—is deeply intertwined with American involvement in that Pacific archipelago. The U.S. took over the islands in the wake of the Spanish-American War of 1898 but, after the Spaniards were defeated, a powerful Filipino insurrection ensued. Counting those who died in combat and those who perished because of outbreaks related to the conflict, hundreds of thousands of Filipinos were killed. A few thousand Americans lost their lives too. The Philippines were an American colony until 1934, after which a Commonwealth was established, only interrupted when the Japanese took over. Full independence did not come until the end of World War II, although a military presence was kept by the United States.[21] In its capacity as a colonial power, the United States triggered significant migration from the Philippines to America.

Other source countries also trace their emigration to North America to military involvement by Washington. Between 1961 and 2001, more than 800,000 Dominicans were admitted to the United States. The fact that they were the second-largest group moving north in the Western Hemisphere is not a mere caprice of history. The United States occupied the Dominican Republic in 1916 and withdrew in 1924, a period during which the Dominican Republic was introduced by the foreign power into a global network of economic and cultural relations; ties between the two nations became intense. Naturally, during the atrocious dictatorship headed by Rafael L. Trujillo between 1930 and 1961, many Dominicans wanted to flee to the United States. Not many actually did because the regime placed draconian restrictions on those wishing to leave, but as soon as Trujillo's dictatorship collapsed, a steady flow of migrants was initiated.

After a period of chaos and violence, leftist Juan Bosch was elected president of the Dominican Republic in 1963. His government lasted no more than a few months, after which a military dictatorship was established, giving rise to an insurrection heavily loaded with radical leftists. The United States intervened militarily once more in 1965 and remained until the election of Joaquín Balaguer in 1966. During that period, a generous policy of granting visas to Dominicans was put in place by President Lyndon Johnson with the aim of providing a safety valve and diffuse the radicalization of anti-government forces. Dominican migration to the United States took on new dimensions—and remained so until the end of the twentieth century, explaining the high numbers of Dominican immigrants.[22]

The nexus between the United States and Mexico is much older and more profound. Spain did not begin to settle Mexico's northern border until the end of the sixteenth century, when it sought to defend the region from the Russians and the English. After Mexico gained its independence in the early nineteenth century, the Mexicans continued to settle the border. Americans were able to migrate to the area, from which they had been previously banned. The process led to the proclamation of an independent Texas by Americans and their Mexican allies in 1836. The tension sparked off by this development eventually led to the war between the United States and Mexico a decade later, and to the capture and annexation by Americans of a large swath of Mexican territory. Approximately 100,000 Mexicans were given the option to remain north of the new border and become American citizens. That large community of Mexicans was American in name only. Their background, their family connections, and their language were Mexican.[23]

For generations, people were free to travel back and forth across the border. For people on both sides, the border was a mere formality. Ties and exchanges between the two sides of the dividing line were much more meaningful than a political border that felt like an artificial boundary. It took a particular economic event—the discovery of gold in California—to attract a surge of northbound Mexican migration. The natives, fearful of competition, pushed back and relations soured.[24]

Those old connections—a tradition of cross-border flows—set the framework for a lasting migratory dynamic. It gathered steam later and continued intermittently, depending on the circumstances prevailing in Mexico and the labor needs of the United States. Large-scale northbound migration from locations that were not close to the border started around 1900, induced by funding in the United States for linking Mexican railroads to the railroads north of the border. Americans charged with enlisting Mexican labor workers followed the rail lines deep into Mexican territory looking for recruits. In the wake of the Mexican Revolution, in which almost 1 million people were killed, the United States willingly received hundreds of thousands of immigrants from its southern neighbor.[25] And after World War I, when American industrialists were cut off from traditional source of foreign workers in the southern, eastern, and central parts of Europe because of movement restrictions, the businessmen went back to looking for Mexican workers. Their efforts redoubled in the following years.[26]

A few decades later, circumstances derived from international conflict again created an urge to recruit large numbers of Mexican laborers. Between the early 1940s and the mid-1960s, the United States, reeling from labor shortages in agriculture brought about by World War II, invited millions of Mexican workers to settle in some twenty different states. They did so under the so-called *Bracero* program, an agricultural guest-worker scheme. The stay was meant to be temporary, and in most cases it was, but many workers legalized their situation and remained in the United States permanently, while others came back from Mexico illegally after they had left.[27] A very important reason why so many Mexicans have steered towards California in recent decades—even if they have also fanned out across their adopted nation—is that a disproportionate number of workers hired under the *Bracero* program went to work in Californian agriculture.

The military, political, and commercial presence of the United States in Central America in the first half of the twentieth century played a major role in establishing the communicating vessels that later facilitated and encouraged the northbound migration from that region. In the early twentieth century, Honduran migration was linked to the banana trade that arose from investments by American companies strongly supported by the authorities in Washington. The expansion of commerce between the United States and Central America brought Hondurans and others to New York and New Orleans. For a very long time, and even as late as the beginning of the 1980s, New Orleans had a large Honduran population. During World War II, due to labor shortages, Central Americans were among those hired to work in shipyards in San Francisco. Most of them had worked in the construction of the Panama Canal and later in American shipping lines—even the United Fruit Co. had hired Hondurans in the merchant marine.[28] The fact that so many Hondurans work in the United States today cannot be dissociated from these historical antecedents. The diastole of expansionary American foreign policy and American business has become the systole of immigrants coming from nations with a past of American influence.

By contrast, countries with which the United States had little involvement were the source of quite small or only modestly significant migration to North America. South American countries are among them. According to official data, no more than 132,103 South Americans settled in the United States in the almost sixty years from 1891–1950.[29]

Of all the foreign communities now settled in Spain that originated in Africa, it is not difficult to see why the Moroccans more numerous than any other. Spain had a colonial presence in Morocco going as far back as 1906 when the Algeciras Conference was held in Spain, in which the European powers gave Madrid and Paris joint policing responsibilities in Morocco. A few years later, in the wake of disputes among European countries over French dominance in Morocco, Spain was granted "protective" powers over the northern and southern Saharan zones. It became known as Spanish Morocco, and it lasted until France and Spain recognized the African country's independence in 1956.

Many Moroccans fought under Francisco Franco in the Spanish Legion against Moroccan rebels. They were rewarded with Spanish citizenship. That explains in part why so many Muslims in the Spanish North African enclave of Ceuta are Spanish citizens today. Moroccan soldiers also fought alongside Franco's nationalist camp during the Spanish Civil War of the 1930s. In a quirky turn of history, independent Morocco would later give refuge to many Spanish exiles who fled Franco's Spain. The old ties derived from Spain's involvement with Morocco help to understand why Spain is a preferred destination for so many Moroccans searching for a new home.[30]

In December of 2009, I visited the city of Ceuta, still part of the Spanish kingdom despite its location and its Muslim flavor. Situated on the North African side of the Strait of Gibraltar, Ceuta is a small but proud enclave whose Mount Hacho is thought to have been one of the pillars of Hercules, the demigod fabled for smashing through the mountains and connecting the Atlantic to the Mediterranean. I was surprised to find a Spanish military barrack, but perhaps it is an appropriate reminder that the enclave has been at the center of disputes between Spain and Morocco over Ceuta.

Today, Morocco wants sovereignty over Ceuta, but Spain will have none of it. History has come back to haunt Spain, as many Africans for whom Ceuta is part of their heritage see Spain as a legitimate destination. Benzú, a settlement bordering Morocco in the northern part of the enclave, is the preferred point of entry for those crossing illegally into Ceuta, and from there across to the Iberian Peninsula. It was shown to me by someone who has helped many Africans sneak into Spain by swimming around the border fence between Morocco and Ceuta, under the peaceful gaze of the "Dead Woman," a gorgeous rock formation on the African side.

Active encouragement of immigrants from certain nationalities is also at the heart of the disproportionate presence of some nationals in "receiving" countries. As a consequence of post-war settlements, Germany received more than 9 million ethnic Germans seeking refuge or expelled from Central and Eastern European countries. Another 3 million left the German Democratic Republic to settle in the western part of the divided republic. It took a couple of decades for all these immigrants to be integrated into the economy, but following the economic "miracle" to which historians of post-war Germany refer, the country found itself in need of labor. It then began to actively recruit other, poorer Europeans.[31]

Migration into Britain from its former colonies was the result of a deliberate policy dictated by the need for labor. I remember, during the few years I spent at a British boarding school in the early 1980s, being puzzled by the extent of the racial contempt that Indians and Pakistanis inspired among so many of my fellow students. The word *wog* was the most common epithet used, but there were others. Young kids can be particularly nasty and may not be representative of sentiments across the adult population, or even of juveniles at large. But the tense atmosphere of the school was not, by the accounts I received from people familiar with the wider context, entirely unrepresentative of what went on in schools across the country. I remember being prompted by this experience to do some perfunctory research on the historical origins of the relationship between Britain and the Indian subcontinent. I was amazed to realize that the presence of Indians and Pakistanis in Britain was centuries old, a product of forceful British involvement in that part of the world, as well as encouragement—to say the least—of labor migration.

Indian servants and *ayahs* (nannies) were brought over to Britain as far back as the seventeenth century by British families returning from India (the East

India Company had been chartered by the Queen in 1600). Indian sailors, known as *lascars*, had also been part of the crew in English ships. Other types of migrants augmented the flow in later years. In the middle of the nineteenth century, exiled princes, student adventurers, political activists, businessmen, entrepreneurs, and others lived in England.[32] By the twentieth century, Indians were, or should have been seen as, anything but an alien presence among British subjects.

After World War II, the United Kingdom placed virtually no restriction on immigration from the colonies. Even as the rest of Europe put impediments to Asian immigrants, London went out of its way to welcome them. The policy had been very open earlier in the century—as was evident in the Nationality Act of 1914, limited only by the fact that the Home Secretary had the power to refuse entry to those who were not able to support themselves. Later on, the flow was reduced by the imposition of various barriers. During World War II, as we saw in the case of the United States, circumstances led to active encouragement of immigration. Indians were even enlisted to serve in the British Army (the "color bar" that previously impeded non-whites from serving was removed). More generally, Asians from the subcontinent were recruited to work in forestry, munitions factories, and all sorts of services. This significant migration set the stage for the post-war arrival of dozens of thousands of Indians and Pakistanis.[33]

How many British critics of immigration today know that in 1948 a policy of open borders for immigrants from Britain's colonies was officially announced? In little time, Britain was viewed in the former colonies as part of a wider territory in which they were relatively free to move about. At the beginning, the flows were very small, but by 1988 more than 2.5 million people from the former colonies were settled on the island.[34]

Other connections between "sending" and "receiving" countries are more immediate. The influx of Algerian immigrants experienced by France from the 1960s onwards bears an umbilical relation to the Algerian War of Independence.[35] The relationship between France and Algeria was not merely that of an occupying force and a suppressed people. It was a colonial presence that involved a large population of French origin, including a generation of French men and women born in Algeria, known as *pieds noirs*. Ironically, the 75,000 *pieds noirs* who returned to France after Algeria obtained its independence suffered discrimination by French society, which saw them as North African. An involuntary product of French colonization, *pieds noirs* were perceived more as undesirable immigrants than as compatriots who had been living abroad.

In the early twentieth century, the United States encouraged the importation of Filipino agricultural laborers. They were needed in Hawaiian sugar cane fields as well as in Californian fields, picking grapes, asparagus, lettuce, and other vegetables. Although they operated under legal restrictions, the Filipinos were not an unwanted presence. It was only during the Great Depression that a backlash against them took place in California, when they were accused of displacing native workers and undercutting local wages. Another quite different United States-induced source of Filipino migration was the encouragement given by American colonizers to the study of medicine among a group of highly qualified men as well as nursing schools that followed the academic trends from back home. The Americans recruited Filipino nurses to work in the United States, where the need for new professionals had been felt.[36]

After World War II, a new series of programs helped create opportunities for many Filipinos interested in employment in American hospitals. They were recruited both as military personnel and as healthcare workers by the United States.[37] That is how Filipino nurses became a high-profile community here in the latter part of the twentieth century. One century of close American involvement in the Philippines and of active encouragement explains in part the fact that today millions of Filipinos constitute the third-largest foreign-born community in the United States.

• • •

These historical realities should be taken into account when "receiving" countries react to immigration. Extreme poverty is not a driver of international migration. Except for periods in which economic disparities played a major role, when the direction of migratory flows has remained constant for a long time, it has often been because of historical ties.

None of the precedents, however, seem to mitigate the distrust and antipathy toward immigrants on the part of contemporary "receiving" societies. In this they are not very different from the societies that confronted the previous migratory flows. Contrary to common wisdom, the reaction to immigration, as we will see next, was not largely welcoming then—and it is not today.

Notes

1. Hans Magnus Enzensberger, *Civil War* (London: Granta Books, 1994), 129.

2. Benjamin Pinkus, "The Germans in the Soviet Union Since 1945," in *The Soviet Germans: Past and Present*, ed. Edith R. Frankel (New York: St. Martin's Press, 1986), 138.

3. Joel Millman, *The Other Americans* (New York: Viking, 1997), 211–214.

4. Richard R. Hofstetter, "Economic Underdevelopment and the Population Explosion: Implications for U.S. Immigration Policy," in *U.S. Immigration Policy*, ed. Richard R. Hofstetter (Durham, N.C.: Duke University Press, 1984), 55–79.

5. Richard Lamm and Gary Imhoff, *The Immigration Time Bomb: The Fragmenting of America* (New York: Truman Tally Books, 1985).

6. Elizabeth McLean, "Some Thought on the Study of Immigration Patterns Within the Modern World Economy: Established and Alternative Data Sources," in *Quantitative Data and Immigration Research*, eds. Stephen Couch and Roy Bryce-Laporte (Washington, D.C.: Smithsonian Institution, 1979), 99–133.

7. Philip Q. Yang, *Post-1965 Immigrants to the United States: Structural Determinants* (Westport, Conn.: Praeger Publishers, 1995), 29.

8. Nana Oishi, *Women in Motion: Globalization, State Policies, and Labor Migration in Asia*, (Stanford, Calif., Stanford University Press, 2005), 5–6.

9. Oishi, *Women in Motion*, 113.

10. Philip Martin, "There is Nothing More Permanent than Temporary Foreign Workers," Center for Immigration Studies, April, 2001, http://www.cis.org/articles/2001/back501.html

11. Illsoo Kim, "Korea and East Asia: Pre-migration Factors and U.S. Immigration Policy," in *Pacific Bridges: The New Immigration From Asia and the Pacific Islands*, eds. James T. Fawcett and Benjamin V. Carino (New York: Center for Migration Studies, 1987), 327–345.

12. J. S. MacDonald and L. D. MacDonald, "Chain Migration, Ethnic Neighborhood Formation and Social Networks," in *An Urban World*, ed. C. Tilly (Boston: Little Brown, 1974), 226–236.

13. George Ayittey, "The African Development Conundrum," in *Making Poor Nations Rich* (Stanford, Calif., Stanford University Press for The Independent Institute, 2007), 139.

14. Manuel Ruben N'Dongo, *Regard sur l'Immigration Africaine en Europe: Les Dictatures Africaines, Causes et Effects de l'Emmigration* (Paris: Éditions des Ecrivains, 1999), 135–136.

15. N'Dongo, *Regard sur l'Immigration Africaine en Europe*, 27.

16. N'Dongo, *Regard sur l'Immigration Africaine en Europe*, 10.

17. Joseph Conrad, *Heart of Darkness* (New York: Signet Classics, 1950), 90.

18. Yasuo Wakatsuki, "Japanese Emigration to the United States, 1866–1924," *Perspectives in American History*, 12 (1979): 440.

19. Alvaro Vargas Llosa, *El exilio indomable* (Madrid: Espasa Calpe, 1998), 85–86.

20. Norma Stoltz Chinchilla and Marilyn Espitia, "Colombia," in *The New Americans: A Guide to Immigration Since 1965,* eds. Mary C. Waters and Reed Ueda (Cambridge: Mass., Harvard University Press, 2007), 338.

21. Yang, *Post-1965 Immigrants to the United States*, 51.

22. Jorge Duany, "Los Países: Transnational Migration from the Dominican Republic to the United States" (paper presented by Professor Duany from the University of Puerto Rico, Río Piedras, at the seminar on "Migration and Development: Focus on the Dominican Republic," sponsored by the *Migration Dialogue*, in Santo Domingo, the Dominican Republic, on March 7–9, 2001) http://migration.ucdavis.edu/ceme/printfriendly.php?id =19_0_6_0

23. Albert M. Camarillo, "Mexico," in *The New Americans: A Guide to Immigration Since 1965,* eds. Mary C. Waters and Reed Ueda (Cambridge: Mass.: Harvard University Press, 2007), 505–506.

24. For an account of the international impact, including the effect on Mexicans, of the American Gold Rush, see Ralph J. Roske, "The World Impact of the California Gold Rush, 1849–1857," *Arizona and the West* 5 (1963): 187–232.

25. Camarillo, "Mexico," in *The New Americans*, eds. Waters and Ueda, 506.

26. Jorge Durand, Douglas S. Massey, and Rene M. Zenteno, "Mexican Immigration to the United States: Continuities and Change," *Latin American Research Review* 36, no. 1 (2001): 109–112.

27. *Bracero History Archive*, Center for History and New Media, 2010, http://bracero archive.org/history

28. Catherine Ceniza Choy and Nora Hamilton, "Central America," in *The New Americans*, eds. Waters and Ueda, 329–330.

29. Catherine Ceniza Choy, "Philippines," in *The New Americans,* eds. Waters and Ueda, 561.

30. An excellent account of Spanish Morocco can be found in Part III (chapters 17–25) of *Historia de Marruecos: De los orígenes tribales y las poblaciones nómadas a la independencia y la monarquía actual* (Madrid: La Esfera de los Libros, 2006.)

31. Zig Layton-Henry, *The Politics of Immigration: Immigration, "Race" and "Race" Relations in Post-War Britain* (Oxford, U.K. and Cambridge, Mass.: Blackwell, 1992), 215.

32. Rozina Visram, *Asians in Britain: 400 Years of History* (London: Pluto Press, 2002), 2.

33. Layton-Henry, *The Politics of Immigration*, 7, 9–10, 12, 14.

34. In 1953, only 9,300 Indians or Pakistanis; 15,000 West Africans; and 1,600 Arabs were in the United Kingdom. Migration to Britain intensified later, despite restrictions placed in the early 1970s in response to the surge and to changing circumstances. See Layton-Henry, *The Politics of Immigration*, 7, 9–10, 12, 14.

35. Abdelmalek Syadi, *l'Immigration ou les Paradoxes de l'Alterité* (Paris: Raison d'Agir Editions, 2006), 70.

36. Choy, "Philippines," in *The New Americans,* eds. Waters and Ueda, 560.

37. Mark Krikorian, *The New Case Against Immigration: Both Legal and Illegal* (London: Sentinel, 2008), 58.

4

The Reaction

A STRONG MOVEMENT against immigration made comprehensive immigration reform impossible in Congress during the George W. Bush administration in the first decade of this century and during the 2009–2012 Obama administration—despite the fact that both presidents had come into office promising such reform. This indicates how much resistance there is to finding a path to legalization for millions of undocumented foreigners in the country now and to opening the gates to substantial numbers in the future.

Attitudes, however, are not uniform throughout the country. States with high numbers of immigrants have tended to harbor much less prejudice against foreign residents than states with fewer immigrants. According to a survey conducted by Bendixen & Associates at the end of 2008, attitudes towards foreign workers were relatively positive in Florida, Colorado, New Mexico, and Nevada. The respondents were predominantly so-called white Anglos, by a wide margin over immigrants or blacks, reflecting the composition of the population. Majorities between 55 and 65 percent said that they believe foreigners come to America to work and find better living conditions, not to profit from social services; that the economy would collapse without their contribution; and that they do not take jobs from American citizens, but mostly jobs the natives do not want.[1] These attitudes contrast with national surveys that include states with fewer immigrants, in which anti-immigrant sentiment is high. More generally, pro-immigrant views in states with large numbers of immigrants drop from time to time, just as the intensity of anti-immigrant feelings in the other states is sometimes more tempered.

It would be a mistake, to believe that all immigrants, or even the overwhelming majority of them, favor open borders. It is usually the case that large numbers of foreign residents tend to differentiate between their particular circumstance, or those of their parents, and those of more recent arrivals.

In the first half of the 1990s, I worked as a journalist at the Miami Herald Publishing Co. and witnessed firsthand—in local surveys, media programs, and general conversation—the rejection that established immigrants tended to express towards different groups of newcomers. The older Cuban generations thought that the socioeconomic background of new Cuban immigrants would degrade the quality of South Florida's population of Cuban origin. They also resented the excessive number of non-Cuban Hispanics—Nicaraguans, Salvadorans, Colombians, and so on—who were setting up camp in Miami and other parts of Dade and Broward counties at such rates that the balance between Cubans and non-Cubans seemed to be moving towards parity. Many Central and South Americans, for their part, saw with dismay that Haitians and other non-Spanish-speaking black immigrants were also a growing presence in the state. These tensions occasionally erupted into violence, but more often they were cloaked under disputes of a minor nature that were occasionally very petty. Our newspaper saw them reflected in the polls that we commissioned from time to time.

These sentiments have been noticeable for quite some time. Polls taken in the 1980s showed that two-thirds of Hispanic Americans in California were against illegal immigration, favoring severe restrictions. According to a survey of Hispanic Americans taken by Roper in 1985, nine out of every ten interviewees supported stopping all illegal entries into the country. A decade later, in a poll commissioned by a group called Negative Population Growth, half of the respondents who were Hispanic supported the view, held by a majority of Americans, that less than 300,000 immigrants—a considerably smaller number than the estimated total number of arrivals at the time—should be allowed in every year.[2]

Those attitudes changed to some extent in the new millennium, in the wake of the heated debate on immigration reform, when the irate reaction that came from some quarters of the United States against immigrants instilled in many foreigners the fear that nobody, not even residents or naturalized citizens, was secure. A survey conducted by New American Media among legal immigrants in 2006 indicated that two-thirds of them were following the ongoing debate "very closely"; more than half of those who responded said they obtained their information from foreign language media, while two-thirds perceived that anti-immigration sentiment in the country was growing and felt insecure. Although the community that expressed this feeling strongly was Hispanics, other immigrant communities tended to agree: Asians (58 percent), and Africans and Europeans (52 percent). The feeling of insecurity was clearly much stronger among Hispanics, Asians, African, and Europeans than among, for instance, Muslims-Americans prior to the terrorist attacks in New York and Washington, D.C., of September, 11, 2001.[3]

The sense of threat among Hispanics had been incubating for years. Numerous high-profile political developments served as flashpoints of anti-immigrant anger, particularly the California ballot initiative known as Proposition 187 designed to prohibit undocumented immigrants from using social services, which was approved by more than 58 percent of the state's voters in 1994. Proposition 187 was never enforced because the courts put it on hold while the legal and political wrangle ensued. In July 1999, Governor Gray Davis announced that he would not appeal a federal court ruling that declared it unconstitutional.[4] But the social and political message was heeded by Hispanics and other residents of foreign origin.

Hostility to immigrants is by no means uniquely American. In many developed countries, large numbers of citizens are at least wary and often hostile to immigration in its present form. In some countries that are part the Organization of Economic Cooperation and Development (OECD), fewer than one in ten favor immigration.[5] Interestingly, attitudes to immigration have become similar even in underdeveloped nations in recent decades. In the 1995–1997 World Values Survey, the top five countries wanting to prohibit or place strict limits on immigration were the Philippines, Taiwan, South Africa, Poland, and the United States.[6] A series of studies conducted by the Pew Global Attitudes project in 2002 and 2003 found that anti-immigrant sentiment was high not only in North America and Europe, but also in Latin America, Africa, and Asia.[7]

Not only are anti-immigration attitudes present in most societies, developed or underdeveloped; they have been strong throughout history in many types of societies. In ancient Athens, *metics* was the name given to people who were treated as resident aliens and not considered citizens.[8] They were obliged to defend the city militarily, that is, to put their lives at risk for the survival of the polity, but were deprived of all political rights. Even their children, despite being born in the city, were not allowed to become citizens. The ancient republic of Rome also distinguished very starkly between citizens and non-citizens. The ruthless discrimination was weakened when Rome became an empire and designed an expansionist system whereby new citizens were incorporated each time a new land was captured.

For all the talk about the United States being a country of immigrants, the truth is that the parents and grandparents of today's Americans, many of them European, awakened in their native U.S. contemporaries strong negative reactions. The argument that past immigration was "good" and contemporary immigration "bad" implies that previous waves of immigrants were generally welcomed. But in fact, many of the nationalities and creeds that most Americans regard as the heritage of this nation were at one point the object of native resentment. The Irish, the Italians, the Hungarians, the Jews, the Catholics, and others were perceived by Americans at the time of their arrival similarly to how some Americans perceive Mexican immigrants today: lowly, uncivilized, unreliable—in one word, "different."

The Irish stereotype, strongly impressed in the mind of ordinary folks in the second half of the 1800s, was that of a rowdy, quarrelsome drunkard. These attitudes probably originated in the gang conflicts that involved Irish members in earlier decades. "No relation except combat was possible or thought of between our gangs and the 'micks'. . . ." recalled Henry Seidel Canby. "They were still alien and had to be shown their place."[9] For decades, the Irish were the target of intense nativist vitriol. Their disproportionate presence in public houses and slums served as a pretext for considering them human scum. It was not until the end of the century that the image of the Irish changed, as they moved up the social ladder and became integrated with native society.[10]

The reception awarded to Central, Eastern, and Southern Europeans from the 1880s onwards in many quarters was no less ferocious. Their culture and appearance were mocked, their actions were considered threatening, and their inability to assimilate and become prosperous was taken as a sign of inferiority. Many were lynched, a scenario that prompted Italy to withdraw its minister from Washington at one point. Unlike what happened with the Irish, intellectuals also partook in the backlash against Italians and Central Europeans.

The reaction against these newcomers was felt all around the country. In the early stages of the immigrant arrivals from Italy, Hungary and other places, the Pacific coast was particularly prominent in its antipathy. Until then, the targets in California and other Western states had been the Asians. Now it was the turn of the Southern, Central and Eastern Europeans. Later, as more Italians were hired to work in the South, southern states became the focal point of anti-immigrant reaction. Italians were considered a challenge to white supremacy.[11]

Tensions between natives and foreign workers got worse due to Prohibition, an era that gave rise to another immigrant stereotype. The ban on alcohol was a boon to organized gangsters who had been recruiting children in poor immigrant quarters. Some of those young recruits grew into what would later become the archetypical Italian mobster. But bootlegging also affected the image of other foreigner communities, particularly Jews from Central and Eastern Europe.[12]

Jews were a vilified immigrant group in nineteenth- and twentieth-century United States. In 1862, in the midst of the Civil War, General Ulysses Grant banned Jewish merchants from his military zone, an order that Abraham Lincoln revoked three weeks later. The Jews had been banned after being accused of profiting from the war. This accusation stemmed from rumors that Jewish traders smuggled southern cotton. In fact, only a small minority of cotton traders who sought to benefit from the need for cotton from the South in the mills of the North were Jews.[13]

Unlike the Irish and the Italians, who became more accepted as they moved up the social hierarchy, the Jews became even less popular as they progressed. Most Jewish immigration in the late nineteenth century was from Central and Eastern Europe and—unlike Jews from Germany and other parts—was associated with an enclosed, insular Yiddish culture. The fact that Jews were eventually assimilated should have meant that suspicions and fears tied to their cultural origin were largely dispelled. However, their social acceptance did not take place until well into the twentieth century.[14]

At the beginning of the twentieth century, a time when some 100,000 Jews were migrating to the United States every year, restrictive laws were finally adopted against them. That did not quell anti-Jewish sentiment. According to credible surveys conducted between 1938 and 1946, Jews were considered greedy and dishonest by more than half of the population of the United States; more than one-third was in favor of imposing discriminatory rules, including the use of separate public restrooms and voting limitations. During a visit to the Yad Vashem museum in Jerusalem in 2010, I was profoundly stirred to learn how

Israel preserves the memory of the 1,000 refugees on the *St. Louis* who left Hamburg on May 13, 1939, but were refused entry into Cuba or the United States, and were forced to return to Europe. Many of them were deported to concentration camps and murdered by the Nazis.[15]

Other immigrant communities were also scorned and suffered discrimination in the early history of the United States. By 1851, the Chinese population lured by the Gold Rush and working in California amounted to 25,000. They owned restaurants, laundries, and shops; they supplied firewood, fruit, and flowers; some worked as domestic servants or in the construction business. Later they diversified and many went to work on the transcontinental railroad.[16] The reaction against them began to be felt in the mid-1800s and reached grotesque proportions in the 1870s and 1880s. A labor union referred to them as "more slavish and brutish than the beasts that roam the fields," adding that they were "groveling worms."[17] Lynchings, boycotts, and mass expulsions were carried out even after the federal government barred people of Chinese origin from coming into the country.[18]

The Japanese were also targeted with special laws that would make any civilized conscience cringe today. However, history reserved a fascinating twist to that infamous story: many Americans helped the Japanese survive those laws. The focal point of anti-Japanese hysteria was California—on whose shores the Asians arrived after crossing the Pacific on their way to establish themselves in America. Anti-Japanese sentiment broke out in the latter part of the nineteenth century, gained new strength after the Russo-Japanese war of 1905, and grew to horrible proportions in the 1920s. Because the Japanese were paid much less than their native counterparts, they sought ways to become farm tenants and sometimes owner-operators. The authorities responded in 1913 with land laws making it illegal for Japanese to lease or own farms. The Japanese in turn came up with schemes to circumvent the prohibition. They leased or purchased land through their native-born children. By requesting the guardianship of their own native-born children at the county office, they could in effect lease or purchase land through their sons and daughters. Some went as far as creating "dummy" corporations whose ostensible owners were Americans.[19]

Today's organized anti-immigration movements are in fact the heirs of a nativist tradition, whether they know it or not. Nativism as a movement was born in the mid-1800s precisely in response to immigration. The original nativists were members of the Star-Spangled Banner, a secret patriotic society. Its members, who came from the upper-middle class, were obliged to maintain total silence about its existence—hence their name, Know-Nothings. They morphed into the American Party in the 1850s and were able to achieve big successes soon before the Civil War. The Governor of Massachusetts was one of the high-profile Know-Nothing members. The movement, as he himself stated, proposed to "nationalize before we naturalize" any new immigrants. Some major figures of the Civil War, including General Ulysses S. Grant, were members of the movement, as were noted intellectuals, Jack London among them. Being against slavery, they fought against the South. Their most long-lasting legacy was probably America's system of public schools, created largely in response to their concern about nationalizing foreigners who had not been Americanized.[20]

John Higham has maintained that the nativist movement was in turn the child of three traditional strands of anti-foreign sentiment that came together at a particular point in time. The oldest, informed by a profound hatred of Catholicism and fueled by the notion of popery as moral depravity, descended from the shock of the Reformation.[21] Anti-Catholic passions were imported by the English colonies, wedged between Catholic France and Catholic Spain. Although the American Revolution, based on pluralism, tolerance, and ideas of individual liberty, tempered anti-Catholicism somewhat, the animosity persisted. Catholics were excluded from public office and subjected to stiff naturalization laws.[22]

A second anti-foreign tradition can be traced back to the 1790s and has to do with the fear of European radicals. Conservatives Americans, distrustful of political agitation, found immigrants inclined to stir political trouble. Since the American Revolution had not been an anarchic, iconoclastic elan against authority, but rather an effort of institutional affirmation, anything that might entail violence against the status quo was seen with suspicion. European and Latin American-style revolution was seen as inimical to American values, which led those who distrusted the backward ways of foreign political activism to adopt a nativist attitude.

The third antecedent of nativism, which emerged in the first part of the nineteenth century, differed from the other two—the anti-Catholic and the anti-radical—in its assertiveness. While the previous ones declared what America was not, the third wave of nativism sought to define Americanism. Although it began as a liberal idea, it developed into a nationalist reaction. The "concept that the United States belongs in some special sense to the Anglo-Saxon 'race' offered an interpretation of the source of national greatness."[23]

The word "nativism" was coined in the 1840s and the first manifestations of this new phenomenon, as mentioned, took the form of the Know-Nothing movement and the American Party. After a period of relative calm, a wave of nativist hysteria struck the Northeast and Midwest of the United States when a group of anarchists caused an explosion in Chicago's Haymarket Square, a development that was seen as proof that foreign radicals were getting busy. Part of the media stoked up xenophobic opinion, calling foreigners "long-haired, wild-eyed, bad-smelling, atheist, reckless foreign wretches, who never did an honest hour's work in their lives . . . crush such snakes."[24] Various nativist groups raised their profile, notably the Order of Railway Conductors and, later, the Grand Army of the Republic, made up of Civil War veterans. New groups, such as the The Order of United American Mechanics and the Patriotic Order Sons of America, came into being. Soon the sentiment began to catch on in mainstream organizations: The Republican Party pushed for immigration restrictions. Business interests that had brought European workers into the country were cowed by the general environment and participated in the backlash against immigration too. They had a good excuse—foreign workers were taking part in labor strikes.[25]

By the 1890s, nativism had become very powerful in the country. Many of the arguments being made at the time were very similar to those one hears today. They broadly involved cultural and economic objections—a fear that the Anglo-Saxon tradition was being eroded by other cultures, and the conviction that immigrants took jobs away from natives, lowered salaries, and generally threatened the conditions under which Americans could work and prosper.

A particularly sordid aspect of nativism was the issue of eugenics, which began to have a presence in the debate in the 1890s and caught the public ear in the following decade. Eugenicist Charles B. Davenport was a leading voice spreading the notion that Europeans represented a biological threat to the survival of the racial purity of the nation. The influence of this pseudoscientific racialist attack on immigration was not negligible. Madison Grant, one of the most important American nativists, declared that "new immigrants," as the Southern, Central, and Eastern European foreigners became known by contrast with the earlier Northern European immigrants, were racially inferior.[26]

A powerfully active force against Jews and Bolsheviks, and later Catholics, was the Ku Klux Klan, the reincarnation of a group of ex-Confederates that had caused much suffering in the post-Civil War Reconstruction with acts of intimidation and violence against carpetbaggers and blacks. It represents one of the extreme forms of nativism at the time. The new version of the organization began in 1916 in Atlanta, when William Simmons, a preacher who had been an organizer of fraternal orders in the rural South, created the Invisible Empire of the Knights of the Ku Klux Klan and appointed himself Imperial Wizard.[27] His group accepted only white Protestants and quickly recruited 5,000 members; by 1923, the membership had grown to a staggering 3 million and expanded to the Midwest and other parts of the country, where anti-immigrant opinion and fear of the large northbound migration of blacks offered perfect conditions. Convinced that the organization's mission was to protect the descendants of the founders and creators of the great nation, the Klan attacked even more whites than blacks. Catholics, Jews, and "Bolsheviks" were targeted continually. Most violent actions against them took place in the South. The KKK had enough clout to influence the results of a few elections; it had one governor elected and set moral standards in some parts of the country—despite Simmons, a modern Torquemada, being a drunkard.[28] In the late 1920s, the movement was torn by internal divisions and eventually withered away.

World War I helped fuel anti-immigrant fervor—as wars tend to do—and rekindled nativism in the early twentieth century. Germans in the United States, including famous ones such as conductor Karl Muck, were interned until the end of the conflict. Theodore Roosevelt openly scolded German-Americans, referring in powerfully nativist language to the "politico-racial hyphen that is the badge and sign of moral treason."[29] As soon as the war was over, nativists found another useful xenophobic pretext—the campaign spearheaded by organizations such as the American Legion to winnow out closet Bolsheviks from society. It mattered little that only a tiny segment of the immigrant population had such leanings: in fearful minds, all immigrants were potential Russian agents.

The social and political climate resulting from the confluence of the various anti-immigrant forces led to the 1921 Immigration Act, a veritable watershed, that imposed immigration quotas for the first time in the history of the United States.[30]

Nativism as an ideological force stems, whether consciously or unconsciously, from the collectivist myth regarding national identity. If one compares the data on attitudes to immigration to the data on attitudes to perceived national identity in the surveys conducted by the Pew Global Attitudes project, a clear connection between those who dislike immigration and those who feel strongly about the uniqueness of their perceived national identity stands out. The attachment to a certain view of collective cultural identity and the discomfort with immigration is very high among those aged 65 or older and considerably lower among those in their 20s. This gap may augur a sea change in the prevailing attitudes in the future, but, for the moment, the strength of anti-immigrant sentiment is in no doubt.

Fear of the other, embodied in a defensive reflex against perceived intrusion, the impulse to preserve the community through antagonism towards newcomers, and the attempt to preempt contagion from the outside world, is an instinct that can be traced to the beginning of human kind. Animosity towards strangers, or beings perceived as such, is a conduct that cuts across all the ages and all sorts of communities, primitive and sophisticated. But it was the modern idea of national sovereignty and the nation state that provided the ideological, moral, and political framework that lent legitimacy to the protection of national borders against foreigners, even if they do not represent a government or an army, and are therefore not a military threat. It elevated the collectivist protectionism of the horde into a legitimate instrument of civilization.

The official birth of the idea of national sovereignty is usually associated by scholars with the Peace of Westphalia of 1648, the two treaties that put an end to the Thirty Years' War among most European powers. Those treaties are generally credited with fixing national sovereignty as a political extension of cultural identity, although notions of nationhood predated the nation state. Historians differ as to whether Westphalia inaugurated the concept of "nation-state," or it was the symbolic culmination of a long process.[31] We do not know whether the latest phase of globalization will definitively erode the nation state. Previous phases, such as the Age of Discovery in the fifteenth century, did not prevent its emergence nor, as in the case of nineteenth century free trade, its subsistence. We know that in many domains, the current phase of globalization entails the gradual dissolution of national borders. But for the moment that idea of a national sovereignty is still the most powerful intellectual, moral, and political instrument in the hands of those who reject the notion of open borders.

The persistence of the idea of national sovereignty as a basis for closed or restricted borders places free societies in a dilemma. Having reduced or eliminated discrimination in their statute books—and even tried to compensate for past injustices by protecting and promoting specific groups in society through so-called positive discrimination—the modern state accepts nationality as a basis for the differentiated treatment of citizens by the law. The rights of human beings in modern states depend on whether they were born there or not. The contradiction between individual rights and liberties, and national sovereignty is nowhere more evident than in the case of unwanted immigrants.

A superstitious notion of nationhood is almost everywhere the basis for the fear and rejection of immigrants. This is true well beyond the most developed and prosperous countries. And it is a potent thread linking anti-immigration sentiment today with anti-immigration sentiment in the past.

In his book *Pandemonium*,[32] the late Senator Daniel Patrick Moynihan, who was an intellectual as well as a politician, defined nation as "a group of people who *believe* they are ancestrally related. It is the largest grouping that shares that belief." The key word is "believed." Americans did not think of themselves as "Americans" until the third quarter of the eighteenth century. The Declaration of Independence did not mention the word "nation," referring only to "free and independent states." Unlike Europe, where the state imported the idea of nationhood, in America the state was a loose entity that succeeded, rather than preceded, the common experiences that gave rise to the American Revolution.

The idea of an American nation, as the American political scientist Samuel P. Huntington argued, did not really come into being until the Civil War. But once it did, it was followed by associations that lobbied for the use of national symbols, as occurred in other countries. Finally arisen, the "national spirit" began to be transmitted through public education, the creation of official holidays, and the language of politics.[33]

Myth and ideology play a significant part in forming a nation's idea of its ethnic roots. America was no different.[34] The nativist reaction against immigration is an extreme offshoot of the national myth.

The State Against the Tide

The modern history of immigration is the history of the state. This history is based on ideas of national identity and includes efforts to stem the tide of immigrants, to use the mechanism of force to impede the natural flows, the comings and goings, of people for whom physical frontiers and official borders had much less significance than for the authorities.

The restrictions adopted by states in the past were most often against people wishing to move out. Influenced by mercantilist economic theories, the government of Louis XIV closely guarded the borders to prevent the French from leaving—the belief being that the drain would ruin the economy. Similarly, until the mid-nineteenth century, the British banned qualified artisans from leaving the country, while Germany imposed a tax on those wishing to emigrate. It was not repealed until 1817.[35]

In current times, some Asian countries have also opted to restrict emigration, for different reasons. The ostensible objective is to protect women from being the victims of abuse in the countries to which they wish to travel. But these arguments lose weight if contrasted with the levels of abuse suffered by women domestically. India, Bangladesh and Pakistan are three such countries.[36]

The actions by the state against incoming migrants, however, have been more numerous than those targeting emigrants. International law in the last half-century, from the Universal Declaration of Human Rights (1948) to the European Convention of Human Rights and Liberties (Protocol of 1962) and the African Charter of Human and People's Rights (1981), has therefore tended to emphasize the right of citizens to leave their countries, rather than movement in the opposite direction. The major reasons informing most restrictive actions against would-be newcomers have been cultural and economic, as well as related to security. Under those broad areas of argumentation and justification, many norms have been passed whose real motives cover a range of attitudes from racism to nationalism to economic protectionism to fear of disorder—attitudes that, as we have seen, have been present for a very long time even if they did not always inform public policy.

After centuries of relatively free circulation, migration in Europe started to be seriously restricted only in 1918 as a result of World War I, when empire after empire collapsed and the continent fragmented itself into various political entities along arbitrarily-defined ethnic lines that incubated new rivalries and contributed to a bunker mentality. The effect of this fragmentation and division based on arbitrary notions of ethnicity was devastating for the relative freedom of movement that people had enjoyed hitherto. Until 1924, France placed no control on the entry of Algerians. After that year, those who wished to emigrate to France needed a labor contract, which was not hard to come by. In 1936, the Popular Front reestablished freedom of circulation and made French Muslims, as they were called, equal citizens. Until the 1960s, the limits imposed were quite minor.[37] For its part, Britain placed minor restrictions during the first half of the twentieth century, and certainly much smaller ones than has been the case in the past three decades.[38]

In the nineteenth century, there were areas of Africa in which people from one country felt welcomed by the state in another, and vice versa. That was the case between Nigeria and Ghana. Migration of Ghanaians to Nigeria started in the latter part of the nineteenth century and the pattern continued with sporadic interruptions well into the twentieth century.[39] A paragraph in V.S. Naipaul's novel *A Bend in the River* gives a sense of how artificial the national borders imposed by Europe in the nineteenth century were:

> Nazruddin had cut down on his business on the coast and begun to move inland. The colonial boundaries of Africa gave an international flavor to his operations. But Nazruddin was doing no more than following the old Arab trading routes to the interior; and he had fetched up in the center of the continent, at the bend in the great river.[40]

By contrast, almost wherever one looks today in the era of globalization, the state seems to be trying to stem the tide of immigrants with deportations, quotas, limitations, and penalties that are increasingly aimed not only at dissuading or punishing illegal foreigners, but also at cracking down on native accomplices who facilitate their presence. With the exception of spaces such as that comprised by the Shengen Agreement among some European countries, the tendency is against the free movement of people. The policies are conceived and implemented under the conviction that there are no natural limits to immigration—that a relatively open border policy would inevitably flood the receiving country with more foreigners than it could possibly accommodate. Peaceful coexistence among immigrants is seen as impossible, even with a generally permissive response to would-be newcomers on the part of the government, given the intensity of anti-immigrant feelings.

In pursuit of the effort to stem the tide, the state has come up with many types of highly visible and well-known barriers that are often the object of scandal in the world media: walls (Israel-Egypt), high-tech barriers and movement sensors (United States-Mexico), barbed wire (Spain-Morocco), electronic fences (Zimbabwe-Botswana), and tubes filled with concrete (Saudi Arabia-Yemen.) The same kinds of actions taken by states in rich nations have been adopted in poor ones against people coming from even poorer lands.

Countries that were once known as particularly welcoming are now restrictive. Australia changed its laws in the early 1990s (for years, they had been lenient towards some groups although tough against others, such as the Chinese). Australia has hardened its immigration restrictions periodically ever since, granting visas according to a points system based on educational attainment, age, and occupational background. Canada, a vast territory with a scarce population and a long history of immigration from whom Australia partly took its cue in recent years, also changed course in the 1990s. Its government announced in the middle of the decade that it would reduce the number of immigrants it would accept, giving preference to skilled professionals and business people, and severely restricting family unification.[41]

Countries such as France, where the stated policy was integration under certain republican values rather than exclusion based on ethnic-based national identity, have nonetheless acted more according to the latter than the former ethos. To describe French policy as "assimilationist" would fly in the face of the evidence that has emerged in the last three decades. The frustration and violence visible in French communities of African origin speak to us of an entire generation of second-generation immigrants who have grown up with a sense of disenfranchisement and marginality. Those youth have turned their lack of opportunity and mobility into a pretext for violence. Assimilationism may have been the stated policy, but absent many factors necessary to make assimilation possible, including an economic environment prone to colorless upward mobility, the translation of that policy, and of the leaders' uplifting rhetoric, into real life is improbable. Arguably, the consistent underperformance of the

European economy in recent decades, and more widely the crisis of the welfare state in France and other European countries evident since the latter part of the twentieth century, bears more influence on how immigration is perceived and treated, and how immigrants assimilate themselves, than official discourse. The contradiction at the heart of the immigration issue pits the republican ideals of the Revolution against the dire government interventionism of its legacy as well as its social elitism.

Others have been more open about the idea of using restrictive immigration policies to preserve so-called national character by making it very difficult even for second- or third-generation immigrants to become naturalized. German-born children of foreigners—including those who had come in under guest-worker programs—were not eligible to become citizens until 2000.[42] In the early 1980s, Great Britain raised the bar considerably for those wishing to acquire British citizenship, scrapping *jus solis* as a basis for becoming eligible.[43]

The need by governments to be seen as tough on immigration cuts across the ideological and political spectrum. It has turned left-wing and socialist governments into custodians of the nation's borders whose zeal matches that of the right. Spain's tough contemporary laws on immigration started under Felipe González, a long-time darling of European socialism, who in 1985, keen to rise up to the occasion of his country's accession to what was called the European Community the following year, approved and implemented a *Ley de Extranjería* that set the tone for the next two decades. To be sure, between then and now, there have been periods of partial legalization of undocumented foreigners, and a law was passed by the right-wing government of José María Aznar in 2000 that placed foreigners already in the country on an equal legal footing with Spaniards. But the general provisions regarding immigration have become more stringent under both the right and the left in Spain.

The fourth *Ley de Extranjería*—in and of itself a symptom of the failure of the previous three—was approved in 2009, establishing a 60-day confinement for "illegals," in Spain, banning family reunification for those under 65 years old and cutting back their access to housing and the electoral registry. In principle, someone who requests asylum, for instance, is allowed to work after six months while he or she awaits a response. In practice, that response may take more than three years, so that the would-be refugee is kept in legal limbo, as was explained to me in Málaga, in southern Spain, in December of 2009, by several people who were in that very situation in a guest house managed by CEAR.

In the United States, the political divide over immigration, at least among the mainstream parties, is also more theoretical than real. Some of the toughest laws have been passed under the Democratic Party, the organization that supposedly takes a more lenient view of this social phenomenon. Particularly notable were the measures taken by the Clinton administration in the mid-1990s. They were mostly adopted under the Illegal Immigration Reform and Immigrant Responsibility Act. The number of border agents was doubled; the construction of physical barriers was ordered in areas with heavy traffic; civil and criminal penalties were stiffened; the authority of state and local officials to enforce the law was buttressed; and the removal of undesirable people at the border was expedited.[44]

The U.S. government decided to clamp down on seasonal migration and build walls along the border, creating an incentive for many immigrants, especially those from Mexico, to remain permanently in U.S. territory rather than risk being kept out of the country, as former Mexican Minister of Foreign Affairs Jorge Castañeda has pointed out. Another effect of the Clinton policies was that points of entry moved east, from California to Arizona and Texas. Between 1997 and 2007, on average one immigrant perished every day but 1,500 succeeded in entering the United States.[45]

The various measures adopted, subsequently reinforced by the Bush administration and kept in place by the Obama administration, have made it possible to deport hundreds of thousands of people, or to prevent from coming into the country. The net flow of immigrants into the country, however, continues to be positive, even if in some years more than 200,000 immigrants have been sent back or returned at the point of entry.

Nearly 180 communities in states all around the country have passed laws requiring police and state officials, in addition to employers, to investigate the migratory status of people who might be undocumented.[46] These laws have in effect given legal cover to raids in places deemed to be concentration points for low-skilled foreigners, or even actions against suspected "illegals" who might simply be stopped in the streets. Some states, Arizona and Oklahoma for example, and Prince William County in Virginia, to mention but one county, have passed "enforcement norms" that have forced many people of foreign origin to move elsewhere.[47]

Reports of mass detentions in the country seem to match the testimonies I obtained in Ciudad Juárez, Mexico, at the foot of the bridge through which dozens of deportees pass every day. The International Human Rights Federation, founded in 1922 and representing groups related to migration issues all around the world, states that on any day in 2007, the number of people that were in detention under control of the U.S. Immigration and Custom Enforcement was as high as 26,500. At least 84 percent of them had no legal representation.[48] A few years later, Obama confronted widespread criticism from pro-immigration groups when it became obvious that mass round-ups and deportations were kept up despite a marked fall in the number of foreigners coming in.

Forceful state action against immigrants is taken even in countries where immigration is needed and encouraged because of acute labor needs. In the Persian Gulf countries in which Arab immigrants have been gradually replaced with Asian workers through restrictions or disincentives aimed at the former, ideological fear has also played a part. Some of these governments wanted to preempt radical left-wing ideas in the times of the Soviet empire, and of pan-Arabism, both of which directly threatened the existence of the Gulf monarchies that harbored immigrants from fellow Arab lands. Those monarchies were the target of pan-Arabist calls for all Arab nations to partake in their oil wealth in the 1960s. Radical activists, Palestinians in particular, agitated for their various political causes and organized strikes that went beyond purely economic claims, raising in the countries that hosted them the specter of instability. The authorities of the Gulf states reacted by persecuting many Arabs in the 1970s and 1980s.[49] Their actions serve as precedents for the more recent efforts of Arab dictatorships aligned with Western liberal democracies to stem fundamentalist Islam and its violent offshoot, Islamic terrorism.

In the light of the progressive hardening of laws relating to immigrants throughout the last decades, many historical analysts have sought to develop theories on immigration policy, mostly along ideological lines. Eytan Meyers has divided the theories into various categories.[50]

The Marxist approach focuses on the short-term relationship between immigration policy and the economic cycle. This approach fails to explain or take into account the variations of policy according to the ethnic origin of immigrants. Its predictions regarding the long-term growth of immigration arising from the demands of the capitalism is simplistic.

The "domestic politics" approach focuses on how the pressure of economic and social factors is reflected in the political response to immigration. There is truth to this, but the proponents of this view prefer to analyze particular cases rather than elaborate on a wide-ranging theory.

The "institutional" approach looks at the complex, contradictory, and gradual process that leads to policy. It too fails to explain why the process by which immigration policies have been adopted in countries with similar institutions has varied so much.

The "liberal" approach looks at immigration policy in the context of globalization—especially the supranational regimes and organizations that it says have replaced the sovereign state. But this is only really true in the European Union, and even there, significant policy differences among some member states still exist.

Other approaches have been offered, particularly in relation to the treatment given to immigration by different European governments. William Brubaker addressed the importance of nationhood and national self-understanding—a mystique enforced by the nation state—in the development of immigration policies. According to him, differences in the way nations understood themselves resulted in two distinctive immigration policies in Europe: "State-centered and assimilationist" in France, "*Volk*-centered and differentialist in Germany."[51] But time has eroded some of the differences, to the effect that in recent years the tendency has been for the various governments to converge. Ironically, time has also undercut the original intentions of immigration policy. A few years ago, who would have thought that more than one-fourth of Germany's powerful starting lineup at the 2010 World Cup in South Africa would be made up of Turks and Ghanaians?

On the whole, theories on what determines immigration policy fail to establish models that fully explain and predict what is in essence an extremely complex process in which a multitude of people with different experiences and psychologies, and under varying stimuli, make decisions or inform the decisions made by others.

Stopping immigrants altogether—drying up the immigration well completely—would require turning the United States or European countries into a totalitarian state. And even under totalitarian conditions, it is unlikely that the control of the borders would be one hundred percent effective. No totalitarian state has managed to be one-hundred-percent effective at prohibiting whatever it was that they tried (or continue to try) to prohibit. The failures of alcohol prohibition in the U.S. or emigration restrictions in the Soviet Union are well known. But assuming the goal of complete immigration prevention was attainable, it would require the kinds of government controls on the movements and personal choices of individuals, communications, hiring practices, and other aspects of daily life that would be intolerable in a liberal democracy such as that of the United States. The massive intrusion into the lives of citizens and the decisions of private businesses would be incompatible with the free enterprise system and the liberties currently protected by the Constitution.

The fact that anti-immigration laws, many of them stemming from nativist pressure, are ineffective in attaining the purported goal does not mean, of course, that many people are not directly affected by them. They are—a tragic reality that is not just statistical but—as I had a chance to witness on the border with Mexico—very real in individual terms. That and other borders where people used to come and go naturally have seen an artificial construct come in the way of tradition.

Notes

1. The survey commissioned by New Democrat Network (NDN) in September 2008 can be seen at http://ndn.org/sites/default/files/paper/statewide-surveys-on-immigration-policy-combined.pdf

2. Georgie Anne Geyer, *Americans No More* (New York: The Atlantic Press, 1996), 76, 223.

3. A poll taken in 2000 among likely Muslim voters showed that 31.9 percent, certainly a high number but not a majority, felt that America treated their religion and their community with respect. The poll, conducted by Zogby and commissioned by the American Muslim Council, was released on August 28, 2000, and reported the following day on page 5 of the *Pittsburgh Post-Gazette.*

4. Samuel T. Francis, *America Extinguished: Mass Immigration and the Disintegration of American Culture* (Monterey, Va.: Americans for Immigration Control, 2002), 76, 91.

5. Lant Princhett, *Let Their People Come* (Washington, D.C.: Center for Global Development, 2006), 8.

6. The World Values Survey is an academic project that gauges values around the world. Its surveys, including the ones to which I refer, can be found on its website at http://www.worldvaluessurvey.org

7. "A Global Generational Gap," Pew Global Attitudes Project, *Pew Research Center*, February, 24, 2004, http://pewglobal.org/commentary/display.php?AnalysisID=86

8. Peter D. Salins, *Assimilation, American Style* (New York: Basic Books, 1997), 23.

9. Henry Seidel Canby, *American Memoir* (Boston: Houghton Mifflin, 1947), 22–24.

10. Kevin Kenny, "Irish Immigrants in the United States," *Journal USA* 13, no. 2: 10.

11. One of many incidents illustrative of feelings at the time involved five Sicilian storekeepers in Tallolah, Louisiana, who caused the fury of local whites by treating blacks as equals. These Italians suffered various acts of contempt. Eventually they were lynched with the pretext of a quarrel over a goat. Primal passions also flared in the Midwest. In August, 1920, a mob attacked a group of foreigners in the Italian quarter of the mining town of West Frankfurt, Illinois. There had a been a strike in the coal mines where some Italians and a large part of the natives worked, as well as an incident involving the kidnapping of two children. The mob blamed the Italians and staged a pogrom-style attack against them, stoning and burning their homes. Labor strikes in other cities also gave rise to acts of xenophobia against the Italians, the Hungarians, and the Poles. Ironically, many of the Southern and Central Europeans had originally been hired by American businesses to offset native strikes. A large number had not been recruited from Europe but from states such as New York, where the Italian community was long established. See John Higham, *Strangers in the Land: Patterns of American Nativism 1860–1925* (New Brunswick: N. J.: Rutgers University Press, 1955), 95, 169.

12. Michael Burgan, *Immigration to the United States: Italian Immigrants* (New York: Facts on File, 2005), 59–62.

13. "General Grant's Infamy," *Jewish Virtual Library*, http://www.jewishvirtuallibrary.org/jsource/anti-semitism/grant.html (Based on material from the American Jewish Historical Society and Abraham Karp, *From the Ends of the Earth: Judaic Treasures of the Library of Congress* [Washington, D.C.: Library of Congress, 1991]).

14. For a comprehensive history of Eastern European Jews who migrated to the United States at the end of the nineteenth and the beginning of the twentieth centuries, see Jeffrey S. Gurock, ed., *East European Jews in America, 1880–1920: Immigration and Adaptation: American Jewish History,* vol. 3, (New York: Routledge, 1998).

15. Alex Tabarrok, "Economic and Moral Factors in favor of Open Immigration," September 14, 2000, http://www.independent.org/issues/article.asp?id=486

16. Jack Cher, *The Chinese of America* (San Francisco: Harper & Row, 1980), 57–60, 70, 72.

17. Jules Alexander Karlin, "The Anti-Chinese Outbreaks in Seattle, 1885–1886," *Northwest Quarterly* 39 (1948), 103–30.

18. "Chinese Immigration and the Chinese Exclusion Acts," *U.S. Department of State*, http://www.state.gov/r/pa/ho/time/gp/82014.htm

19. Robert Higgs, "Landless by Law: Japanese Immigrants in Californian Agriculture to 1941," *The Journal of Economic History*: 38, no. 1 (March 1978): 207–218.

20. Peter Brimelow, *Alien Nation: Common Sense About America's Immigration Disaster* (Random House: New York, 1995), 12–13.

21. Ray Allen Billington has explored this first manifestation of nativist sentiment in *The Protestant Crusade, 1800–1860: A Study of the Origins of American Nativism* (New York: Quadrangle Books, 1938). Also see John Higham, *Strangers in the Land: Patterns of American Nativism 1860–1925* (New Brunswick, N. J.: Rutgers University Press, 1955), 5.

22. Higham, *Strangers in the Land*, 5–7.

23. The fact that Sharon Turner's *History of the Anglo-Saxons* was wildly popular in America provides some context to the emergence of this third strand of nativism. See Higham, *Strangers in the Land*), 9.

24. Dennis Wepman, *Immigration: American Experience"* (Facts on File: New York, 2007), p. 189.

25. As is usually the case in times of collective phobia, the suspicion against foreigners extrapolated relatively minor threats from foreigners onto the wider immigrant community and disregarded the community's many contributions, of which some of the very same people and interests that suddenly turned against it had been very conscious earlier. Different sources valued the monetary contribution of the immigrants to the United States at the time. The U.S. Treasury Department valued it at $800 per person. Andrew Carnegie raised the estimate to $1,500. If the general public had any sense of that contribution, attitudes would have to change once the air was cleared. See Andrew Carnegie, *Triumphant Democracy or Fifty Years March of the Republic* (New York: Charles Scribner's Sons, 1886), 34.

26. The first edition of *The Passing of the Great Race*, by Madison Grant, was published in New York by Charles Scribner's Sons in 1918.

27. For a good account of the Ku Klux Klan, see David M. Chalmers, *Hooded Americanism: The History of the Ku Klux Klan,* 3rd ed. (Durham, N.C.: Duke University Press, 1987).

28. Higham, *Strangers in the Land*, 286–293.

29. Frederick C. Luebke, *Bonds of Loyalty: German-Americans and World War I* (Dekalb, Ill.: Northern Illinois University Press, 1974), 174.

30. Philip Q. Yang, *Post-1965 Immigrants to the United States: Structural Determinants* (Westport, Conn.: Praeger Publishers, 1995), 12.

31. For the two differing views see, for instance, Martin van Creverd, *The Rise and Decline of the State* (Cambridge: Cambridge University Press, 1999), and Roger Scruton, *The West and the Rest: Globalization and the Terrorist Threat* (Wilmington, Del.: Intercollegiate Studies Institute, 2003).

32. Daniel Patrick Moyniham, *Pandaemonium: Ethnicity in International Politics* (New York: Oxford University Press, 1993), 1.

33. Samuel Huntington, *Who Are We? The Challenges of America's National Identity* (New York: Simon & Schuster, 2004), 111.

34. As early as 1639, the Pilgrims, who had landed nineteen years earlier, had set fines for shipmasters who brought paupers—ironically, a form of discrimination against Anglo-Saxon immigrants. Two centuries later, after it became known that most of the

residents of the New York municipal alms house were foreigners, the authorities faced popular pressure to do something about it. In 1839, they expelled Scottish paupers whose passage had been paid by the city of Edinburgh and who had arrived wearing clothes from poorhouses in Edinburgh. See Peter Brimelow, *Alien Nation: Common Sense About America's Immigration Disaster* (New York: Random House, 1995), 148.

35. Hans Magnus Enzensberger, *Civil War* (London: Granta Books, 1994), 118–119.

36. Nana Oishi, *Women in Motion: Globalization, State Policies, and Labor Migration in Asia*, (Stanford, Calif.: Stanford University Press, 2005), 57–60, 87.

37. Abdelmalek Syadi, *l'Immigration ou les Paradoxes de l'Alterité* (Paris: Raison d'Agir Editions, 2006), 193–194.

38. Zig Layton-Henry, *The Politics of Immigration: Immigration, "Race" and "Race" Relations in Post-War Britain* (Oxford, U.K, and Cambridge, Mass.: Blackwell, 1992), 9.

39. Adepoju Aderanti, "International Migration in Africa South of the Sahara," in *International Migration Today*, vol. 1, *Trends and Prospects*, eds. Reginald Appleyard and Charles Stahl (Paris: UNESCO, 1988), 160.

40. V. S. Naipaul, *A Bend in the River* (New York: Vintage International, 1989), 20.

41. The degree of severity with which "illegals" are punished still varies considerably around the world. Brazil does not provide criminal sanctions for the undocumented entry and presence of foreigners, opting instead to fine them. Japan, at the other end of the spectrum, applies a three-year prison sentence. In peak years, such as 2004, the Tokyo authorities deported more than 50,000 people. Another state that is tough on immigrants, Switzerland, has been turning away more than 100,000 people per year. See "Immigration Law: Sanctions And Enforcement In Selected Foreign Countries," *Report For Congress*, The Law Library of Congress, April, 2006.

42. Thomas Donland, *A World of Wealth: How Capitalism Turns Profits into Progress* (Upper Saddle River, N.J.: Pearson Education, 2008), 76.

43. Layton-Henry, *The Politics of Immigration*, 190.

44. The text of the law can be found on the following website: http://frwebgate.access .gpo.gov/cgi-bin/getdoc.cgi?dbname=104_cong_public_laws&docid=f:publ208.104.pdf

45. Jorge Castañeda, *Ex Mex: From Migrants to Immigrants* (New York: The New Press, 2007), 3, 43–45.

46. Donland, *A World of Wealth*, 70.

47. "U.S.: Is Illegal Tide of Immigrants Finally Easing?" *Hispanic American Center For Economic Research (HACER)*, January 17, 2009, http://www.hacer.org/report/ 2009/01/us-is-illegal-tide-of-immigrants-html

48. The information is provided in the Autumn 2008 issue of *Frontera Cero*, a newsletter published by CEAR in Madrid.

49. Andrzej Kapizewski, "Arab Labor Migration to GCC States," in *Arab Migration in a Globalized World* (Geneva: International Organization for Migration, 2004), 119–121.

50. Eytan Meyers, "Theories of International Immigration Policy: A Comparative Analysis," *International Migration Review* 34, no. 4 (2000).

51. Oishi, *Women in Motion*, 82.

5

Unnatural Borders

CIUDAD JUÁREZ IS known as the most dangerous city in the world because of the drug war, and it feels like it. Half of Juárez looks like a ghost town; the other resembles a battle zone briefly gone quiet so that cars can get out. Many assembly plants are silent, commercial centers are as lifeless as the cotton fields east of town, restaurants and bars are half-empty, and even the facade of the morgue is riddled with bullets. Thousands of run-down cars seem to be just cruising aimlessly, their drivers having no destination in mind. Street vendors in the small plaza where the cathedral stands do little more than talk to each other, and the soldiers riding around with their fingers on the triggers look more tense than the civilians.

On the morning I arrived, a woman was found buried in her own backyard a few blocks from where I was staying; two bodies were also identified in Anapra, a nearby slum with houses made of cardboard, surrounded by the desert; a fence put up by the U.S. authorities can easily be seen from there. One evening when I went to dinner, I learned that four people had been shot earlier outside the same restaurant. Another shootout had left a couple of victims on the Paseo Triunfo de la Republica, a major artery. Someone mentioned that a child had been found hanging from a bridge earlier in the week, just another corpse adding to the numbing statistic: 2,300 people killed in 2009. As I write this in the middle of 2011, some 1,339 people have already been killed in the first half of the year.[1] No wonder a quarter of the population has fled.

There was a time, before the mass deportations of Mexicans from the United States, when human traffic flowed copiously in a south-to-north direction between Juárez and El Paso—the Casa del Migrante guesthouse would receive an average of 60 guests per day, who would stay up to a couple of weeks. A couple of decades ago, vehicles transporting workers would drive back and forth crossing the low river, as many Mexicans worked for El Paso employers and came back in the evening.

Nowadays, Mexicans wanting to travel to El Paso need a permit; the consulate gives it to them under heavy restrictions, the main one being that they are not allowed to go beyond El Paso itself. Crossing illegally through this heavily guarded border area is almost impossible now, although a few daredevils are known to make it across at Anapra, the nearby desert slum facing a hill on top of which stands a "black Christ" that looks perfectly white from a distance. Most of the migrants who try to cross from Anapra—a very long shot considering the fence, the highly visible border patrols on the other side, the high-tech sensors, and the powerful lights that shine on the area at night—are Central Americans whose information with regard to the possibilities of crossing from Juárez to El Paso are outdated or, in some cases, who have been misled by mischievous—or cruel—*polleros.*

The levees of anti-immigration policy and enforcement are fighting to contain, along the border between the U.S. and Mexico, a tide as natural as the flow of the sea and the rivers. The border is an almost 2,000-mile stretch. No other first-world country shares a land border with a third-world nation. The closest comparison might be the border between Spain and North Africa via Gibraltar, and the border between Italy and Albania, but in both cases there is water in between, and the length of the border is much smaller. For a very long time, people living near the U.S.-Mexico border treated it as a bridge, not a rampart. It feels very different now. Nowhere is the anti-immigration reaction, which is discussed in the previous chapter, more poignant than at America's southern border, where it takes on real meaning for countless human beings. What used to be a natural crossing is now an unnatural construct working against people's impulses to come and go freely.

In recent decades, the cross-border dynamic has been a cat-and-mouse game. Border patrols catch Mexicans or other immigrants soon after they traverse the border and, instead of processing them through the legal system, they send them back to Mexico, so as not to clog the court system. U.S. authorities know full well that the would-be migrants will try to come back, which is why the U.S. often expels them through a different entry point than the one they used coming in, so as to make their journey back more arduous and long, hopefully discouraging future attempts. My interviews with Mexicans in Ciudad Juárez, the Chihuahua and Sonora border towns, and very specifically in Sásabe, left no doubt.

The cat-and-mouse game has moved the center of gravity of illegal crossings along the border over the past couple of decades. At the end of the 1990s, a little-known town by the name of Douglas, in Arizona, was the busiest point. It was soon displaced by others, such as Nogales, and much more recently by Sásabe, from where aspirants trek two or three days through the Arizona desert aiming to get to Tucson, or even Phoenix. Nobody even mentions Tijuana, the legendary stepping-stone of Mexican crossing for years, as a point of illegal entry today.

Those migrants to whom I talked were performing what amounted to a ritual attempt to cross, because others had done so before. Before the establishment of the U.S. border patrol with just a handful of agents in the 1920s, no one really guarded the border. Well into the 1940s, those wanting to enter illegally could do so without much hassle.[2] Even in the 1970s, the U.S. border patrol had no more than a couple of thousand agents. For generations of Americans, Mexicans were not really alien. Generation after generation of Mexicans have related to the U.S. side of the border with familiarity. The result is evident in the most basic data relating to the population of the border areas. In 2000, the populations of six out of twelve important cities on the U.S. side of the border were over 90 percent Hispanic, in three others the proportion was more than 80 percent Hispanic, and in one it was more than 70 percent Hispanic. Only two—San Diego and Yuma—were less than 50 percent Hispanic.[3] Those lands did not become Hispanic overnight. They were historically Hispanic. The sociological composition of these cities has withstood the shifting borderlines derived from war as well as politically directed efforts to "Anglicize" it. While California's nineteenth-century population was overwhelmed by Anglo immigration from other parts of the United States, big Spanish-speaking enclaves survived in Texas and New Mexico. But even California partially reverted to a mix with a strong Hispanic component.

Nowadays, more people cross the border from El Paso into Juárez, one of several entry points for deportees along the border between the U.S. and Mexico, than go the other way.

Before being sent back to Mexico, the deportees spend time in jail in the United States—sometimes a week, oftentimes a few weeks, in many cases several months. Afterwards, they are removed to a town like Juárez. At the Paso del Norte border bridge (the formal name of the Santa Fe Bridge), which lies at the end of the Benito Juárez Avenue, a once-bustling commercial artery and now a run-down figment of its former self, overlooking the Rio Grande, a sliver of water melancholically belying its mighty name, they are handed to the Mexican police most afternoons in groups of several dozen people. The authorities present them with various options, one of which is to head towards the Casa del Migrante guesthouse, in the outskirts of Juárez, with a land ticket to their hometown in their pockets. If they choose the Casa del Migrante—and some 7,000 of them did in 2009—they get a roof for one night, a meal and a shower, and they head for the bus the following morning, bound for their final destination. That destination can be anywhere: Guerrero, Michoacán, Jalisco, Zacatecas, San Luis Potosí—wherever.

The vast majority of the deportees are men in their twenties and thirties who work in agriculture or construction; to judge by my conversations with them under the cold, windy conditions of December, a significant number left Mexico as children with their parents. For most of them, "home" has little to do with Mexico, a country they left many years ago, sometimes decades ago, from which they have become disconnected, even if they have kept up communication with family members. The deportees enter the bridge in handcuffs on the U.S. side and arrive in Mexico with free hands, but with the disconcerted look of someone who is not quite sure whether he really is free to go anywhere.

Few spectacles are more telling about the degradation of life here than the sight of the migrants expelled from the United States coming in over the Santa Fe Bridge every evening. As soon as they walk in, dozens of people, including mean-looking thugs and attractive girls, mob them and try to force them toward the foreign exchange bureaus on Benito Juárez Avenue, where sometimes they are briefly kidnapped for a small ransom and oftentimes cheated into buying pesos at inflated rates. Some of the girls are trained to flirt with the migrants, get themselves invited out for a drink, then take the migrants to bars where they are subsequently skinned of whatever money they have brought with them.

Because many of the deportees have done time in U.S. jails, they enter their own country with a sullied reputation that makes them social outcasts in the eyes of many Juarenses, as residents of Ciudad Juárez are called. Some of the deportees were picked up by the U.S. police in routine raids on business sites or simply hangouts where the authorities suspect they will find illegal aliens. Others came to the attention of the cops for misdemeanors that brought their migratory status into the open; after spending some time behind bars, they were offered the chance to leave the country before any court case was initiated. The fact that some of the deportees have criminal records has extended a shadow of undesirability over all of the deportees, prompting politicians in this city run by the Partido Revolucionario Institucional (PRI) political party—as is the state of Chihuahua to which it belongs—to stigmatize them. And, at least initially, they are easy to spot: They all wear a prisoner's wristband.

The Mexican federal police, known as Grupo Beta, who are in charge of handling the deportees once the U.S. authorities hand them over, try to counsel and protect them. "But once they are in Mexico, they know they are on their own, so they have to face the new reality," says Marcos, a 22-year old Honduran who came to Mexico with the intention of heading north because his family only has employment a couple of days a week back home, but who accepted an invitation from the Casa del Migrante to remain there and work at the guesthouse. "Migrants are despised on both sides of the river, just as Central Americans are mistreated here by people who complain how Mexicans are mistreated in the United States."

His journey was gruesome—by land to El Salvador and then Guatemala, by boat across the Río Suchiate and into southern Mexico, and by train to Querétaro, where he was briefly hired to paint a house in exchange for a roof under which he could sleep before he headed to Juárez, naively convinced that one could still cross over to the other side from there. His journey was a success compared to the gruesome nature of what happens to many of the others who attempt to travel from the south to the north of Mexico. Some are raped, others killed on the "death train," as they call it—and many, many are arrested.

Some of the deportees—unshaven, unkempt, weary, some dressed in rags— look like a Court of Miracles, the Paris district that used to provide refuge for France's crooks. But they are not crooks. Their stories are the stuff of heroism: the relentless pursuit of a dream; so relentless that, despite the hardships endured and the colossal odds against them, many still want to try it again.

Emilio, who comes from Guerrero, in southern Mexico, entered the United States fifteen years ago from San Luis Río Colorado into Yuma, a city on the state's border with California. He lived in California for ten years and then moved to the state of Washington, where he spent the next five years. He has two children, a nine-year-old and a six-year-old who speaks virtually no Spanish, with his partner, also Mexican, who has stayed behind and whom he might never see again—if his plans to cross illegally once more do not work out, that is.

Emilio, an agricultural laborer who worked for an apple grower, had a driver's license thanks to Washington's lax laws regarding the issuing of state documents, but he managed to get into trouble for drunk driving. The second time he was sent to the county jail, the police checked his status. He was deemed to be an illegal alien and handed over to immigration officers, who initiated a deportation process that took almost three months, during which he was transferred to another prison in Tacoma. In the course of that process, Emilio was offered a $5,000 bail, which he was not able to pay despite the money he earned working in the prison's kitchen. He then became persuaded that waiting for the trial was useless since he had no chance of being allowed to remain in the country. Immigration officers explained to him that the fact that his children were U.S. citizens did not constitute any sort of attenuating circumstance. A few weeks later, he was taken to the airport and made to board a plane that subsequently picked up other detainees in various stopovers on the way to Texas.

"I entered with my all heart," he says, "because this is my country, but I do not belong here anymore. My entire life is over there. When I came into Juárez, I took a taxi to the bus terminal, and the Mexican police arrested me because I had no papers." They probably thought he was Central American. "I was only able to persuade them that I was Mexican by showing them the certificate that the U.S. immigration officers gave me."

Emilio's mind is totally made up: As soon as possible, he will attempt to make it back to the United States. When I point out to him that Juárez is—together with Tijuana, another traditional staging point for migrants—probably the most heavily monitored border crossing between the United States and Mexico, he calmly shrugs his shoulders. "I know where to go," he says. "Other deportees told me where I could find help. I will be heading west with that help." For a moment I think he means "help from the smugglers," but I can see his index finger pointing upwards and realize he must be talking of Father Romo. "West" to Emilio means Mexicali, facing Calexico on the U.S. side. "My desire to go back is stronger than my fear."

The nuns tending the small guesthouse's living room go about their business totally unperturbed as Emilio shares his plans with me. They have heard it all before and they need to get things ready for the next wave of visitors. They have just received word from Manuel, the Casa del Migrante's van driver, that a new bunch of deportees are on their way and they need to have supper ready to welcome them to their (new) country.

At the Santa Fe Bridge—historically known as El Paso del Norte, an inscription that still dominates the entrance—more deportees come in later that evening. Jaime, a man in his mid-twenties, seems the most restless of the lot; he looks uncomfortable. He was able to sneak into the United States six years ago and headed straight for Las Vegas, where he had heard there was work. After a short search, he found employment at a restaurant. Soon he fell in love with a Colombian girl and moved in with her. His life seemed pretty stable—until he made a big mistake. Tired of his old car, he arranged for it to be burnt so that he could claim the indemnity payment from the insurance company and buy a brand new one. He was arrested for insurance fraud and sent to a county jail, where the immigration officers were brought in to take his fingerprints and ask him questions. He was transferred to a prison further north eight days later.

"I spent three days with seventy other people crammed into a room that smelled like hell," he recalls. "We could not shower, and if we wanted to use the bathroom we had to do our stuff right there, in front of everybody. The difference is that the county jail does not treat immigrants like immigrants, but just like any other type of inmate, while the immigration police, who take control of illegals as soon as authority is transferred over to them at the prison, want to make them feel like less than dirt. And I did, I felt like less than dirt."

Conditions became better once the immigration officers left and prison life resumed its routine. He was offered an almost immediate deportation. He took the offer, he says, "because I had no chance of winning the case, and I would have had to spend three months in the fish tank, as they call it, for nothing. I had never been anywhere near the slammer before, and I hated every moment of it. The humiliation was unbearable for me." Eighteen days after his arrest, he was ready to go. He was asked to stay up all night; in the wee hours of the morning, he boarded a plane that flew him straight to El Paso. Unlike Emilio, he is not going to try it again. "I am terrified of being caught again. This time I could be inside for a very, very long period. They have managed to get me very scared. I am trying to persuade my girlfriend to go back to Colombia, where I can marry her, and see if I can get her some papers to come and live in Mexico with me. I need her. I have little family here that I can relate to. It will not be easy setting up camp here."

The procession of deportees continues. The small crowd that had gathered to see them into the country at the bridge's entrance seems more eager to lay hands on the few dollars they presume will need to be exchanged and spent in Juárez than on the deportees' plight, the lost jobs, the broken families left behind, the shattered dreams, the humiliating time spent in jail, the shock of finding out that the country of their younger years is no longer really theirs because, as in the opening lines of Leslie Hartley's *The Go-Between*: "The past is a foreign country: they do things differently there."

A Casa del Migrante spokesperson tells me that, according to the Instituto Nacional de Migración, the government body that deals with migrant issues, some 559,453 people were deported from the United States in 2008, one-fourth of them to Chihuahua, one-fourth to Baja California, 43 percent to Tamaupilas, and the rest to other places.[4] In 2010, the number of immigrants who were kicked out of the United States just to Baja California reached 186,575.[5] According to the same source, the number of Central Americans who were deported from Mexico in 2008 was just under 5,500. "Someone is always another country's Mexican," says Miguel wryly later on that evening, when he hears these statistics.

The morning after the deportees walk into Mexico, the same bridge presents a surreal aspect, with a long line of Mexicans heading in exactly the opposite direction—towards El Paso, Texas. The daily ritual involves hundreds of locals crossing into the United States on foot over the old El Paso del Norte Bridge. They enter the country long before they have reached the checkpoint at the other end because exactly in the middle of the walkway that runs alongside the bridge road, a plaque divided into two sections fixes the limits between Mexico and the United States. For a few hundred meters, then, the migrants are technically in the United States even though not a single officer has checked their papers. The "papers," which get checked at the bottom of the bridge, are nothing but a limited pass given by the U.S. consulate in Juárez that allows Mexicans to visit El Paso but does not grant them authorization to go beyond the city limits. It is the way the bureaucracy has found to maintain the tradition of free passage between the twin cities while keeping with the times. The visitors can stay a few nights on the other side.

Just minutes away from there, in the dusty northwestern outskirts of Juárez, the few who still think they can make it to the other side in clandestine form through the Anapra slums, the most violent part of town, are likely plotting their next move. There are no paved roads, or basic services, including water. The streets, if one can call them so, are lined with cardboard-and-tin shelters that pass for houses, the occasional power line hanging from the sky—an illegal connection that seems to be coming from, and going, nowhere. But this godforsaken corner of the world where murders, score settling, and gang warfare are part of daily life, is still a tempting proposition for some whose aspirations go beyond the temporary, restricted visit to El Paso that so many others make by crossing over the Santa Fe Bridge. Despite the overwhelming evidence that crossing over from Anapra is nearly impossible nowadays, dreamers looking to defy the odds still lurk in these premises at night wanting to wiggle their way around the lights, the fence, and the statistics that speak of, well, the nearly impossible. Those who try are fewer and fewer, but they think Father Romo will give them a hand if they run into trouble. It has happened before.

One evening, after accompanying Manuel to the Santa Fe Bridge to pick up migrants, I ride back to Casa del Migrante with him. There are twelve migrants crammed into the van sitting behind us. This is the last one of Manuel's three trips this evening. The passengers have all gone through the motions—the walk across the bridge in the cold winter night, the assistance from the Grupo Beta, the instructions on how to proceed into the country, the money for the bus, the "welcoming" mob, the daze that follows the shocking realization that the expulsion has been consummated, and then Miguel, out of nowhere, smiling and comforting, offering to drive them to the Casa del Migrante for a night's rest, warm food, and some clothes.

I pay close attention, during the 25-minute ride, to the chatter behind me—everyone is telling their personal stories to everyone else. Although they have been deported together, most of them only met at the end of the journey back to Mexico, having come from different parts of the United States and spent time in jails all over the country. "I am never going back," says one. "It is not worth the risk." Another pledges to cross back in less than a week. A third one explains that his sources tell him the cost has gone up because the dangers have multiplied at both ends: the gangs at the Mexican end, the border patrol at the other. Jail stories abound—"I worked and worked trying not to think of where I was," says one; "I just prayed," another one chips in, "and got little sleep because the other guy snored." They laugh a little—mostly a nervous laughter. No one really kids around or tries to loosen the tension. They are mostly exhausted and disconcerted.

"Look, no license plates," says one of them pointing to a van out the window. "It's dangerous; you never know if it is the police or the gangs, or both," warns another. "It smelled awful back there," interjects another one, referring to the Mexican end of the Santa Fe Bridge, where street vendors hawk fried snacks that fill the air with the scent of burnt grease, and small heaps of garbage seem to stare at the procession of deportees from street corners. "Traffic is chaotic; I could never drive here," announces a small, stocky Mexican who has kept quiet for most of the way. "Did you see those maniacs trying to mob us to take our money?" recalls the one who seems to be emerging as the leader of the group in that little laboratory of human interaction that the van headed to the Casa del Migrante seems to become every evening, with all those castaways expelled by the tide of politics suddenly forced by circumstance into a tight fraternity whose members need to sort out temporary hierarchies and roles.

"That would never happen back home," I hear someone comment. The sudden silence in the van says it all. This act of cultural identification with the United States coming from the back of the van sounds disturbingly awkward and ironic in the mouth of a Mexican deported from the United States in the midst of a national revulsion against an invasion of brown-skinned aliens that—according to voices calling for implacable anti-immigrant measures—threaten to destroy the country's WASP tradition. "Yes," someone finally breaks the silence after a few seconds that feel like an eternity. "You don't see this kind of stuff back there," he adds with a twinge of disdain in his voice. "It's going to take a while to get used to this place."

Notes

1. "Estadística criminal 2011," Larednoticias.com, Edición no. 168, año 4, http://www.larednoticias.com/detalle.cfm?s=33

2. Albert M. Camarillo, "Mexico," in *The New Americans: A Guide to Immigration Since 1965,* eds. Mary C. Waters and Reed Ueda (Cambridge, Mass.: Harvard University Press, 2007), 506.

3. The information is contained in an article published in *The Economist Magazine* on July 7, 2001, 29.

4. The Instituto Nacional de Migración's website is http://www.inm.gob.mx/

5. The official figures given by the National Migration Institute were reported in the press. See "Cerró 2010 con 186 mil deportados: INM," *El Mexicano,* January 2011, http://www.el-mexicano.com.mx/informacion/noticias/1/3/estatal/2011/01/06/447847/cerro-2010-con-186-mil-deportados-inm.aspx

6

The Law as Fiction

THE REACTION AGAINST immigration discussed in earlier chapters has determined to a large extent the legal treatment given to this social phenomenon. The effect has been a permanent divorce between the law and reality. Because of the chasm that separated what the governments tried to do through the legal system and what the reality at the grassroots level was dictating, the laws have been constantly changed and reversed. They have been updated at a pace that failed to anticipate, catch up with, and sometimes even significantly affect, the flow of immigrants. Of the laws that were effectively enforced, many resulted in unintended consequences, including unpleasant side effects, the emergence or worsening of new social ills, and new problems that created the need for more laws.

An even more perverse symptom of the divorce between the law and real life was the fact that the authorities themselves often acted in ways that contradicted their own policies, either turning a blind eye to what was happening on the ground or sending subtle signals of tolerance to would-be immigrants.

As is often the case when government norms and real life are wide apart, comical absurdities have periodically taken place. A so-called Texas Proviso in the United States made it legal for thirty years to hire an unauthorized worker, for instance, to mow someone's lawn, yet illegal for the employer to harbor him or her—i.e., to bring the worker into the house to drink a glass of water.[1] No less absurd is the fact that, nowadays, a large number of immigrants pay some $7 billion in annual taxes in vain—to false Social Security accounts.[2]

Abdelmalek Sayad, a late sociologist of Algerian origin who wrote extensively about the North Africans in France, succinctly summed up the divorce between the law and reality as regards immigration:

Because it cannot always make the law and the fact conform to each other, immigration is condemned to engender a situation that seems to doom it to a double contradiction: One no longer knows if it is a provisional state that one likes to prolong indefinitely, or, on the contrary, if it is a more durable state that one likes to live through with an intense sense of the provisional.[3]

If a person remains undocumented for decades but manages to make a decent living and happens to benefit from a period of relatively low intensity of enforcement—or even of blind eye enforcement,—that person will be, regardless of legal issues, in a very different condition and frame of mind from the foreigner who devotes most of his or her energy to evading the law-enforcement machinery of the state because he or she entered the country at the "wrong" time.

In the past, Mexicans were hired to replace other less-desirable immigrants, only to find themselves in the position of being the most undesirable foreigners in the United States years later. After the Gentlemen's Agreement between the United Stats and Japan that restricted Japanese immigration in 1907, employers in the United States began to recruit Mexicans in big numbers, unleashing a sequence of events whose lasting consequences the U.S. government did not anticipate. The pattern was repeated when Central, Eastern, and Southern Europeans were directly targeted by the new laws of the early 1920s. Towards the end of that same century, the Clinton laws had the effect of increasing the number of illegal Mexican residents not because of a surge in entries, but because of a precipitous drop in the number of departures by people who would otherwise have continued to come and go based on seasonal demand for their labor. The unforeseen ripple effects of measures designed to stem certain migration flows have periodically forced legislators to address perceived problems created by other legislators.

Failure to anticipate unintended consequences is a constant in U.S. immigration policy. In 1965, the new watershed legislation eliminated the national origins formula prevalent since the 1920s, established some hemispheric limits, and emphasized family reunification. The authorities failed to see that, given the fact that Americans of European origin had few foreign relatives still alive, there would be a very significant increase in annual admissions from other parts of the world once the backlog of applications was disposed of. In 1964, Attorney

General Robert Kennedy, closely involved with the immigration bill being discussed at the time, wrote that "it would increase the amount of authorized immigration only a fraction."[4] Regardless of one's views on immigration, this was a clear misunderstanding of the consequences of the law. Because the number of visas for family reunification was virtually unlimited, legal admissions increased by half, from 3.3 million in the 1960s to 4.5 million the following decade. The dynamic led to several amendments in the 1970s and 1990s; the law was always a few steps behind.[5]

At all times, immigrants have found ways to circumvent the law. After the Chinese Exclusion Act of 1882 went into effect, the Chinese continued to smuggle themselves into the United States despite the great geographical distance marked by the Pacific. In one decade alone, more than 7,000 Chinese citizens entered the country illegally.[6] Eventually the law was repealed—a belated attempt by those who made law to accommodate reality. The ending of the *Bracero* program by a Democratic administration under pressure from unions in the mid-1960s was a clear failure to recognize the reality of an American agribusiness dependent on Mexican labor. Media stories had highlighted cases of worker abuse in the years leading up to the decision by the U.S. Congress; a report by Edward R. Murrow, "Harvest of Shame," had denounced, for instance, scandalous living conditions by migrant workers in Florida.[7] The program was indeed ended, but the effects, i.e., the growth of illegal channels for migration flows linked to labor needs, were worse than the original problem.

In subsequent years, in a twisted recognition that reality had surpassed the perceptive powers of legislators, the government often turned a blind eye to the inflows of agricultural laborers. Some time later, the informal tolerance of undocumented foreigners on the part of those who were supposed to uphold the law was followed by yet another belated attempt by the authorities to adapt the law to a reality they had previously failed to heed: in 1965, the Immigration and Nationality Act opened the doors to more newcomers. Today, that law is denounced as the original sin behind illegal immigration.

Of course, in the new millennium, the new ceilings imposed by the amendments would be questioned by anti-immigrant politicians, academics, and activists as proof of excessive permissiveness on the part of the state. Their howling would show total disregard for the fact that those new ceilings were established in extremis, as an attempt to accommodate a reality that had made a mockery of previous limits, including the needs of an economy whose bosses desperately lobbied the government for a substantial increase of the quotas. This was an imperfect accommodation, I might add. In 1999, even after raising the ceilings, the government felt compelled, in practice, to relax enforcement of the rules of the Immigration and Naturalization Service so that it would only go after illegal foreigners who committed crimes, not people who were simply undocumented. This decision would be the object of much criticism in the next decade.[8]

The debate, then, is not, as many people thought in the new millennium, between amnesty—of the type given by President Ronald Reagan, a conservative, in 1986—and enforcement, which had failed to stem the tide in the period when law-enforcement agencies had applied themselves to the task. The real debate is between accepting and negating reality. The root of the problem is that too many foreigners have been chasing too few visas. This occurs in good part because the legal ceiling included a very small number of low-skilled workers (no more than 5,000); the quota applicable in the new millennium was out of sync with the reality of the roughly eight hundred thousand immigrants who were coming in illegally every year before the 2007–08 debacle, and finding opportunities in an economy clearly able to sustain them.

The more than 3 million undocumented foreigners granted amnesty in 1986 were absorbed by the market, but the market continued to grow and attract foreign workers, no matter what the laws and the quota system said. Those who benefitted from the 1986 amnesty married, bought homes, and laid down roots in the United States. Bringing them into a discussion about the appropriate number of foreigners for the United States in the new millennium, as so many have done in recent years, misses the vital point that the reality of the decade 2000–2009 outgrew the legal arrangements of the 1980s.

Guest-worker programs have tended to be outgrown by reality no less than partial amnesties. In the last few years, a comedy of errors born out of the disconnect between the law and reality seems to have been happening in relation to the case of 500 metalworkers imported from India in 2006 to help repair some off-shore oil rigs damaged by Hurricane Katrina in the Gulf of Mexico. Hundreds of those workers filed a lawsuit against Signal International, owner of the rigs, alleging they had been promised permanent residency by representatives of the employer. Instead they were sent to an isolated workplace that according to the U.S. Equal Employment Opportunity Commission seemed "laced with ridicule and harassment." According to the *New York Times,* when the Indians protested against the work conditions and their ambiguous status, the Immigration and Customs Enforcement suggested that Signal should send the workers back home. After the workers refused to be sent back, the Department of Justice started an investigation, while the company sued the American and Indian agents who had helped it hire the foreign workers.

This is only one of many cases that have arisen from small guest-worker programs presently functioning in the United States with many limitations that turn would-be solutions into problems. Ironically, the effects of these limitations are precisely the kinds of ills to which people on both the left (unions) and the right (nativists) point as intolerable abuses when arguing against the programs. But as Edward Schumacher-Matos, co-author of a documentary on the issue, together with Anne Morriss of Harvard University's Center for International Development, has argued, the problem is not the hiring of foreign workers such as these much-needed Indians, but the potential for abuse precisely because of the imposed limitations—including the inability to change jobs and earn a path to permanent residence or citizenship.[9] Middlemen exploit opportunities created by the law.

As is well known, many of the engineers and PhD's driving much of the technological innovation in Silicon Valley in the late twentieth and early twenty-first centuries have been Indian. But according to the Department of Homeland Security, there are more than 300,000 illegal Indians in the United States, many of them having arrived on H-1B visas (work permits) or student visas and overstayed them in the hope of getting a residence card—which means that they were educated and professional. The jarring juxtaposition of the large number of illegal Indians in the country alongside their vast technological contributions illustrates the incongruence that results from a dissonance between the law and reality. One-quarter of American Nobel Prize winners since 1901 have been immigrants, and four out of every ten PhD scientists working in the United States are foreign-born.[10] A system that limits potential contributors to America's technological supremacy in the name of "the law" is obviously divorced from the real world.

Only when the law has successfully adapted to reality has illegal immigration dropped. Regardless of the merits of the *Bracero* program or lack thereof, the mechanism for matching legal arrangements with real life—in that case the demand for labor in agriculture—dramatically reduced the number of un-documented foreigners entering the country after World War II. The drop in illegal entries at times amounted to 95 percent.[11]

Examples of the unreality of the law as regards immigrants abound elsewhere too. In the early and mid-1990s, European countries passed an array of norms attempting to stem the human tide. While in Germany, immigration declined by half, in France it rose by 38 percent.[12] It appears that the various norms had the effect of reshuffling entry points and preferred choices; net numbers signal that. And yet, despite stringent efforts to enforce the laws, they were not effective. Meanwhile, some countries accused others of being too lenient and affecting overall conditions across Europe. Various interests hurt by the restrictions on the hiring of foreign labor complained that competitors in other countries of the European Union were benefiting from their governments' reduced or inefficient enforcement.

There is a more tragic dimension to the disparity between legal norms and real life than the ones hitherto discussed. It has to do with the creation of conditions that place human beings in situations of violence, privation and absence of protection from the violation of basic freedoms. Human trafficking and the criminalization of social conducts that do not entail murder, theft, fraud, or any other form of real harm are two manifestations, as far as immigration is concerned, of the ill effects of passing and enforcing laws that bear little connection with social reality.

Many developing countries in Asia employ foreign females in sexual industries tolerated and sometimes encouraged by the government.[13] Since 1996, a majority of registered foreigners in Japan have been women. However—unlike most migrant women in West and Southeast Asia who are domestic workers, nurses, and factory workers—in Japan, the majority are "entertainers," a category that sometimes entails outright prostitution, but is often limited to bar hostesses and performers. The category of "entertainers" (called *japayuki*, a derogatory name) was created in 1981 in response to strong demand. It has since expanded, and the government has used immigration as a tool to satisfy that new demand. The late 1990s and early years of the next decade saw a boom in the industry.[14]

The Japanese government has accepted the need for a disproportionately high number of women immigrants in that particular industry, even as it has banned immigration in most other areas. However, the ceiling it has placed is unrealistic, which gives rise to a significant number of illegal females. Despite official sanctioning for the activities that employ them and tolerance for the use of immigrant workers, female entertainers do not enjoy the kinds of legal protections that one associates with lawful activities. This is partly because immigration is mostly banned in every other industry and the foreign women find themselves isolated in a tainted social activity, and in part because of the unrealistic quota. Given the legal conditions under which their activities take place, crime syndicates such as the Yakuza have exploited the situation of these women entertainers.[15]

Other cases of human traffic or abuse derived from, or made worse by, migratory policy derive from the system that in many countries binds workers to employers beyond normal contractual duties. In all Arab states, there is a practice known as *kafala*, a type of sponsorship that attaches the foreign worker to a local employer through a legal as well as financial dependency. In these states, Asian and African workers find it impossible to arrange their legal papers without assistance from local nationals, particularly recruitment agencies. When the universally accepted individual rights of immigrants are violated, they cannot go to the police because their illegal status means that they will be detained.[16]

The tendency of immigration law to criminalize otherwise law-abiding behavior has served to distort the debate on immigration by playing into the hands of those who point to high numbers of inmates who are immigrants among the prison population in some developed countries. But the truth is that criminal behavior among immigrants is not disproportionate compared to many native groups. Ron Unz, publisher of the *American Conservative*, wrote an article based on detailed analysis of incarceration data compiled by the 2008 Bureau of Justice Statistics in the United States. He discovered that the Hispanic incarceration rate, though far lower than that of blacks, was higher than that of white Americans, largely because a much larger fraction of Hispanics falls within the gender category (male) and age group (18–44) in which a majority of those who break the law originate than is the case with whites. The median white age is 40, putting nearly half the population above the likely age range for committing crimes, while the median Hispanic age is 27. Once the national imprisonment rates are adjusted for age, Hispanic incarceration rates are only moderately above those of whites; in many states with large Hispanic populations, the rate of white incarceration is greater.[17]

Between 1995 and 2002, a project by scholars from Harvard, the University of Chicago and the University of Michigan studied 3,000 young inhabitants of Chicago, a large number of them first or second-generation immigrants. They found that a person's immigrant status was much less relevant to violence than other factors. First-generation immigrants were 45 percent less likely to commit violence than third-generation immigrants. Mexican-Americans were the least violent. In the 2000 decade, about one-fourth of federal prisoners were immigrants. According to observers of the prisoner population, this statistic resulted from the high numbers of immigrants among the population and the high number of young men among them, as well as from the enhanced enforcement of immigration laws.[18]

Other studies have led to similar conclusions.[19] Tim Wadsworth, a professor of sociology at the University of Colorado, conducted a study of U.S. cities with more than 50,000 residents and cross-referenced statistics relating to population size, crime, and immigration. His conclusion was that immigrants had been a significant factor in the drop in New York's crime rate during the 1990s: "The cities that experience the greatest growth in immigration were the same ones that were experiencing the greatest declines in violent crime." He attributed this connection to a number of factors, including that homogeneous immigrant enclaves produce tight social communities, and that the people who tend to migrate have certain characteristics that set them apart.[20]

A contributing reason for the number of immigrants in prison in recent years has been the government's increased enforcement of immigration laws in response to social and political pressure. In 2007, according to the United States Sentencing Commission, Latinos accounted for 40 percent of all sentenced federal offenders in the U.S., more than triple their share of the adult population. Those without U.S. citizenship represented 29 percent of all offenders. The figures were the result of a decision, since the early 1990s, to make the enforcement of immigration laws a federal priority.[21] The deportees, for one, as mentioned in a previous chapter, spend weeks or months in jail before they are deported, impacting the statistic significantly. A large number of those immigrant inmates had not committed crimes other than being in the country illegally.

The criminalization of human conduct has been the extreme effect of laws dictated by the social reaction against inflows of foreigners. But the real problem has been the unreality of the law—its tendency to try to determine, rather than reflect, the ebb and flow of human society, and to mold that flow to the whims of law, which are often the result of passionate native reactions to what they perceive and fear. As we will see next, these reactions are based, among other things, on the premise that foreigners are culturally incompatible with the host society.

Notes

1. Frank D. Bean and B. Lindsay Lowell, "Unauthorized Migration," in *The New Americans: A Guide to Immigration Since 1965*, eds. Mary C. Waters and Reed Ueda (Cambridge, Mass.: Harvard University Press, 2007), 72.

2. Jorge Castañeda, *Ex Mex: From Migrants to Immigrants* (New York: The New Press, 2007), 34. Also see Thomas Donland, *A World of Wealth: How Capitalism Turns Profits into Progress* (Upper Saddle River, N.J.: Pearson Education, 2008), 118.

3. Abdelmalek Syadi, *l'Immigration ou les Paradoxes de l'Alterité* (Paris: Raison d'Agir Editions, 2006), 31.

4. Mark Krikorian, *The New Case Against Immigration: Both Legal and Illegal*, (London: Sentinel, 2008), 196.

5. In 1976, an amendment imposed a 20,000 ceiling for any Western Hemisphere country, in effect extending the single-country limits imposed on Eastern Hemisphere nations. In 1978, an amendment finally established a unified immigration system to merge the two hemispheric ceilings into a single worldwide quota of 290,000 visas each year. Following the pattern of dissonance between politics and real life, the quota soon proved to be unrealistic given the needs of a vibrant economy that was about to be transformed by the new information technology. The number of people who could legally be admitted was raised to 700,000 in the early 1990s, and had to be raised to 675,000 in 1995. The amendment maintained family reunification as the main path into the country but, forced by economic reality, it also increased employment-related inflows. An entire new category of immigrant—the investor category—had to be created for those who brought more than $1 million into cities or $500,000 into rural areas and created at least ten jobs. See Philip Q. Yang, *Post-1965 Immigrants to the United States: Structural Determinants* (Westport, Conn.: Praeger Publishers, 1995), 15–16.

6. Stanford M. Lyman, *Chinese Americans* (New York: Random House, 1974), 106.

7. Edward Schumacher-Matos, "Good Night and Good Luck, Guest Workers," *The Washington Post*, April 17, 2010, A11.

8. Samuel T. Francis, "America Extinguished: Mass Immigration and the Disintegration of American Culture," (Monterey, Va.: *Americans for Immigration Control*, 2002), 71–72.

9. Schumacher-Matos, "Good Night and Good Luck, Guest Workers," A11.

10. Alex Nowrasteh, "Let Immigrants Power America's Scientific Prowess," *Competitive Enterprise Institute*, December 2, 2009, http://cei.org/articles/2009/12/02/let-immigrants-power-americas-scientific-prowess

11. Jason Riley, "Obama and the Amnesty Trap," *The Wall Street Journal*, April 20, 2009, http://online.wsj.com/article/SB124018650616333437.html

12. "Trends in International Migration: Continuous Reporting System on Migration," 2000 ed. (Paris: Organisation for Economic Co-operation and Development [OECD], 2001.)

13. Between 20,000 and 30,000, Burmese women work in the "entertainment" industry in Thailand, some 100,000 Nepalese do so in India, and as many as 200,000 Bangladeshis are similarly employed in Pakistan. In Japan, it is estimated that hundreds of thousands of migrant women, principally, but not only, from the Philippines and Thailand, work in Japan's sex industry as "entertainers." The sex industry accounts for 1 percent of that country's Gross National Product and employs much higher numbers of women—in relative terms—than it does in many other countries. See Nana Oishi, *Women in Motion: Globalization, State Policies, and Labor Migration in Asia*, (Stanford, Calif.: Stanford University Press, 2005), 4.

14. Elif Kaban (International Labor Organization) "UN Labor Body Urges Recognition of Sex Industry," *Reuters*, August 18, 1998.

15. Oishi, *Women in Motion*, 34–35.

16. Ray Jureidini, "Human Rights and Foreign Contract Labor: Some Implications for Management and Regulation in Arab Countries" in *Arab Migration in a Globalized World* (Geneva: International Organization for Migration, League of Arab States, 2004), 207–208.

17. Ron Unz, "His-Panic: Talk TV Sensationalists And Axe-Grinding Ideologues Have Fallen For a Myth of Immigrant Lawlessness," *The American Conservative*, March 1, 2010.

18. Carl F. Horowitz, "An Examination of U.S. Immigration Policy and Serious Crime," *Center for Immigration Studies*, April, 2001, http://www.cis.org/articles/2001/crime/tocoh.html

19. According to a report by Ruben Rumbaut and Walter Ewing conducted on behalf of the American Immigration Law Foundation and the Immigration Policy Center in February of 2007, the undocumented population doubled between 1994 and 2006, but the violent crime rate declined 34 percent. See Castañeda, *Ex Mex: From Migrants to Immigrants*), 34. Also see Donland, *A World of Wealth*, 128–129.

20. Aaron Rutkoff, "Do Immigrants Bring Down Crime Rates?", *The Wall Street Journal*, May 27, 2010, http://blogs.wsj.com/metropolis/2010/05/27/are-immigrants-responsible-for-new-yorks-crime-drop/

21. Mark Hugo Lopez and Michael T. Light, "A Rising Share: Hispanic and Federal Crime," *Pew Hispanic Center*, Washington, D.C., February 18, 2009, http://pewhispanic.org/reports/report.php?ReportID=104.

PART II

Immigrants and Culture

7

Immigrant Values versus Native Values

FROM THE VERY beginnings of the republic, there have been those who viewed with worry the traditions of foreigners who might import their mindset and way of doing things. In his *Notes On The State Of Virginia* (Query VIII),[1] Thomas Jefferson warned against the danger of immigrants from absolute monarchies because they might bring their ways with them or, if they shed those ways, they might go to other extremes—such as licentiousness, rather than temperate love of liberty. Well-meaning critics of immigration have always pointed to similar cultural dangers, all the way to Samuel Huntington's *Who Are We?,*[2] in which the late essayist argues that the basic tenets of the American way of life are gravely threatened by the type of immigrants the United States receives today. American history has proven those fears to be mostly unfounded, but their persistence tells us something about the protectionist instinct that inhabits even open societies. The argument that immigrants pose a threat to the cultural underpinnings of a free country such as the United States has been made by respected scholars and is shared by many well-meaning people, who deserve a thorough response.[3]

When the cultural underpinnings that immigration is supposed to threaten are described in depth and traced to their roots, religion emerges as a key tenet. The Christian foundations of Western, and specifically American, society, taken to mean a set of general values, are at the center of the discussion. The so-called Religious Awakenings that punctuate important periods of American history are said to have played a crucial part in shaping political and social developments in the United States, and therefore in the formation of the nation. To-day's society, according to this point of view, is partly a legacy of that history. Newcomers with different formations will, if they overwhelm the natives, erode and ultimately kill the legacy.[4] Contemporary immigration, critics contend, challenges the Protestant legacy and its value system.

There is no denying the part played by religion in the formative era of the United States. Even foreign observers identified religion as a major force in the republic in the nineteenth century. Alexis de Tocqueville called it "indispensable to the maintenance of Republican institutions."[5] And yet there has always been a strongly secular penchant in society moderating and limiting the religious influence as well. The religious dissenters who had fled Europe to establish themselves in America did so in the name of the liberty to worship God in whatever way they wanted, not according to one particular dogma. Later, some of the leaders of the Revolution were called "atheist" because they spoke strongly against a hegemonic church—for instance, Thomas Paine in *The Age of Reason*. Thomas Jefferson was accused by Calvinists of being a heretic, as was James Madison. The Constitution itself, although not quite as clear as some European constitutions about the separation between church and state—protects freedom, among other things, by not giving preponderance to any particular religion and not imposing religion on society. The citizens are free to decide whether they worship a spiritual being or authority, or not.

These safeguards were not observed in practice, of course, in many cases. Discrimination against Catholics was notorious for a long period in American history. But in time, Catholicism assimilated some features of the Protestant environment. Catholicism was in turn assimilated into the American mainstream, with the exception of Maryland, whose distinctly Catholic flavor was preserved more intact, although it comported with the general value system of the country. Claiming that any one of the strands of America's legacy regarding spiritual matters is definitive constitutes a mutilation of American history. Protestantism's dominant presence in the spiritual landscape of the United States notwithstanding, freedom of cult, a significant degree of separation between state and church, and religious pluralism are at the heart of American democracy. This is something that should be borne in mind when assessing the cultural impact of any segment of American society, including large ones such as those comprised of contemporary immigrants.

But even if we accept, for the sake of argument, the predominance of religion in the cultural underpinnings and institutional framework of American society (as opposed to other formative elements in the American way of life), the case of Latinos is indicative of how little resemblance to reality the theories about the cultural threat to America by immigrants bear. The overwhelming majority of Latinos who moved to the United States between 1990 and 2003 were Christian—70 percent Catholic, 23 percent Protestant. More than one in every five Catholics describe themselves as "born again," as do 85 percent of Protestants. There is a heavy evangelical, Pentecostal, and Charismatic influence among them. Protestant evangelism has made inroads in many Latin American countries in recent decades, prompting the Catholic Church to fight back. The influence of Protestant denominations and evangelical cults is partly due to the work done over the years by missionaries from the United States and by the grassroots efforts of native groups.

The influence of religion and, more generally, of family values may account for the fact that the fertility rate among Mexican-American women is 60 percent higher than it is among native women in the United States.[6] For decades, Christian groups have decried the decline of the family in America, pointing, among other things, to the low fertility rate of married women and the disproportionate number of children born out of wedlock. Latino, and specifically Mexican, immigrants exhibit the opposite pattern. That said, the tendency in Mexico and Latin America has been for the fertility rate to decline in the last few decades due to the modernization of those economies and the social changes brought about by globalization. This means that future waves of immigrants will probably conform to the prevailing patterns in the United States—which should put to rest the argument that high fertility rates among immigrants, taken to be a sign of backwardness, ensure the definitive Mexicanization of U.S. society.

Some have argued that religious communities are more important to immigrants than they are in the immigrants' countries of origin. As a scholar has aptly put it, "[In] encountering America, immigrants have also encountered the diversity of their own communities of faith." They have found, one might add, earlier immigrants who are already assimilated, who help them ease the transition either deliberately or by their mere example.[7] Anyone familiar with immigrant networks realizes how important religious communities are in the process of adaptation of newcomers to the host society. If we accept that Christianity is a predominant factor in the American way of life, the role played by religious communities among immigrants would appear to run contrary to the argument that immigration is undermining the spiritual legacy of the republic.

To make matters more interesting, the assimilationist current actually flows both ways when it comes to religion. Many churches in the United States have started to incorporate elements familiar to immigrants in mass, probably anticipating that Hispanics will provide in the future a foundation on which to perpetuate the Christian churches' social relevance and leadership. It is as yet unclear how much this process will influence the spiritual and religious life of natives, but historical precedent indicates that host countries are never immune to cultural influence by newcomers. The enriching effect of the spiritual and religious diversification of the United States on American Christianity is undeniable. American Christians now include members of the Mar Thoma Syrian Church from India, Haitian and Vietnamese Catholics, Korean Presbyterians, Nigerian Anglicans, and many more groups connected to the spiritual legacy of other nations. Catholic parishes have not only incorporated new aspects to their mass; they have also adopted festivals such as the Day of the Dead and the Feast Day of Our Lady of Guadalupe. The National Conference of Catholic Bishops estimates that by 2020, more than half of all American Catholics will be Latinos.[8]

Especially intriguing is the resonance of family values among immigrants. For as many as eight out of every ten Hispanics, it is preferable to spend as much quality time with the family as possible than work longer hours in order to make as much money as possible. Clearly, illegal foreigners are obliged to work longer hours because of their lower productivity and income, and because first-generation immigrants usually strive for progress with redoubled keenness in order to make up for their initial disadvantage. It is ironic that in America, a country that encourages family values, Hispanic immigrants are more likely to live with a spouse and a child than natives are. Nearly half of undocumented foreigners in the United States in 2008 were couples with children.[9] As mentioned, Hispanics have tended to have more children than natives, something that will gradually change in the future if demographic patterns occurring in Mexico and other Latin American countries are sustained.

It would seem that, among communities that share fundamental outlooks on issues as vital as family values, conditions are in place for cultural cross-fertilization. Those who think that the cultural fabric of America is disintegrating because of immigrants tend also to be those who think that the post-1965 America represents a degeneration of traditional values. They should take notice of the fact that single-parent households represent only 13 percent of undocumented households, while they constitute nearly one-third of households whose members were born in the United States. Immigrant values in this and other cases are more in tune with pre-1965 American society than with post-1965, or post-modern, America, a fact that should give comfort to those who decry the decline of traditional values in the United States and, more generally, in the West.[10]

Other important traits related to the American way of life speak to us of a high level of cultural compatibility between immigrants and natives. Immigrants and natives show a remarkably similar level of entrepreneurship in the United States: 11.3 percent of immigrants and 12.6 percent of natives are self-employed, and the average self-employment income is almost identical. (Koreans, Italians, Vietnamese, and Iranians are significantly more likely to be self-employed than natives.)[11] In the states with the highest concentration of immigrants, certain national groups have tended to become dominant in particular businesses. Dominicans, a relatively poor group, control New York City's bodegas (grocery stores); in Washington, D.C., taxicab owners and drivers are African, while in New York they are South Asian and Haitian; as Jews and Italians in New York moved on from owning fruit and vegetable stores, Koreans took over ownership of those businesses and later expanded them into other areas—the reason why Korean stores are prominent in black neighborhoods; Indians and Pakistanis have tended to focus on the motel and newspaper businesses, as well as owning convenience stores. And so on.

In the country at large, multiple stories abound of black entrepreneurs of foreign origin who have lived the American dream. A Nigerian, Kase Lawal, founded an international oil exploration, refining, and trading company that has more than 1,000 employees worldwide. By 2006, the time of its twentieth anniversary, his business, which trades crude oil and natural gas in Africa and Europe, as well as wholesale electric power in the United States, was already the second-largest black-owned firm in the *Be Industrial/Service 100* list, with sales of $1.5 billion. By 2009, Lawal's firm CAMAC Holdings, which had been in existence for a quarter of a century and become an icon for blacks around the United States, was named the second-largest black-owned company in the entire country. In recent years, Lawal also entered the world of finance by buying a stake in the only black-owned bank in Texas.

The founder and CEO of CAMAC often tells the anecdote that when his son was in school, he would be asked what his dad did for a living. Because he was used to his father traveling (Lawal was seeking funding at the time) and had done a fair amount of traveling himself, the kid responded, "He works at the airport and passes around peanuts!"[12] Today, Lawal is an emblem of both the immigrant self-made man and the black self-made man. His story—the Nigerian from a modest background who came to study in the United States and dreamed of establishing his own business—has a validating effect for millions of immigrants and blacks in America.

A key economic characteristic of immigrant household behavior that echoes native practices at the heart of this country's success since the nineteenth century is saving money (the cruel irony is that this healthy tradition was painfully lost on natives in the last couple of decades; it seems to be gradually coming back since the 2008 financial debacle). The immigrants' thriftiness ought to give comfort to those who fear criminal behavior on the part of foreigners—savers are not people who tend to plant bombs or kill fellow men. All immigrant groups exhibit high savings rates; even low-income groups, such as Mexicans, do.[13] The fact that immigrants have fewer bank accounts than natives has to do with the illegal status of many of them. In this and other cases, what passes for a cultural difference has to do with impediments that hinder what would otherwise be a conduct similar to that of native groups or to previous waves of immigrants. For years, Mexicans did not become naturalized at the same rate as other groups, in part because they feared losing their native citizenship. When Mexico recognized double citizenship, the proportion of Mexicans who took up the citizenship of the United States shot up. A couple of other factors contributed too, among them the 1986 amnesty and the obstacles placed on circular migration in the Clinton years.[14]

It is not uncommon for immigrants to express optimism about their lives in the United States—perhaps a symptom of a psychological Americanization. Surveys show that Asians and Hispanics believe hard work will be rewarded and that the "system" works for everybody. Hispanics are the ones who have by far the most faith in the notion that every American—of whatever background—has the opportunity to succeed; their numbers are followed by Asians and blacks.[15] In various surveys, both Asians and Hispanics have claimed to be highly patriotic regarding their adopted country.[16]

Some of America's successful professionals, investors, and business people have recognized the potential of immigrants today. "Those people who are ambitious and brave enough to risk it all here," the globetrotting investor Jim Rogers has written, "are exactly the kind of people we want in this country. They are certainly the kind of people I would want working for me."[17] Many others, including Bill Gates, a symbol of American capitalism and, more recently, philanthropy, have expressed similar sentiments regarding the virtues of immigrants. In their observations regarding the contribution of foreigners to America, they all seem to point to characteristics—working hard, saving, seeking personal and familial betterment, establishing safe communities with high degrees of mutual cooperation—that cut across nationality and time, because people of very different backgrounds and at very different periods seem to have possessed them. This would seem to comport with the notion that the American way of life was traditionally informed by people from different origins and backgrounds, including millions of immigrants, who were able to shape the kind of environment in which the American way of life—as it is now regarded—became possible.

The economic contribution of immigrants stemming from hard work, saving and investing, entrepreneurship, and private initiative is felt and recognized by other countries apart from the United States. Immigration has expanded markets in many Western societies to the benefit of the native population. An annual fair in Madrid named *Integra Madrid* (Madrid Integrates), for instance, is the biggest such event for products and services aimed at immigrants, attracting more than 80,000 visitors, both native and foreign. Spanish banks, telecom companies, tourism agencies, food firms, state entities, and other concerns take part in it with increasing enthusiasm, targeting immigrants as if they were natives.[18] It has become not just an economic event, but also a cultural one, bringing together natives and foreigners.

Oftentimes, high achievement beyond the realm of the economy has generated a sense of pride among natives who recognize a cultural contribution by foreigners through various activities. One of them has to do with the highly sensitive area of national sports, for instance. The French soccer team that won the World Cup in 1998 was a multicultural team made up of players of various origins, including Africa. The leader, Zinédine Zidane, was the son of Algerian parents; one of its other stars, defender Lillian Thuram, was a child of the *banlieue* [public housing], having moved to France from the Antilles. The slogan that celebrated their national and cultural diversity—*black, blanc, beur* (black, white and Arab)—expressed the belief, since proven highly optimistic, that total integration had been achieved. But, regardless of how accurately or inaccurately this slogan reflected reality, it expressed a high-minded integrationist aspiration on the part of many French people and a celebration of success by immigrants or descendants of immigrants whose achievements could be perceived by natives as a source of common pride. Conversely, of course, a reprehensible conduct on the part of a high-profile immigrant can generate a backlash that goes beyond that individual. Nicolas Anelka, a black Frenchman of Caribbean origin whose unpleasant dispute with the coach during the 2010 World Cup held in South Africa won him the expulsion from the team, reportedly had that kind of effect on many French people. Alan Finkielkraut, a reputed intellectual, referred to Anelka's upbringing in a *banlieue* as the reason why he had no sense of patriotism.[19]

Gentrification

The process of gentrification—the resurrection of neglected neighborhoods—in the United States indicates the extent to which immigrants can actually help host societies overcome urban decay if the system is less rigid than in Europe. As some observers have pointed out, for some years abandoned areas of New York, among them parts of Harlem, offered the spectacle of blocks with a supply of run-down houses, but no inhabitants. The houses were burned by charcoal and looked shabby, but they were waiting for someone with the initiative and entrepreneurial intuition necessary to turn the neighborhoods into something better. It fell on the immigrants of New York to do just that. They bought very cheaply these structures that others did not want and undertook the challenge of renovating them. The same process was replicated in other parts of New York, including the South Bronx.[20]

In other states, communities of foreign origin have also resurrected neighborhoods that others had abandoned and to which no one else seemed interested in giving the kiss of life. Illegal Chinese immigrants have brought new life to Chinatowns and developed the Chinese-American community, in some cases, out of slums and downtrodden parts of major urban centers. The service provided by poorer Chinese men and women in the Chinatowns of America has made the price of Chinese food less expensive, thereby making it possible for wealthier, professional immigrants to enjoy a reasonable standard of living. In Los Angeles, immigrant businesses—from corner butchers and styling salons to manufacturers of ethnic food that export products to other states and restaurants with franchises around the country—have generated the supporting environment necessary for the regeneration of former slums and depressed neighborhoods. That is the case of Pico Union, a district of Los Angeles, for instance, or of Valley Boulevard, in Monterey Park, also in the County of Los Angeles.[21]

There are numerous examples of very poor communities that blossomed into models of entrepreneurship, social cooperation, and economic development, thanks to immigration. Delray Beach, in the southeast corner of Palm Beach County, is a successful community with a very large Haitian presence—many arrived in rafts and were extremely poor back home. It became prosperous in a relatively short period of time after the effort to regenerate it began with a handful of families in the late 1980s to mid-1990s. There was already an old tradition of blacks in Delray Beach. In the segregated South, being "colored" doomed Delray Beach to poverty for years. By the late 1970s, most of the farmland was bulldozed to make room for retirement villages and the many tract-home developments sweeping south from West Palm Beach. In 1990, Delray Beach was a crack zone. The power structure was "redneck," meaning that whites controlled it and discriminated against people of color. Blacks who worked in the resorts and the mansions on the beaches were expected to be back on the mainland by nightfall.

All of that changed in a short time after the Haitians moved in. According to Joel Millman, they were lured to Palm Beach County by the demand for farm laborers. Farmers desperately needed them to work in the fields situated between Lake Okeechobee and Interstate 95. But then the Haitians fanned out along the coast, where they found work in hotels and other facilities on the beaches, providing the kind of service that other black people had done before. They rented houses from absentee lords. Other Haitians joined them a bit later, mostly from the Bahamas, located just 40 miles away, which became a back-door entrance into south Florida. These boat people began their journey in makeshift shelters and ended up being members of the up-and-coming Haitian community.[22]

Gradually, Haitians and other Caribbean immigrants who followed them settled in the area, pushing away drug lords and other emblems of the low life. They rekindled the dying fire in those neighborhoods with their entrepreneurial zeal and their sense of mutually cooperating community. A new police chief realized he had allies in the new neighbors and fought crime in close coordination with them.

Delray Beach's Pineapple Grove bore the aspect of a ghost town at one point, its storefronts abandoned. Now it is a bustling mall with restaurants and boutiques, which are run by Haitians or employ them. Many small businesses belong to Haitian proprietors, including grocery stores, plumber outlets, textile boutiques, cosmetology schools, money remittance offices, and international phone operators. Working Haitians, rather than welfare recipients, made possible the gentrification of Delray Beach.[23] By 2008, the Haitians obtained representation at City Hall, becoming full participating members in the local democracy.

When immigrants come, they revolutionize the environment of such neighborhoods precisely because they spend money that nobody was able or willing to spend before. They don't earn very much at first, or even for a long while, but their ability to spend and consume what others produce has an automatic impact on the neighborhood. That is why some have argued that focusing on the immigrants' education, skill levels, or the types of jobs they fill—as organizations working to help foreigners assimilate sometimes do—does not render the immigrants justice. The crux of the matter is not how immigrants earn money, but what they spend it on once they have produced it. Therein lies the key to the regeneration of abandoned or downtrodden neighborhoods seen across the country.

Not every part of town can be a high-tech, upper-middle-class neighborhood. The division of labor and the constant mobility of a dynamic economy means that there will always be people of lesser skills than the well-to-do who nonetheless can make a decent living if they have the opportunity. The prosperity of many New York neighborhoods depends less on super-modern industries and yuppies or rich professionals than on the mass consumption of many low earners. These immigrant families earn little but spend much, simply because together they make up a sizable demand for goods and services, or because they have access to some credit. But precisely because they are low-skilled and poor, they tend to move to poor neighborhoods, which they usually transform with their energy and aspirations. The result is that places like Flushing in Queens, New York, go from decadence to vibrancy in a short time. Without immigrants of the kind that many people think are culturally incompatible with modern America, the gentrification of slums would not be the same.[24]

This does not mean that no cultural differences can be seen in various immigrant communities vis-à-vis the mainstream society in the United States. One should not romanticize immigrants, of course, or deny the fact that many of them come from countries where the general environment has ingrained attitudes and a general outlook that is less conducive to self-reliance and success than the ones prevailing in prosperous societies. Many Mexican immigrants (to take an especially targeted immigrant community in today's anti-immigrant environment), as well as other Latinos, exhibit some beliefs or customs that are not those of the mainstream society in the host country. A study conducted in southern California compared Mexican-Americans with four other cultural groups and concluded that the Mexican-American orientation towards five basic human issues differed from the rest. Their relationship to nature was one of "subjugation" to it rather than mastery over it; they saw nature as good or evil, but not perfectible; their attachment to the group or larger family was stronger than their individualism; they preferred "being" to "doing"; they valued the present, no so much the future.[25] Lionel Sosa, a consultant of Hispanic origin who played a key role in identifying cultural groups, including Hispanics, as consumer targets and later as political constituents, maintains that certain traits hold Latinos back. Among them, he cites the mistrust of people outside the family, the acceptance of poverty as a virtue necessary to enter heaven, and a lack of self-reliance and ambition.[26]

These cultural traits have been present in parts of society throughout Latin America for a long time and partly explain the difficulty in overcoming poverty. I was reminded by Stanford scholar William Ratliff of the story of Spanish barbers in Mexico City who, as far back as 1635, petitioned the government to move Chinese barbers to the outskirts of the city, claiming that the long work hours of the Chinese constituted "unfair business practice." But these cultural traits are not genetic flaws; they are a historical legacy that modern life will gradually dissolve. The evidence already points to a gradual evolution, helped by globalization and the information era, as well as by the institutional reforms that have taken part in many parts of the continent aimed at removing some of the obstacles that weighed heavily against entrepreneurship and upward mobility. The economic dynamism of Latin America today and the expansion of its middle classes speak to us of a transformation that proves—not for the first time in the course of civilization—that culture changes and adapts. The economic behavior of immigrants in the United States, as we will see later, indicates that the attitudes and beliefs identified by the aforementioned survey are by no means insurmountable obstacles.[27]

Notes

1. Jefferson's book was published in Paris in 1784 in a private edition; the English edition did not appear until three years later. Numerous electronic versions are available. http://etext.virginia.edu/toc/modeng/public/JefVirg.html

2. Samuel Huntington, *Who Are We? The Challenges of America's National Identity* (New York: Simon & Schuster, 2004).

3. Huntington made this argument most notably in his book *Who Are We?*

4. The Religious Awakening dating back to the 1730s and 1740s was led by George Whitefield and other preachers. Congregationalists, Presbyterians, and Baptists played a prominent role. John Adams later stated that those years, credited with informing the minds and hearts of the patriots who led the Revolution, marked "a change in their religious sentiments" and in "their duties and obligations." The Second Awakening, which took place in the 1820s and 1830s, was especially notable because from it stemmed the abolitionist movement. The following period of religious fervor, in the 1890s, was also politically influential and probably helped to bring about the Progressive Era. The last one, in the 1950s and 1960s, generated two ideologically opposed movements. One, on the left, morphed into the Civil Rights struggle; the other, a reaction to the counterculture of the 1960s and 1970s, turned into the powerful Christian right that influenced, among other institutions, the Republican Party and is still very much alive today. See Huntington, *Who Are We?*, 77–78.

5. Alexis de Tocqueville, *Democracy in America* (New York: Vintage, 1945), 316.

6. Albert M. Camarillo, "Mexico," in *The New Americans: A Guide to Immigration Since 1965,* eds. Mary C. Waters and Reed Ueda (Cambridge, Mass.: Harvard University Press, 2007), 510.

7. Diana L. Eck, "Religion," in *The New Americans,* eds. Waters and Ueda, 215–217.

8. Eck, "Religion," in *The New Americans,* eds. Waters and Ueda, 219.

9. Jeffrey S. Passel and D'Vera Cohn, "A Portrait of Unauthorized Immigrants in the United Sates," Pew Hispanic Center, March 2008. The research is based on the March Current Population Surveys conducted by the U.S. Census Bureau through 2008. http://pewhispanic.org/files/reports/107.pdf

10. There are already signs that an impact is happening even before illegal immigrants become legal. A study by the Sutherland Institute in Salt Lake City says that the

arrival of Latino immigrants strengthens families and marriages in Utah regardless of their legal status (about 12 percent of the population of Utah consists of people of foreign origin). Almost seven out of every ten Hispanic immigrants in Utah, a very conservative state, get married, against 66 percent of Anglos who tie the knot. The number of children per family is similar in either case. Just 3 percent of immigrants get divorced, against 9 percent of Anglos who break up their marriage. See Passel and Cohn, "A Portrait of Unauthorized Immigrants in the United States." Also see "Inmigrantes hispanos fortalecen familias," *La Opinión*, Los Angeles, September 6, 2009.

11. Steven A. Camarota, "Immigrants in the United States, 2007—A Profile of America's Foreign-Born Population," Center for Immigration Studies, November, 2007, http://www.cis.org/immigrants_profile_2007

12. Alan Hughes, "Black Gold," *Black Enterprise,* June 1, 2006, http://www.blackenterprise.com/magazine/2006/06/black-gold/ Also see CAMAC's press release of May 18, 2009, http://www.camacholdings.com/downloads/CAMAC%20named%20Second%20Largest%20African-American%20Owned%20Co.%20in%20US,%2005.18.09.pdf

13. Jorge Castañeda, *Ex Mex: From Migrants to Immigrants* (New York: The New Press, 2007), 128.

14. Whereas in the 1960s no more than 5,000 Mexicans opted for U.S. citizenship every year, by 2005, almost 80,000 Mexicans did so. See Castañeda, *Ex Mex*), 137.

15. The survey was ordered by New America Media, conducted by Bendixen & Associates, and published, under the title of "Deep Divisions, Shared Destiny," on December 12, 2007.

16. The survey was ordered by New America Media, conducted by Bendixen & Associates, and published, under the title of "Deep Divisions, Shared Destiny," on December 12, 2007.

17. Jim Rogers, "Open the Doors," December 3, 2002. The article is available at http://www.jimrogers.com

18. "Feria y fiesta de la inmigración," *El País (Negocios)*, November 29, 2009.

19. Laurent Dubois, "France's Soccer Empire in Ruins?" CNN (International Edition), June 25, 2010, http://edition.cnn.com/2010/OPINION/06/25/dubois.football.france/index.html#fbid=VsrxSxXn891

20. Joel Millman, *The Other Americans* (New York: Viking, 1997), 48.

21. Jonathan Bowles and Tara Colton, "A World of Opportunity," Center for an Urban Future, February, 2007, 48, http://www.nycfuture.org

22. Millman, *The Other Americans*, 301.

23. Millman, *The Other American*, 286–296.

24. Millman, *The Other Americans*, 50.

25. Florence R. Kluckhohn and Fred Strodtbeck, *Variations In Value Orientations* (New York: Row, Peterson, 1961), 353.

26. Lionel Sosa, *The Americano Dream: How Latinos Can Achieve Success in Business and in Life* (New York: Plume, 1998). Chapters 1 and 6 are particularly relevant to his assessment of cultural traits that, in his opinion, hold Latinos back.

27. Evelyn Hu-Dehart, "The Chinese of Peru, Cuba, and Mexico," in *The Cambridge Survey of World Migration* (Cambridge, U.K.: Cambridge University Press, 1995), 220.

8

Islam, Ghettos, and Slums

MANY CITIZENS WHO find foreigners culturally suspect associate immigration with social degeneration. Sporadic riots, such as the ones that took place in the Mount Pleasant neighborhood in Washington, D.C., in 1991 after the District's police shot a Latin immigrant over a quarrel about drinking in public, have become engraved in the psyche of American mainstream society. No less pervasive, on both sides of the Atlantic, is the image of slums populated by foreign gangs full of hatred for the rest of society and immigrant neighborhoods that have the aura of ghettos in which few natives dare to tread. These images travel very fast internationally in all directions, courtesy of the new phase of globalization. The horrific violence in the new millennium in French immigrant neighborhoods, particularly the *banlieues* surrounding Paris (low-income neighborhoods in the outskirts of the city), have become, in the minds of many people on both sides of the pond, symbols of the cultural divide—the unbridgeable chasm that separates the native people from the alien intruders.

The presence of a disaffected, marginal generation of young people who bear a grudge against the mainstream society is a feature of most developed countries. Sometimes this group includes immigrants or the descendants of immigrants. The result is a permanent tension between people perceived as alien to mainstream culture and the host society. Many of the arguments about the cultural incompatibility of contemporary immigrants and their host societies stem from the images and news that periodically come out of violent immigrant slums on the margins of European society. The cultural tension is more acute in those countries than in the United States. In parts of Europe, some strands of Islamic immigrant culture seem to pose a challenge to basic safeguards of liberal democracy and modern society—partly because of the rigidities germane to a statist, protectionist system that hinders upward social mobility, and partly because of the influence exercised in marginal communities by religious fanatics with a political agenda. The reaction by some of those societies and governments has led to attempts to curtail Muslim-related impositions on women and children by male-dominated households. This, in turn, has opened a fascinating discussion in nations built on the notion that individuals are free to make personal decisions.

To the extent that there is an immigrant threat to liberal democracy and to its cultural underpinnings in Europe, it comes from attempts by Islamic fanatics to impose on their women and children horrific customs in the context of free societies that have constitutional safeguards against abuse of power. Although the perceived threat is highly exaggerated, it bears some discussion because some of the tensions are real.

Numerous testimonies have been given of what this threat entails. Ayaan Hirsi Ali is one of the most well-known cases throughout the world. I don't remember being more emotionally affected—or more persuaded—by a memoir since college than I was by her book *Infidel*.[1] She became world-famous in 2004, when Dutch filmmaker Theo van Gogh was murdered by an Islamic fundamentalist for making a documentary critical of Islam. The killer pinned a note to his victim's body with a death threat against Hirsi Ali, who had collaborated with him. She had taken refuge in Holland after a life of oppression under her Islamic family, made worse by her native Somalia's clan-based structures and forced relocations to Saudi Arabia, Ethiopia, and Kenya. Not only was she a devout Muslim, but she had also been a close sympathizer of the Muslim Brotherhood, the fundamentalist movement that was sweeping the region. After escaping to Holland to avoid an arranged marriage, she became a Dutch citizen and began to speak out against the culture of oppression affecting women in the Islamic world. She denounced "multiculturalism," in which Western countries tolerate and encourage—often at taxpayers' expense—cultural practices among immigrant groups even when they violate individual rights.

Today, many North African immigrants find a sense of belonging in the Islamic fundamentalist groups active in their midst; through them, they feel connected to the *umma*, the larger Muslim community. This does not necessarily mean that they identify ideologically or politically with radical Islam. They are, after all, intent on making a living in the liberal democratic societies they have chosen.² But certain rules that are part of liberal democracy clash with the customs adopted by some in the Muslim immigrant community, or that traditional households have imposed on women and the younger generations. To complicate matters, there are also grey areas—customs not directly linked to religious fundamentalism that still conflict with legal norms. This is true not only of Islam but also of other religions practiced by immigrants in Western societies. Should Sikhs be exempted from wearing crash helmets, it has often been asked, because their religion prescribes the turban?

It is a matter of historical irony that the symbiosis of the Islamic faith and the Algerian state was favored and encouraged by Paris for political purposes long before Europe confronted the challenge of Muslim immigrants wanting to maintain religious traditions that run contrary to liberal democracy. In 1905, a law was passed in France separating state and church totally and establishing complete freedom of worship, but the government decided not to apply this policy in the Algerian colony because Islam was considered an important tool for the control of the population. From 1905 until 1962, Islam, therefore, was the official religion in Algeria under French rule. Once Algeria gained its independence, Islam was a culturally strong, but politically innocuous, presence in French society throughout the immigrant population. Only in contemporary times, particularly in the wake of the Iranian Revolution, did the fundamentalist version of Islam become symbolized by the use of the veil (*hijab*) in North Africa and, through emigration, in French *bidonvilles* (city outskirts).

Since 1989, when it first appeared in public, there has been a vigorous debate about the veil—*la voile*. In Nanterre, Roubaix, Marseille, and Strasbourg, many Muslim girls adopted the veil and the scarf. Some wore them to make a rebellious statement against their parents, who practiced more traditional and less affirmative forms of Islam. The French authorities ruled that local teachers were at liberty to decide whether the use of the veil and the scarf was compatible with the separation of state and church. Attempts to prevent this manifestation of what many teachers and authorities considered a symbol of the oppression of women in certain Islamic societies were subsequently met with strong legal resistance by Muslims, including women who defended the right to abide by these religious customs.

The French school authorities, sometimes at the local level, sometimes higher up, responded to the protests, arguing that women were being forced under various forms of domination to accept something that symbolizes their demeaned position in Muslim societies. They pointed, for instance, to the fact that the FIS (Islamic Salvation Front), Algeria's violent fundamentalist organization, imposed the veil on women through the use of terror In the 1990s. However, the courts did not always accept these arguments. Between the late 1990s and the first few years of the new millennium, they reinstated many of the girls who had been suspended or expelled.[3]

The authorities in Paris eventually decided to intervene more forcefully. In the name of the deeply held principle of the *laicité* (secularity) of the French state and disregarding those who called for an "Anglo-Saxon" approach placing individual choice above even the separation of state and church, a law was passed in 2004 making it illegal to show "ostensible" religious articles, including the Muslim veil, the Jewish *kippa,* and the Christian cross in public schools and colleges.[4] More discreet symbols were allowed. The law, criticized by some Muslim countries and Islamic organizations in France, was upheld by the European Court of Human Rights four years later.

Although cultural differences between Muslim immigrants and host nations sometimes come across in milder fashion (in France, some Algerians have been less economically active than Moroccans and Tunisians, probably because the latter have tended to be single),[5] the differences mentioned above can be an obstacle to adaptation. Some North Africans, as African observers themselves have pointed out, exhibit a difficulty to assimilate within a lay state where religion is not part of the political culture. Many Muslim immigrants also resist adaptation to the lay society in Western Europe. Whereas in countries governed by Islamic law, including those that are allies of the West, visitors from Western countries are obliged to follow local rules and, as happens in Saudi Arabia, foreign women have to wear a veil.[6]

In France, some Africans go to Europe with their many wives, shunning monogamy, and practice other customs banned in the West. Their children are sometimes taught in school that the West is a departure from God, but also that they have the same rights as Westerners. Their parents try to inculcate in them the "clan" culture, telling them that Christians are impure—with the effect that the children do not even want to attend school. "Taking the Western culture of the country in which they are as an enemy, the parents of immigrant children have denounced a fictitious enemy," observes Manuel Ruben N'Dongo.

"In reality, the enemies of these adolescent youth are hateful obscurantism and rampant atavism transmitted from generation to generation."[7] In some parts of France with heavy concentrations of immigrants, Muslim customs have been imposed in public schools. Under pressure from Muslim bosses in the neighborhood, a primary public school in the XIXe Arrondissement banned pork in meals.[8]

One should not, however, draw precipitous conclusions from the difficulties encountered by certain European countries with regard to the assimilation of Muslim communities. Radical Islam is represented by a minority of Muslim immigrants in Europe. A vast majority of Muslims do not challenge the basic tenets of liberal democracy and respect for individual liberty among their own family members. Furthermore, the existence of many liberal democracies with substantial Muslim populations that are by and large well-adjusted to the basic tenets of the laws and the prevailing culture of the host nations indicate that the cultural difference is by no means an insurmountable challenge for the few European countries in which it has become a national issue.

In the aftermath of 9/11, researchers set out to study—in Mosques, Islamic centers, universities, and Muslim communities in areas such as California, New York, and Michigan—how well Muslims have been assimilated in the United States. They found few signs of European-style Muslim radicalism, although they also identified a growing religious sentiment caused by several factors: the isolation that Muslims felt as a result of the attacks, the need generated in Muslims by that traumatic event to look more deeply at their faith, and the resurgence of fundamentalist Islam elsewhere. Scarves, enrollment in Islamic centers, the learning of Arabic and Urdu were some of the signs of this growing Muslim religious sentiment.[9] However, Islam has not generally become a vehicle of violent radicalism or illegal conduct for significant numbers of immigrants or their descendants, nor is it associated with ghettos.

It is true that in many slums in developed countries, there is a high concentration of immigrants, and anger and violence are part of daily life. Once again, France is a case in point. Despite decades of discussions, the French system clearly has some built-in blockages that impede the kind of mobility that has made it possible for people of foreign origin to transform or transcend some ghettos and slums in in the United States. But these blockages do not necessarily imply that a cultural incompatibility makes integration impossible. If foreign values were incompatible with native ones, the United States would not have been able to incorporate so many black immigrants into its economy and society. It can be argued, of course, that immigration in France is of a very specific origin—mostly North African. But it wasn't always so, and the troubles in the *banlieues* have not involved immigrants, but their children or grandchildren, the overwhelming majority of whom were born and brought up in France. I would argue that obstacles to assimilation by the host country have played a major role in creating the ghettos and the ghetto-like mentality to which critics point as proof of cultural incompatibility.

In the 1970s, most immigrants in France went to live, upon arrival, in *foyers*, tiny apartments into which nine or ten of them were crammed, built by Sonacotra with some funding by employers and government help. They were part of a more general pattern of low-rent housing that the government had subsidized since the 1950s. After the 1970s, under a program known for the French acronym for "priority urbanization zones," these housing projects grew quickly and gradually became immigrant ghettos. The crammed conditions improved somewhat—after 1974, the rooms became slightly bigger—but the ghetto quality only worsened. Both the government and the employers steered foreign workers towards these enclaves that had been created with good intentions but had an isolating effect on immigrants, deliberately separating them from the rest of society.

The living arrangements, as some critics have pointed out perceptively, held an important contradiction. While the integration of these workers into the economy pulled them in an individualistic direction, their lodges, where everything was shared and common, pushed them towards collectivism.[10] Immigrants felt protected by the housing projects' collectivist environment, even if it was notoriously grim and, yes, insecure. Eventually, their integration into the economy also waned, as they ceased to work in the businesses that had brought foreign labor into the country or their relatives found few avenues for progress in them. The rigidity of France's labor laws and business climate coupled with the widespread resistance of French managers to hire foreigners compounded the problem.

Most immigrants today live in so-called *HLMs* (*habitation à loyer modéré*), the French acronym for a euphemism that means rent-controlled housing, a type of facility available also to many French people. This housing is subsidized by the government through direct help given to builders and to tenants. Family patterns in those neighborhoods, as was the case in welfare-dependent families in the United States before the welfare reform of the 1990s, are depressing. The children of immigrants grow with little guidance and an absence of values that is reflected in their generally hopeless lives. It is not surprising that nihilism and blind hatred seem to abound among the youth in some of the worst slums.

These factors may play a part in the wider society, beyond the purely immigrant community, where unemployment among young people is high and the rigidity of the economic system also affects the ability of French kids to move up. In the United States, although some cultural differences may stand in the way of swift integration, other factors, namely a more porous and flexible political economy, help dissolve whatever cultural constraints were pulling immigrants away from the rest of society.

The rigidities to which some economists have pointed in France have to do with socialist and corporatist norms in the economic system, particularly the minimum wage, taxes, and business regulations. Other rigidities pertain to the realm of general native attitudes towards foreigners. Economic institutions and discriminatory attitudes have combined to narrow the avenues of progress for young people of immigrant origin. The high minimum wage affects young immigrants in particular because it discourages employers from hiring low-productivity workers, a group that is overrepresented by the children of immigrants. The ratio of the cost of the minimum wage for the employer to the cost of the mean wage has been much higher in France than in the United States as a result of successive forms of government intervention that were supposed to help the poor. The periodic raise of the minimum wage itself and the introduction of the 35-hour week are two examples.[11]

A middle-of-the-road case is that of Britain, where the economic system has been more open and enterprise-friendly than in France, but where the constraints—both legal and cultural—placed on immigrants have made assimilation difficult. Although Asians from the former colonies are more integrated into British society than Africans are in France, they have had a tougher time than immigrants in the United States. For decades, it was very difficult for immigrants to buy or rent a house from a local authority—the path many Britons of lower economic standing used in order to have access to housing. Before a 1968 law banning racial publicity, it was common to read in advertisements warning such as "Europeans only." For a long time, reality failed to catch up with the 1965 Race Relations Act, which outlawed precisely that kind of conduct in response to a social tension that dated back to the Nottingham and Noting Hill riots of the late 1950s.[12]

Between 1972 and 1975, the British government carried out a series of surveys to gauge the extent of racial-based inequality across the country. Lack of qualifications was not an explanation for the differences in the quality of employment among white natives and the rest of the population. While 79 percent of white men with college or university degrees were in professional or managerial jobs, only 31 percent of non-whites who had similar qualifications enjoyed a similar type of white-collar employment.[13]

Notes

1. Ayaan Hirsi Ali, *Infidel* (New York: Free Press, 2007).

2. Roger Fauroux and Hanifa Chérifi, *Nous Sommes Tous Des Immigrés* (Paris: Éditions Robert Lafont, 2003), 175.

3. Fauroux and Chérifi, *Nous Sommes Tous Des Immigrés*, 143–145.

4. The text of the law can be found in English in the following website: http://www .legifrance.gouv.fr/affichTexte.do?cidTexte=JORFTEXT000000417977&dateTexte=

5. Abdelmalek Syadi, *l'Immigration ou les Paradoxes de l'Alterité* (Paris: Raison d'Agir Editions 2006), 74.

6. Manuel Ruben N'Dongo, *Regard sur l'Immigration Africaine en Europe: Les Dictatures Africains, Causes et Effects de l'Immigration* (Paris: Editions des Ecrivains, 1999), 126.

7. N'Dongo, *Regard sur l'Immigration Africaine en Europe,* 119–120.

8. N'Dongo, *Regard sur l'Immigration Africaine en Europe,* 167.

9. Geneive Abdo, liaison for the Alliance of Civilizations at the United Nations, conducted a two-year study. He shared some of his conclusions in an article in the *Washington Post* titled "America's Muslims Aren't As Assimilated As You Think," published on August 27, 2006. He is also the author of *Mecca And Mainstreet: Muslim Life in America after 9/11* (New York: Oxford University Press, 2006).

10. Syadi, *l'Immigration ou les Paradoxes de l'Alterité,* 85.

11. Bernard Salanié, "The Riots In France: An Economist's View," June 11, 2006, http: //riotsfrance.ssrc.org/Salanie/

12. Zig Layton-Henry, *The Politics of Immigration: Immigration, "Race" and "Race" Relations in Post-War Britain* (Oxford, U.K., and Cambridge, Mass.: Blackwell, 1992), 49.

13. Layton-Henry, *The Politics of Immigration,* 56.

9

The Multicultural Fallacy

MUCH OF THE cultural bias against contemporary immigration in the United States has to do with the shift that occurred in the origin of the majority of newcomers in recent decades. That shift can be traced back to 1965, when the Immigration and Nationality Act abolished the discriminatory national origins quota system and replaced it with hemispheric ceilings—170,000 from the Eastern Hemisphere with a maximum of 20,000 from any one country, and 120,000 from the Western Hemisphere. The real cornerstone of this new law was family reunification because it expanded the categories of relatives who could enter without numerical limits.[1] This family reunification partly offset the numerical limitations on permanent legal immigration from Mexico, which were imposed for the first time by the ceiling on Western Hemispheric immigrants.

Regardless of its merits or lack thereof, the Immigration and Nationality Act cannot be fully understood without taking into account the domestic context, heavily influenced at the time by the Civil Rights movement. Racial restrictions relating to immigration had been repealed in 1952, but a quota system remained in place.[2] After the Civil Rights Act of 1964 that prohibited discrimination on the basis of race and other criteria, keeping national quotas and the Asian exclusion provisions was unthinkable. For years, Catholics, Jews, and liberals (in the American sense of the term) had criticized the preference given to Northern and Western Europeans. Seen through the prism of the egalitarian 1960s, laws that favored Nordic Europeans over Alpine Europeans, Alpine Europeans over Mediterranean Europeans, and Mediterranean Europeans over Asians or Jews were unacceptable. The provision regarding reunification, in turn, was the result of a change of opinion partly influenced by lobbies. President John F. Kennedy had pushed for a skill-based system of the kind envisioned nowadays by proponents of a Canadian- or Australian-type approach, but under the Johnson administration, various groups fought for family reunification to be one of the central criteria of the new policy.[3] The new immigration law was one of many expressions of the ideological evolution experienced by the generation that came of age during World War II. These were the children and grandchildren of the last great immigrant wave (mostly European). For them, reform meant embracing diversity and allowing families to follow immigrants into the United States—thinking that not many would do so.

As is usually the case with legislation, the sponsors and promoters of the 1965 law did not anticipate the full effects of their decision. Senator Edward Kennedy, the Immigration Subcommittee chairman, promised: "Our cities will not be flooded with a million immigrants annually. Under the proposed bill, the present level of immigration remains substantially the same. . . . Secondly, the ethnic mix of this country will not be upset."[4]

In subsequent decades, the number of immigrants rose and their composition changed, impacting the mix in the country at large. Although the rise in immigrant numbers had less to do with the provisions of the law than with illegal immigration attracted by a market that demanded more foreign labor, the law did have an effect. Between 1820 and 1924, some 34 million Europeans had moved to the United States. Between 1965 and 2000, some 23 million new immigrants arrived in this country, mostly from Latin America and Asia.[5] The shift in the origin of immigration to the United States was momentous. In 1950, more than two-thirds of legal immigration originated in Europe or Canada, 25 percent in the Western Hemisphere (other than Canada), and 6 percent in Asia. By the 1980s, only 13 percent of immigration originated in Europe or Canada, 47 percent in the Western Hemisphere (other than Canada), and 37 percent in Asia; eight out of every ten immigrants were from Latin America and Asia, a proportion that would be maintained into the new millennium.[6]

The 1965 law also left its mark in the proportion of immigrants who arrived through family reunification visas as compared to those who did so based on employment.[7] A majority of Asian and, to a lesser extent, Middle Eastern and African, immigrants, who came after the new law was enacted had a middle- or lower-middle-class backgrounds.[8] Asians made use of occupational preferences favored by the statutes—scientists, engineers, and doctors were able to stay in the country after studying in the United States—although many Indians, especially Sikhs and Punjabis, went into agriculture. Latinos overwhelmingly came through the reunification channel, and most were low-skilled workers or farmers.[9]

The modern immigration era, generally assumed to have started in 1965, coincided with the emergence of a new paradigm regarding "minorities" and "ethnic groups" in the developed world, especially in the United States. Various expressions—multiculturalism, cultural relativism, ethnic collectivism—have come to describe an ethos informed by intellectual and political circles that started as a genuine effort to correct discrimination, whether in the law or in social attitudes, but ended up enthroning new ills. I refer to the process whereby all values became acceptable as long as they could be associated with an underprivileged group, and the focus on individual rights and identity was replaced with a focus on minority rights and ethnic identity. These groups, in turn, vied for power and influence with the help of native ideologues invoking those collectivist rights.

Although multiculturalism became particularly influential in the post-1965 world and established itself as a new paradigm, it does have older roots. The European immigrants who moved to the United States between 1880 and 1920 were no strangers to it, although its influence was much weaker. Their political groups engaged in the same competition for power and resources in which contemporary "ethnic groups" often take part under the incentives provided by multiculturalism.[10] But in the post-1960s world, "ethnic groups" are more numerous or at least politically visible. There is a greater effort to accommodate them, and race consciousness is a more determining factor at play in minority-related issues; the result is a much greater presence of identity politics.

Although immigration was not the sole or even the primary source of multicultural thinking, it was caught up in this ideological deformation through the focus on ethnicity and minority rights. The effect was that those who championed immigrants oftentimes contributed, wittingly or unwittingly, to the gradual undermining of some of the values of the free society—for example, limited government, self-reliance, individualism, the sanctity of contracts, and private property. They did so by giving ideologues—who considered such notions ethnocentric, discriminatory, or even imperialistic, a panoply of arguments with which to combat them—in both academia and political life.

In 1963, a little before the sea-changing immigration act, Nathan Glazier and Daniel Patrick Moynihan had already signaled the change of paradigm taking place in the United States and the Western world in their book *Beyond The Melting Pot*. Immigrants and so-called minorities—blacks (still called Negroes), Jews, Italians, and Puerto Ricans—had become "ethnic groups."[11] Foreigners ceased to be just individual immigrants and became part of those collective entities that academics and activists began to identify as worthy of special attention in society. The identity of immigrants, in the eyes of social engineers, ceased to be personal or individual—they were now identified as part of a larger body, a multicultural entity, and therefore attitudes and policies that affected them had to be shaped by multiculturalism.[12] For decades, the new multicultural paradigm would rule supreme, only to become questioned in intellectual circles in any meaningful way in the second half of the 1980s, and especially in the 1990s.[13]

In 2010, a new cartoon show called "Ugly Americans" on Comedy Central, the cable channel belonging to Viacom, made brilliant fun of the twisted way in which the original melting pot concept turned, in recent decades, into a chaotic scene in which social workers spend their time trying to pander to the foreigners' cultural idiosyncrasies through the notion of shared civil rights. The result is anything but the integration that the fictional "Department of Integration" on the show is supposed to facilitate. The scene is a Manhattan peopled by zombies, monsters, and mutants, with a few remaining humans. A human social worker with a liberal heart and an alcoholic wizard try to help the non-humans assimilate, but the two demons that oversee the Department of Integration have cut the staff to almost nothing, while the demand for help from minorities is almost unlimited. The show illustrates the critical perceptions that multiculturalism generates in many Americans these days.

Multiculturalism was one of the political offshoots—perhaps the most powerful one—of the intellectual trend that questioned the traditional values and approaches of the Western canon in the years after World War II and the concurring wave of decolonization. Ray Jureidini reminds us that, after a period beginning in the nineteenth century when colonial anthropology had classified traditional cultures as "naive," "primitive," or "barbaric," the other extreme—cultural relativism—became the normative anthropological concept in the study of non-Western societies.[14] Influenced by the idea that imperialist impositions or cultural standards dating to the colonial era were to be eradicated, anthropologists such as Claude Lévi-Strauss argued that all cultural groups and societies have a cultural and thus moral equivalence.[15] This premise translated into the principle that because distortions arise from stereotypes, prejudice, and racism, it is important to "step back" from the values imposed by one's culture when studying other cultures. Only thus can the social scientist who studies another community be as objective as possible.[16]

The moral equivalence of all cultural groups and societies is the philosophical premise that forms the basis of multiculturalism. According to the ideology of multiculturalism, society is parceled out into collectivist entities given equal ethical and moral validity, each with "rights" that create an obligation on the part of the rest of society. Multiculturalism came to influence education in ways that undervalued the traditional search for truth and knowledge in the process of learning. Students were brainwashed with all sorts of "post-modern" sophistry according to which all authority is suspect, children are alien to their parents, and classical teaching is a form of indoctrination. Self-expression became an end in itself, regardless of what was being expressed. Teaching minority-related differences, inculcating ethnic nationalism, and singing the virtues of victimhood and redistributive justice became in many schools and universities more important than helping kids become free, responsible citizens who understand equality as the protection of equal rights before the law, and who value individual achievement.[17]

This ideological erosion of the Western canon took place in many other parts of the developed world at more or less the same time, on the heels of a self-critical and ashamed look at their colonial pasts, old and recent. Traditional patterns of authority at home—of domestic colonialism, as it were, in the country at large and within the family itself, were also impugned. In Europe, the rebellion of the period known as "May 68" went beyond a healthy revision of traditional patterns and saw a questioning of all parental authority, leading, in the view of many observers, to a revision of basic principles of discipline that ultimately generated an overly permissive environment in which new generations had a hard time discerning what was important and true.

In the United States, by adopting a guilty conscience, the academic, intellectual, and political elites gradually devalued their own society and culture in the eyes of large numbers of people from younger generations. Those elites recoiled from the idea that newcomers should be encouraged to adopt the language of the host nation and their customs because such a process was ethnocentric. I am not referring to the imposition of English on new immigrants, but simply to encouraging the adoption of the language among people aspiring to make a living in this country. Small groups devoted to the protection of the collective identity of minorities made it their task to "deconstruct" (to use the chic verbiage employed by proponents of such views at the time), the moral and ideological edifice of modern society in developed countries—i.e., expose the patterns of "domination" implicit in individual rights, free markets, and free exchange, which were seen as fig leaves for a system aimed at keeping minorities in their place. The assertion of a cultural identity by those minorities through their highly politicized spokespersons discouraged assimilation on both sides of the Atlantic. If liberal democracy was no better than the regimes that had kept the migrants poorer than they needed to be back home, why should assimilation be a condition for getting one's hands on the pie of a prosperity that had been achieved through imperialist rapacity by the United States, Europe, and others?

The idea of assimilation came under attack as far back as the 1960s, the time when the shift in paradigm that we call multiculturalism began. It was seen as an outdated, patronizing imposition. By the 1980s, the new approach had pretty much reversed the teachings of, for instance, the School of Chicago and other sociologists who had defined assimilation not as the erasure of all ethnic origins, "but a process of interpenetration and fusion in which persons and groups acquire the memory, sentiments and attitudes of other persons and groups, and, by sharing their experience and history, are incorporated with them in common historical life."[18] Interpenetration and fusion were no longer desired objectives because they amounted to disfiguring the uniqueness of the cultural identity of minorities.

The multicultural zeitgeist of the 1960s influenced the political world early on. In its Title VII, the Civil Rights Act of 1964, for instance, prohibited refusing to hire people on the basis of race or gender, and required that "intent" to discriminate be proven. Soon, judges, bureaucrats, and activists focused their interpretations of the law on the historical consequences of discrimination, rather than on the intent of those who committed discrimination. This shift paved the way for initiatives aimed at correcting the social legacy of old injustices through affirmative action and other such means. What started as an anti-discrimination legislation became an exercise in social engineering through "positive discrimination," an avenue with no end in sight that gradually turned good intentions into a panoply of legal and social weapons aimed against some tenets of the free society, among them private property. Even bodies created by the act of 1964, such as the Equal Employment Opportunity Commission, became tools for redesigning society.[19]

The deformation was seen in multiple government actions. For instance, in 1968–70, the Department of Labor issued orders requiring contractors who hired workers to take into account the proportion of races in the geographic area of business. Those orders were a distortion of the Executive Order signed in 1961 by John F. Kennedy, which stated, "The contractor will take affirmative action to ensure that applicants are employed and that employees are treated during employment without regard to their race, creed, color or national origin."[20]

Similar distortions took place with regard to the Voting Rights Act of 1965 that prevented Southern states from denying blacks the right to vote. In 1969, the Supreme Court interpreted the law to mandate systems of representation that would ensure the election of minority candidates. The result of this interpretation was gerrymandering based on ethnic considerations, that is, the creation of electoral districts with boundaries drawn to provide safe seats for blacks and Hispanics.[21]

The Bilingual Education Act of 1967 also embodied the spirit of the times and gave rise to policies that in time would lead many Americans to resent immigration and view minorities as invasive. The bill was designed to provide help to Mexican-American children who were poor and at an educational disadvantage because they spoke little English. From this small beginning emerged a complex structure of federal regulations, court decisions, and further legislation favoring the use of the Spanish language. In 1975, Congress amended the Voting Rights Act to prohibit state and local governments from imposing any qualifications or prerequisites that would deny or abridge the right of any citizen of the United States to vote because he or she was a member of any "language minority group." Local governments in voting districts where five percent or more of the population belonged to a language minority group, defined as American Indian, Asian, Alaskan, or "of Spanish heritage," were forced to cater directly to them. By the mid-1980s, the language programs were designed, according to a survey published in *Time* magazine, "to maintain a student's original language indefinitely."[22]

Early in the new millennium, more than 330 jurisdictions in 30 states were already forced to provide written materials and oral assistance in various languages. Two-thirds of these jurisdictions were providing material and assistance in Spanish. By then, the Equal Employment Opportunity Commission had filed countless suits against employers who required employees to speak English only. (Henry Ford must have been turning in his grave!)[23]

Multiculturalism was bound to provoke a reaction among natives in the United States sooner or later. The perception that natives were being in turn discriminated against by the disproportionate effort to cater to minority groups was certain to stoke up resentment. Naturally, the larger the minority perceived as benefitting from multiculturalism, the greater the resentment against it. Hispanics were a natural target, given their numbers. Before the multicultural ethos became dominant, Europeans and Latin Americans who moved to the United States had generally been seen as belonging to a common heritage by virtue of Latin America's European legacy (the region was colonized by Spain and Portugal for centuries and became part of the Western world through colonization). The arrival of African and North African immigrants, in turn, was seen as culturally challenging, in contrast with Europeans and Hispanics, who were considered more akin.[24] Now, in multicultural America, partly as a result of the deep resentment that multiculturalism has caused, Hispanics have come to be perceived by many as a deviation from the Western immigration of yesteryear, as a minority that has encroached on native rights and is bent on undermining the Western traditions. Those perceptions have by and large overshadowed the evidence that points to a gradual assimilation by Hispanic immigrants and those from the West Indies or Haiti—and to the lack of evidence that today's immigrants are developing permanent non-English-speaking enclaves.[25] Hispanics are perceived by many as belonging to a totally alien culture, and by some as a different race altogether.

The obsession with race, again a legacy of multiculturalism, has generated so much profiling confusion that an entire category—that of non-Hispanic whites—had to be created to distinguish between native whites and people from a Hispanic background who either think of themselves as white or are considered white in their native countries—and this is not a small number of people. By 2000, 63 percent of Colombians identified themselves as white, as did 42 percent of all Latinos.[26] Among Cubans, 90 percent of people identified themselves as white.[27]

What to an American white may seem a shade of brown, to a Hispanic may seem white by comparison to darker-skinned fellow nationals or, as is often the case, in accordance with the social position the family maintained back home: Social status, not skin color, is sometimes a determinant of race, or at least of how people think of race, in highly stratified countries. I have black Dominican friends who think of themselves as being more white than black and firmly categorize Haitians as black. The Peruvian term *cholo* is supposed to refer to a mixed-race person, but is often used pejoratively to refer to someone of lower standing regardless of skin color. Many Latinos identify themselves as white in the United States because they fear being perceived as alien to the mainstream of society, a paradoxical consequence of profiling and an implicit—and ironic—effort to assimilate.

Race is an almost meaningless concept in today's world, of course. Time has reduced to absurdity the pseudo-scientists who invented racial demography, beginning with Arthur de Gobineau, whose famous *An Essay On The Inequality Of The Human Races*[28] inspired Hitler's view of the Aryan master race. A race would be a genetically homogenous group of individuals—genes being the only biological element parents pass on to their children. What "race" fits that description in any modern society? What passes for race is largely skin color combined with background, but the various "races" are really the product of multiple, heterogeneous combinations of genes that—except in very secluded, isolated, and small communities—are impossible to trace. Even ethnicity, which is really an extended family on a much larger scale, is a suspect concept given the genetic combinations that have taken place over the years, centuries, and millennia. But the multicultural fallacy has managed to turn ethnicity into a goal in itself and paradoxically generated by way of reaction an antipathy that seeks to set immigrant minorities apart—culturally, but also, to some extent, racially.

Much is written and debated around the issue of race tensions in the United States in relation to immigration. The focus on ethnic identity has not helped diffuse those tensions and may have contributed to exacerbating them by placing excessive emphasis on race, which is often confused with ethnicity. I do not refer only to tensions between white Americans and immigrants, but also between immigrants and various other groups, particularly the black community. Real but sporadic incidents tend to take on disproportionate dimensions and generate resentment.[29]

It cannot be denied that tensions exist among minority groups, and between them and the native population—something that is true in almost any society. Many of us remember how in 1992, after the verdict acquitting the police officers in the Rodney King trial, African-Americans sacked and looted Korean groceries, Cambodian shops, and Indian newsstands in very tough parts of Los Angeles. But these episodes are not common. The multicultural fallacy has rendered those tensions more acute than they would otherwise be by focusing on ethnicity and race, rather than the individual, when discussing and enforcing "rights." A survey conducted in 2007 showed that 79 percent of Hispanics considered racial tensions a "very serious problem," while 65 percent of blacks and 37 percent of Asians thought the same. More than 60 percent of Hispanics said they prefer to conduct business with whites than with Asians and blacks, while 47 percent of blacks and 53 percent of Asians said the same thing.[30] The irony of these results is that they are evidence of a bias on the part of immigrants in favor of mainstream white America—the same society in which large numbers of natives see immigrants as culturally different and unwilling to assimilate.

As we will now see, patterns of assimilation on the part of contemporary immigrants are not very different from those of yesteryear who are judged by current critics to have been more culturally compatible. If we look beyond the fog created by the multicultural fallacy, we will see that assimilation by contemporary immigrants echoes the process of acculturation followed by other waves of immigrants in the past.

Notes

1. Harry Johnson, "An International Model," in *The Brain Drain*, ed. Walter Adams (New York: Macmillan, 1968).

2. Thomas Donland, *A World of Wealth: How Capitalism Turns Profits into Progress* (Upper Saddle River, N.J.: Pearson Education, 2008), 68.

3. Many Americans see the 1965 Immigration and Nationality Act as a Trojan Horse that allowed third-world nationals to replace Europeans as the primary source of immigration in the United States. But in fact, the 1965 law was the result of domestic, that is, profoundly American, politics, not of foreign pressure, or even primarily domestic

organizations led by foreigners. Apart from the Civil Rights movement, the context in which the law came into being was one of low unemployment and economic boom. The Democrats from big cities—where so-called minorities were emerging as potential electoral constituencies—were keen to accommodate their local interests. Philip Hart, the act's sponsor on the Senate side, came from Michigan; Emmanuel Celler, from Brooklyn, sponsored the legislation on the House of Representatives side. See Joel Millman, *The Other Americans* (New York: Viking, 1997), 60–61.

4. Peter Brimelow, *Alien Nation: Common Sense About America's Immigration Disaster*" (New York: Random House, 1995), 76.

5. U.S. Immigration and Naturalization Service, *2000 Statistical Yearbook of the Immigration and Naturalization Service*. Unpublished selection available online: http://uscis .gov/graphics/shared/aboutus/statistis/yearbook2000.pdf

6. George J. Borjas, *Friends Or Strangers: The Impact Of Immigrants On The U.S. Economy* (New York: Basic Books, July, 1991), 4.

7. In 1992—to name but one year in a decade with abundant immigrants—55 percent of the more then 900,000 people who moved to the United States entered under family reunification visas, whereas no more than 13 percent arrived because they were granted permits to work. See Peter Brimelow, *Alien Nation*, 141.

8. Pyong Gap Min and Mehdi Bozorgmehr, "Immigrant Entrepreneurship In The United States: Trends, Research And Theory," in *Venturing Abroad: Global Processes And National Particularities of Immigrant Entrepreneurship In Advanced Economies*, eds. Robert Kloosterman and Jan Rath (Oxford, U.K. and New York: Berg/New York University Press, 2003).

9. By 1980, more than 387,000 Indians or Americans of Indian ancestry were in the country. A decade later, the Indian or Indian community in the United States had grown to 786.000, of whom no more than one-quarter were naturalized Americans. See U.S. Census Bureau, *Asians And Pacific Islanders in the United States* (Washington, D.C.: Government Printing Office, 1993), 13.

10. Herbert J. Gans, "Ethnic and Racial Identity," in *The New Americans: A Guide to Immigration Since 1965*, eds. Mary C. Waters and Reed Ueda (Cambridge, Mass.: Harvard University Press, 2007), 102.

11. Nathan Glazer and Daniel Patrick Moynihan, *Beyond The Melting Pot* (Cambridge, Mass.: MIT Press, 1963).

12. A little later in the decade, Harold Cruse, the famous black nationalist, wrote that the United States "is a nation of minorities ruled by a minority of one—it thinks and acts as if it were a nation of white Anglo-Saxon Protestants." See Harold Cruse, *The Crisis Of The Negro Intellectual* (New York: William Morrow, 1967).

13. Some examples of this include: Joshua A. Fishman et al., *The Rise and Fall of the Ethnic Revival* (Berlin: Mouton Publishers, 1985); David A. Hollinger, *Postethnic America: Beyond Multiculturalism* (New York: Basic Books, 1995); Pnina Werbner and Tariq Moddod, *Debating Cultural Hybridity, Multicultural Identity and the Politics of Antiracism* (London: Zed Books, 1997); and John Miller, *The Unmaking of Americans: How Multiculturalism Has Undermined the Assimilation Ethic* (New York: Free Press, 1998.)

14. Ray Jureidini, "Human Rights and Foreign Contract Labor: Some Implications for Management and Regulation in Arab Countries," in *Arab Migration in a Globalized World* (Geneva: International Organization for Migration, League of Arab States, 2004).

15. Jonathan Shestack, "The Philosophical Foundations of Human Rights," in *Human Rights Concepts And Standards,* ed. Janusz Symonides (Paris: Ashgate and UNESCO, 2000), 31–66.

16. This type of approach, which also has roots in Max Weber's famous essay *Objectivity In The Social Sciences*, is at the root of the cultural relativism that has led to the justification of human rights abuses and tyranny in underdeveloped countries. The reaction to this deformation of objectivity in the study of other cultures has prompted some social scientists to respond that there is a case to be made against moral relativism with the argument that almost all human societies "show a concern for the value of human life. . . . In none is the killing of other human beings permitted without some fairly definite justification. In all societies there is some prohibition of incest, some opposition to boundless promiscuity and to rape, some favor for stability and permanence in sexual relations. All human societies display a concern for the truth. . . . All societies display a favor for the values of cooperation. All know friendship." If this is true, the premise that some human rights are absolute and universally accepted should allow cultural relativists the means to express moral outrage against certain abhorrent practices without losing their unbiased attitude and objectivity. Hopefully, as international law regarding human rights becomes increasingly accepted and various countries incorporate it into their domestic legislation, social pressure will be brought to bear on those who perpetrate or condone human rights abuses, and universal standards of respect for the lives and property of others will cease to be tolerated under cultural pretexts. We will still be left with the discussion about what exactly is a human right, a field that has also seen a toxic contemporary deformation—but that is another matter.

17. Georgie Anne Geyer, *Americans No More* (New York: The Atlantic Press, 1996), 128.

18. Carola Suárez-Orozco and Marcelo Suárez-Orozco, "Education," in *The New Americans,* eds. Waters and Ueda, 124–125.

19. Hugh Davis Graham, *The Civil Rights Era: Origins and Development of National Policy, 1960–1972* (New York: Oxford University Press, 1990), 250.

20. Andrew Kull, *The Color-Blind Constitution* (Cambridge, Mass.: Harvard University Press, 1992), 200–203.

21. Kull, *The Color-Blind Constitution*, 214–216.

22. Samuel Huntington, *Who Are We? The Challenges of America's National Identity* (New York: Simon & Schuster, 2004), 158–166.

23. Huntington, *Who Are We?*, 164.

24. Daniela Flesler, *The Return of the Moor: Spanish Responses to Contemporary Morrocan Immigration* (West Lafayette, Ind.: Purdue University Press, 2008), 131.

25. David López ans Vanesa Estrada, "Language," in *The New American,* eds. Waters and Ueda, 241.

26. Luis Eduardo Guarnizo and Marilyn Espitia, "Colombia, " in *The New American*, eds. Waters and Ueda, 378.

27. Max Castro and Thomas D. Boswell, "The Dominican Diaspora Revisited: Dominicans and Dominican-Americans in the New Century," *The North-South Agenda*, paper 53 (Miami: North-South Center, University of Miami, 2002).

28. Joseph Arthur Comte de Gobineau's *Essai sur L'inégalité des Races Humaines* was first published in Paris between 1853 and 1855, and dedicated to George V of Hanover.

29. Millman, *The Other Americans*, 74.

30. The survey was ordered by New America Media, conducted by Bendixen & Associates, and published under the title of "Deep Divisions, Shared Destiny" on December 12, 2007.

10

Culture Changes

EXPERIENCE TEACHES THAT total assimilation takes only two or three generations, a period when viewed from a distance is short, but when viewed from an immediate perspective feels like an eternity. In exiled communities, made up of people who aspire to return to their homelands and who have a political motivation to keep their presence in a foreign land transitory, the time frame can be different. But even in that case, if the duration of the regime from which they flee is prolonged, exile communities eventually assimilate, as subsequent generations transition from exiles to immigrants. The children of Cubans who arrived in the United States during the 1960s and 1970s may feel an attachment to the island because of the trauma suffered by their parents, but they view the United States as their country. Cubans who arrived in the 1980s and 1990s have a very different attachment to the island than do the older generations. I witnessed as much during my stay in south Florida in the early 1990s as editor of the op-ed pages of *El Nuevo Herald* and member of the board of the Miami Herald Publishing Co. The level of interest in Cuban issues among young writers of Cuban origin was well below that of the previous generations.

Students of assimilation conclude that the first generation of immigrants usually makes progress in speaking English but predominantly speaks the native tongue; the second generation is bilingual but is generally more comfortable in English; and the third generation tends to be monolingual in English. A study conducted among 14,000 Hispanic adults over a span of years indicated that only one-quarter of first-generation immigrants spoke English well, while 88 percent of their children spoke it very well. The proportions are similar across various nationalities. In the next generation, the percentage of those who speak

English very well rises to 94 percent. This pattern can also be seen among immigrants of much higher economic standing.[1]

Sociological studies based on the 2000 census indicate that among immigrants from non-English-speaking countries, only 10 percent do not speak any English, and 40 percent arrive in the United States already able to speak it reasonably well. The studies find a strong correlation between the length of time a foreign-born person has been in this country and his or her ability to speak English well. Almost all native-born children speak English. Only about one-third of third- and fourth-generation immigrants are still able to speak the language of their immigrant grandparents. The consensus is that the standard three-generation linguistic assimilation still holds.[2]

Researchers who looked at immigrant assimilation in the United States in the early twentieth century reached similar conclusions. The so-called "Hansen Law" enthroned the idea that adaptation to the host country was a process completed by successive generations. The first generation emigrated, the second "escaped" towards assimilation, and the third one came back to the origins, not by renouncing the adoptive culture, but by embracing the legacy of the old homeland from the security of the country to which their elders migrated and to which they naturally belonged.[3] The third generation, therefore, exhibited a cultural paradox. The more it valued is distant roots, the more assimilated it was. This is something easily seen today among Americans from families that have been in the country for several generations but who celebrate festivities linked to their ancient roots, be they Irish, Italian, German, English, or another culture.

In the last couple of decades, assimilation on the part of immigrants has comported with the three-generations pattern. One way to confirm this is to gauge the percentages of foreigners who marry natives in the first, second, and third generations. In the mid-1990s, more than 18 percent of first-generation Asian females and more than 8 percent of first-generation Hispanic females had married outside of their group. Among second-generation females, the numbers were higher: more than 29 percent of Asians and 26 percent of Hispanics. The percentages rose to more than 41 and 33 percent, respectively, among the third generation.[4] Generally, at the turn of the millennium, intermarriage between whites and other groups had quadrupled to more than a million.

An interesting effect of the three-generation process of assimilation is that once a community of foreign origin is established, newcomers tend to achieve upward social mobility quite quickly. Many new immigrants in the United States move to homes in suburban areas following the native middle-class trend of the post-war decades, a progress facilitated by the fact that previous waves of fellow nationals are already assimilated. By almost any measure, second-generation immigrants—approximately one in ten people living in the United States[5]—do much better than their parents. They also do better than comparable workers who are first-generation immigrants. In the 1990s, the median income for a Dominican born in the United States, some $26,000, was more than $6,000 higher than that of a comparable worker who arrived before 1990.[6] The children of immigrants tend to do very well by comparison with natives. In 2006, a typical second-generation person was earning 6 percent more than other native-born workers.[7]

The educational success of the children of immigrants also points to assimilation over time. Second-generation immigrants have between 0.3 and 0.4 more years of education than people whose parents were born in the United States. Even in immigrant communities whose economic performance is unremarkable, the educational drive is notable. Only one in nine Dominicans born in the United States who were 25 years or older did not complete high school, compared to 53 percent of those who arrived before 1990.[8] The evidence has led a reputable scholar to state: "The fear that post-1965 immigrants will never assimilate is belied by the rather surprising educational success of their children."[9]

Even so, the system places onerous obstacles on the educational assimilation of immigrants. Although the Supreme Court has mandated that illegal immigrant children be allowed to go to school, only ten states permit them to go to college paying in-state tuition rates. Even in those states, a person who settled in the United States illegally as a child, almost always because of his or her parents, will be able to obtain a good education in college but will face a tough reality after graduation: He or she will continue to be undocumented even if one parent is a citizen.[10] There are some 4 million children who, despite having one parent who is a citizen, remain undocumented because the other parent is an illegal alien.[11] The ability of the 65,000 undocumented kids who graduate from high school every year to positively impact the adoptive country is limited by the legal status of the one parent.

Nonetheless, the fact that an illegal immigrant child can go to school everywhere in the country and then to college in ten states enhances his or her opportunity to absorb the mainstream culture. These kids are keen to contribute to America's greatness. They even started a movement—"Dream University"—that led them to organize marches in Washington, D.C., to try to persuade Congress to pass a law that would offer a path to citizenship to those who graduate from college or serve in the military. The message the kids are sending is that they want to reverse the statistics that speak of a 25-percent high school drop-out rate among native-born Latino adults and a 52-percent drop-out rate for foreign-born Latino adults.[12] Sadly, in December of 2010, the Senate voted against the proposed Dream Act, which would have given residency to illegal immigrants who came to the United States as minors, provided they had spent at least five continuous years in the country prior to the enactment of the law and had served at least two years in the military or studied at least two years at a four-year institute of higher learning. In view of this, the Obama administration issued in 2012 the Deferred Action for Childhood Arrivals memorandum that defers the deportation of immigrants who came as children to the United States as long as they meet some requirements, among them being under the age of 31 as of June 15, 2012 and having come into the country before turning 16.[13]

Cultural Suspects of Yesteryear

The cultural argument against current immigration maintains that new immigrants, mostly low-skilled, uneducated people from countries with dubious political and economic institutions cannot be absorbed and assimilated in the way previous generations of foreigners were. A comparison between previous waves of immigrants and new ones indicates that many of the observations made about today's immigrants were also made in relation to newcomers in the nineteenth century and the first half of the twentieth century. In time, those foreigners became integrated with the natives and were so well accepted that critics of immigration eventually posited that they represented a "different" kind of immigrant wave from recent ones, who were supposedly much less compatible with the host culture.

Partly as a result of the influx of people from the Mediterranean area and Central and Eastern Europe, there were many illiterate people among the low-skilled immigrants in the United States during the late nineteenth and early twentieth centuries. In 1896–97, President Grover Cleveland stopped a law that sought to limit immigration by including only those who could read and write. President William Taft tried to persuade Americans that they needed immigrant workers, and that those workers could be taught to read and write later on.[14] These presidents understood the value of the various types of immigration, the complexities of the division of labor, and the mutable nature of cultural backgrounds.

Italians who migrated in the nineteenth and early twentieth centuries took many customs with them that differed from those of host nations, such as having their children work and their wives abstain from work, and treating education as less than a priority because it was not seen as beneficial in the long term.[15] They often sought and performed work with a labor contractor of their own nationality and culture, something which critics of immigration today say is indicative of a reluctance to assimilate and an insurmountable cultural gap on the part of contemporary newcomers. Over the years, the Italians rose up the economic scale largely through acquiring job skills in low-skilled occupations rather than by becoming educated and entering the professions. Eventually, they began to succeed in activities such as wine growing and fruit growing, before spreading to a cross-section of activities.[16] Their children and grandchildren, who were better educated and eager to succeed, subsequently completed the assimilation cycle.

For a very long time, Germans remained quite distinct from the rest of society and were notoriously slow to learn English. Who is aware of this today? How many Americans realize that the once culturally suspect Germans gave the United States lager beer, coleslaw, delicatessen, the Christmas tree, oatmeal, and hamburgers? How many know that songfests, beer gardens, bowling, parades, target shooting, and swimming—activities German immigrants practiced on Sunday—were taken as signs of strange cultural habits?[17] When the temperance issue was revived in the 1870s, the *Chicago Tribune* thought that enforcing a Sunday closing law was necessary to prevent the "German conquest of the city." Eventually, the German example was popularized and helped "relax America's Sunday habits"—an interesting example of cultural osmosis between immigrants and the host country.[18]

Among first-generation Japanese families living on the mainland, a majority began either as laborers or domestic servants. Less than 4 percent owned or managed farms, let alone other kinds of businesses. Strivers that they were, and despite the cultural differences and language disadvantages, three out of every five members of the first generation eventually became owners or managers, but it took a long time, during which this community was seen as culturally suspect.[19] The success of Japanese farm laborers challenged the widely held beliefs regarding the historical causes of the poverty of so-called ethnic minorities and their prospects. Neither political activities nor biological assimilation played a significant role in the rise of the Japanese. Although there was some political action and some intermarriage, assimilation took place as the Japanese community rose economically and acquired a certain social standing.

The ability of first-generation Japanese to speak English was limited, as is the case today with immigrants from non-English-speaking nations. The second generation rose further than the first one through different occupations, including the educated professions. It was not so much specific skills, but a general human capital conveyed through work habits, perseverance, social cohesion, and respect for the law that helped facilitate this process.[20] When restrictive immigration laws went against them, first-generation Japanese immigrants showed that respect for the law is not incompatible with circumventing immigration norms—a paradox that critics of immigration refuse to accept today and denounce as criminal behavior. The cultural qualities that made the Japanese a contributing factor in the prosperity of the United States was only noticed or acknowledged by the country at large when Japanese immigration was reduced. Post–World War II Japanese language assimilation followed the traditional pattern previously described. By 1980, three out of every four Japanese Americans spoke only English. Some have argued that perhaps in this case, the internment of the war years served as an additional cultural "incentive," but the similarity with other immigrants in terms of generational adaptation to the new language suggests that this cannot have been the main reason.[21]

The cultural acceptance of Jews in America was also gradual and followed the gradual socioeconomic rise. Only after much suffering and constant speculation as to their cultural inability to assimilate did the Jews begin to rise first in business, then professionally. It became customary for Central European and Russian Jews to work long hours for low pay in much criticized "sweatshops" owned by German Jews. In many cases, because a good deal of the work was done at home, many Jewish immigrants saw little need to speak English. They saved part of their money in order to bring over their families; two out of every three Central and Eastern European Jewish immigrants arriving in the early twentieth century had their passage paid by family members.[22] The children struggled at school in the beginning. Only later did they become overrepresented among those who graduated from high school and went to college. Eventually, three-quarters of the students at the College of the City of New York were Jewish.[23] By the 1930s, more than half of the physicians working in New York were of that same heritage.[24] A similar pattern on the part of immigrants today, especially Hispanics, is seen by critics of immigration in the United States as signaling a qualitative difference between current immigration and the kind of immigration that contributed to the rise of the country.

Some researchers argue that the post-1965 immigrants have come to a different America than the one experienced by earlier immigrants, and can therefore afford to resist assimilation. According to this view, the second and third generations retain more loyalty to their origins because they have a greater support system among fellow nationals, and because the host nation is currently more tolerant of cultural deviation. But now that the second generation of the initial wave of post-1965 immigrants has reached adulthood, we are learning that assimilation has been proceeding much as it did among the second generation of earlier European immigrants. The loyalty to the language of their parents is not greater among today's second generation than it was among second-generation immigrants in the past. Today, as the second generation assimilates, some of its members may compensate for having distanced themselves from immigrant groups and cultures by stressing their so-called ethnic identity. But this has few practical implications in terms of values and daily conduct. People who seek to identify with their heritage do not modify their behavior or relationship with the country in which they were born, in this case the United States, but merely make up for having become assimilated. In that sense, the adoption of a symbolic ethnicity is indicative of assimilation, not of separation from the host nation.[25]

Tensions will be defused as people from different backgrounds mingle, intermarry, and coexist, a social mélange that modern life and globalized cities make almost inevitable. The signs that immigrants will integrate into mainstream America are already there—so much so that even speaking of mainstream America as "white" is to mutilate some of its component parts and disregard the human wealth that is the multinational and multicultural United States: in California, Hawaii, Houston, and New York, native whites are no longer an absolute majority.

Another way in which immigrant cultural patterns today echo those of the past is intermarriage. A century ago, among Italians born between 1886 and 1900—that is, second-generation Italian Americans—17 percent of women out-married. Among second-generation Mexican-American men at the turn of the new millennium, the proportion was 20 percent, while it was 11 percent among women.[26] If one takes into account the fact that it was six times as hard to limit one's choice of spouse for an Italian a century ago than it is for a Mexican today (given the much larger population of Mexican origin), it is hard to say that this, or other groups of Hispanics, represent a very different cultural challenge to mainstream America than past immigrant waves did.

Today, in the era of instant global communications, immigrant communities are able to maintain close contact with people from their villages, towns, and cities back home. The evidence, however, points to the fact that the first generation has much less active attachment to the country of origin than is generally thought, if we take into account the three main transnational activities: remittance sending, weekly phone calls, and travel to the native country.[27]

As is well known, some immigrant communities like to concentrate in certain areas. Two-thirds of the families in Miraflores, a village of 4,000 people in the Dominican Republic, have relatives in the Jamaica Plain area of Boston.[28] There is no essential difference between this phenomenon and the concentration of first-generation Italian or Irish immigrants from a particular region of their home countries in certain neighborhoods or cities in America in the nineteenth and early twentieth centuries.

In contemporary times, the concentration of Cubans[29] and other Latin Americans in South Florida has not essentially modified the "American way," however much of a flavor it may have given it. Even the political convictions of the powerful Cuban old guard are being challenged by younger generations, as suggested by the South Florida 2008 presidential victory of Barack Obama, who proposed a dialogue with the Castro regime. In undergoing such a generational transformation, the concentrated Cuban community of South Florida has clearly followed a national trend that has proven stronger than national affinity. Even organizations traditionally associated with hardline views, such as the Cuban American National Foundation, have supported a more flexible foreign policy towards Cuba in recent years. Regardless of one's own convictions about immigration, this indicates the extent to which communities of foreign origin are vulnerable to change and adaptation.

In general, the more flexible, porous, and open a society, the better chance it has of creating a peaceful environment in which different groups can cooperate and eventually mix. Despite the United State's many flaws, including the multicultural fallacy that has exercised such influence on academia and the body politic, this country is one of the pinnacles of peaceful, cooperative, and creative coexistence among peoples of different backgrounds. The European Union, despite its bureaucratic edifice and pockets of immigrant violence and native counter violence, is increasingly a successful multicultural space (the term should not be confused with the ideology of multiculturalism) if for no other reason than its decision to open the borders of 27 member countries with very different populations and histories. Those countries that are best able to understand that the multicultural society, as opposed to the multiculturalist one, is largely blind to color, race, nationality, and religion, and is therefore more focused on the rights of every individual rather than on the collective identity of the various groups, will stand to benefit most from the times in which we live.

The American system has not been perfect at assimilating foreigners. There are ghettos or enclaves still mired in underachievement and even poverty, and certain highly concentrated groups, such as Puerto Ricans in New York, have experienced much more difficulty than others in moving up the social scale. But studies show that those immigrants or children of immigrants who combine access to education and English-language skills with strong personal and cultural attachments to family and to the immigrant community that surrounds them often do better than the assimilated peers, who end up in drug-infested neighborhoods.[30] The issue suggested by this complex state of affairs, then, is not so much the cultural inability to assimilate, as it is the differentiated achievement levels on the part of various groups given the opportunities available in the prevailing economy and social environment. The issue also involves successive waves of immigrants who temporarily lower the average level of preparation and achievement. Would the Japanese in the United States have been considered as prone to assimilation by mainstream America as they are now if successive waves of poorer, less educated Japanese had continued to migrate to the United States well into the latter part of the twentieth century? Would the ability of Central, Eastern, and Southern Europeans to acculturate in the United States be brandished as proof that earlier waves of immigrants were more culturally compatible with the natives if the average income, education level, and English skills of that community were lowered by the arrival of new immigrants of similar heritage? Probably not.

Would it have been obvious that Asians were willing to become integrated through intermarriage if new waves of Asian immigrants—who tended to start their journey in America within the protective network of fellow nationals—had continued to offset statistically the significant number of marriages between Asians and natives? By 1990, half of Asian-American men and an even higher percentage of Asian-American women were married to non-Asians. For those under 25 years of age, the percentage was as high as 66 percent for women. This is the same community that was seen, for decades, as a "yellow peril" threatening mainstream America.[31]

Other countries exhibit the same patterns that successive waves of immigrants have exhibited for decades in the United States. French people who regard North African immigration with horror forget that Charles de Gaulle, an icon of modern France, spoke about the "integration of the souls" and placed Algerians in high government positions.[32] This move symbolized a rise in Algerian status that was already underway and that, in time, dispassionate observers saw as a successful assimilation and likely part of the reason why Algerians, who began to migrate much earlier, are more integrated today than Moroccans and Tunisians. In fact, until the arrival of fundamentalist Islam to Muslim immigrant communities in France, the Muslim religion was not seen as a cultural threat. In 1926, when the mosque of Paris was built, North Africans protested because they saw it as a colonialist symbol of French domination! Algerians who migrated with their families in the 1950s educated their children in the proud schools of the republic. Later, mixed marriages ceased to be a taboo among Algerians.[33]

After World War II, some 85,600 Central and Eastern Europeans brought in by the United Kingdom from Germany to work in agriculture, mining, and textiles became the object of cultural mistrust. Poles were not even allowed in pubs; complaints about mills being "full of foreigners" were common. Only when Asians began to migrate to the United Kingdom did the Brits accept Central and Eastern Europeans as culturally compatible immigrants.[34]

Former Spanish Prime Minister Felipe González has written about the racism against Spanish migrants in Europe, recalling how signs could be seen in Brussels saying, "No entry for Spaniards, Africans and North Africans."[35] Those who criticize contemporary immigrants in some European countries compare them unfavorably to previous migratory flows, including Spaniards, who they now say were much more culturally akin to their mainstream societies.

Perhaps the ultimate irony of cultural arguments against immigrants is not that similar charges were leveled at past immigrants who are now lauded as part of America's heritage, but this: Many people who leave their land of origin cite, as the reason for moving from developing countries to more accomplished ones, cultural constraints among their fellow countrymen that hold them back from making progress at home. But these constraints are very similar to ones that many people in their adopted countries accuse those same migrants of carrying with them. In 1999, a survey conducted by cultural associations of French institutes in Morocco among high-skilled people who had migrated to France revealed that 88.7 percent of respondents did not contemplate returning home. They cited dissuading factors in their home countries that had more to do with the general environment than with salaries: the archaic mentality, the lack of transparency regarding social and economic rules, and the inadequacy of career opportunities.[36]

Culture Changes Both Ways

Regardless of where one stands in the immigration debate, the cultural argument against immigration implies that values, habits, customs, and mindsets are self-perpetuating and permanent. But contemporary and ancient history are replete with examples of peoples that evolved and transformed themselves, of cross-fertilization between very different kinds of peoples. Institutions that had been strong and validated by centuries-old traditions disappeared in a nick of time and the people who had lived under them found themselves perfectly able to adapt to new circumstances. Countries that were backward turned themselves into universal models and others that were at the pinnacle of civilization let themselves fall into the dark ages.

In the eighteenth century, the Scots, who had been on the fringes of European civilization, burst onto the scene as leading figures in a variety of fields of endeavor. The Japanese, who had been a closed society, were able to adopt Western civilization so effectively that they became, in the course of a few decades, a leading world power.[37] In 1914, a monarch headed nearly every European state; a couple of decades later, practically all the monarchs were gone. Institutional changes reflected and reinforced cultural ones. Colonialism had been a fact of life for millions of people generation after generation; yet in the years following World War II, colonialism crumbled to bits in Asia and Africa.

Cultural change takes many forms and originates in different ways, ranging from the repressive and brutal to the spontaneous and smooth. It often involves a social chemistry that effects change on all sides, including the dominant culture, subtly influenced by foreign cultures with which it comes into contact through immigration and other means.

Reform Judaism is an interesting case of change affecting both the immigrants and the natives. In the early nineteenth century, as Germans sought to regain the civil equality enjoyed under the French occupation during the Napoleonic Wars, the way Jews dressed and other customs constituted barriers to their social and legal acceptance. Some of the wealthier Jews converted to Christianity (Karl Marx's father was one of them). Others promoted efforts to reduce the differences between Jews and Gentiles, while retaining the main religious tenets. Reform Judaism and the modernization of Jews grew out of this effort. Among many other signs of assimilation, Synagogue services began to be conducted in German. Such changes were anathema to Orthodox Jews and made little headway in Central and Eastern Europe. But Reform Judaism quickly spread as far as the United States, where the more open and progressive system enabled this updating of old religious practices.[38] It is tragically ironic, as Raphael Patai pointed out, that the German Jews exterminated by Hitler were among the most assimilated Jews in the world. Half of the Jews who got married in Germany during the 1920s married Gentiles.[39]

The pace of assimilation and cultural change involving immigrants from different countries has varied according to how tenacious certain cultural traits were. German culture was particularly tenacious among immigrants from that nation, while the Scots were readily absorbed into American or Australian culture. Host cultures were probably more influenced by immigrant cultures that were particularly resistant to assimilation, such as the Germans, than by more malleable immigrant cultures. Much depended on how willing influential agents of the immigrant culture were to encourage assimilation. The Irish Catholic Church, for example, worked very hard to assimilate the Irish to America, while it was much less involved in Argentina, a country that hosted a notable Irish immigrant community.

Host societies tend to perceive the immigrant as "different," however they choose to interpret the concept. This has always been, and perhaps will always be, the case. As Alfred Schutz, the prominent social scientist, put it in somewhat mangled language, "When the migrant goes to another place, he becomes essentially the man who has to place in question nearly everything that seems to be unquestionable to the members of the approached group. To him the cultural patterns of the approached group do not have the authority of a tested system of recipes because he does not partake in the vivid historical tradition by which it has been formed."[40] When the stranger arrives, he or she tends to do things in his or her usual way, unless some power dictates otherwise. The cultural clash soon forces the stranger, under what anthropologist Klavero Oberg calls "shock," to adapt or leave. If the stranger chooses the former, there is a period of adjustment. Interestingly, the host society also learns, less consciously, to adjust to the stranger—which is one of the reasons why culture means movement and change, a dynamic process in which host societies also adopt novel ways and means, or sometimes rediscover old ones.[41]

Each community of people—allowing for many individual idiosyncrasies—has its own patterns of conduct and relationship, and therefore knowledge and achievement, as a result of multiple factors, including the very basic one of geography. The differences between various human groups and communities are not dictated by genetics, as was once thought. "Over long spans of history," wrote Thomas Sowell, "the radical reshuffling of the relative technological rankings of different races and nations makes it hard to conclude that such standings are genetically determined. China was far in advance of Europe a thousand years ago and Southeastern Europe was far more advanced than northwestern Europe 2000 years ago."[42] Precisely because the destiny of a group is not predetermined, there is no guarantee that the leading nations of today will forever continue to set the cultural trend of humanity. And precisely because culture is malleable, host nations are also open to foreign influences, however unconscious such osmosis may be for any particular generation.

Although cultural adaptation is a trait of most communities exposed to others, it can be a difficult process to spot at any one moment. Any migratory group that produces successive waves of immigrants will appear, in the eyes of the host nation, not to be able to adapt at any one point in time because recent arrivals will overshadow or seem to average down the types of cultural traits that the host nation may judge indispensable for adaptation. To be sure, this is the case for Mexicans in the United States.

Scholars of immigration have argued that a policy of "Americanization" of foreigners is a prominent factor in the exceptional way in which the United States was able to absorb large numbers of immigrants over long periods of time. Turning foreigners into Americans—which is what Americanization is normally taken to mean—differed from the treatment preferred by other nations, which employed foreigners as a labor force without making an effort to absorb them. Unlike Germany, where Turkish workers were never considered worthy of "Germanization"; or the Persian Gulf sheikdoms, where foreign labor was and remains a business proposition; or, in a very different scenario, indentured labor in the American way, despite the initial backlash against newcomers, gradually sought to lodge the aliens in the heart of mainstream society, transforming them into Americans.

Americanization also meant, to a lesser extent and much less deliberately, letting America be influenced and shaped by people from overseas. Except in periods of exclusion of certain nationalities and of backlash against a sudden surge in immigration, Americanization was a process whereby foreigners ceased to be aliens. They were supposed to provide the ultimate proof of allegiance by rooting themselves profoundly in American society. As one future Supreme Court Justice put it in 1915, "however great his outward conformity, the immigrant is not Americanized unless his interests and affections have become deeply rooted here."[43]

This transformative process was much more than a government policy. It did not stem so much from political decisions as from a social and cultural vision. Ironically, whenever a backlash against immigration occurred in the last couple of centuries, the accusation against the groups that critics of immigration chose to target was that they deviated from Americanization; these critics charged the permissive authorities of departing from a time-honored tradition. Americanization was both a porous system that accepted and absorbed the "refuse" of the rest of the world in exchange for thorough assimilation, and a convenient tool used by anti-immigrant groups to denounce the cultural incompatibility of certain foreign communities with native society. Today's many critics of immigration attack what they perceive as permissive authorities who have renounced Americanization and decreed a sort of cultural surrender to immigrants.

There are two very different ways of understanding Americanization. Nobel Laureate Friedrich Hayek, an economist and thinker who was one of the great minds of the twentieth century, wrote, "[T]hat the United States would not have become such an effective melting pot and would probably have faced extremely difficult problems if it had not been for a deliberate policy of 'Americanization' through the public school system seems fairly certain."[44] This version of Americanization refers to the general awareness of values and institutions of a functioning liberal democracy and a capitalist economy, and of the history of the United States, inculcated primarily through education and to some extent at the workplace. A more chauvinistic version usually invoked in order to attack immigration interprets Americanization as a discriminatory process that weeded out culturally incompatible foreigners and preserved the rest, subjecting them to a near-magical process that ipso facto turned them into perfect Americans. This latter interpretation has little historical backing. Assimilation, as we have seen, involved people from all kinds of cultural backgrounds at different times, and their Americanization was a gradual generational process.

This is not to say that Americanization did not involve a renunciation of old attitudes and even beliefs on the part of foreigners—assimilation is always a transformative experience. Nor is every accusation made by anti-immigration critics against the prevailing ethos entirely unfounded. Multiculturalism has indeed distorted the view of culture and, more to the point, blurred the significance of adaptation by minorities and newcomers to the basic heritage of American society, particularly as regards its political, social, and economic institutions. But let us keep in mind that the distorted interpretation of Americanization is less an attempt to correct the evils of multiculturalism than an ideological lie aimed at delegitimizing certain kinds of immigrants, or even immigration in general.

The attack on immigration through a reinterpretation of Americanization appears also to stem from the deterioration of the American education system, which critics of immigration rightly see as a peril for the future competitiveness of the United States. But the decadence of the education system is a problem originating in America's decision-makers and opinion shapers, not in the cultural penchant of the immigrants themselves. Some immigrants who use the system as pupils, parents, or teachers probably do reinforce its features, as do some natives themselves. The decline of public education is something that does not separate foreigners from natives, but quite the contrary—both groups are mostly its victims. This truth emerges from research such as that conducted by the Intercollegiate Studies Institute, which found that American students arrive at college knowing very little about American history and government, and they learn virtually nothing about either during the four years of higher education.[45]

The word "Americanization" was invented in the 1850s by Orestes A. Brownson, a Vermont native who converted to Catholicism and became conservative after having espoused Utopianism and socialism. He argued in his quarterly review that the nativists had a point. The Irish should assimilate to the American nation that was already established, he maintained, and the Roman Catholic Church should not identify itself with autocracy. However, Americanization as both a policy and a social ethos did not appear until a few decades later, mostly in response to Southern, Central, and Eastern European immigrants.

There are different versions of how the Americanization program was initially launched, but one of the early manifestations is traced back to the town fathers of Lawrence, Mass., after a bitter 1912 strike involving immigrants. One local group published a pamphlet titled "Lawrence—Here She Stands: For God and Country," while the local public school developed an "American Plan For Education in Citizenship" that included lessons in history in order to teach "love and loyalty for America."[46] Less chauvinistically, public schools in other parts of the country adopted similar policies of Americanization. One school principal in New York declared that "education will solve every problem of our national life, even that of assimilating our foreign element."[47] Important leaders echoed these sentiments. Woodrow Wilson said, "You cannot dedicate yourself to America unless you become in every respect and with every purpose of your will thoroughly American."[48]

There are those who maintain it was not so much the public school system, but civic associations, that caught on to the trend and gave it renewed and decisive impetus. The case has been made that civic-minded groups on opposite sides of the political spectrum both had major impacts on spreading Americanization throughout the territory. Social settlements that looked at the issue from a humane perspective, as well as patriotic hereditary societies such as the Daughters of the Revolution, were both involved. The first group—on what we would today call the political left—acted through social workers; the second—on the right side of today's political spectrum—worked through scholarships and courses.[49]

Even the world of business began to adopt initiatives aimed at Americanizing foreigners. Henry Ford, one iconic example, made it a policy in his company to ingrain in foreign workers not only the language, but also the values that he considered part of the essence of his country. The first words foreign workers in his company were taught were: "I am a good American."[50] Ford compelled his employees to attend the Ford English School that he himself set up before and after work, two days a week. In 1916, he organized a pageant centered on a gigantic melting pot. A large number of immigrant workers appeared dressed in typical foreign clothes and carrying items alluding to their respective fatherlands; another group of men appeared from either side of the pot, elegantly dressed and waving American flags.[51]

The movement in favor of Americanizing foreigners reached its apex in the Progressive Era. It became confused, in the wake of World War I, with the more forceful and authoritarian Americanization triggered by the conflagration and, subsequently, the Red Scare that followed the triumph of Communism in Russia. The Americanization fervor died down after 1920, when it was replaced by the anti-immigration sentiment that eventually led to the restrictive laws of that decade. The public school system, for its part, continued with varying degrees the Americanization drive until the mid-twentieth century.

Perhaps the one lesson that can be extracted from the process of Americanization is that people change and adapt, and that immigrants influence the host country even as they assimilate. The impact of the Hispanic community in the United States today is such that cultural influence is probably working in both directions, although numerous indications point especially to the assumption, by new generations of Hispanics born or raised in the country, of some essential traits of American mainstream society. The existence of consecutives waves of Hispanic immigrants—predominantly, but not only, Mexican—makes any study of assimilation and progress difficult unless narrow segments of that wide community are considered based on birth, time of immigration, age, citizenship, language, religion, education, and other factors. But by and large, the Hispanic community can be seen as part and parcel, not an excrescence, of the American cultural body.

The sheer economic power of Hispanic consumers and producers speaks precisely to that fact. The number of Hispanic-owned businesses has surpassed 3 million. Between the late 1990s and the early part of the 2000 decade, the number grew at almost three times the native rate. By 2012, the sum of Hispanic businesses is expected to increase to 4.3 million; these businesses will generate $539 billion in revenues, a figure higher than the GDP of all Latin American and Caribbean countries except two. The top Hispanic business alone—Brightstar Corp., a provider of services to wireless industries headed by Marcelo Claure— has sales of $3.5 billion. The top ten companies are headquartered across six different states. Hispanic consumers have a purchasing power of nearly $1 trillion already; the figure will reach $1.3 trillion by 2015.[52]

These staggering numbers tell us two stories. One story has to do with the entrepreneurial, self-reliant, wealth-producing nature of immigrant communities. The other story points to the familiarity that American natives have, as producers and consumers, with Hispanic producers and consumers. The economic interaction is already having an impact in cultural terms by influencing the way natives look at foreigners and vice versa. Even tastes, language, and idiosyncratic forms of expression are suffering modifications of which ordinary citizens may not be immediately aware, but which will become more evident with time. That cultural interaction has also been the case on the other side of the pond. Spaniards have adopted various linguistic twists from the very immigrants at whom, according to surveys, they look with increasing discomfort. Every time I travel to Spain, something I do at least once a year, I am struck by the expressions that Castillians, Andalusians, or Catalans have picked up from Venezuelan soap operas, Peruvian cooks, Dominican domestic employees, or Ecuadoran taxi drivers.

An American of immigrant parents born three decades ago was raised in a country where only one in twenty children had a foreign-born mother compared to one in four today. Eight times more children are born to Mexican mothers in the United States today than in 1970. Evidently, this entails an increased potential impact by immigrant children on native students; it also foreshadows a much larger number of Americans of Mexican origin eventually becoming part of the cultural matrix of America.[53]

At some point, a growing immigrant community—particularly in an environment that is porous and flexible—becomes aware of the possibilities of influencing the system either for its own benefit or simply because of a natural desire to organize with a view to achieving common goals. One vehicle for this is political participation, through civic associations, votes, and the election of officials of immigrant background. For instance, the first U.S. Congressman born in India, Dalip Singh Saund, from California's Imperial Valley, was elected in the United States in 1956. He was also the first Asian American to serve in the United States Congress. By 2007, many in the Indian community in the United States were celebrating the election of Bobby Jindal, a Republican Catholic of Indian descent, as governor of that state. A few years later, San Francisco elected it first Chinese-American mayor, Ed Lee.

There are signs that Hispanics are becoming more aware of their potential as a community. Although they have formed several organizations, most of them single-issue ones, Hispanics have so far lacked an organizational capacity that reflects their numbers. Even in the wake of the immigration debate, Latinos were poorly organized to fight back, which is why their powerful May Day demonstrations in 2006 and 2007 had little continuity (new demonstrations took place in March of 2010 to push for immigration reform, but again the effect died down soon).

This is bound to change sooner or later; the climate is already one of increased desire for civic and political participation. The electoral impact of Hispanics is already very strong. The election that made Barack Obama president in November of 2008 was the first election in modern times in which an immigrant community may have been decisive in the result. More than 10 million Hispanic voters played a crucial role in the 2008 presidential election, voting for Barack Obama by a 2-1 margin, and giving him a decisive push in four states—Florida,

Colorado, Nevada, and New Mexico—that he wrested back from the Republican Party.[54] In 2012, some 12.5 million Hispanics, 10 percent of the electorate, cast a ballot in the presidential election, expressing an overwhelming preference for Obama once again.[55]

Hispanics have tended to side with the Democrats in the past, but the margins in 2008 and 2012 were very large. According to 2004 exit polls, President Bush had obtained 44 percent of the Hispanic vote in his re-election bid,[56] which means that a few million Hispanics deserted the Republicans in the following years. One would think that by almost any measure—upward social mobility, church attendance, marriage patterns—Latinos would be a dream electoral target for a party that champions enterprise, self-reliance, and family values. But in 2008 and 2012, the Republican Party did not seem interested. Even accounting for the fact that in 2008 Hispanic voters, like other demographic groups, wanted to punish the Bush administration and were eventually seduced by a candidate who courted them intensely, the shift in their vote was tectonic. The relentless anti-immigration voice on the right managed to turn millions of Hispanics who were not illegal immigrants into a community-conscious force acting in fear of a perceived threat. This fear even produced the irony of California Hispanics voting for the center-left of the political spectrum in the general election, while siding with the conservative right on social issues, as shown by their vote against Proposition 8—the anti-gay marriage initiative.[57]

It is simplistic and naive to think that immigrants vote as a group. But if circumstances instill enough fear in them, they can behave as a group for purely protective reasons. Historically, it was not so much fear that drew people of recent foreign descent to the Democratic Party, but rather a deliberate effort on the part of the political machine of the Democratic Party to bring immigrants into the process. The political machines of big cities such as Boston, Newark, Chicago, or New York forged so-called ethnic coalitions to push through certain key pieces of legislation, many of them related to Roosevelt's New Deal and, later, Lyndon Johnson's Great Society. The momentous 1965 law regarding immigration was partly a child of those political connections.[58] However, given Ronald Reagan's amnesty, the arrival of successive waves of immigrants, the changes experienced by American society, and the increase of the Hispanic vote, those antecedents by no means determine that Latino voters will always side with the Democrats.

In 1996, Bill Clinton obtained around 70 percent of the Hispanic vote, and Hispanics represented 5 percent of the electorate—not an insignificant number in any closely contested election. The trend was already beginning to insinuate itself: The 1996 Hispanic vote reflected a 135-percent jump in the number of votes cast by Latinos since the 1965 immigration law against a 21-percent rise in the number of other voters.[59] By the time George W. Bush was reelected, Latinos constituted 6 percent of the turnout. When Obama became president, 7.4 percent of voters were of Hispanic origin. The number of immigrant voters was much smaller in the case of other communities. Asians, for instance, constituted 2.5 percent of the electorate.[60]

Politicians of all parties and persuasions will eventually be forced to look closely at some important trends among Hispanics. I don't mean the obvious fact that they represent 16 percent of the population and by the year 2050 will probably make up one-quarter of the nation. Almost 4 million Hispanics— nearly one in ten—are financially well off, and about forty percent are middle-class. This is not a small achievement for people whose beginnings are, for the most part, quite humble. Treating them as alien to the mainstream American experience and culture is risky from a purely electoral point of view. In a radio address given in 1977, Ronald Reagan mocked "the illegal alien fuss," asking: "Are great numbers of our unemployed really victims of the illegal alien invasion, or are those illegal tourists actually doing work our own people won't do?" If only in the interest of political survival, those who claim to idolize the Gipper need to take stock of what the Hispanic voter behavior in the 2008 election meant.[61]

Since congressional districts are apportioned on the basis of total population, including legal and illegal, rather than on the basis of the total number of citizens, the impact of large communities of foreign origin on the electoral process is felt even before those who are citizens, either through birth or naturalization, are allowed to vote. The fact that there is a high concentration of such voters in swing states with a disproportionate bearing on the outcome of elections means that immigrant communities have potentially a strategic political power that parties and leaders will want to tap. The many Republicans who have in recent years advocated a more immigrant-friendly policy (including former President George W. Bush) have strong evidence with which to counter anti-immigrant Republicans.

The United States has more experience with immigrant groups playing a key role in Washington policy towards their countries of origin than with communities of recent foreign descent playing a key role in electing a president, members of Congress, and other officials. For decades, Jews and Cubans have been very influential in shaping the U.S. government's policy towards Israel and Cuba, respectively.

The wider Hispanic community has not been able to exercise focused, well-organized influence in the political process yet. Hispanics have lacked the single-issue focus that Jews and Cubans have had for many years. The influence of the Hispanic community has more to do with numbers than with the ability to navigate the waters of the legislative and executive decision-making process. But, in recent times, there have been various shows of force that have given the country a taste of its potential influence. In December of 2005, the approval by the House of Representatives of the Border Protection, Anti-terrorist and Illegal Immigration Control Act triggered a backlash by pro-immigration groups that led, in 2006, to mass demonstrations from coast to coast. The bill never became law because there were enough votes in the Senate to filibuster an attempt to bring it to a vote. A year and a couple of months into the Obama presidency, Hispanic groups took to the streets once again to press the administration for comprehensive immigration reform, a promise that they felt was being side-stepped by other legislative priorities.

Groups such as the National Council of La Raza, founded with funding from the Ford Foundation in 1968 and originally supported by government agencies and left-leaning foundations,[62] have a high profile after years of involvement with immigrant-related issues. However, no group has gained enough national notoriety as a commanding voice on the matter to be able to pressure the politicians effectively. The crucial element in any lobbying effort—a large system of campaign donations parallel to the advocacy effort—has so far been non-existent or negligible among pro-immigration groups. Perhaps this lack of campaign support explains in part why there is less awareness than there should be in the country about the obvious similarities between the cultural process of adaptation by contemporary immigrants and that of past waves of immigrants. It may also help to explain why political and legal bodies seem so detached from the real world, where cultural integration is much more profound than the decision makers seem to realize.

Notes

1. Shirin Hakimzadeh and D'Vera Cohn, "English Usage Among Hispanics In The United States," Pew Hispanic Center, Washington, D.C., November 29, 2007, http://www.pewhispanic.org/reports/report.php?ReportID=82

2. The studies were conducted by sociologists Frank Bean and Gillian Stevens from the University of California at Irvine and the University of Illinois, respectively. See David López and Vanesa Estrada, "Language," in *The New Americans: A Guide to Immigration Since 1965,* eds. Mary C. Waters and Reed Ueda (Cambridge, Mass.: Harvard University Press, 2007), 229–230.

3. Marcus L. Hansen, "The History of American Immigration as a Field for Research," *American Historical Review* 32:3 (April 1927): 500–518.

4. Gregory Rodriguez, *From Newcomers to Americans: The Successful Integration into American Society* (Washington D.C.: National Immigration Forum, 1999), 22.

5. Nancy Foner and Philip Kasinitz, "The Second Generation," in *The New Americans,* eds. Waters and Ueda, 272–273.

6. Peter H. Shuck, "Citizenship and Nationality Policy," in *The New Americans,* eds. Waters and Ueda, 44.

7. George J. Borjas, "Making It In America: Social Mobility In The Immigrant Regulation" (Working Paper 12088, National Bureau Of Economic Research, Cambridge, Mass., March 2006).

8. Shuck, "Citizenship and Nationality Policy," in *The New Americans,* eds. Waters and Ueda, 44.

9. David Card, "Is The New Immigration Really So Bad? Working Paper 11547, National Bureau of Economic Research (Cambridge, Mass., 2005), 1. http://www.nber.org/papers/w11547

10. Mary Sanchez, "The Impossible Dream," *Poder 360°,* March, 2010, http://www.poder360.com/article_detail.php?id_article=3886

11. Jeffrey S. Passel and D' Vera Cohn, "A Portrait of Unauthorized Immigrants in the United States," Pew Hispanic Center, March 2008. The research is based on the March Current Population Surveys conducted by the U.S. Census Bureau through 2008. http://pewhispanic.org/files/reports/107.pdf

12. Richard Fry, "Hispanics, High School Dropouts and the GED," Pew Hispanic Center, May 13, 2010, http://pewhispanic.org/reports/report.php?ReportID=122

13. http://www.dhs.gov/deferred-action-childhood-arrivals

14. Nancy L. Green, *Repenser Les Migrations* (Paris: Presses Universitaires de France, 2002), 55. Also see Georgie Anne Geyer, *Americans No More* (New York: The Atlantic Press, 1996), 46–47.

15. Leonard Covello and Francesco Cordaso, *The Social Background Of The Italo-American School Child* (New York: Rowman & Littlefield, 1972), 230.

16. Thomas Sowell, *Migrations and Cultures* (New York: Basic Books, 1996), 166.

17. Sowell, *Migrations and Cultures,* 78.

18. John Higham, *Strangers in the Land: Patterns of American Nativism 1860–1925* (New Brunswick, N. J.: Rutgers University Press, 1955), 25.

19. Eric Woodrum, Colbert Rhodes, and Joe R. Feagin, "Japanese American Economic Behavior: Its Types, Determinants, and Consequences," *Social Forces*, June 1980, 1238.

20. Sowell, *Migrations and Cultures*, 138.

21. Peter Xenos, Herbert Barringer and Michael J. Levin, *Asian Indians in the United States: A 1980 Census Profile,* (Honolulu: East-West Population Institute, East-West Center, 1989), 29.

22. Moses Rischin, *The Promised City: New York's Jews, 1870-1914* (Cambridge, Mass., Harvard University Press, 1962), 63.

23. Thomas Kessner, *The Golden Door* (New York: Oxford University Press, 1977), 98.

24. Arthur Goren, "Jews," in *Harvard Encyclopedia of American Ethnic Groups*, ed. Stephan Thernstrom et al. (Cambridge, Mass., Harvard University Press, 1980).

25. As an important study of post-1965 immigration states, this symbolic ethnicity is "normally worn light, does not interfere with everyday American ways, and can therefore be given up quickly and easily if people chose." See Herbert J. Gans, "Ethnic and Racial Identity," in *The New Americans*, eds. Waters and Ueda, 106–107.

26. Joel Perlmann and Mary C. Waters, "Intermarriage and Multiple Identities," in *The New Americans*, eds. Waters and Ueda, 118.

27. According to the Pew Hispanic Center's 2006 National Survey of Latinos, only 9 percent of Hispanics can be considered highly attached to their country of origin, if we use the three common criteria: remittances sent, weekly phone calls, and travel to the native country. Roger Waldinger, "Between Here and There: How Attached Are Latino Immigrants To Their Native Country?" Pew Hispanic Center, Washington, D.C., October 25, 2007, http://pewhispanic.org/reports/report.php?ReportID=80

28. Peggy Levitt, *Transnational Villagers* (Berkeley: University of California Press, 2001), 2–3.

29. In the years immediately following Fidel Castro's triumph in Cuba, 260,000 Cubans fled the island, mostly to South Florida. In the 1970s, another 265,000 went the same way, followed by 140,000 in the 1980s and 170,000 in the 1990s. By the new millennium, two-thirds of Miami residents spoke a language other than English. See "Summary Social, Economic and Housing Characteristics," PHC-2 report series, U.S. Census Bureau 2000: Census Of Population and Housing, 2003, 27–28, http://www.census.gov/census2000/pubs/phc-2.html

30. Norma Stoltz Chinchilla and Nora Hamilton, "Central America," in *The New Americans,* eds. Waters and Ueda, 337.

31. Eric Liu, *The Accidental Asian: Notes For a Native Speaker* (New York: Random House, 1998), 188.

32. Roger Fauroux and Hanifa Chérifi, *Nous Sommes Tous Des Immigrés* (Paris: Éditions Robert Lafont, 2003), 85.

33. Fauroux and Chérifi, *Nous Sommes Tous Des Immigrés*, 65–66.

34. Inge Weber-Newth, "Narratives of Settlement: East European Migrants In Post-War Britain," in *Histories And Memory: Migrants And Their Histories In Britain*, eds. Panikos Panayi and Kathy Burrell (London: I.B. Tauris, 2006), 78–85.

35. Matthew Carr, "Spain: Racism At The Frontier," *Race & Class* 32, no. 3 (1991): 93.

36. Mohamed Mghari, "Exodus of Skilled Labor: Magnitude, Determinants, and Impacts on Development," in *Arab Migration in a Globalized World* (Geneva: International Organization for Migration, League of Arab States, 2004), 79–80.

37. Sowell, *Migrations and Cultures*, 381.

38. Louis Wirth, *The Ghetto* (Chicago: University of Chicago Press, 1958), 107–108.

39. Raphael Patai, *The Vanished Worlds Of Jewry* (New York: Macmillan, 1980), 57.

40. Alfred Schutz, "The Stranger: An Essay In Social Psychology," *American Journal of Sociology* 49, no. 6 (1994).

41. Kalvero Oberg, "Cultural Shock: Adjustment To New Cultural Environments," *Practical Psychology* 7 (1960): 177–182.

42. Sowell, *Migrations and Cultures*, 376.

43. The quote is from a speech by Louis Brandeis, the son of Jewish parents, who served as a Supreme Court Justice, after president Woodrow Wilson nominated him, from 1916 until 1939. Mark Krikorian, *The New Case Against Immigration: Both Legal and Illegal* (London: Sentinel, 2008), 11–12.

44. Friedrich V. Hayek, *The Constitution of Liberty* (Chicago: University of Chicago, 1960), 377.

45. Krikorian, *The New Case Against Immigration*, 31.

46. John Miller, *The Unmaking of Americans: How Multiculturalism Has Undermined the Assimilation Ethic* (New York: Free Press, 1998), 49.

47. Higham, *Strangers In The Land*, 235.

48. John Fonte, "Dual Allegiance: A Challenge to Immigration Reform And Patriotic Assimilation," Center For Immigration Studies, November 2005, http://www.cis.org/articles/2005/back1205.html

49. Higham, *Strangers In The Land*, 236.

50. Higham, *Strangers In The Land*, 247–248.

51. Conrad Cherry, "Two American Sacred Ceremonies: Their Implications for the Study of Religion in America," *American Quarterly Review* 21 (Winter 1969).

52. California, Texas, Florida, and New York are the states with the largest number of Hispanic-owned businesses. In Los Angeles, immigrants in recent years have started 80 percent of all new businesses. While this includes thousands of taco trucks, carnicerías, and other micro businesses, immigrant entrepreneurs in Los Angeles have funded nationally renowned firms such as El Pollo Loco, Panda Express, Lulu's Dessert, and Forever 21. At least one-quarter of Los Angeles' fastest-growing companies in 2005 were started by first-generation immigrants. That same county hosts more than a third of the country's largest 500 Hispanic-owned companies, but many other cities are being flooded by torrential entrepreneurial activity on the part of Hispanics. Some of the statistics were given to the author directly by the United States Hispanic Chamber of Commerce and the research department of *Hispanic Business* magazine in personal interviews conducted over the telephone in March of 2010. The list of the top 500 Hispanic businesses is available online. See http://www.hispanicbusiness.com/research/500/ Also see "Hispanic-Owned Firms: 2002," 2002 Economic Census (Survey of Business Owners), U.S. Census

Bureau, August, 2006, 4–18; the *Los Angeles Business Journal* (containing detailed lists of the fastest-growing businesses in L.A. County), http://www.labusinessjournal.com; and 2009 Hispanic Business 500 Directory," *Hispanic Business Magazine*, 2009. http://www .hispanicbusiness.com/research/research_HB500.asp

53. Jorge Castañeda has written, for instance, about how well Mexican women in particular have assimilated. See Jorge G. Castañeda, *Mañana Forever: Mexico and the Mexicans* (New York: Alfred A. Knopf, 2011).

54. Mark Hugo López, "How Hispanics Voted In The 2008 Election," Pew Hispanic Research Center, November 5, 2008, http://pewresearch.org/pubs/1024/exit-poll-analysis -hispanics

55. Paul Taylor, Ana Gonzalez-Barrera, Jeffrey Passel and Mark Hugo Lopez, "An Awakened Giant: The Hispanic Electorate is Likely to Double by 2013," Pew Hispanic Center, Washington, D.C., November 14, 2012, http://www.pewhispanic.org/2012/11/14 /an-awakened-giant-the-hispanic-electorate-is-likely-to-double-by-2030/

56. According to the *Washington Post*, 31 percent voted Republican and 67 percent voted Democrat (based on network exit polls). See "Democrats See Immigration Stance as Key to Latino Votes," *Washington Post*, July 20, 2010, A5. Also see Dick Morris, "The Hispanic Vote Elects Bush," November 5, 2004, http://archive.newsmax.com/archives/ articles/2004/11/4/203450.shtml

57. Daniel Cubias, "Not So Fabuloso: Latinos and Proposition 8," *The Huffington Post*, November 16, 2008, http://www.huffingtonpost.com/daniel-cubias/not-so-fabuloso -latinos-a_b_144070.html

58. Joel Millman, *The Other Americans* (New York: Viking, 1997), 62.

59. Michael Jones-Correa, "Ethnic Politics," in *The New Americans*, eds. Waters and Ueda (Cambridge, Mass.: Harvard University Press, 2007), 198.

60. Mark Hugo Lopez and Paul Taylor, "Dissecting The 2008 Electorate: The Most Diverse In History," Pew Research Center, April 30, 2009, http://pewresearch.org/pubs /1209/racial-ethnic-voters-presidential-election

61. Alvaro Vargas Llosa, "Hispanics At The Polls," The Washington Post Writers Group, November 12, 2008, http://www.postwritersgroup.com/archives/vargo81111.htm

62. Geyer, *Americans No More*, 193.

PART III

Immigrants and the Economy

11

Immigrants and the Economic Seesaw

HAVING EXPLORED IN previous chapters the cultural assault on immigration, let us now turn to economics, another major front in the attack on the social phenomenon of immigration.

There has been human migration since time immemorial. Before the rise of agriculture, a horde's or a tribe's survival was synonymous with movement. Although the nature of migration changed, the need for movement did not cease with agriculture and the sedentary life. As the exchanges of the economy grew in size and complexity, the need for labor mobility also increased. That was true before the Industrial Revolution, after the Industrial Revolution, and in today's global services economy.

Peter Bauer, one of the foremost development economists of the twentieth century, explained in interviews and written texts that increases in labor and capital accounted for no more than 10 percent of the Western world's output growth over the past two centuries; the balance was caused by technical innovation and new ideas.[1] His statement was not aimed at belittling labor and capital, but at debunking the myth that a country can automatically achieve prosperity simply by augmenting the factors of production. If an increase in the factors of production is not the key agent of output growth, then progress does not depend on a set number of workers, but instead on a country's ability to find new ways to produce more with less, thereby raising productivity. The potential for production growth is virtually unlimited, as is the potential for new jobs. This entails periodic movement by workers from certain jobs to others. In some cases, this movement is due to the disappearance of obsolete types of jobs; in others, it occurs because workers move in to fill a vacuum left by other workers who move on. The industries or services abandoned by those workers who move on continue to exist, meaning that there is still a certain level of demand for them. This process of worker movement and their replacement takes place not just at the national level, but also on an international scale.

In countries where workers are idle against their will, there are not enough jobs available for all those wishing to work. Something is standing in the way of these countries creating more businesses, or of the businesses that already exist being able or willing to hire more workers.

Conversely, there are countries in which the economy needs more workers for certain jobs than are immediately available domestically, either because there are not enough workers to do all the jobs available, or because workers in the country are not willing to perform certain jobs. Workers who do not want to take jobs that they may have taken in the past might be the beneficiaries of upward social mobility due to improvements in education. Also, there may also be skilled jobs that may not have enough takers, which therefore need foreign labor. When an economy needs workers from the outside—whether from an outside state within a country, or from an outside country— many businesses cannot function or realize their potential unless they can tap those remote sources of labor. The inflow of workers from out of town solves that problem, creating opportunities for investment—and therefore more jobs. By increasing the supply of labor, migrant workers—whether domestic or international—raise the productivity of resources that need labor. They allow capital, land, and natural resources to be exploited more efficiently.

Economically driven migration is the way in which the above-mentioned imbalances are adjusted nationally or internationally. This does not mean that other factors are not part of the migration story. As we have seen, there are many factors involved, and their complexity defies the simplistic analysis often heard in the discussion on immigration. Anyone with an opinion on immigration needs to understand the relationship between immigration and the economy. Either encouraging or persecuting immigration has a direct impact on a country's economic functioning, and on its well-being. The recurring economic argument against immigration is simply misplaced.

As mentioned, migration is one way in which labor adjusts the asymmetries between countries, or between states or regions within a country. Although the adjustment can take place across long distances, one obvious flow takes place across land or sea borders shared by neighboring territories that are very unequal.

When domestic labor is not enough to fill the needs of a country's economy, it makes sense that it taps the nearest international sources of labor—which usually means neighboring territories. Among the most unequal borders in the world are those that separate Oman and Yemen, Saudi Arabia and Yemen, South Africa and Mozambique, Thailand and Myanmar, Botswana and Zambia, Israel and Egypt, Spain and Morocco, Israel and Jordan, Russia and Mongolia, Greece and Albania—and, of course, the United States and Mexico. It comes as no surprise that flows of workers between many of these pairs of countries are intense, or that governments place much effort to block those flows precisely because the governments are aware of how closely migration flows are connected to imbalances between countries.

There are many cases of unequal neighbors whose asymmetries have been impressively adjusted through labor migration, among other factors. One of the most successful efforts to redress a balance in economic and social terms between two countries that share a border involves Germany and Poland. The inequality ratio between the two, which was has high as 10 to 1, went down to 3 to 1 after the end of communism. This was achieved not by erecting the infamous Berlin Wall, which kept Poland poor, but by getting rid of it two decades ago.

Conversely, in many cases, disparities between neighbors have increased in places where barriers limit the cross-border movement of people. Although migratory restrictions are not the only reason for these disparities, their increase does tend to correlate with places where barriers limit cross-border movement.

There used to be an economic gap of 4 to 1 between Spain and Morocco in the 1970s; by the new millennium, it had widened to 15 to 1.[2] The reaction in those places where disparities have grown, as Ana María López reminds us, has not been to make the movement easier, but quite the opposite: it has taken the form of physical restrictions including high-tech and not-so-high-tech walls, sensors, barbed wire, cables, electric fences, and tubes filled with concrete. But the "pull" effect of the market has continued to operate in the face of these obstructions, which is why many Moroccans have migrated to the Iberian Peninsula despite extraordinary efforts to keep them out.

Mexico's lamentable twentieth century became the United States' opportunity. Land reforms in Mexico after the Revolution never reached the intended goal of providing land and resources to peasants; families, therefore, could not live on farming. The country's attempt to industrialize attracted more workers to its cities than could be incorporated into its inflexible labor markets—hence the appeal for them of the northern neighbor's job-hungry economy. This disparity created the opportunity and the need for certain flows of labor, capital, and goods across the border. The free trade agreement between the two countries in the 1990s was one response to this obvious fact. Illegal Mexican immigration in the U.S., the need for which grew with this pact, is another. Although, contrary to perceptions, the average Mexican immigrant household that migrated to the United States in the 2000 decade had an income of between $35,000 and $40,000,[3] clearly a large portion of Mexican migration to the United States is made up of low-skilled workers for which the American economy has a need. This need reflects the fact that the economy of the United States is ten times the size of the Mexican economy and its per capita GDP is four times that of Mexico.

Estimates indicate that just before the financial and economic debacle of 2007–08, illegal workers constituted more than 10 percent of the 3-million-plus workers of Arizona, a state with only 4 percent unemployment at the time. The fact that there were two and a half times as many illegal workers in Arizona as unemployed residents looking for work suggests that the economy needed something that those illegal workers were able to provide.[4] A study from 2007 estimates that the state's annual economic output would fall by 8.2 percent if all foreign workers were kicked out—a loss of $29 billion, without counting the cancelation of business licenses for those companies employing them.[5] Foreign labor was a necessity, not an imposition from outside—a tax on the local economy or a form of charity, but a necessity.

The relationship between poor Arab nations and the richer Persian Gulf countries is illustrative of how migration helps to adjust international economic imbalances. Oil-producing states (Saudi Arabia, Kuwait, Bahrain, the United Arab Emirates, Oman, and Qatar) have long imported workers from other Arab states that lacked oil. Immigration to Saudi Arabia and Kuwait started in the 1930s, when crude was discovered, but full-scale production did not begin until after World War II, which is when the need for foreign workers picked up. Before 1973, the inflow of foreign workers was not very large, but after the rise in oil prices known as the second "oil shock," all the Mashreq countries except Iraq (Egypt, Jordan, Lebanon, Palestine, Syria, and Yemen) became a source of large migratory flows to the Gulf nations. The oil-producing states needed these workers in order to build oil fields and infrastructure (later tourism and banking attracted some foreigners too) and the poorer, unemployment-riddled Arab states needed them to work abroad so they could send money back home because their economic system did not provide opportunities for them locally. By 1990, foreigners outnumbered natives in the Gulf region.[6] They were no longer just from Arab countries—millions of Asians were pouring in by then.

Since the 1950s, the industrialized world has needed a large, relatively unskilled force that could perform repetitive, physically demanding tasks. This force needed to renew itself periodically, which meant that the pool from which it was drawn had to be kept up. Even though technological advances made some of the low-skilled work force redundant, other functions, sometimes directly resulting from the new technologies, still necessitated unskilled workers for purposes of assembly (electronics) or printing (circuit boards). Some labor-intensive industries (construction) have periodically boomed, offsetting the lower demand caused by certain technological developments in other industries. There were times when the level of automation reached a ceiling (agriculture in the 1970s), with the effect that low-status labor was still indispensable. At all times, the large migration of middle-class Americans to states where a job sector was particularly attractive (e.g., high tech in the West) triggered a greater demand for childcare, gardening, and health care for the aged, which were typically performed by Hispanics, Mexicans in particular.[7] Again, migration was the process by which economic adjustments took place between "receiving" and "sending," first among states, and later, countries.

The economic story of Western Europe after World War II is impossible to tell without discussing the role played by immigrant workers constantly redressing imbalances brought about by economic change and progress. The physical and economic rebuilding of nations devastated by the war and eager to march on the route towards full industrialization led Western European countries to recruit several million laborers from Southern and Eastern Europe, North Africa, Turkey, and the Middle East. Without migrant workers, it would not have been possible for Western Europe to adjust after the war.

The story is no different on other continents. Hong Kong started to industrialize after the 1949 communist takeover of China. Many Chinese refugees who had been capitalists moved to Hong Kong. But unskilled workers were needed in order to sustain business expansion. In 1947, only 10 percent of Hong Kong's exports were manufactured goods; by the 1950s, they constituted 70 percent of the overseas sales. Immigrants—women in particular—were a big part of that story. They were originally brought because of their "docility, obedience and manual dexterity," according to an in-depth, on-location study of Asian migration. By 1981, a time when the economy began to shift to services, half of Hong Kong's workers were females.[8] The economic miracle for which the region became known is inextricably mixed with the influx of female labor from outside.

One way to understand how international imbalances create a need for international migration is to understand that there is no essential difference between domestic migration and international migration. After the decline of an industry in a city that is dependent on it, the emigration of redundant people to another city helps keep income close to the national average over time. The key to ending income gaps within a country is labor mobility. For instance, in parts of Kansas and North Dakota, in the Great Plains, the population decreased 28 percent from 1930 to 1990 because of the decline in farming. Labor mobility helped keep the income per person in those states at 85 percent of the U.S. national average as workers sought opportunities elsewhere.[9] On a world scale, similar imbalances naturally encourage migratory flows that would in time have similar effects internationally, were it not for the many barriers that stand in the way.

Imbalances sometimes are related to demographic trends, not just social mobility in a prosperous country, technological innovation, the obsolescence of certain industries, or the emergence of new ones. A United Nations study used population projections to estimate how many immigrants would be required to compensate for negative demographic trends in developed nations between 2000 and 2050. (Not that reversing or compensating for those trends is in and of itself a desirable thing, but in an industrialized world built on the highly questionable premise that young workers need to sustain the older generations from a low retirement age onwards, the upkeep is crucial for those who are already part of the system.) In scenario 1 of the United Nations study (maintaining the size of the total population), the conclusion was that almost 50 million immigrant workers would be needed in the European Union—still comprising 15 countries, not 27, at the time; in scenario 2 (maintaining the size of the working age population), 79 million would be needed; and in scenario 3 (maintaining a support ratio of 15–64 years old/65+ years old), 674 million immigrants would be necessary.[10]

Given the connection between migration and the needs of the economy, the realities of the market—not policy—have dictated migratory flows to a large extent around the world, even in the face of great obstacles. The market connects supply and demand in the case of migrants, as it does in other cases. The fact that we are speaking of humans does not reflect the commoditization of persons, but, rather, the fact that an economy, which is made of people, has certain laws that cannot be disregarded. Market forces weigh heavily on migration and help connect those who want jobs with those who offer them.

Of course, the black market does not operate in a way that is entirely insensitive to the incentives and disincentives of the law. The international labor market is a "buyer's market" and labor-exporting nations have scant leverage over importing nations. The degree to which governments are efficient in keeping illegal immigrants out is a major factor influencing the workings of the international labor market. The fact that rich nations have placed severe restrictions in recent decades has contributed to the fact that many Asian migrants, for instance, have preferred to go to other Asian countries where they have identified a more institutionally friendly environment. Since the 1970s, as a consequence of rapid economic growth, temporary migration schemes were adopted that attracted millions of workers from the same continent. Ten times as many Filipino migrants went to other Asian nations than to North America (even though Filipinos still constitute one of the largest immigrant communities in the United States).[11] But even if government restrictions can influence the way in which the international labor market works and legal incentives and disincentives weigh heavily on the comings and goings of migrant workers, the market is a force so powerful in this domain that it has been able to function in the face of major obstacles.

In general, it can be said that the market tends to find ways of circumventing rules that stand in the path of smooth flows or of exploiting loopholes. In the Great Depression, Malaysia sent back to China many Chinese men who were illegal workers. Since China was also a victim of the Great Depression and unemployment was high in that country, the market adjusted itself by generating a new phenomenon: Chinese women emigrants. More than 190,000 females left Guangdong between 1933 and 1938, finding work in other parts of the region.[12]

Market realities have been decisive in determining the size of migratory flows in the United States too. The need for Mexican labor dates as far back to the nineteenth century. During the construction of the railroads from Mexico City into the Midwest of the United States, so-called *enganchadores* working for U.S.-based contractors would travel to Mexico in the 1870s and pay the Mexican military or police to arrest potential laborers and ship them over to their new job. A less violent recruitment began to take place at the turn of the twentieth century, when Japanese immigrant labor was restricted and American businessmen needed to replace it with Mexicans.[13] In the early twentieth century, American agricultural interests were instrumental in the U.S. government's decision to keep an open back door for workers from the Western Hemisphere—Mexican or otherwise—when migratory restrictions were imposed on Southern and Eastern Europeans. That "back door" turned, by the middle of the century, into the official guest worker programs discussed in earlier chapters. The underlying market needs determined the size and pace of border crossings, much as they do now.

The proximity of the United States and Mexico has created over the years a labor market that is much more unified than the national borders would suggest. The United States is able to tap the Mexican labor market in order to sustain certain activities that require what is commonly known as "stoop labor"—such as landscaping and harvesting. Some of these activities can only be produced at home and therefore cannot be outsourced, while others are maintained through protectionist measures and would probably be more efficiently produced overseas. But since large parts of the country seems to want to maintain activities for which there is not enough domestic labor, Mexican and Central American labor is desperately needed. Without immigrants, many products would either disappear or be more expensive.

Just as demand for labor affects migration flows, supply is also linked to the fortunes of the economy, in this case in the countries where migrants originate. A country's population size encourages emigration when the number of young people entering the labor market exceeds the number of jobs it can offer. When the economy cannot absorb young people after they reach working age, usually because of inefficient economic institutions derived from the wrong kinds of policies, net migration and the birth rates of the previous twenty years tend to be linked. In the late 1970s, the fertility rate of North African countries was high—about six children per woman. Hence, in the late 1990s, the number of departures was also high—126,000 emigrants per year.[14]

There is nothing unusual about business interests, i.e., the demand for labor, deciding the movement of workers from one country to the other. This has been the pattern worldwide for a very long time in all types of economic environments, which is why the business community tends to be pro-immigration, even as the pro-business right of the political spectrum tends to be anti-immigration. Those on the right who are pro-business and anti-immigration misread historical experience and pay little attention to what wealth creators tell them through their daily activities, including the hiring of foreign labor. They fail to see that business interests have by and large been very pro-immigration because their interests were closely tied to migratory flows that leveled the seesaw, so to speak, when imbalances emerged.

Governments have often accepted reluctantly the need for foreign labor because of pressure from businesses. Until 1991, the Dominican Republic government routinely negotiated with Haiti the flow of Haitians across the border precisely because Dominican businesses wanted workers from the neighboring country; after 1991, private contracts substituted for government agreements.[15] No less significant was the role played by South African businesses in migration to that country from neighboring African states, but also from Britain, China, Zimbabwe, Zaire, and others. In the mines of the South—Basothos, Mozambicans, Swazis, and Botswanas have been hired periodically. By the 1990s, there were more than 2 million illegal workers in South Africa, in great part as a result of business needs.[16] The market told business people that they needed to hire workers from other places, and the business community in turn pressured governments to be allowed to hire foreign workers—or at least turn a blind eye to their hire.

In Europe after World War II, British businesses were behind the policy that encouraged Jamaicans, Pakistanis, and Indians, as well as Southern Europeans, to move to "Perfidious Albion"—as England was sometimes pejoratively called. In the 1960s, there were shortages of labor in Britain that could not be filled by British, Irish, or other European workers. Acutely aware of such a need, the business community engaged in significant hires. In order to match the various needs, Afro-Caribbean workers settled in Greater London and the West Midlands; Indians settled mainly in Greater London, the West Midlands and, in smaller numbers, in West Yorkshire and Greater Manchester; Pakistanis moved into the West Midlands, West Yorkshire, London and Manchester; and Bangladeshis settled mainly in East London.[17]

In France, business interests obtained government licenses that allowed them to bring in more than 800,000 Algerians in the 1960s, followed by Moroccans and then black Africans in the 1970s (one-quarter of Algerians went back in great part because the permissive policy did not "lock" them in); their influence on government was such that the authorities provided help with lodging facilities through the *Société Nationale de Construction Pour Les Travailleurs.*[18] After the mid-1950s, German businessmen were also behind the recruitment of foreign workers through government-to-government agreements, including the 2 million Turks who came in the 1960s and beyond.[19]

Business leaders have understood the economic value of migration far better, it seems, than multilateral bodies that redistribute wealth, or pressure rich nations to redistribute it, from the developed to the developing world. Ironically, one of those very multilateral bodies, the World Bank, estimated in 2005 that the annual benefit of allowing a tiny 3 percent rise in the labor force through the relaxation of current immigration restrictions in developed countries would amount to $300 billion in poor countries and $51 billion in rich ones.[20] Considering that foreign aid totaled $70 billion in the year before the 2007–09 financial and economic debacle, the payoff seems evident.[21]

There are those who, even accepting that migration has helped to fill a vacuum in industrialized countries, maintain that migration creates its own imbalances and disruptions by triggering outflows of people in places that receive immigrants—a sort of "white flight" in the case of the United States. The connection between foreign-originated immigration in certain parts of one country and native out-migration from those same parts has not been definitively and conclusively established. In flexible, dynamic systems, the connection is even more difficult to ascertain. Because the United States has historically been a country with much internal mobility of people as a response to evolving economic circumstances in different states (many business people credit that flexibility in part for the country's prosperity[22]), it is impossible to determine exactly how much immigration has contributed to native out-migration in some parts of the country. For instance, how much of the so-called "white flight" out of California to the Mountain West in the 1990s was related to the heavy presence of immigrants, as some critics contend, and how much was due to the deterioration of economic conditions resulting from an environment that many businesses considered unattractive?

Film star Arnold Schwarzenegger's election as governor of California in 2003 was in great part a reaction against an economic state of affairs that had pushed many businesses and people out of that state. He based his campaign, which I had the chance to witness firsthand as a resident of California's San Francisco Bay Area at the time, in large measure on the promise to redress the business climate. The connection between foreign immigrants and native out-migration did not even feature in that heated gubernatorial campaign. At the same time that some people moved out, others moved in. Asian immigrants, for instance, moved from other states to California despite the fact that Latino immigrants continued to make their strong presence felt in the state.[23]

I am not suggesting that no native white Americans have moved out of California because of the large foreign-originated community. Some undoubtedly have. But there have been many reasons, historically, why Americans have been constantly on the move within their country, and the economy has been a major one; the evidence suggests that many factors besides the presence of immigrants have been at play. By the end of the twentieth century, 17 percent of Americans, almost one in five, moved homes every year on average.[24] Again, in 2005, more than 39 million people changed residence, of which one in five changed states.[25] The notion that this native flux is caused by low-skilled immigrants who leave Americans without a job or sully their neighborhoods requires a stretch of the imagination better left to artistic minds.

The movement of black Americans out of the South to largely urban areas of the Northeast and Midwest in the twentieth century was comparable in magnitude to the mass migrations across the Atlantic from Ireland or Germany at their peaks in previous centuries.[26] And even in the late twentieth century, migration by Americans from one region to another was greater than the migration of all people from all foreign countries to the United States.[27] Mobility of labor is a major feature of the U.S. economy, not a recent event related to a particular inflow of foreigners.

Other critics who accept the role played by migrants in certain periods contend that, by making it easy to hire cheap labor, foreign workers hold back the capitalization of the economy because they give businesses an easy alternative to investment in automation and mechanization. Two of the foremost scholars on immigration, Philip Martin and Michael Teitelbaum, wrote that, "Japan [was] getting robots while Germany [got] Turks."[28] To judge by the economic slowdown of Japan in the last two decades and the extraordinary productivity of the German economy—the world's number-one exporter—Turks were not such a bad deal; they do not seem to have got in the way of German mechanization. By the same token, the fact that after 2006, only 5 percent of Florida's orange groves used mechanical harvesting has not prevented the agriculture of the United States from being the most productive in the world, making it possible to feed some 300 million people with a shrinking proportion of labor being employed in that field.[29]

The fact that migration is part of an adjustment process—the constant correction of imbalances that take place in fluid economies—also means that, as countries develop, they send out fewer and fewer migrants, and receive immigrants in turn. Such is the case of Chile, a South American country that is today the home of dozens of thousands of Peruvian, Bolivian, Paraguayan, and even Argentinean and Uruguayan workers—one more case of a formerly backward nation that became a country of destination for migrants after having been a nation of emigrants (in the 1970s and 1980s many Chileans left their country for political reasons).

A similar turnaround has taken place in Puerto Rico. When Leonard Bernstein wrote *West Side Story* in the 1950s, it seemed that the flow of Puerto Rican immigrants would have no end. By 1961, however, when average incomes on the island amounted to one-third of the level of the mainland United States, net migration from the island dropped to almost zero.[30] If the Mexican economy were to grow at a minimum rate of 6 percent a year in the near future, the number of new jobs could roughly equal the size of the workforce in three years, bringing relief to migratory pressures in that country as well—fewer people would want to risk migrating to the other side of the border.[31] By then, of course, the labor needs of the U.S. economy will be supplied by migrants from other countries who will inspire a similar response to the one that Mexicans get today from anti-immigration groups.

A good way to gauge how immigration responds to adjustment needs is to observe how recessions impact the flow of workers across national boundaries. The recent recession in the developed countries serves as an illustration.

What Happens to Immigrants in Times of Recession?

In general, illegal migration and the black market are more responsive to market forces than legal flows because they are less affected by bureaucratic interference. In times of economic boom, immigration picks up, while in times of economic downturn the opposite happens.

The adjustment in times of recession tends to be almost immediate. If labor demand falls in a particular country and workers are trapped by national boundaries, there will still be many people wanting work—labor supply will be inelastic, economists would say—and all the adjustment will happen through a drop in wages. But if workers can go elsewhere to find jobs, wages will stay more or less the same, as happened in Ireland during the potato famine in the nineteenth century. Wages relative to the United Kingdom and per capita income never fell, thanks to emigration.[32]

In times of recession, flows into stagnant economies naturally ebb. In recent years, hundreds of thousands of Latin Americans have left Spain and returned home because of the lack of jobs due to the ongoing crisis in that European country. The population fell by 28,000 in the first half of 2011. If the trends were maintained, Spain would see its population drop by half a million people in the current decade. In 2008 and 2009, immigration plummeted in the United States because jobs that were available in construction and other industries before the recession no longer existed. The housing bubble had been like Christmas for immigrants—they built, renovated, painted, and landscaped the millions of houses and backyards that were bought and sold. Once the housing market collapsed, those jobs disappeared and the "pull" factor disappeared with them. Other industries also saw the domino effect.

It is estimated that annual illegal immigration in the United States was two-thirds smaller in the period between March 2007 and March 2009, when the number of undocumented entries averaged 300,000 per year, than between March 2000 and March 2005.[33] This means that the immigration market probably felt the impact of the recession long before many other markets, since the recession was not officially proclaimed until 2008, and it is generally believed to have begun in earnest late in 2007. Furthermore, a study published in 2012 showed that net migration from Mexico to the United States had fallen to zero from 2005 to 2010 (in fact, more people moved from the United States to Mexico in that period than vice versa).[34]

Admittedly, the enhancement of enforcement mechanisms—a doubling of the border patrols to 16,500 and the doubling of detention beds used to hold undocumented foreigners since 2000—played a part in discouraging immigrants. But to judge by historical precedent, the time frame in question, subsequent events, and the observations of experts, the recession was the primary factor.[35] In the years immediately following the enhancement of border patrols, there was a rise in illegal immigration in various states; the drop began when the economic impact was felt in industries employing Hispanics. Between 2006 and 2007, one year after President George W. Bush enhanced border security, the top ten states in terms of undocumented foreigners saw the number of illegal immigrants rise by 470,000. In October of 2006, President George W. Bush, a supporter of immigration, signed, under pressure from his party and a big part of public opinion, the Secure Fence Act authorizing the construction of 700 miles of fencing along the border, more vehicle barriers, checkpoints, and lighting to prevent entries. Regardless of the efficacy of these measures and of the fact that the fence may never be finished as it was intended to be (as I write in 2011, work on it has practically stopped), the fact is that the numbers of immigrants really began to drop as soon as the recession set in. In California, for instance, the proportion of undocumented foreigners dropped by 8.4 percent between 2007 and 2009; in Florida, where the bursting of the real estate bubble was particularly catastrophic, the drop amounted to as much as 25 percent.[36] When greater Las Vegas, one of the fastest-growing areas in the last twenty years, started to decline in 2007, the inflow of workers dropped too. Net annual immigration was reduced by 16 percent in the 2007–08 period, compared to 2000–2007.

A student and critic of low-skilled immigration, Harvard Professor George Borjas, has concluded that when the Mexican economy improves—and salaries rise and unemployment drops south of the border—fewer illegal foreigners are arrested in the United States. This is not to say that the economy changes match the arrest records perfectly. But generally speaking, there is a resonance between the state of Mexico's economy and the number of arrests north of the border. Given that the government interferes in that market through the mechanism of the law and its enforcement, the converse is also true: when the economy improves in the United States, law enforcement increases with regard to illegal immigrants; more of them tend to be arrested.[37]

The impact of the recession was felt among high-skilled workers too. For the first time since 2003, demand for H-1B visas—work permits granted upon request by American companies wishing to hire qualified foreigners—dropped. In 2008, the quota for those types of visas ran out in one day, but in 2009, there were only 46,700 applications six months after the new ones were made available. The fact that growth declined in the high-tech sector, which is usually where most applications are concentrated, explains in part the reduction in the number of applicants. Similarly, applications to universities by foreigners for master's degrees dropped by 17 percent.[38]

The recent recession was not an exception. Similar effects have been caused by other periods of economic stagnation. Although the previous recession produced in essence the same effect on immigration as the latest one, its intensity was different. From 2000 to 2003—the period following the bursting of the dot-com bubble—annual illegal immigration dropped by almost one-third in the United States.[39]

Although seldom, cases do occur in which migrants are resistant to recessions. That resistance occurred among Asian women migrants in Arab countries during the financial crisis of the end of the 1990s, when Arabs kept their nannies and domestic employees, probably in part as a sign of status.[40] Even in the United States, there have been a few instances in which migratory flows have not shadowed closely the needs of the economy because certain vested interests interfered. The ending of the *Bracero* program in the 1960s, in part due to pressure from unions and religious groups, created a temporary dissonance. But policy is not able to stem flows effectively if the needs of the economy hunger for imported workers—hence illegal migration and a great deal of blind-eye tolerance on the part of those supposed to enforce the law. In the conclusion of a scholar who has researched one century of Mexican migration: "There is no evidence that any steps by the U.S. government in the last one hundred years to restrict immigration from Mexico has had any appreciable effect on the underlying, structural demand for Mexican labor in the U.S. economy."[41]

The economy is not the only factor in migration; most people tend to look at immigrants in ways that are influenced by a host of considerations, not solely economic utility. But a greater awareness of the connection between migration and the international economy would help to clarify the many misunderstandings informing the debate on immigration and the political decisions related to it. An inflexible application of the fundamental tenets of the nation state is incompatible with the functioning of the real economy as regards the movement of people. Either the former adapts to the latter openly in the way it has increasingly done with regard to the movement of capital, goods and services, or the adjustment takes place illegally.

Migration is a factor of production that adjusts itself to the economic environment, including the forces of supply and demand. We have seen this adjustment, for instance, in the case of recessions, but also in the opposite type of environment, i.e, when the economy needs workers to expand. Interfering with those forces can, in the debatable case that restrictive measures are effective, produce effects similar to those intended, but they will always generate other, unintended results as well—precisely because migratory flows are connected to market forces. Many supporters of the market economy understand that excessive interference with it has negative consequences. It should not be hard to understand that, given that migration is a labor component of the market economy, the kind of interference we are seeing in many countries, including the United States—if effective—will impede the adjustments for which the economy clamors. The consequences will not be pretty.

Notes

1. Peter Brimelow, *Alien Nation: Common Sense About America's Immigration Disaster"* (New York: Random House, 1995), 166.

2. Ana María López, "La ley de la frontera: migraciones ilegales y la ley de flujos," *Revista de Occidente*, no. 316, September 2007, 103–105.

3. Richard Fry, "Gender and Migration," Pew Hispanic Center, July 5, 2006, http://pewhispanic.org/reports/report.php?ReportID=64

4. Thomas Donland, *A World of Wealth: How Capitalism Turns Profits into Progress* (Upper Saddle River, N.J.: Pearson Education, 2008), 71.

5. Donland, *A World of Wealth*, 71.

6. Nana Oishi, *Women in Motion: Globalization, State Policies, and Labor Migration in Asia*, (Stanford, Calif.: Stanford University Press, 2005), 43.

7. Wayne A. Cornelius, "Mexican Migration to the United States: The Limits of Government Intervention" (*Proceedings of the Academy of Political Science* 34, no. 1 (1981): 6. http://www.jstor.org/stable/1174031

8. Oishi, *Women in Motion*, 22–25.

9. Lant Princhett, *Let Their People Come* (Washington, D.C.: Center for Global Development, 2006), 49.

10. Philippe Fargues, "Arab Migration to Europe: Trends and Policies," in *Arab Migration in a Globalized World* (Geneva: International Organization for Migration, League of Arab States, 2004), 140.

11. Oishi, *Women in Motion*, 4.

12. Oishi, *Women in Motion*, 23.

13. Jorge Castañeda, *Ex Mex: From Migrants to Immigrants* (New York: The New Press, 2007), 33.

14. Bullent Kaya, *The Changing Face of Europe—Population Flows in the 20th Century* (Strasbourg: Council of Europe Publishing, 2002), 54.

15. Félix Manuel Angomás, *Los efectos de la inmigración haitiana hacia la República Dominicana* (Santo Domingo: Editora Universitaria, 2006), 17.

16. Aurélia Wa Kabwe-Segatti, "South African Discourses on Immigration: Changes and Continuity in the Transition Period," in *Etre Etranger et Migrant en Afrique au XXe Siècle: Enjeux Identitaires et Modes d'Insertion,* vol. 1, ed. Catherine Coquery-Vidrovitch (Paris: l'Harmattant, 2003), 39.

17. Zig Layton-Henry, *The Politics of Immigration: Immigration, "Race" and "Race" Relations in Post-War Britain* (Oxford, U.K, and Cambridge, Mass.: Blackwell, 1992), 12–13.

18. Oishi, *Women in Motion*, 45.

19. Maxime Tandonnet, *Le Grand Bazar ou l'Europe Face à l'Immigration* (Paris: l'Harmattan, 2001), 17–22.

20. "Global Economic Prospects: Economic Implications of Remittances and Migration," World Bank, Washington, D.C.: 2005, http://econ.worldbank.org/external/default/main?pagePK=64165259&theSitePK=469372&piPK=64165421&menuPK=64166322&entityID=000112742_20051114174928

21. Pritchett, "Let Their People Come," Center For Global Development, Washington, D.C., 2006, http://www.cgdev.org/content/publications/detail/10174

22. Jim Rogers, "Open the Doors," December 3, 2002. The article is available at http://www.jimrogers.com

23. Peter Brimelow, *Alien Nation: Common Sense About America's Immigration Disaster"* (New York: Random House, 1995), 71.

24. Jason Schachter, "Geographical Mobility: Population Characteristics," Current Population Report*s,* U.S. Census Bureau, May 2001, 1–2, http://www.census.gov/prod/2001pubs/p20–538.pdf

25. "Geographical Mobility Between 2004 and 2005," Current Population Survey, U.S. Census Bureau, March 2005.

26. "Historical Statistics of the United States: Colonial Times to 1970," U.S. Bureau of the Census (Washington, D.C.: Government Printing Office, 1975), 105–106.

27. "Geographical Mobility: March 1990 to March 1991," Series P-20, no. 463 (Washington, D.C.: Government Printing Office, 1992), xiii.

28. Philip Martin and Michael Teitelbaum, "The Mirage of Mexican Guest Workers," *Foreign Affairs* (November-December 2001), http://www.foreignaffairs.com/articles/57422/philip-l-martin-and-michael-s-teitelbaum/the-mirage-of-mexican-guest-workers

29. Julia Malone, "Farmers, Inventors, Explore Automation as Answer to Labor Shortage," Cox News Service, June 1, 2006.

30. Michael Barone, "Is Illegal Tide of Immigrants Finally Easing?" Hispanic American Center For Economic Research, January 17, 2009, http://www.hacer.org/report/2009/01/us-is-illegal-tide-of-immigrants.html.

31. Frank D. Bean and B. Lindsay Lowell, "Unauthorized Migration," in *The New Americans: A Guide To Immigration Since 1965*, eds. Mary C. Waters and Reed Ueda (Cambridge, Mass.: Harvard University Press, 2007), 70–83.

32. Princhett, *Let Their People Come*, 57.

33. Jeffrey S. Passel and D'Vera Cohn, "U.S. Unauthorized Immigration Flows Are Down Sharply Since Mid-Decade," Pew Hispanic Center, Washington, D.C., September 1, 2010, http://pewhispanic.org/files/reports/126.pdf

34. Jeffrey Passel, D'Vera Cohn, and Ana Gonzalez-Barrera, "Net Migration From Mexico Falls to Zero—and Perhaps Less," Pew Hispanic Center, Washington, D.C., May 3, 2012,

35. Steven A. Camarota and Karen Jensenius, "Homeward Bound: Recent Immigration Enforcement and the Decline in the Illegal Alien Population," Center for Immigration Studies, Washington, D.C., July, 2008, http://www.cis.org/trends_and_enforcement

36. Shikha Dalmia, "Obama's Immigration Distraction: Even Immigrants Are Shunning America's Sputtering Economy," *Reason*, July 13, 2010, http://reason.com/archives/2010/07/13/obamas-immigration-distraction

37. See chapter 4, in particular, of George J. Borjas, *Friends or Strangers: The Impact of Immigrants in the U.S. Economy* (New York: Basic Books, 1991).

38. Miriam Jordan, "Slump Sinks Visa Program," *The Wall Street Journal*, October 29, 2009.

39. Jeffrey S. Passel and Roberto Suro, "Rise, Peak and Decline: Trends in U.S. Immigration 1992–2004," Pew Hispanic Center, September 27, 2005, http://pewhispanic.org/reports/report.php?ReportID=53

40. Oishi, *Women in Motion*, 21.

41. Cornelius, "Mexican Migration to the United States," 9.

12

What Immigrants Do to Jobs, Wages, and the Economy

THE FACT THAT low-skilled immigrant jobs are menial jobs that most natives consider poor and mediocre does not mean that the economic contribution of these jobs is not important. In order to continue to be increasingly productive at the low end of the spectrum, the economy generates the need for low-skilled employment.

It is only natural that some groups fulfill the low-skilled roles in the United States because the division of labor is part and parcel of a market economy, domestically and internationally. The occupational status of Mexicans and Puerto Ricans lags the furthest in comparison to native whites in the United States. If Mexicans were removed from these occupations, others would fill the gap. An increasing degree of separation between Hispanics in general and native whites could be seen in the 1990s, confirming the skill distribution across the economy: While native whites increased their representation in professional occupations, and Hispanics tended towards construction and service occupations. The length of time that foreign-born Latinos have been in the United States contributes to narrowing the gap in occupational status with respect to native whites. But others take the place of those that move up, in a permanent cycle that has to do with the requirements of the economy, helping maintain a balance in terms of skill distribution.

The number of native workers available for low-skilled, entry-level jobs has declined sharply in the last few decades because of the falling birthrate, the higher level of education, and the job aspirations of people who used to perform those jobs, such as Chicanos and blacks. Low-skilled immigrants are filling a gap, rather than forcing America's economy to take them.

More recently arrived Hispanic immigrants have a lower occupational status in the United States than previously arrived countrymen, even if the recent arrivals have the same level of education and experience. The jobs are there for the taking. The issue is not so much that Hispanics are highly represented in low-paying jobs, but that the productive economy of the United States is in need of employing low-skilled workers, of whatever nationality and background.

The function performed by foreign workers is a net plus for the economy. Even academic critics of immigration admit that foreign additions to the workforce enlarge the size of the economy. A few years ago, George Borjas calculated that the net benefit of immigration in the United States amounted to $22 billion. Using his method of calculation and updating the information to the present, Benjamin Powell estimates the figure to be $36 billion today. It may sound small compared to the overall size of the economy, but that only begs the question: How much larger would the net contribution be with more immigrants?[1]

A widely held view of immigrants maintains that they take jobs away from native workers. Even people well inclined towards them think of the job market as a given quantity, a zero-sum game in which new workers displace old ones. If a foreign newcomer takes a job away from a native, a young person entering the job market for the first time poses the same threat. How could any society renew or expand its workforce under the premise that any new addition to the labor market is a job thief or a wage killer? If new additions to the workforce have a negative effect, as Powell has explained, why is it that between 1950 and today, a period in which the workforce grew from 60 million to 150 million people with the massive entry of women and baby boomers into the economy, has there been no long-term increase in the unemployment rate in the United States?[2]

There is scant connection between illegal workers and native unemployment. Except in very critical times—such as the 2007–09 recession—most unemployed Americans do not stay out of work for long, which means that the composition of the relatively small proportion of the working-age population that is jobless changes continually. Those who remain without a job tend to be the few million "discouraged" workers who do not look for work. And except in very unusual circumstances, illegal workers outnumber unemployed Americans (both those actively seeking a job, and those who are not).[3]

Critics who blame immigrants for taking jobs away from natives sometimes overlook two essential facts. First, they fail to realize that the job market is a flexible, malleable, ever-changing creature whose limits, in terms of the number of jobs available, no one is a priori able to establish. And, second, they lose sight of an obvious reality: Like native workers, immigrants are both producers and consumers, influencing the overall economy in both capacities.

The immigrant tide is indifferent to the projections for job growth prepared by agencies such as the Bureau of Labor Statistics. The mass of people rolls in sensing that there is a need for their labor, and they find work; the collective earnings engender new businesses or boost established ones. The 10-cent phone call, the dollar jitney, and the Bengali buffet—as a journalist who has researched low-skilled parlors and outlets aptly puts it—are more than discount consumer services—they are also job creators. Every new minivan that hits the street represents three new drivers, plus the incremental demand supporting gas stations, mechanics, auto parts salesmen, and other related services.[4]

No matter how large, immigration will not cause unemployment in a highly productive economy. It will simply mean that workers will be freed from certain jobs in order to pursue others, although, of course, it might not always mean that people will find a job they like better than the previous one. The process is similar to what happens when technological changes lure workers away from old occupations and towards much better opportunities elsewhere in the economy.[5] These workers are usually trained in new technologies by the companies employing them, and they are able to shift from one type of occupation to another rather smoothly. Technology destroys jobs, but it creates many more. As economist Alex Tabarrok has written, "Edison destroyed more jobs with his light bulb than immigrants have ever done; the same goes for Henry Ford, who destroyed the horse and buggy industry."[6] Similarly, immigrants facilitate the rise of natives through the skills ranks. In Spain, between 2000 and 2007, the number of native *peones* went down at the same time that immigrants came in. By 2007, no more than 14 percent of Spaniards were doing low-skilled work.[7]

Of course, the fact that immigrants fill certain gaps in the economy allowing natives to trade up does not mean that ample mobility does not take place within the low-skilled community, or that certain occupations will permanently be dominated by some foreign groups—hence the constantly changing taxicab scene in New York, for instance. The Chinese and Japanese began as plantation laborers in the United States triggering similar complaints to the ones that haunt Hispanics today, but they moved on to become small businessmen and later entered fields such as engineering and medicine.

Some goods and services consumed in rich nations have to be produced domestically and people would still want them if immigration were severely restricted. If fewer foreigners were employed in their production, natives would have to be paid higher wages, which in turn would force prices for those goods and services to rise. People would then consume less of them, leading to a loss of jobs for natives.

Everywhere, immigrant workers willing to work cheaply help natives to trade up. The fact that in the post-war environment, millions of women have been able to move from housework to professional occupations, or that many blacks have moved into the middle class owes not a little to the "undesirable" low-skilled foreigners. This dynamic has been true in the United States and in many other countries. In Switzerland, the arrival of immigrants in the 1960s allowed nationals to switch to more skilled occupations, with better wages.[8] Even countries that had severely restrictive—and reasonably effective—anti-immigration policies eventually had to relax their rules in order to help create conditions for the native population to move up the scale. Taiwan revised its immigration policy for foreign domestic workers in 1992. By 2001, there were 114,519 caregivers and domestic workers from abroad. South Korea was a labor-exporting nation until the 1980s but has evolved into a migrants' destination since 1991. In November 2002, it started admitting foreign domestic workers, albeit only Chinese citizens of Korean descent, with the aim of facilitating the upward mobility of natives who no longer wanted certain jobs.[9] When Singapore became independent in 1965, it gradually opened up the country to foreign investment. At first, it had abundant cheap labor, but because the population was small it eventually had to allow foreign workers into the country. By the early 1970s, it had dozens of thousands of immigrant workers who despite their low skills contributed to the general prosperity of that emerging nation by making it possible for natives to be more productive.

Moroccans who picked vegetables and spread fields with fertilizer in Almería made it possible for Spaniards, who were once so poor that they emigrated themselves, to disdain such "lowly" occupations and become professionals.

The Spanish baby boom finished in 1976. After 1993, when those born in 1976 reached working age, the economically active population started to fall. By 2007, the number of people between the ages of 17 and 32 had dropped in Spain, and yet the overall number of employed people had risen from 13 million people in 1996 to 20 million. Two-thirds of them were natives, mostly because women started to work, but one-third of the new jobs were performed by immigrants. With their willingness to do menial work and their greater geographical mobility, these workers who had come from overseas helped occupy spaces that natives did not want for themselves and fulfill activities for which there was not enough native labor supply for whatever other reason.[10]

As of 2004, some 89 percent of American workers had a high school degree or more.[11] Therefore, roughly nine in ten working Americans gained from the fact that someone else—mostly, but not only, immigrants—was available to perform roles that they did not want or could not play. The number of natives with no degree has been shrinking fast. If the trend continues, virtually all manual labor will be performed by foreign-born workers. This implies wage gains for natives since they will able to specialize in language-intensive and managerial tasks that are better paid. The need for foreign workers, then, promises to be even greater in the future than it has been in the past. In the context of an increasing backlash against low-skilled workers from abroad, this prospect does not bode well.

Do Wages Come Down?

What is often touted as a large influx of immigrants between 1990 and 2004 in the United States reduced the real wages of natives lacking a high school education by less than 1.5 percent, according to solid calculations, but it cut the wages of earlier immigrants by about 10 percent. Because different levels of education complement each other, in that period immigrants also caused a raise in the wages of native workers with at least a high school degree by an average of 2 percent. Taking into account the gains of the more educated (89 percent of workers born in the United States) and the losses of the less educated (11 percent), the net impact was to increase average wages of native workers by about 1.8 percent.[12]

It is true that illegal immigration tends to be connected to low salaries. But the low salaries have to do with productivity. In the long run, average wages are related to average labor productivity, which is determined by technology and institutions. In the last half-century, real wages in the United States have risen even as the labor force has doubled. Since it takes time to adjust production capacity to increases in the labor force, a sudden huge influx of immigrants would lower wages somewhat for a short period. However, the current influx is smaller than 0.5 percent of current employment. Each year for the last three decades, new investments have added between 2 and 3 percent to the existing stock of capital in the United States.[13] This increase in capital has allowed more people to be employed with better salaries.

According to the Department of Labor, more than half of the growth in labor demand in the top 25 occupations in the United States will take place in low-skilled services that cannot be outsourced, including such jobs as janitors, fast food workers, cashiers, and health aides. This reality points to the fact that the need for low-skilled workers in this country will increase in the future. Labor-intensive activities continue to play a large role in employment, however much the technological advances help many parts of the economy expand, grow in productivity, and generate new industries. Some of these labor-intensive activities are not outsourced because of protectionist measures, while others, such as the ones cited by the Department of Labor, simply cannot be imported. Because many labor-intensive services do not grow in productivity, their price goes up relative to goods and services that do cheaper because of improvements in productivity. Paradoxically, the salaries of people employed in these activities tend to go up in time because their employers need to compete with high-productivity activities that may lure workers away. Immigrants help keep these salaries lower and those services cheaper than they would otherwise be because of the "Baumol effect," named after economist William Baumol. Immigrants also provide the supply for a labor demand that is always high relative to more technology-intensive parts of the economy that require fewer workers.[14]

In general, the inflow of less-educated workers generates competition for workers already in that group but also increases the demand for highly educated workers because businesses need to manage the resulting higher numbers of unskilled employees. In time, technological advances make those unskilled workers more productive—thereby eventually raising their wages. Ironically, because foreigners are important at the high end of the economic scale, they also contribute to the rise of productivity among low-skilled immigrants. While two-thirds of workers with no degree were foreign-born in 2004, almost one in three of those with doctorates in science, technology, and engineering were also foreign-born.[15]

The overall beneficial effect of migration on wages can be seen in countries between which there is free circulation of people. For instance, Giovanni Peri and Susana Iranzo created a migration model matching Western and Central Europe in view of the expansion of the European Union to countries that were formerly part of the Communist bloc. They concluded that migration in the expanded union increases the relative specialization between East and West. The total westward emigration rate from Central Europe predicted in the model is 30 percent of the population, a rate similar to the historical long-term migration rate of Puerto Ricans to the United States between 1950 and 2000. In terms of real wages, free migration from one country to the other is beneficial to both countries, and to most groups in each. The highly educated Central Europeans are used more efficiently in the West and help create a wider range of varieties of goods. These efficient gains spill over into Central Europe in the form of reduced prices of traded goods.[16]

What Does the Research Say?

Various approaches to measuring the impact of immigration on native workers have been pioneered over time. Jean Grossman has studied how wage structures compare in different local labor markets and relates the differences to those in the relative supply of immigrants. But the study fails to see that people, goods, services, and ideas will flow between cities.[17] Any analysis needs to take those active forces into account.

A second approach to measuring immigration's impact compares changes over time in the number of immigrants to the rate of employment across the country. But it does not spell out the skill implications of technological changes experienced by specific industries.[18] According to George Borjas, Richard Freeman, and Lawrence Katz, natives tend to move out of cities with large numbers of foreigners, so that the effect is spread out across the country. For that reason, he and others proposed in 1992 an approach comparing the nation's actual supply of workers in different skill groups to the one the country would have had without immigrants, and then calculating how the increase in supply derived from immigrant workers affects the wages of different skill groups. Their conclusion was that immigration is responsible for almost half of the 10.9 percentage point decline in the relative wages of high school dropouts between 1980 and 1995.[19]

But other approaches have gone beyond the Borjas, Freeman, and Katz method. David Card, for instance, assigns immigrants and natives to skill groups and assumes they are perfect substitutes. The first step is to assess the effect of immigrants on the relative supplies of different skill groups in different cities. Then he relates the relative wages for different skill groups to the relative supplies in the same cities. He concludes that the proportion of immigrants in U.S. cities has roughly doubled since 1980 to 18 percent; that in both 1980 and 2000, slightly more than one-third of immigrants had less than a high school education; and that the percentage of natives with less than a high school education has fallen sharply, more than offsetting the inflow of less-educated foreigners.[20]

Card also found that that the number of low-skilled natives who left the cities was smaller than the number of low-skilled immigrants who flowed in. The number of low-skilled workers seeking jobs therefore increased. But there was almost no connection between the relative wages earned by native workers and the proportion of low-skilled immigrants, while unskilled foreigners caused only a slight increase in the employment rate of native dropouts.[21] The reason is that most of the unskilled labor was absorbed by industries willing to hire more unskilled workers in certain cities. Capitalism is a creature that adapts to, and profits from, increases in factors of production. If more unskilled workers are available, businesses innovate in ways that allow them to tap those resources. This adaptability and the fact that the reshuffle takes place without affecting relative wages indicates that high school graduates offset high school dropouts.[22]

Other studies have confirmed that immigrants have very small effects on native employment and wages (of course, once undocumented foreigners become legal, their salaries rise as well). The influx of 125,000 Cuban migrants from the 1980 Mariel boatlift did not harm the local employment rate or wages in Miami. While many immigrants moved on, half of them settled in that city, causing a 7 percent rise in the supply of labor and a 20 percent rise in the number of Cubans working there. They were younger and less educated than the Cubans already residing in Miami, and a majority were males. At first, unemployment rose from 5 percent to 7 percent in a few months, but the same rise took place at the national level, which probably means that the Mariel boatlift was not responsible. The *Marielitos* earned 18 percent less than other Cubans, and yet, except for a short period in 1982–83, the salaries of black workers during the five years following the influx remained fairly stable, as did those of non-Cuban Hispanics.[23]

Some purported free-market conservatives who decry immigration, such as Mark Krikorian, maintain that immigrants create a supply shock of labor that lowers wages because employers can pick and choose. Contradicting his own assertion that they have a negative effect on Americans, the author cites a National Research Council Report according to which natives as a whole receive a benefit of between $1 billion to $10 billion per year from immigration, an effect that he attributes to redistribution away from the poor, because the poorest of American workers suffer a 5 percent wage cut. It is not at all clear how these figures are reached, especially considering that the skilled workers only see their wealth increase by two-tenths of 1 percent.[24] As explained, many studies have confirmed that any impact on wages is very small and temporary. In any case, the lowering of wages at one end does not redistribute wealth by raising wages at the other end. Wages are not a given quantity that is parceled out. They are determined by productivity in a competitive economy.

By the author's logic, and that of other pro-market critics of immigration who use similar arguments, government policies that raise wages in the United States should be favored. However, raising wages is exactly what unions and minimum wage policies seek to do—and these are two things free-marketeers actively dislike. The same author states that union membership has declined because it is an old-fashioned, industrial-age institution. He postulates that immigrants are like nineteenth-century workers trying to get into a twenty-first-century economy. Presumably, the erosion of unions is hurting wages and allowing employers to pick and choose, which are exactly the charges he levels against immigrants. Moreover, why nineteenth-century immigrants should find jobs so easily in a twenty-first-century economy that does not need them is mystifying.[25]

Some anti-immigration advocates on the left see Mexican labor in the United States as the fault of greedy employers intent on protecting profit margins and middle-class consumers intent on protecting their restaurants meals, clothing, agricultural produce, and maid service. The universe of people cited by these critics as beneficiaries of foreign-born labor is so huge that it begs the question: What is wrong with so many people being better off? But the contention misses an important point: The supposed conspiracy against the little guy also takes place in periods of very low immigration. If the search for profit margins and widespread, affordable consumption is a bad thing, that is a charge that can be leveled not at immigration, but at the free-enterprise system and the capitalist and consumer societies—an altogether different proposition that begs the question: Is socialism a better system? Immigration is not about stealing jobs or making the rich richer. It is about having the workforce necessary to meet different needs, from highly skilled scientists and program developers to harvest pickers, to nannies, to nurses.

Yes, the areas of the economy—hotels, construction, commerce—in which immigrants are highly concentrated in various developed countries tend to command lower salaries, which in turn helps keep those costs down. But this was also true before immigration. The evidence belies the mantra that the salaries of immigrants, who are heavily represented in the areas described, are the ones that rise the slowest. Between 2000 and 2006, salaries in Spain rose 21.4 percent on average, but in the construction and hotel industries they rose 24 and 23.5 percent, respectively.[26] In many parts of the United States, the scarcity of workers is such that market rates for illegal workers are above the legal minimum wage. In prosperous cities such as Phoenix, it is difficult in normal times to hire anyone for less than $15 an hour in cash. With lower costs, occupations that employ immigrants can produce more efficiently and therefore keep prices down, which increases real wages, even if nominal wages drop slightly with a sudden influx of immigrants. The temporary drop also attracts new firms into an area, generating economic expansion and ultimately more job opportunities.

What hurts employment and wages in any economy is a system—a set of institutional arrangements—constraining the ability of people to generate businesses, of businesses to expand and hire labor, and of technology to augment the productivity of workers. Taxes and fiscal constraints placed on small and midsized enterprises in France, for instance, have kept unemployment high by comparison to the United States (up until the 2007–09 recession, when the U.S. unemployment rate reached European levels). For many years, the U.S. unemployment rate was half of France's, and yet both economies harbored high numbers of immigrant workers. What has kept French unemployment rates high is the labyrinthine system of wealth redistribution, protectionism, and disincentives that is the French economy (despite it all, some heroic French corporations are extremely competitive worldwide). Subsidies given by the government to jobless Frenchmen and women who create businesses, for instance, are handed out between three to six months after the businesses are created. These kinds of absurdities—not the considerable number of African immigrants employed in France—have hurt the labor market by keeping the economy inefficient and postponing real reform.

In open economies, flexibility and mobility constantly help adjust domestic asymmetries, diffusing economic and social tensions that might have translated into a less peaceful coexistence in different periods.

The flexibility of the system—including the drop in immigration in hard economic times and native mobility in response to evolving opportunities and fortunes—has been a strong safeguard against unrest, unlike some European countries where rigid institutions have stood in the way of job creation and generated an underclass of immigrants. The fact that immigration is no longer concentrated only in the six states mostly associated with it—California, New York, Florida, New Jersey, Texas, and Illinois—but spread out in all regions is making immigration part of the population mix in the imagination of most Americans.

Immigrants Mirror the Natives

Contrary to conventional wisdom and conspiracy theories, immigrant workers tend with time to mirror native workers in terms of their employment patterns. Male immigrants, for example, over time tend to mirror native workers in certain key areas: participation in the labor force, unemployment rates, the rate of office or manufacturing work, and salary per hour.[27]

The fact that so many immigrants work in low-skilled occupations reflects the continuous need for those workers and the continuous arrival of low-skilled foreigners willing to take those jobs. But there is no law that says that immigrants cannot progress. They do, and it is not unusual for foreign communities to rise from low occupations to become successful. History is replete with examples. Attitudes toward work can transform an environment for a certain number of people, even when that environment is not conducive to prosperity and generating mobility. Virtually all the wealthy Indians in Africa made their fortunes from humble beginnings.[28] In South Africa, while agriculture was the obvious destiny for those who had worked on plantations, Gujaratis set up small businesses to compete with whites in Natal, the Transvaal, and the Orange Free State. As elsewhere, the Indian retailer was willing to adjust to the special needs of his clientele, often made up of poor Africans. Indian stores were open long hours, charged lower prices than Europeans, and extended credit. The Indian owners were soon denounced by Europeans for engaging in "unfair" practices, and by Africans as "exploiters."[29]

Differences among immigrant groups can be starker than people who paint them with a broad brush realize, just as there are differences in terms of skill and achievement between groups of natives. Among Central Americans, who tend to be the most disadvantaged Hispanic immigrants in the United States after the Mexicans, Nicaraguans do much better than other nationals from that region. They are twice as likely to be employed in managerial, professional, technical, or sales positions—almost 45 percent of them are in that category.[30] Furthermore, at the turn of the new millennium, the poverty rate among Salvadorans, 20 percent, was not much higher than among the Vietnamese, of whom 15 percent were poor. The disparity between Mexicans and Chinese was much higher—31 percent against 10 percent.[31] Many factors account for these rates, including the obvious fact that different groups started from different positions in their country of origin and have varying degrees of education. Again, each immigrant group has a role to play in a modern economy, irrespective of nationality.

If we look at those who are college-educated, we find that Hispanics are more likely to change occupations than other workers. Recently arrived immigrants and immigrants who do not speak English usually switch occupations within five years. But there are differences among the various groups of immigrants. Cubans in general resemble the occupational trends of native whites closely. A Dissimilarity Index based on the 2000 Census measuring the difference in occupational distribution concluded that 31 percent of male, foreign-born Hispanic workers would have to change occupation in order to resemble the occupational distribution of native whites. However, for all Hispanics in general, the proportion was 22 percent, exactly the same as with blacks and Asians. This means that, even as new immigrants take up lower-skilled roles in need of fulfillment, Hispanics assimilate in ways that translate into occupational distributions similar to those of other minorities.[32]

The "Mexicans" of Yesteryear

In discussing the low-skilled component of a modern economy and the high representation of immigrants in it, one should never lose sight of historical precedent. If we consider past waves of immigrants, including those whose contribution to society we tend to value and compare advantageously with current immigrants, it becomes much clearer that what is happening today is no different in essence from what happened in the past.

Gross statistical disparities in the representation of groups in different occupations, industries, income levels, and educational institutions have been the rule, not the exception, across the planet. Sometimes those disparities have existed for generations, even centuries.[33] The international economy has accommodated such disparities, allocating the crucial resource that we call labor accordingly. With time, those disparities have changed. Some groups have caught up and others have replaced the previous laggards. Immigration is a bellwether of international disparities. Many of the groups that we associate with high achievement in American society today were the "Mexicans" of yesteryear.

Individuals who first arrive in the United States from poor countries earn about 55 percent as much as native Americans of the same age, sex, and years of schooling in contemporary times.[34] But that disparity in income is not new. A very sizeable gap has been a constant in the United States since the nineteenth century. One century ago, the Immigration Commission presented a report to the Congress of the United States based on an investigation in 23 states. More than half a million wage earners, almost 300,000 of them foreign-born, were interviewed. One major focus was on "new" immigrants from Southern, Central, and Eastern Europe who were earning less than the "old" immigrants from Northwest Europe because they were willing to accept lower standards of living. It concluded, "[T]hey were content to accept wages and conditions which the native American and immigrants of the older class had come to regard as unsatisfactory." Restrictions were recommended that had a bearing on immigration laws of 1917, 1921, and 1924. Obviously, immigrants were not paid less because they had a low standard of living, but, rather, they had a low standard of living because they were paid less.[35] The reason for the lower pay was the difference in skills and therefore—as economists like to say—marginal productivity.[36]

If we look at different immigrant groups at the time, the high incidence of agricultural work, a feature still salient a century later, is blatant. According to records of Japanese associations in California, two-thirds of Japanese immigrants with work labored in agriculture in 1910.[37] Before that period, they had been employed in railroads, logging and lumbering camps, mines and domestic service. Eventually the Japanese moved up, but after the internment of some 110,000 of them (most were American citizens) in the wake of the attack on Pearl Harbor, they went back to the low ranks of society. By the end of the war, among first-generation Japanese immigrants to America, the number of people who owned their own business was less than half that of the pre-war years, while the proportion of house servants and farm laborers increased significantly. Again, as has always been the case, it would take the second and third generations to catch up. The fact that twenty-five years after the internment, the income of Japanese males was still between 9 and 13 percent below its pre-war years highlights that the rise, impressive though it has been, has been gradual.[38]

The story of Chinese immigrants is also one of early generations struggling with low-skilled jobs. At one point, four-fifths of agricultural workers in California were Chinese.[39] After the backlash that ensued, the Chinese retreated into two main occupations—laundries and restaurants. Hundreds of Chinese laundries opened in San Francisco in the second half of the nineteenth century, concentrating that community in one particular line of work—much like Koreans in New York many decades later.

After World War II, the Chinese who migrated to the United States through Hong Kong spoke no English and began their new life in low-wage jobs in Chinatown restaurants and garment factories. Crime rates soared in some Chinatowns for a good while. By 1990, their median income was still lower than that of Chinese immigrants who had arrived in the country earlier. Eventually, the Chinese moved up and others took their previous positions.[40]

The Irish who migrated to the United States in the nineteenth century were in mostly unskilled or semi-skilled activities.[41] Those who arrived after the potato famine were three-quarters literate, and their fares were paid by established extended families. Similarly, Italian migration to the United States was overwhelmingly from the underdeveloped, rural South, rather than from Italy's much more industrialized North.[42] They began in the United States at the very bottom of the social ladder—as bootblacks, sewer workers, ragpickers. Both in 1880 and 1905, three-quarters of Italians working in New York City were blue-collar worker; the rest were peddlers, shopkeepers, and barters.[43] Like taxicab operators after them, they eventually moved up and others filled the gap.

The vast majority of pre-1965 Filipinos in the United States came from agricultural and unskilled backgrounds, although an early wave had been made up of a privileged part of that Asian economy. After the 1924 law banning Asians, Filipinos were still able to move to the other side of the Pacific because of the colonial relationship. The agricultural occupations that other Asians had filled were those occupied by Filipinos in the Western states. In the 1920s and 1930s, Filipino men were also employed in other unskilled jobs in hotels and restaurants, or as domestic servants, bellmen, cooks, dishwashers, and janitors.[44]

In many places of the Western Hemisphere, Indians remained agricultural workers for a long time, in contrast with the urbanization of the Indians who settled in Africa, where they quickly undertook commercial activities. Part of the explanation may lie in the origin of the different migratory waves. Most Indians who went to Africa were Gujaratis from Western India, a group that excelled in some professions and in commerce, while those who went to the Western Hemisphere, for instance, many Caribbean islands, were from the Ganges River basin in Eastern India.[45] The stereotype of the Indian migrant is a high-tech genius, an image born out of the extraordinary contribution of Indians to the Silicon Valley revolution in the United States. This stereotype runs contrary to the diversified history of that country's emigrants and points to the changing roles that different national groups have played in the international economy throughout the centuries. Their case should help put into perspective the story of immigrants who currently occupy the lower rungs of the social ladder.

Critics of immigration observe economic enclaves—certain activities or certain areas of a particular city—dominated by today's immigrants and intuit an immigrant conspiracy to stake out positions from which to exclude natives, with a view to expanding into other areas of the country later. Such opinions run contrary to historical experience and basic economics. They indicate little awareness of the similarities between what can be observed today and historical precedent, and therefore little awareness of the fact that immigration dynamics are constantly evolving. These opinions betray a misunderstanding of how markets work and of the benefits of constantly evolving enclaves determined through economic dynamics, rather than conspiracy.

The Koreans are one of the most enterprising immigrant groups in the United States. They also generate some animosity for their dominance of some niche markets. But their rise to dominance of certain neighborhoods was the product of effort, opportunity, and competition. In the 1960s, they discovered in Harlem a market for one of Korea's earliest export industries—the weaving of women's hair for wigs. They became wholesalers, attracting African immigrants who found an opportunity trading hairpieces, and eventually skin lighteners and other cosmetics in high demand among African-Americans. By the 1970s, Koreans had moved out of Harlem and replaced Jews as subcontractors of Manhattan's Garment District, between Fifth and Ninth avenues from 34th to 42nd streets, also known as the Fashion District because it has traditionally been a center of fashion manufacturing and design. Eventually, the Koreans moved to the Gift District, where they warehouse cheap manufactures from Asia that are stacked by Mexicans, and sold by Iranians, Iraqis, Indians, Chinese, and others.[46]

Other niche markets illustrate how certain immigrant groups came to dominate some activities because the original group moved on. In the 1970s, as Millman reminds us, one found mostly second-generation Italians, Jews, and the Irish people operating taxis in New York. They could afford to send their kids to college and lived mostly in Queens. They owned "medallions," a lifetime license that was hard to obtain. Because new ones were not issued and the fleets became old, the prestige of the occupation was eroded while other activities became more attractive, and less-well-off immigrants took over. Five or six Pakistanis, or Afghans, or Egyptians, or Bangladeshis would work one cab as a family. They would lend one another money to invest in buying expensive licenses from those who already had them. Eventually, more medallions became available. In the 1980s, Russian immigrants acquired most of them. But they were replaced in turn by Haitians when new ones were issued—and in the 1990s

Pakistanis came to dominate the market when they got their hands on a bunch of new medallions given out by New York's authorities.[47]

The popular image of immigration as an out-of-control invasion ignores the tight organization that actually takes place, reflected in part in the emergence of neighborhoods with clusters of fellow nationals specializing in certain trades—as can be seen by walking down Western Market Street, a center of Peruvian life in Paterson, N.J., for example, or taking the bus line from Paterson to Union City, owned by and heavily used by Peruvians—or showing up at the Brownstone, a restaurant in Paterson where presidential candidates from Peru often make an appearance in the run-up to elections. The concentration of Peruvians in Paterson started in the 1960s but gained momentum particularly in the 1980s and 1990s. It prospered because fellow Peruvians found it easy to transact with each other, replace a community member who was ready to move up or move on, and overcome the kinds of barriers that newcomers find. Economies of scale were helped by their concentration. By keeping costs reasonable—for instance, by pooling resources and acting as family units rather than single individuals—and by expanding output, they helped bring more business to Paterson. Peruvians also had an impact in East Newark, Harrison, and Kearny for similar reasons, as I have been able to confirm in visits to the area.

Clusters of fellow nationals not only help to increase production; they also boost general consumption, helping bring more business to an area. Individual members of concentrated immigrant communities may earn low income, but collectively they spend significant amounts as well. Figures from the U.S. census, for instance, show that New York's median household income in 1990 was just under $30,000, with males earning slightly above the median and females slightly less. Even though most New York households are comprised of two earners, the average income was similar to the single-person wage, revealing that many families earned small incomes. But the same census figures reveal that in the case of immigrants, the median household income is higher than that of the median single-earner income, and that generally immigrant households earn more than natives. How is that possible if single immigrants earn less than single natives? because the most likely explanation is that several people in the family work, and those who have a job work long hours. The Guyanese are a case in point. Most live in families with at least two wage earners, and one-third of them live in homes with three or more wage earners.[48]

The "Good" Immigrants

The term "high-skilled," or even "skilled," is confusing and relative. It covers a broad range of educational backgrounds, job preparation, and work experience, ranging from semi-skilled to scientific, high-tech, or simply academic proficiency. By some measures, some of the old waves of immigrants in the United States were relatively skilled, even if they are described as "low-skilled" when judged by today's superior standards. Such was the case of Jewish immigrants between 1899 and 1914, two-thirds of whom had artisan skills, particularly in shoemaking and clothing.[49] But, generally speaking, today the term "skilled" usually refers to professional, technical, or managerial activities, and to higher education credentials.

The new phase of globalization has intensified the mobility of ideas, goods, economic capital, and, to a lesser but increasing extent, human capital. Before the financial and economic crisis of 2007–08, affiliates of foreign companies in the United States employed more than 5 million workers directly. Between 2003 and 2007, foreign companies in America invested some $184 billion to create 447,000 new jobs, many of them in struggling cities of the Midwest.[50] But not only foreign capital moved in. Educated immigrants came in significant numbers too, albeit at a much lower rate than would have been the case if the restrictions on the number of work permits issued to high-skilled workers had not been in place.

Due to the growing perception that in an intensely competitive world the mobility of high-skilled labor will be beneficial to developed economies, there are currents of opinion postulating policies that would award "points" to aspiring guest workers for meeting certain proficiency standards. Canada and Australia have carried out such policies for some time (both countries award roughly two-thirds of their visas for reasons linked to employment, whereas only one in six visas is given for that purpose in the United States). Some countries even propose to "auction" or simply "sell" visas at expensive prices, thus attracting people with a certain level of income, who would then be forced to work hard in the country of destination in order to recoup the "investment." Of course, the fact that in many emerging nations, income per person is rising meteorically means that the return on education will be ever higher so long as the right policies continue, lowering the incentive for high-skilled people to emigrate permanently. As far back as the 1970s, the return on education in countries in which migration originated was between 10 and 15 percent higher than in the 1950s.[51] That was still not enough to prevent many people from wanting to leave since they had started from a very low bottom and the improvement was insufficient for them. But this is now appearing to change, as emerging nations begin to prosper and opportunities expand.

If things continue along that path, there will be competition for scarce high-skilled migration by many countries aspiring to attract them. It is not hard to foresee a world in which many incentives will be given to high-skilled migrants, who will for the most part go through the legal process, while unskilled immigrants, whose role in the economy of host nations is much less understood, continue to use illegal means. Conversely, countries from which high-skilled migrants will want to leave will face the dilemma of either transforming their own political economy to enhance the domestic environment and keep their people or lose them to competitors.

A substantial study found that holders of H-1B visas (three-year, once-renewable work permits sponsored by companies in the United States) add to innovation and help increase patent registrations by Americans. The conclusion was that increased numbers of H-1B visas strongly shadow increased numbers of patents for which immigrant inventors applied. They found no evidence that this affected U.S. applications negatively—i.e., there was no crowding-out effect, as some critics maintain.[52] No wonder major CEOs of American corporations, among them, and very publicly, Bill Gates, the former head of Microsoft, have been pleading with the U.S. government to augment the quota of H-1B visas issued each year.

Most of the ire directed at immigration is focused on low-skilled immigrants. One wonders, however, what the reaction would be in rich countries, both at the grassroots level and among the elites, if high-skilled immigration acquired much greater proportions than it has today. By definition, high-skilled immigrants are visible and influential, which can, in certain circumstances, arouse nationalist and nativist fears and prejudices. The persecution of Jews in Central and Eastern Europe at certain times had to do with resentment towards their high-skilled success. No one truly likes too much competition, even if they pay lip service to it, much less if that competition comes from a group of people that can be broadly painted as alien to a national tradition.

Groups or minorities that have owned or directed the lion's share of certain industries in some countries range from the Lebanese in West Africa, to the Greeks in the Ottoman Empire, the Britons in Argentina, the Belgians in Russia, the Spaniards in Chile, the Chinese in Southeast Asia and the United States, the Italians in Latin America, and the Jews in New York. Skills are widely distributed throughout the world, but they can be highly concentrated in specific nations in particular circumstances for a host of reasons. This concentration brings both an extraordinary expansion of wealth and opportunity, but also envy and suspicion, especially if those perceived as monopolizing the opportunities are foreign.[53]

In the late twentieth century, migrations tended to involve many people with more education, higher skills, and greater job experience than the general population of the countries they left. In 1989, for instance, more than one-fifth of the migrants from all regions of the world to the United States were professionals or technicians, while an additional 10 percent were in executive, administrative, and managerial positions.[54] This distribution was reinforced in subsequent years.

It is highly debatable whether a nation from which high-skilled emigrants leave loses much more than if they stayed behind. Emigrants, as has been the case of Chinese Americans in recent decades, contribute in many ways through trade and investment to their own home countries. Remittances sent by Africans in Europe or Latin Americans in the United States have amounted to much more than foreign aid and, for some countries, more than foreign investment. In any calculation, moreover, one would need to take into account how much wealth high-skilled people would have been able to create at home had they preferred to stay there, under an environment not necessarily conducive to exploiting their skills.

In the early 1970s, when this same debate was taking place, the Research Service of the Congress of the United States calculated that America gained $20,000 a year from each qualified migrant from a developing country. Applied to Africa, this would imply a "loss" of over $1.2 billion invested in the education of some 60,000 African specialists who emigrated between 1985 and 1990. The estimate put forward much later by the United Nations Conference on Trade and Development (UNCTAD), based on 1979 prices, assigned a value of $184,000 to each African professional migrant—counting those between the ages of 25 and 30.[55]

The problem with these outdated calculations is not so much that they were made a few decades ago, but that they do not take into account the limitations back home for those who migrated, or the many ways in which emigrants contributed to their adopted country. These calculations do, however, give us a sense of how the perception that a "brain drain" would hurt poor countries and benefit rich countries has been around for much longer than people realize today.

Critics of the 1965 immigration law in the United States often fail to notice an interesting side effect of that same legal watershed—the growth of educated migration from poor nations, both Asian and Latin American, to the United States. The number of new PhDs in science and engineering working in the United States increased between 1973 and the end of the twentieth century only because of the influx of foreigners. Many factors aside from the 1965 law have played a key part in the influx of educated migration into the United States, among them the rise of Asia and the relative progress made by some Latin American countries, as well as the globalization of knowledge and information. There have been periods before 1965, for instance the 1940s, when the average immigrant had more years of education than native people. But the 1965 law unwittingly helped attract high-skilled migration in the following decades by making migration easier for Asians and Latin Americans, among whom there were also educated people wanting better opportunities.

Indian immigration post-1965 has been made up of predominantly well-educated, urban professionals migrating with their families. Their contribution to the Silicon Valley high-tech phenomenon is the stuff of legend. In the 1980s, there were some 5,000 Indian engineers in that corner of northern California, while the number was four times larger nationwide.[56] Indian and Chinese enterprises in Silicon Valley provided more than 70,000 jobs by the turn of the century. More than 900,000 Asian-owned firms in the country at large employed 2 million people and generated $161 billion in receipts.[57]

Indian immigrants went—and have continued to go—mostly to California, New Jersey New York, Illinois, and Texas.[58] These new waves of Indian immigrants tended not to be clustered in residential areas but dispersed, with residential patterns similar to those of natives of the United States. This dispersal can be explained by their relatively small numbers, their skills, and the absence of concentrated Indian neighborhoods prior to their arrival.[59] The relationship between the relative prosperity of Indians in the United States and their level of education is evident. The median income of those who arrived in the 1980s was more than \$40,000.[60]

The impact of Indian high-skilled migration has also been felt in other countries. Among the nearly three-quarter million Indians who settled in modern industrial nations in the late twentieth century, 44 percent went to Britain, of whom nearly half were highly-skilled professionals—a proportion that belies the stereotype of the Indian grocer. By contrast, only 10 percent of those who chose underdeveloped countries were high-skilled migrants.[61]

Other Asian groups have contributed immensely to the post-1965 high-skilled migratory influx in the United States. Nearly half of the flow from Hong Kong since the 1980s has comprised major international financiers, executives of multinational corporations, and global traders.[62] A disproportionate number of scientists and scholars have also moved from Taiwan to America. While one-quarter of Chinese immigrants from the mainland are not high school graduates, according to the 2000 census, the Chinese from the mainland are on average more educated than American natives.

Many Latin American countries have also exported relatively educated and skilled people to the United States because of the perennial political and economic problems they inflicted on themselves in the last decades of the twentieth century. In the new millennium, one-sixth of all Latinos were employed in jobs classified as managerial, professional, technical, or related to sales. Half of all Colombian immigrants aged between 25 and 64, for instance, were thus employed.[63] Studies have shown that three-quarters of Dominican migrants were not from rural backgrounds and had skilled, blue-collar, or white-collar positions before leaving the island.[64] By 1990, migration included a cross section of society's mostly urban working class, but one out of four held a relatively skilled and well-paying job in the Dominican Republic.[65]

Notes

1. Benjamin Powell, "An Economic Case for Immigration," Library of Economics and Liberty, June 7, 2010, http://www.econlib.org/library/Columns/y2010/Powellimmigration.html. George Borjas's original calculation is in George Borjas, "Immigration," in *The Concise Encyclopedia of Economics*, ed. David R. Henderson (Indianapolis: Liberty Fund, 2009).

2. Powell, "An Economic Case for Immigration."

3. Thomas Donland, *A World of Wealth: How Capitalism Turns Profits into Progress* (Upper Saddle River, N.J.: Pearson Education, 2008), 77.

4. Joel Millman, *The Other Americans* (New York: Viking, 1997), 44.

5. Alberto Benegas Lynch, *Estados Unidos Contra Estados Unidos* (Guatemala City: Fondo de Cultura Económica, 2008), 257.

6. Alexander Tabarrok, "Economic and Moral Factors in Favor of Open Immigration," The Independent Institute, September 14, 2000, http://www.independent.org/issues /article.asp?id=486

7. *Segundo Libro Blanco de la Integración Sociolaboral de Refugiadas, Refugiados e Inmigrantes* (Madrid: CEAR, 2008), 34–35.

8. Bullent Kaya, *The Changing Face of Europe—Population Flows in the 20th Century* (Strasbourg: Council of Europe Publishing, 2002), 64.

9. Nana Oishi, *Women in Motion: Globalization, State Policies, and Labor Migration in Asia*, (Stanford, Calif., Stanford University Press, 2005), 32.

10. *Segundo Libro Blanco*, 31, 32.

11. Giovanni Peri, "America's Stake in Immigration: Why Almost Everybody Wins," *The Milken Institute Review* (Third Quarter 2007), 45.

12. Peri, "America's Stake in Immigration," 47.

13. Peri, "America's Stake in Immigration," 43.

14. Lant Princhett, *Let Their People Come* (Washington, D.C.: Center for Global Development, 2006), 6, 38.

15. Peri, "America's Stake in Immigration," 45.

16. The income per person regardless of where he or she resides increases by 0.8 percent in Western Europe and by 38 percent in Central Europe. The greater freedom of movement helps the less educated in Western Europe with a 2.1 percent increase in real wages and hurts the most educated only slightly—with a 0.9 percent drop— who are negatively affected by the greater number of highly educated people brought about by high-skilled migration. All workers who remain in Eastern Europe also obtain real wage gains of 1.4 percent because of lower prices and the larger variety of goods via trade. See Susana Iranzo and Giovanni Peri, "Migration and Trade: Theory with an Application to the Eastern-Western European Integration" (Working paper, March 2009), 26–27, http://www.econ.ucdavis.edu/working_papers/09-7.pdf

17. Jean Grossman, "The Substitutability of Natives and Immigration in Production," *Review of Economic Statistics* no. 64 (1982): 596–603. http://www.jstor.org/pss/1923944

18. George J. Borjas, Richard B. Freeman, and Lawrence F. Katz, "How Much Do Immigration and Trade Affect Labor Market Outcomes?" (Brookings paper no. 1, Harvard University, 1997), 1–67, http://www-personal.umich.edu/~jdinardo/Pubs/comment _on_borjas_freeman_katz97.pdf

19. Borjas and Freeman et al., "On the Labor Market Impact of Immigration and Trade," in *Immigration and the Work Force: Economic Consequences for the United States and Source Areas*, eds. George J. Borjas and Richard B. Freeman (Chicago: Chicago University Press, 1992), 213–244.

20. David Card, "Is The New Immigration Really So Bad?" (Working paper 11547, National Bureau Of Economic Research, (Cambridge, Mass.: 2005), 5, http://www.nber .org/papers/w11547

21. Card, "Is The New Immigration Really So Bad?", 7.

22. Card, "Is The New Immigration Really So Bad?", 16.

23. David Card, "The Impact of the Mariel Boatlift on the Miami Labor Market," *Industrial and Labor Relations Review* 43, no. 2 (January 1990): 245–57.

24. Mark Krikorian, *The New Case Against Immigration: Both Legal and Illegal* (London: Sentinel, 2008), 138. The report quoted by the author is taken from *The New Americans: Economic, Demographic and Fiscal Effects of Immigration*, eds. James P. Smith and Barry Edmonston (Washington, D.C.: National Academies Press, 1997).

25. Krikorian, *The New Case Against Immigration*, 138.

26. *Segundo Libro Blanco*, 34–35.

27. George J. Borjas, *Friends or Strangers: The Impact of Immigrants on the U.S. Economy* (New York: Basic Books, 1991) Chap. 3, "A Statistical Portrait of Immigrants," contains comparative data.

28. Agekananda Bharati, *The Asians in East Africa: Jayhind and Uhuru* (Chicago: Nelson-Hall Company, 1972), 108.

29. T.H.R. Davenport, *South Africa: A Modern History* (Toronto: University of Toronto Press, 1977), 91–93. See also W. H. Hutt, *The Economics of the Color Bar: A Study of the Economic Origins and Consequences of Racial Segregation in South Africa* (London: The Institute of Economic Affairs, 1964), 122.

30. Norma Stoltz Chinchilla and Nora Hamilton, "Central America," in *The New Americans: A Guide to Immigration Since 1965*, eds. Mary C. Waters and Reed Ueda (Cambridge, Mass.: Harvard University Press, 2007), 333.

31. Steven A. Camarota, "Immigrants in the United States, 1998: A Snapshot of America's Foreign-Born Population," Center for Immigration Studies, Washington, D.C., January, 1999, http://www.cis.org/articles/1999/back199.html

32. Rakesh Kochhar, "The Occupational Status and Mobility of Hispanics," Pew Hispanic Center, Washington, D.C., December 15, 2005, http://pewhispanic.org/files/reports/59.pdf

33. Thomas Sowell, *Migrations and Cultures* (New York: Basic Books, 1996), 372.

34. Christopher Claque, "Relative Efficiency, Self-Containment and Comparative Costs of Less Developed Countries," *Economic Development and Cultural Change* 39, no. 3 (April 1991): 507–530.

35. Robert Higgs, "Race, Skills, and Earnings: American Immigrants in 1909," *The Journal of Economic History* 31, no. 2 (June 1971): 421.

36. If we are to believe the report, only 54.9 percent of Armenians, 10 percent of Bulgarians, 11 percent of Croatians, 11.07 percent of Flemish, 8.41 percent of Greeks, and 43 percent of Russians spoke English. Economist Higgs did a regression analysis based on this information to see how the lack of English skills and scant literacy impacted wages. It was very clear that those who spoke no English and had little literacy were paid less, which led him to conclude that those two variables "explain almost four-fifths of the variance

in average earnings among the groups." Because of the relationship between wages and skills in this group and the wages commanded by white natives at the time, "the evidence is quite convincing," he states, "that at least some American employers preferred wealth to the pleasures of discrimination." See Higgs, "Race, Skills, and Earnings," 424–427.

37. Robert Higgs, "Landless by Law: Japanese Immigrants in Californian Agriculture to 1941," *The Journal of Economic History* 38, no. 1 (March 1978): 206.

38. Aimee Chin, "Long-Run Labor Market Effects Of Japanese-American Internment During World War II on Working Age Male Internees" (Working paper, June 2004), 29, http://www.uh.edu/~achin/research/chin_japanese_internment.pdf

39. Jack Chen, *The Chinese of America* (San Francisco: Harper & Row, 1980), 83, 93.

40. Sowell, *Migrations and Cultures*, 227.

41. Kathleen Neils Conzen, *Immigrant Milwaukee, 1836–1860: Accommodation and Community in a Frontier City* (Cambridge, Mass.: Harvard University Press, 1976), 73.

42. Anna Maria Martellone, "Italian Mass Emigration to the United States," *Perspectives in American History* New Series 1 (1984): 405.

43. Sowell, *Migrations and Cultures*, 162.

44. Catherine Ceniza Choy, "Philippines," in *The New Americans,* eds. Waters and Ueda, 559.

45. Sowell, *Migrations and Cultures*, 333.

46. Millman, *The Other Americans*, 30.

47. Millman, *The Other Americans*, 40–41.

48. Those who have studied immigrant enclaves have come to the conclusion that the rate of self-employment among foreigners—about 12 percent—is greater than that of natives. The income gap between self-employed and employed immigrants is also higher than that of natives. On average, self-employed immigrants make 48 percent more than salaried immigrants, while the gap among natives amounts to 28 percent. The range of activities among self-employed immigrants is wide, but mostly involves construction, retail, services, and professional occupations. The existence of Latino enclaves where demand for these types of services is high and there are large pools of recruits for businesses run by fellow nationals weighs heavily on the ability of many foreigners to be self-employed. Six years after their arrival in the United States, for instance, four out of every ten Cubans were employed by other Cubans, and 15 percent of Mexicans were employed by other Mexicans. See Millman, *The Other Americans*, 47. Also see chap. 10, "Immigrant Entrepreneurship and Immigrant Enclaves," in George J. Borjas, *Friends Or Strangers.*

49. Simon Kutnetz, "Immigration of Russian Jews to the United States," *Perspectives in American History* 9 (1975): 104–105, 110.

50. Richard T. Herman and Robert Smith, *Immigrant, Inc: Why Immigrant Entrepreneurs Are Driving the New Economy (And How They Will Save the American Worker)* (Hoboken, N.J.: John Wiley & Sons, 2009), xxvii.

51. For a comparison between the 1970s and the 1950s, as well as an overview of the evolving situation until 1990, see chap. 7, "Why Are the New Immigrants Less Skilled Than the Old?" in George J. Borjas, *Friends Or Strangers.*

52. The authors built algorithms (computer procedures) that recognize likely foreign names on U.S. patent applications. They analyzed 15 years of data to create an estimate of foreigners filing patents in the country. They then cross-referenced the patents held by foreign inventors with the numbers of H-1B visas awarded each year and broke down the regional location of H-1B visa recipients and patent applicants. See William K. Kerr and William F. Lincoln, "The Supply Side of Innovation: H-1B Visa Reforms and U.S. Ethnic Invention" (Working Paper 09-005, Harvard Business School, December 2008), http://www.hbs.edu/research/pdf/09-005.pdf

53. Sowell, *Migrations and Culture*, 372.

54. Robert W. Gardner, "Asian Immigration: The View From the United States," *Asia and Pacific Migration Journal* 1, no. 1 (1992): 78–79

55. Mohamed Mghari, "Exodus Of Skilled Labor: Magnitude, Determinants, and Impacts on Development," in *Arab Migration in a Globalized World* (Geneva: International Organization for Migration, League of Arab States, 2004), 76.

56. Robert Bellinger, "Indian EEs: Torn Between Home, Opportunity," *Electronic Engineering Times*, August 1, 1988, 40.

57. Neeraj Kaushal, Cordelia W. Reimers, and David M. Reimers, "Immigrants and the Economy," in *The New Americans,* eds. Waters and Ueda, 182–184.

58. Karen Isaksen Leonard, "India", in *The New Americans,* eds. Waters and Ueda, 459.

59. In the 2000 Census, 11 percent of them said they were native English speakers, while 65 percent said they spoke English well. English was the home language of 9.6 percent of Indian immigrant households, with 71.3 percent speaking Indo-European languages, and 17.7 percent speaking other Asian languages. See Karen Isaksen Leonard, "India," in *The New Americans,* eds. Waters and Ueda, 461.

60. "Asians and Pacific Islanders in the United States," U.S. Bureau of the Census (Washington, D.C.: U.S. Government Printing Office, 1993), 142, 153.

61. M. C. Madhavan, "Indian Emigrants: Numbers, Characteristics, and Economic Impact," *Population and Development Review*, September 1985, 462, 466.

62. Ewa Morawska, "Transnationalism," in *The New Americans,* eds. Waters and Ueda, 153.

63. Luis Eduardo Guarnizo and Marilyn Espitia, "Colombia," in *The New Americans,* eds. Waters and Ueda, 380.

64. Peggy Levitt, "Dominican Republic," in *The New Americans,* eds. Waters and Ueda, 402.

65. Jorge Duany, *Quisqueya on the Hudson: The Transnational Identity of Dominicans* (New York, CUNY Dominican Studies Institute, 1994).

13

Do Immigrants Cost More than They Contribute?

IT IS NOT infrequent for both critics and defenders to offer a measure of the costs and the benefits that immigrants bring to society. It is impossible, however, to arrive at an accurate estimation because the factors that would need to be calibrated are very numerous and not always measurable in currency terms. The calculations generally tend to relate specifically to the government's finances, not to the impact on society as a whole, which is what any calculation that purported to be accurate would need to be able to ascertain.

Even the fiscal cost of an immigrant is extremely difficult to estimate because it is contingent on factors such as age, education, and family composition—and because immigrants are highly mobile. Younger migrant workers with no children pay far more in taxes than they receive in benefits. Migrants with low education and earnings who bring children constitute a net fiscal cost in the first few years because of public education. Migrants who move from one state to another, from one job to another, and from one source of revenue to another will inflict varying costs on, and make varying contributions to, the rest of society in the course of a short period of time, let alone a lifetime.

The debate, nonetheless, is ongoing and figures are constantly offered. In the new millennium, the cost-benefit arguments from previous decades resurfaced in various forms. One noted anti-immigration critic postulated that high poverty levels among immigrants lessened their contribution substantially. In 2005, 17 percent of immigrants had incomes below the official poverty line, compared with 12 percent of Americans.[1] About 45 percent of immigrant households were in or near the poverty line. Since almost 29 percent of immigrant households use at least one welfare program against 18 percent in the native population who do,[2] one can see how the argument resonated with many people.

One in four uninsured Americans is an immigrant, contended the same critic; they go to emergency rooms and get treated. In the Medicare prescription bill, Congress was giving $250 million per year to the states for treatment provided to undocumented foreigners. Again, because some estimates suggested that in 2006, nearly $600 million in uncompensated care for illegals was provided by New York and $1.4 billion was provided in California,[3] two states with big immigrant populations—this line of argument was music to the ears of superficial observers. The 10-million-plus school-age children from immigrant families, the critic claimed, accounted for all of the growth in elementary and secondary school enrollment nationwide over the past generation—at a huge cost to American taxpayers.[4]

Besides repeating the arguments of the past and making the same errors, this and other detractors forget three things. First, immigrants tend to contribute more resources than they consume, and any analysis that purports to estimate the burden brought by foreigners on natives ought to at least take their contribution into serious account. Second, immigrants save more than natives, a habit that was sorely lacking in the country in the years leading to the bursting of the real estate bubble in 2007–08. In doing so, they provide a boost to investment and therefore future rewards for society as a whole. Third, arriving immigrants are generally in their most productive years, which bolsters their contribution to the economy.

Many people do not realize that undocumented foreigners pay taxes. For instance, they pay the same real estate taxes as natives, whether they own homes or their taxes are passed through rents, as well as the same sales taxes and other consumption-related levies. The majority of state and local costs of schooling and other services are funded by these taxes. Additionally, the United States Social Security Administration has estimated that three-quarters of undocumented immigrants pay payroll taxes and contribute between $6–7 billion in Social Security funds that they will be able to claim[5] (assuming that anyone will be in a position to claim Social Security benefits in the future!).

In 1997, in the midst of a decade with a particularly large influx of newcomers, the National Research Council calculated the fiscal effect of immigration in California and New Jersey. The fiscal burden was $229 per native-born New Jersey household and $1,174 per native-born California household. But after a thorough analysis of the current net fiscal impact, the Council concluded that "immigrants are a net taxpayer benefit to native households." The net benefit took place at the federal level, not the local level, making it convenient for those who attacked immigration to focus on local costs.[6] Also in 1997, a report from the National Academy of Sciences calculated the gains from immigration to be between $1 billion and $10 billion, even if the local and state tax burden of native households was increased by $229 per day nationally and $1,200 in California.[7]

Those who point to the cost of public education for undocumented children also disregard the fact that most undocumented children are in mixed status families—most are citizens, and most have one parent who is also a citizen. While it is true that one out of every five children under 18 has an immigrant parent[8] and that a majority of children in primary and secondary education are children of immigrants, it is also true that a majority of those kids have at least one parent who is legally in the country. The cost that each of those children represents is equivalent to that represented by any native child—under a system that presupposes, rightly or wrongly, that mediocre public education creates a more level field for people of all social strata and therefore will reverberate positively in the form of future social peace and economic success.

In the 1990s, when much of the anti-immigrant fervor of the new millennium was incubated, the authorities stated at one point that immigration cost taxpayers $518 million a year in the United States,[9] in large part because of education and health services to illegals. According to critics, decisions such as the 1982 *Plyer v. Doe* case, in which the Supreme Court of the United States struck down a state statute that denied funding for education to children who were illegally in the country, had contributed to skyrocketing costs through the school system. Dade County schools (Florida) had more than 16,000 undocumented children, a burden of $68 million. Hospital care was also mentioned repeatedly. By the mid-1990s, they contended, two-thirds of births in Los Angeles public hospitals were related to undocumented foreigners and New York hospitals were spending some $500 million on care for illegal immigrants.

Two researchers, Donald Huddle and David Simcox, published a study in 1994 concluding that between 1993 and 2002, immigration would cost the United States $668.5 billion in general. The calculation included not only total public expenditures minus taxes paid by immigrants based on an expected rate of immigration, but also an estimation of the cost to "displaced" natives, a highly debatable proposition.[10] Donald Huddle of Houston's Rice University became widely associated with the annual tax bill that he claimed derived from legal and illegal foreigners in 1992—$42.5 billion.[11] His and Simcox's arguments and figures have continued to be insistently cited (in updated form) into the new millennium.

Huddle failed to take into account several factors. First, because immigrants are harder to count than native-born Americans (the reporting of address changes is much slower than that of natives, for instance), federal disbursements lag behind local needs. The census makes an adjustment every ten years, but by then more immigrants have arrived and a new generation is overlooked. As one writer put it, "What Huddle proves, if anything, is that immigrants generate more short-term costs to states and localities that provide services than the federal government reimburses."[12] Secondly, and more importantly, Huddle's calculation ignored the evidence that immigration generates more tax revenues at all levels of government, including sales taxes and transaction taxes, than the fiscal burden it represents.

As Jeffrey Passel and Rebecca Clarke demonstrated, Huddle used estimation procedures that included many errors.[13] Without them, the post-1970 immigrants actually showed a surplus of revenues over costs of at least $25 billion. The first error Huddle made was to rely on income estimates for legal immigrants in Los Angeles County who entered during the 1980s, whose incomes were lower than those of other groups of immigrants who entered during the period 1970–92. Second, by understating immigrant incomes, he understated their taxes by dozens of billions of dollars.[14] Third, the study omitted several ways in which immigrant money is channeled towards the government—Social Security contributions, unemployment insurance, and gasoline taxes. Finally, he overstated the costs of social services enjoyed by immigrants by almost $10 billion.[15]

In the context of the current fiscal situation of the United States, with the "baby boom" generation beginning to draw on the unfunded liabilities of Medicare and Social Security, the fiscal and economic contribution by immigrants should not be underestimated. Since 1965, the fertility rate of natives has declined, while that of immigrants has been consistently higher—about 3.0 among Hispanics against 1.8 for native whites.[16] In the 1990s, there were periods when one out of every two new jobs were filled by immigrants, a fact that helped lessen the burden on those entitlement programs through their contributions.[17] In this new millennium, unauthorized immigrants are much less likely than United States-born residents to be 65 or older. In the case of natives, the proportion is 12 percent; in that of legal immigrants, it is 16 percent, while among illegal immigrants it is only 1.2 percent.[18]

In most wealthy countries, fertility rates are below the 2.1 percent necessary to maintain a stable population (whether maintaining a stable population is desirable is a different issue). But given the commitments made by the welfare state and their relation to the size of the workforce, the implications of a sustained drop in fertility rates are obvious. Europe, and Japan in particular, are facing an acute problem in that regard.[19] German writer Hans Magnus Enzensberger coined the phrase "demographic bulimia" to describe the contradiction in wealthy societies between decrying the low birth rate and the complaint about too many immigrants.[20]

Since World War II, migration has contributed, directly or indirectly, to two-thirds of the demographic growth in countries with sizable populations of foreign origin, including Germany, Belgium, France, and Switzerland, halving their aging rate. In Italy, a country with a negative migration balance in the three decades following World War II, the birth rate declined much more acutely, raising alarm.[21] Europeans became increasingly worried about this demographic issue for the last couple of decades and began to take stock of the challenge to their age ratios as they entered the millennium, when annual population growth amounted to 0.7 million every year only because of immigration—in a continent in which the net number of births every year adds up to merely 300,000. Without immigrants, the situation would be much worse: Germany, Italy, and Sweden would suffer a net drop in the size of their total populations.[22]

A few years ago, it was estimated that the United States would need between 4 and 10 million immigrants every year, and Germany 1 million, in order for these two countries to restore the traditional age pyramid. In the case of Germany, the conclusion was that by 2050, the ratio of labor force age to retirees would fall from 4 to 1; in Japan, another nation confronting a particularly grave demographic challenge to its statist system, it would drop to 1.5.[23] If trends continue as they are, it looks like older generations of natives will depend on the welfare provided by immigrants!

Those who calculate the cost of immigration often include the expense related to combating illegal immigration—a high cost indeed considering that in Canada, Germany, the Netherlands, the United Kingdom, and the United States, more than $17 billion is spent every year enforcing immigration laws (the care for asylum seekers is included in the figure).[24] In April 2010, the Arizona state legislature passed a statute (SB 1070) aimed at ramping up law enforcement that made it a state crime for "illegals" not to have an alien registration document, obliged the police to question the status of anyone they encounter who might be in the country illegally, and allowed citizens to sue government agencies that they think are hindering the enforcement of immigration laws. Seventeen other states signaled that they wanted to follow suit, while protests erupted across the country, triggering in turn demonstrations of support for the law in many states. The fiscal cost of enforcing it—leaving aside the effects on the economy itself— never seemed to be a problem for those who voted in favor. They did not take into account that in 2010, the enforcement budget was already roughly ten times greater than in 1993.[25]

Entrepreneurs versus the Welfare State

Part of the perception that immigrants inflict a heavy burden on society stems from the fact that newcomers tend to be relatively poor. The poverty rate for immigrants and their U.S.-born children under 18 years of age is 17 percent, nearly 50 percent higher than the rate for natives and their children. Among the poor, Hispanics are disproportionately represented. The poorest people of foreign descent are, in this order, Dominicans, Mexicans, Guatemalas, Hondurans, Jamaicans, Haitians, Koreans, Cubans, Salvadoreans, Vietnamese, Ecuadoreans, Colombians, Chinese, Germans, Brazilians, Japanese, and Peruvians. The lowest poverty rate among immigrants belongs to the Filipinos. Given the incidence of poverty among immigrants, the proportion of immigrant-headed households using at least one major welfare program in the United States is high—33 percent, compared to 19 percent for native households.[26] At the higher end of the spectrum, fewer than 5 percent of immigrants from Britain and Germany went on welfare after arriving in the late twentieth century in America; on the lower end of the spectrum, more than one-quarter of the immigrants from Vietnam and nearly half of those who came from Cambodia received welfare benefits.[27] Hispanics being the largest immigrant group and overrepresented in the poverty map, they are seen as being especially favored by the welfare state.

The perception that immigrants use the welfare system to their advantage and at the expense of the rest of society is a powerful driver of anti-immigrant sentiment both in the United States and in Europe. N'Dongo has written, "Europeans of all ages, victims of unemployment and fiscal injustices imposed by the government, are more sensitive to a certain xenophobic discourse."[28] When Europeans heard in the mid-1990s that 11 percent of pupils in German public schools and 22 percent of pupils in Swiss public schools were foreign, resentment began to incubate.[29] It was a period of immigration surge in Europe, and Europeans were frustrated by a low-productivity economic system overburdened with taxes and regulations. In the next few years, that resentment translated into increasing animosity towards immigrants, with far-right political parties or groups gaining prominence, and sporadic acts of violence catching international attention. We have seen a similar trend in the United States. The increasingly weak fiscal position of the government, saddled with skyrocketing deficits and debt, has reinforced the resentment against foreigners to judge by the strength that anti-immigrant sentiment has achieved in the last decade. The inability of successive administrations to push immigration reform through Congress attests to this.

An overgenerous welfare state and free immigration (something that does not exist today) can become a seriously problematic combination not only from a fiscal point of view but, perhaps more importantly, also because of the emotional and psychological impact on natives. Open borders threaten the welfare state not because every immigrant needs benefits, but because of the way in which benefits are structured in domestic laws. Giving immigrants fewer benefits immediately generates a reaction from those who would rather keep an unsustainable system than open the door to legal discrimination. At the same time, keeping equal benefits for people regardless of their migratory status fuels the anti-immigrant sentiment and provides it with a powerful motive against which the real facts are ineffective.

To make matters even more complicated, there are those who look at the tension between the welfare state and immigrants with high expectations. As Milton Friedman put it, "It's just obvious that you can't have free immigration and a welfare state."[30] Ideas like these have led critics of the welfare state, and even those who simply recognize the system to be unsustainable, to hope that immigration pressures will accelerate the system's final collapse. They see the conflict between the welfare state and immigration as the harbinger of a much healthier relationship between government and society in the future.[31] This may be an exaggeration since most welfare state benefits go to the old—and most immigrants are young—but clearly a disproportionately large welfare system will be used by those who can, including immigrants. Although the welfare state is by no means the prime attraction for foreigners, it might have a "pull" effect on some immigrants. For certain critics, this "pull" may be the best hope of accelerating the collapse of the welfare state.[32]

A century ago, during a previous wave of mass immigration, the federal government spent roughly $178 a year per American in today's dollars, while today it spends close to $10,000—a more than fifty-fold increase. Federal spending accounted for less than 3 percent of the economy in 1900 but grew to 20.1 percent by 2005; the combined spending of all levels of government was 8 percent of the total economy in 1900 and surpasses 31 percent today.[33] Immigrants are not responsible for this exponential growth. Between the 1920s and the end of the 1960s, the period in which the welfare state went from infancy to maturity, there was relatively little immigration compared to the period before and after that. Social Security was established in 1935, Food Stamps in 1964, Medicare and Medicaid in 1965, and the Child Nutrition Act that created the Special Supplementation Nutrition Program for Women, Infants and Children came into being in 1966. These programs spawned incentives for millions of Americans to regard the government as a social safety net. That many immigrants should have seen it in that light too is only natural, even though these programs were not a motivation for migrating to the United States.. The high proportion of foreigners using some of the programs when it was possible for illegal foreigners to do so is tied to the greater incidence of eligibility conditions—i.e., poverty—among undocumented immigrants. But clearly the original sin lies with the explosive growth of government. Given the realities of the marketplace, it is realistic to think that immigration numbers would have been different but for these programs and the welfare state.

There are many examples of countries in which immigrants are or used to be excluded from benefits open to natives. Even in the United States before and during World War II, foreigners were not eligible for relief programs—the few that existed. The labor market, not welfare, was in large measure the incentive to immigrate. If in the 1850s, a family wished to educate its children, it assumed the financial responsibility, just as many people, including poor ones, do today in other countries.[34] Immigrants who migrated to America by the droves simply adapted to that system in the way those who migrate today adapt to the prevailing public school system. Examples abound of poor people and lower middle classes that supplement or replace government-provided services around the world today because of their poor quality, insufficient reach, or politicization. A few years ago, in the process of editing a book related to a project that I directed, I discovered that relatively poor Nigerian women involved in a clothing design industry in Abeokuta are willing and happy to devote some of the earnings from their entrepreneurial activity to educating their kids in private schools, even though they could send them to public ones.[35]

The misconception about the migrants' motivations has overshadowed in part the entrepreneurial and cultural achievements of immigrants in most regions of the world. Leaders and opinion shapers should not lose sight of this truth in these times in which competitiveness is the catch phrase du jour. Anywhere you look, it is obvious that people who move to another country for reasons that do not have to do with crime are for the most part risk takers willing to sacrifice more, work harder, and strive for success more keenly than those who take for granted the relative comfort awarded to them by their native habitat. In 2007, the Google vice president said it all when he told graduates of San Jose State University, "To keep an edge, I must think and act like an immigrant."[36]

Immigrants are almost by definition entrepreneurial. Only in the 1990s did the rate of self-employment among natives of the United States catch up with that of immigrants—about 11 percent—probably because of the fascination with stories of incredible wealth associated with dot-com ventures.[37] Since then, the native rate has lagged that of immigrants again. About 15 percent of highly innovative companies backed by venture capital were founded by foreign-born entrepreneurs.[38] More than one-third of the semiconductor industry and the computer/communications industry, one-fourth of the software industry and manufacturing-related services, one-fifth of the bioscience industry, and even 8 percent of the defense and aerospace industry of the United States were started by immigrants.[39] On the 2009 Forbes list of the greatest 100 venture capitalists, six of the top eleven were immigrants.[40]

Many cities in the United States have been noticeably impacted by the entrepreneurial drive of people of foreign origin. A critical mass of immigrants helped Miami become a hub of financial services, trading, media, and development for the entire Caribbean basin and a big part of Latin America. Personal income growth averaged 11.5 percent a year in the 1970s and 7.7 percent a year in the 1980s in Dade County, which meant that by the 1990s, Miami was a powerhouse of many industries. In that decade, international tourism exceeded domestic tourism for the first time, and Miami became a leading player in the cruise ship industry.[41] Many other groups equaled or surpassed the Cuban story. As early as 1980, Indians in the United States averaged an income that was 10 percent higher than that of Americans—a fact that will surprise those who think that the Indian success story in the United States is a very recent development linked to Silicon Valley.[42]

During the past decade, immigrants have been the entrepreneurial dynamo energizing cities such as Miami, Los Angeles, and New York— starting more businesses than natives; bringing growth to the construction, food, and health-care industries; churning out new jobs; and transforming run-down or declining communities into economic hubs boiling with life and commerce.[43] The welfare state has not been a major motivation for people of foreign origin in these and other cities.

There is nothing surprising in these figures. In every United States census since 1880—a period when today's welfare state was inconceivable—immigrants have been more likely to be self-employed than natives.[44] The constant entrepreneurial infusion brought about by people who wanted to create something for themselves has translated into job opportunities for many Americans. Job growth in immigrant-dominated communities has far outpaced overall employment gains since the 1990s: between 1994 and 2004, overall employment in New York grew by 6.9 percent but rose by 27.9 percent in Jackson Heights, for instance.[45] Between 1995 and 2005, immigrants created 450,000 jobs by founding a quarter of the nation's technological and engineering companies. A quarter of New England's biotech companies had at least one immigrant founder; by 2006 they had produced sales of over $7 billion. More than 1.5 million small businesses provided jobs to 2.2 million people just before the financial and economic crisis of 2007–09.[46] In 2000, foreign-born people—among them Syrians, Iranians, Brazilians, Colombians, Vietnamese, and Dominicans—constituted 36 percent of the total population of New York, but exactly half of its self-employed workers.

Many French people, as well as outside observers, consider Moroccans troublemakers and parasites who are sucking the blood of French society. However, Moroccans' entrepreneurial drive is also in plentiful supply. Some 63 percent of Moroccan immigrants in Europe invest in real estate, and four out of every ten of those established in France own their own home. Almost one in every five Moroccan immigrants invests in commerce. The emergence of a Maghrebi elite in countries to which their parents emigrated reveals a process of adaptation by the second and third generations akin to that seen in other parts of the world. It has translated into intense economic activity. This elite invests in university centers and research laboratories, and can be found at the head of companies in areas as varied as transport, tourism, information, cleaning services, clothes, foodstuff, carpentry, and painting.[47]

The story of migration is replete with epopees of communities that rose from the very bottom to the top. The Ibos in Nigeria, the Indians in Fiji, the Lebanese in West Africa, the Jews in Central Europe, and the Chinese in Southeast Asia are some examples. The rise of communities of foreign origin often led to envy, even hatred, and to stereotypes such as those that plagued the Chinese and the Jews for many years, when they were accused of usury and exploitation because of their dominance of "middleman" activities in many countries. Jews in America may have begun as peddlers, but they rose to command department stores such as Macy's, Gimbels, Abraham & Straus, Bloomingdale's, and Saks Fifth Avenue; to supply miners with Levi jeans during the Gold Rush; to leave their indelible mark on Hart, Schaffner & Marx, Bache & Co, Florsheim, Goldman Sachs, and Simon & Schuster; as well as on the famous award named after Joseph Pulitzer.[48]

The nature of current immigration would be better understood today if the many precedents of immigrant achievement in times and countries without a welfare state comparable to that prevailing in today's rich nations were taken into account. The Japanese created the silk industry in Brazil. Even though they constituted 2 to 3 percent of the population of Sao Paulo and owned only 2 percent of the land, they produced almost a third of the agricultural output in the early 1930s.[49] By 1909, the Northern Italians who moved to Argentina and Brazil owned twice as many food and drinking establishments as natives, and ten times more barbershops.[50] By 1911, they owned half of all industrial enterprises in the metropolitan area of Sao Paulo and 20 percent of them in Rio Grande Do Sul.[51]

Across the Atlantic, the first Indian grocery store, the Bombay Emporium, was established in London in 1931. In a matter of a few decades, the Indian community, as is well known, came to dominate the trade. In 1945, the year when the modern welfare state was founded in Britain, there were only 1,000 Indian doctors in the British Isles; in a few decades, they would number by the dozens of thousands.[52]

The story of how the welfare state in the United States grew during the twentieth century is widely documented and is not the main topic of this book. It is a story that has its fundamental pillars in the New Deal of the 1930s and the entitlements and programs created in the 1960s and 1970s, although many other periods have seen significant additions. Reform has occasionally taken place—for instance, regarding the welfare program in the 1990s—but the net effect of the last century was a colossal growth of the government's size and participation in social and economic matters. In that period, interests became "rights," a distortion that, fed by a political system favoring group interests advanced through the mercantilist machinery of government rather than individual rights, generated an unhealthy level of state power.[53] The 2007–08 financial and economic debacle added newer and deeper forms of statism to the system on both sides of the Atlantic through bailouts, rescues, stimulus programs, monetary expansion, and other forms of spending and government meddling.

At numerous stages in this process, the law, whether through political decisions or through the courts, protected illegal foreigners' access to services on the grounds that not doing so would undermine the principle of equality before the law. The traumatic legacy of race relations in the country accounts in large measure for this. In 1971, the Supreme Court held that being alien ("alienage") was constitutionally a "suspect classification" for states to establish in making distinctions among their residents. Much later, Proposition 187 in California, which sought to deny health, education, and welfare benefits to illegal immigrants and their children, was never put into practice because the courts held it back and eventually struck it down. Even the provisions that prohibited welfare payments and food stamps to legal foreigners in the Welfare Reform Act of 1996 were eroded in just a couple of years.[54]

However, participation by immigrants in welfare programs of one kind or another has declined sharply since then. More generally, the notion that welfare is a primary objective of migration is belied by several facts. The evidence points to work being a much more important motive than welfare. In this, contemporary immigrants do not differ from immigrants in the past, when welfare was much less widely available and pervasive in the developed world. In 2003, to take a not-too-distant year, more than 90 percent of illegal men worked in the United States, a work rate higher rate than that of citizens of the United States or of legal foreigners.[55] At the beginning of the 1990s, a period associated with high immigration, the proportion of foreigners receiving public assistance was only 1.7 percent higher than that of natives—9.1 percent against 7.4 percent.[56] Another fact often overlooked is that, despite the erosion of some of the provisions in recent laws, undocumented foreigners are mostly ineligible for welfare, food stamps, Medicaid, and other public benefits.[57]

There is no reason to think that a system that provided much fewer services funded by taxpayers would significantly alter the attractiveness of the United States or European countries for migrants. Some contemporary examples attest to the fact, moreover, that there is nothing Utopian about conceiving of a modern society without the kind of overextended, bloated welfare state associated with developed nations today—and attracting immigrants at the same time. One of the wealthiest places on earth, Hong Kong, built a very different system from the 1960s onward. The incorporation of women into the labor force led to the need for immigrant women for childcare and eldercare in Hong Kong. Because the state viewed those functions as the responsibility of the family and not the government, the premises for some of the fundamental aspects of the welfare state did not exist in the form they did in other wealthy societies. The government stated its position very clearly: "Social welfare services should not be organized in such . . . a way as to . . . accelerate the breakdown of the national or traditional sense of responsibility—for example by encouraging the natural family unit to shed on to social welfare agencies, public or private, its moral responsibility to care for the aged or the infirm."[58] Contrast this with Germany and Britain, countries that have been paying unemployment benefits for five years, or France, where those benefits are guaranteed for two years.[59]

In 1975, Hong Kong opened a legal immigration channel for domestic workers from other Asian countries. Until that point, they were only allowing unskilled workers in if they were from China. This change in policy occurred in part because of pressure by Western families in Hong Kong, who clamored for domestic service. By 2001, there were 232,000 immigrant domestic workers, a great majority of them Filipinos.[60] Absent from this dynamic was the welfare state that some in Western nations mistakenly identify as the fundamental reason for immigration.

Ecuador is a poor South American country with a stifling economic environment. But stories of Ecuadoran success in the United States abound. Antonio Grijalba's human resources and administration services firm was listed as one of the 500 fastest-growing private companies by *Inc.* magazine.[61] Hector Delgado turned a tiny travel agency into a major operation with two dozen locations in New York and $1 billion in annual revenues just before the 2007–08 financial crisis. These and other Ecuadorans were much more interested in the enabling environment of the United States as a vehicle for their entrepreneurial aspirations than in the welfare state. In 2001, Yet-Ming Chiang from Taiwan, Ric Fulop from Venezuela, Bart Riley from the United States, and Gururaj Deshpande from India founded A123 Systems, a company that made high-tech lithium-ion batteries of the kind that might one day sustain a worldwide electric car industry. By 2009, they employed 1,800 people on three continents and had raised more than $250 million from investors.[62]

Sergey Brin, the co-founder of Google, left Russia as a kid; Pierre Omidyar, founder of eBay, is the child of Iranian immigrants in France; Andrew Grove, founder of Intel, was born in Hungary; Jerry Yang, co-founder of Yahoo, came from Taiwan; and Elon Musk, co-founder of PayPal, is a South African. Carmen Castillo migrated to the United States from Spain when she was 22. Three years on, she launched Superior Design International from her one-bedroom apartment—a consultancy firm that helps corporations source IT experts. By early 2009, she was operating in Fort Lauderdale one of the largest Hispanic-owned businesses in America and one of the largest woman-owned businesses in the world.[63] If the word "welfare" is to be associated with these people, it is only to the extent that they have brought it to millions of Americans who benefit from their achievements—just as these immigrants made the best of the environment they found in this country.

It would be naive to think that all immigrants are equally entrepreneurial, or even that all immigrants from the same place of origin are similarly endowed. Of course, there are differences. Northern Italians, from a region particularly noteworthy for its capitalist tradition, are prevalent among the most outstanding Italian American entrepreneurs of the past. This suggests that the high representation of Northern Italians among migrants from Italy to Argentina and Brazil was also an important factor in the extraordinary role played by Italian immigration in South America. Back then, Argentina offered an enabling environment that allowed these foreigners to exploit their potential. Other immigrants were less successful. But even allowing for major differences in potential and achievement among various immigrant groups in the past and today, the overall result is a general infusion of economic activity. That is true of people from noted capitalist cultures and people from countries much less known for their entrepreneurial potential.

Many years ago, noted economist Mancur Olson compared German and Haitian immigrants in the United States. Using the 1980 census, he saw that self-employed Haitians earned on average $18,900 and salaried Haitians earned $10,900, while the respective figures for foreigners of German origin were $27,300 and $21,900. He inferred from these relative levels of achievement that Germans have twice as much human capital as Haitians. Therefore, with German levels of human capital, the country of Haiti ought to have twice the per capita level of income that it has. But with twice its level of per capita income at the time, Haiti would still have had one-fifth of Germany's level of income per person. Olson concluded that human capital—i.e., cultural factors—were not enough to explain the varying performances of different countries. The other key factor is the prevailing institution environment—i.e., the formal and informal rules of the game, including the enforcement of property rights. When placed in the same environment, in this case the United States, the difference between Germans and Haitians was much less acute in terms of economic performance than it was between the two countries themselves.[64] This kind of evidence should give pause to those who think nationals from certain countries are particularly undesirable given their inability to do something for themselves, and their tendency to live off the rest. People from all kinds of backgrounds do better when the environment in which they act facilitates progress. Of course, the institutional environment itself cannot be totally separated from the cultural environment since culture increases or decreases the prospects of successful implementation of useful ideas. But, again, people with cultural traits that are not prone to generating prosperity adapt to different environments, thereby undergoing a cultural transformation.

The mantra about the exploitation of the welfare state by foreigners is a red herring that preempts a more fundamental discussion about how and why modern society has come to sustain a fiscal and regulatory behemoth. Despite the general prosperity of modern society, the welfare state is gradually undermining the forces of creativity, entrepreneurship, and success, creating perverse incentives not just for immigrants, but for all citizens. Because foreigners have more limited access and more immediate needs, as well as a striving attitude and a desire to do well in the host nation, they have less incentive to depend on the welfare state than poor natives themselves. But ultimately, any citizen to whom redistributed wealth is offered will have a perverse incentive to take it. That is not an immigrant problem. It is human nature.

Few angles of the discussion on immigration are more sensitive than that of the welfare state. Who wants undesirable aliens coming to one's country to live off one's hard work by exploiting public services funded through taxation? As with other aspects of the matter at hand, many factors contribute to obfuscating the truth—among them are (1) the consequences of having a law that is fiction, (2) the growth of a welfare state that provides very little welfare and very much state, and (3) the prevalence of a system that prefers to spread its excesses evenly rather than be seen to discriminate against a group of citizens. And if a way were found to exclude immigrants from the welfare system altogether, and to let them come into the country on the condition that they pay for those things we associate with the welfare state—surely this would be called discrimination. Issues are confused, facts distorted, and principles blurred. This confusion makes the arguments over welfare state and immigration reflective of ideological or sentimental bias to such an extent that people who have certain beliefs end up supporting ideas and programs that would in practice undermine those very beliefs. Thomas Sowell warned many years ago that the "combination of immigration laws, welfare state benefits and schemes to keep foreigners foreign are leading to potentially explosive conflicts."[65]

The discussion is not helped by the United States' obsessive focus on inequality—that is, the relative incomes of various groups as opposed to the social mobility and progress of individuals and families in general. By the new millennium, the Gini coefficient that measures inequality on a scale of 0 (total equality) to 1 (total inequality) had risen to 0.466 from a score of 0.399 in the 1960s. This fact has served to fuel academic, media, and popular hostility towards the free enterprise system, blaming it for spreading poverty.[66] While purporting to stand for the free market, the reaction by those on the opposite side has actually reinforced the focus on inequality by feeding the notion that immigrants negatively affect incomes. Free-marketeers have also ingrained in many citizens the conviction that foreigners are a burden on society because they are the disproportionate beneficiaries of the programs and services that we tend to call the "welfare state." Squashed somewhere in the midst of the contentious debate lies the truth about what immigrants want and do, the real origin of the welfare state, and the entrepreneurial contribution of immigration. Somewhere in this debate is the answer to where the real blame should lie for a system that in large parts of the developed world is bankrupt, not only because its liabilities are unfunded, but more importantly because it saps people's ability to create even more wealth.

As we will see next, the discussion about the impact of immigration—its costs, benefits, and general effects—on the United States, Europe, and other parts of the world is not helped by the fact that the ideological waters have been muddied over the years. The lack of clear thinking on both sides of the ideological spectrum has turned facts and information into a very small part of the discussion.

Notes

1. Steven A. Camarota, "Immigrants at Mid-Decade: A Snapshot of America's Foreign-Born Population in 2005," Table 10, Center for Immigration Studies, Washington, D.C., December 2005, http://www.cis.org/articles/2005/back1405.pdf

2. Camarota, "Immigrants at Mid-Decade."

3. For New York figures, see Jack Martin, "The Costs of Illegal Immigration to New Yorkers," Federation For American Immigration Reform, September 2006, http://fairus .org/site/DocServer/NYCosts.pdf?docID=1161. For California, see Jack Martin and Ira Mehlman, "The Costs of Illegal Immigrantion to Floridians," Federation For American Immigration Reform, October 2005, http://fairus.org/site/DocServer/fla_study.pdf?doc ID=601

4. Mark Krikorian, *The New Case Against Immigration: Both Legal and Illegal* (London: Sentinel, 2008), 175.

5. Jeffrey S. Passel, "Unauthorized Migrants: Numbers and Characteristics," Pew Hispanic Center, Washington, D.C., June 2005, http://pewhispanic.org/files/reports /46.pdf

6. Neeraj Kaushal, Cordelia W. Reimers, and David M. Reimers, "Immigrants and the Economy," in *The New Americans: A Guide to Immigration Since 1965,* eds. Mary C. Waters and Reed Ueda (Cambridge, Mass.: Harvard University Press, 2007), 184.

7. Samuel T. Francis, "America Extinguished: Mass Immigration and the Disintegration of American Culture," (Monterey, Va.: Americans for Immigration Control, 2002), 26–27.

8. Mary C. Waters and Reed Ueda, "Introduction," in *The New Americans*, eds. Waters and Ueda, 3.

9. Georgie Anne Geyer, *Americans No More* (New York: The Atlantic Press, 1996), 316.

10. Donald Huddle and David Simcox, "The Impact of Immigration on the Social Security System," *Population and Environment: A Journal of Interdisciplinary Studies* 16, no. 1 (September 1994), 91–97.

11. Donald Huddle, "The Cost of Immigration," Carrying Capacity Network, Washington D.C., July 1993.

12. Joel Millman, *The Other Americans* (New York: Viking, 1997), 49.

13. Jeffrey S. Passel and Rebecca L. Clarke, "How Much Do Immigrants Really Cost: Reappraisal of Huddle's 'The Cost of Immigrants'" (manuscript), The Urban Institute, Washington D.C., February 1994. Cited in Michael Fix and Jeffrey S. Passel, "Immigration and Immigrants: Setting the Record Straight," The Urban Institute, Washington, D.C., May 1994, 60.

14. Jeffrey S. Passel, "Immigrants and Taxes: A Reappraisal of Huddle's 'The Cost of Immigrants'" (Policy Discussion Paper PRIP-II-29, Program For Research on Immigration, The Urban Institute, Washington D.C.). Cited in Fix and Passel, "Immigration and Immigrants," 60–61.

15. Some of the overstated costs involved basing the calculation regarding the cost of providing services to all immigrants on the cost of providing them to legal immigrants in Los Angeles County, overstating the rate of participation of foreigners in certain programs as well as the respective costs, exaggerating the enrollment of immigrants in public schools, and using an estimate of the size of the illegal population that was 50 percent above the real one. Huddle's paper failed to take into account the impacts of programs on natives or society at large—assuming that not all the services were wasted on the immigrants. See Passel and Clarke, "How Much Do Immigrants Really Cost?" 61–62.

16. For the effect of immigration on fertility rates in America and Europe, see "A Tale of Two Bellies," *The Economist* (August 22, 2002); and "Half a Billion Americans?" *The Economist* (August 22, 2002).

17. Neeraj Kaushal, Cordelia W. Reimers, and David M. Reimers, "Immigrants and the Economy," in *The New Americans,* eds. Waters and Ueda), 185.

18. Jeffrey S. Passel and D'Vera Cohn, "A Portrait of Unauthorized Immigrants in the United States," Pew Hispanic Center, March 2008. The research is based on the March "Current Population Surveys" conducted by the U.S. Census Bureau through 2008, http://pewhispanic.org/files/reports/107.pdf

19. OECD, *Trends in International Migration: Continuous Reporting System on Migration* (Paris: OECD, 2001).

20. Hans Magnus Enzensberger, *Civil War* (London: Granta Books, 1994), 117.

21. Bullent Kaya, *The Changing Face of Europe—Population Flows in the 20th Century*, (Strasbourg: Council of Europe Publishing, 2002), 54.

22. Lant Princhett, *Let Their People Come* (Washington, D.C.: Center for Global Development, 2006), 12–13.

23. Enzensberger, *Civil War*, 134.

24. Princhett, *Let Their People Come*, 64. See also Philip Martin, "There is Nothing More Permanent than Temporary Foreign Workers," Center for Immigration Studies, Washington, D.C., April 2001, http://www.cis.org/articles/2001/back501.html

25. Edward Schumacher-Matos, "Try McCain's Border Plan," *The Washington Post*, July 30, 2010, A21.

26. Steven A. Camarota, "Immigrants in the United States—A Profile of America's Foreign-Born Population," Center for Immigration Studies, Washington, D.C., November 2007, http://www.cis.org/immigrants_profile_2007.

27. Peter Brimelow, *Alien Nation: Common Sense About America's Immigration Disaster* (New York: Random House, 1995), 287.

28. Manuel Ruben N'Dongo, *Regard sur l'Immigration Africaine en Europe: Les Dictatures Africaines, Causes et Effects de l'Emmigration* (Paris: Éditions des Ecrivains, 1999), 12.

29. Kaya, *The Changing Face of Europe*, 67.

30. Peter Brimelow, "Milton Friedman at 85," *Forbes*, December 29, 1997, http://www.forbes.com/forbes/1997/1229/6014052a.html

31. Journalist Tom Bethell, for instance, wrote that "a few million more 'undocumented' newcomers may just finish off the welfare state: one more argument for an open border." See Tom Bethell, "Immigration, Si; Welfare, No," *American Spectator*, November 1993.

32. On Friedman, immigration, and the welfare state, see a PowerPoint presentation by Bryan Caplan, from George Mason University, "Immigration Restrictions: A Solution In Search of a Problem," http://econfaculty.gmu.edu/bcaplan/Immigration.ppt

33. Chris Edwards, "Downsizing the Federal Government," The Cato Institute, November 2005.

34. Susan Adler, "Education in America," *The Freeman: Ideas on Liberty* 43, no. 2 (1993), http://www.fee.org/publications/the-freeman/issue.asp?fid=156 Also see Robert P. Murphy, "The Origins of the Public School Idea," *The Freeman: Ideas on Liberty* 48, no. 7.

35. See Thompson Ayodele, "The Nigerian Design Industry, "in *Lessons from the Poor* (Oakland, Calif.: The Independent Institute, 2008), 163–204.

36. Richard T. Herman and Robert L Smith, *Immigrant Inc: Why Immigrant Entrepreneurs Are Driving the New Economy (and how they will save the American worker)* (Hoboken, N.J.: John Wiley & Sons, 2009), xxix–xxx.

37. In 2005, according to a study by the Kauffman Foundation, an average of 0.35 percent of the adult immigrant population created a new business each month, compared to 0.28 percent for natives. Pittsburg, an old industrial town in California, is a good example of immigrant entrepreneurship beyond the traditional centers of economic activity by foreigners. In good part because of the dominant Filipino community, most of its residents are self-employed. The steel mill was able to reopen thanks to Korean money. For the comparison between self-employment among natives and immigrants in the 1990s,

see John Gartner, *The Hypomanic Edge: The Link Between (A Little) Craziness and (A Lot of) Success in America* (New York: Simon & Schuster, 2005). Cited in Herman and Smith, *Immigrant Inc.*, 16.

38. Llewellyn H. Rockwell, Jr., "Sad End to the Immigration Issue," *Lewrockwell .com* (blog), May 17, 2009.

39. "Special Report on Entrepreneurship," *The Economist*, March 12, 2009, 12, http: //www.economist.com/surveys/displaystory.cfm?story_id=13216025

40. Among them, Pierre Omidyar, founder of eBay, was born in France to Iranian immigrants; Andrew Grove, founder of Intel, emigrated from Hungary; Jerry Yang, co-founder of Yahoo, migrated to the United States from Taiwan; and Elon Musk, co-founder of PayPal, moved from South Africa to the United States. This is perfectly in keeping with tradition. First-generation immigrants founded Warner Brothers, Anheuser Busch, Goya Foods, Goldman Sachs, Paramount Pictures, Max Factor, Sbarro, and many others. Foreigners founded Dow Chemical, Dupont, Pfizer, Procter & Gamble, Carnegie Steel (later U.S. Steel), and Carnival Cruises. See Herman and Smith, *Immigrant Inc.*, xxvi.

41. Michael Fix and Wendy Zimmermann, "After Arrival: An Overview of Federal Immigrant Policy in the United States," in *Immigration and Ethnicity: The Integration Of America's Newest Arrivals*, eds. Barry Edmonston and Jeffrey S. Passell (Washington, D.C.: Urban Institute Press, 1994), 256–258.

42. Peter Xenos, *Asian Indians in the United States: A 1980 Census Profile* (Honolulu: East-West Population Institute, 1989), 35.

43. Jonathan Bowles and Tara Colton, "A World of Opportunity," Center for an Urban Future, February 2007, 3–4, http://www.nycfuture.org

44. Bowles and Colton, "A World of Opportunity," 4, http://www.nycfuture.org

45. Bowles and Colton, "A World of Opportunity," 6, 9, http://www.nycfuture.org

46. Herman and Smith, *Immigrant Inc.*, xxv, 10–11.

47. Mohamed Khachani, "Moroccan Migration to Europe: What Impact On The Economies of Countries of Origin," in *Arab Migration in a Globalized World* (Geneva: International Organization for Migration, League of Arab States, 2004), 42, 49.

48. Both in the United States and Latin America, Jewish immigrants brought with them from Central and Eastern Europe the skills of the garment industry and changed forever the patterns of clothing for the poor. Most Jews who arrived in Latin America in the early twentieth century, where there was no welfare to sustain them, began as peddlers too, but they created much of the clothing and textile industry in Brazil, Chile, and Argentina. Jews branched out into many other areas across the hemisphere, established Colombia's principal airline, contributed some of Mexico's most prominent doctors, and started hundreds of factories in Venezuela. The success of Jews in Argentina in the early twentieth century and again after 1945 was initially met with resentment but has come to be recognized as one of the great contributions to Argentina's success—before the nation's wealth was squandered by populism in the second half of the twentieth century. See Thomas Sowell, *Migrations and Cultures* (New York: Basic Books, 1996), 295. Also see Robert Weisbrot, *The Jews of Argentina: From Inquisition to Peron* (Philadelphia: The Jewish Publication Society of America, 1979), 176–184.

49. Patrick Makoto Fukunaga, "The Brazilian Experience: The Japanese Immigration During the Period of the Vargas Regime and the Immediate Aftermath, 1930–1946," (PhD thesis, University of California at Santa Barbara, 1983), 36–42, http://searchworks.stanford.edu/view/1578290

50. Carl Solberg, *Immigration and Nationalism: Argentina and Chile, 1890–1914* (Austin, Tex.: Institute of Latin American Studies, University of Texas, 1970), 38.

51. Emilio Willems, "Brazil," in *The Positive Contribution by Immigrants*, ed. Oscar Handlin (Paris: United Nations Educational, Scientific and Cultural Organization, 1960), 133, http://unesdoc.unesco.org/images/0006/000681/068180eo.pdf

52. Rozina Visram, *Asians in Britain: 400 Years of History* (London: Pluto Press, 2002), 278–281.

53. For a description of the gradual creation of legal statuses and entitlements in the course of the last century, see, for instance, Peter H. Schuck and Rogers M. Smith, "*Citizenship Without Consent: Illegal Aliens in the American Policy* (New Haven, Conn.: Yale University Press, 1985).

54. Francis, "America Extinguished," 61.

55. Randolph Capps and Michael E. Fix, "Undocumented Immigrants: Myths and Reality," The Urban Institute, Washington D.C., November 2005. Also see Passel and Capps et al., "Undocumented Immigrants."

56. George J. Borjas, *Friends Or Strangers: The Impact Of Immigrants On The U.S. Economy,*" (New York: Basic Books, July, 1991), P.6.

57. Michael Fix, Wendy Zimmermann, and Jeffrey S. Passel, "The Integration of Immigrant Families in the United States," The Urban Institute, Washington D.C., July 2001, http://www.urban.org/UploadedPDF/immig_integration.pdf

58. For an account of female labor in Hong Kong, see Pui-lan, Kwok, Grace Chow, Lee Ching-Kwan, and Rose Wu, "Women and the State in Hong Kong," in ed. Fanny M. Cheung, *Engendering Hong Kong Society: A Gender Perspective of Womens' Status* (Hong Kong: Chinese University Press, 1997).

59. Samuel Huntington, *Who Are We? The Challenges of America's National Identity* (New York: Simon & Schuster, 2004), 74.

60. Nana Oishi, *Women in Motion: Globalization, State Policies, and Labor Migration in Asia*, 25–27.

61. Bowles and Colton, "A World of Opportunity," *Center for an Urban Future*, February 2007, 53, http://www.nycfuture.org

62. Herman and Smith, *Immigrant, Inc.*, 1–6.

63. Herman and Smith, *Immigrant, Inc.*, 45–50.

64. Mancur Olson, "Why Some Nations Are Rich, and Others Poor," in *Making Poor Nations Rich*, ed. Benjamin Powell (Oakland, Calif.: The Independent Institute, 2008), 42–43.

65. Sowell, *Migrations and Cultures*, 388.

66. "Measures of Household Income Inequality: 1967 to 2001," (Historical Income Tables-Income Inequality, Table 1E.6.), U.S. Census Bureau, Washington D.C., September 2009, http://www.census.gov/hhes/www/income/histinc/ie1.html

PART IV

Open Minds

14

Is Immigration a Left-Wing
or a Right-Wing Cause?

IT IS NOT easy to find an issue that cuts across the ideological divide in the way immigration does. Broadly speaking, the right favors strong immigration controls and forceful assimilation of immigrants who are allowed into the country, while the left favors more welcoming policies, as well as diversity and multiculturalism. But these clear-cut lines of demarcation are misleading. The real divide takes place within each camp and there are, albeit for different reasons, tacit coalitions of leftists and rightists on both side of the issue.

Immigration has opened fissures among conservative as well as liberals in many parts of the world, not just in the United States. This includes Latin America, for instance, where a nationalist right in the Dominican Republic wants to keep the Haitians at bay, but more free-market-oriented classical liberals have traditionally defended them. I used to host a TV program that was produced in Santo Domingo and aired in other parts of Latin America; I remember quite vividly the stark contrast in the positions adopted by people who were otherwise ideologically akin. In Chile, the free-market right has been supportive of the many thousands of undocumented Peruvians who live in that country, but the nationalist right, prone to political conflict with Peru whose own nationalists are obsessively anti-Chilean, has not been as friendly.

In Mexico, the right tends to be very defensive when Mexican immigrants in the United States are mistreated but implacable in *its* treatment of Guatemalans or Central Americans in general. On the left, organized labor has been very slow to defend immigrants in Latin America, but non-governmental organizations (NGOs) have usually been more sympathetic.

On the European left, meanwhile, the unions have been a bellwether of evolving and sometimes conflicting attitudes to immigrants, as they have in the United States. There was a time when immigrants from Asia and the West Indies were still the objects of some discriminatory practices in Britain, a similar situation to the one that, in the view of Britain's labor unions, was affecting part of the native population too. And yet the unions often propped up policies and practices that discriminated against immigrants in the workplace.[1] Today's unions in Britain, as in other parts of the developed world, have a more amenable view towards foreign workers. Most unions don't take an activist role against foreign workers or put together lobbying efforts on a large scale, but the anti-immigrant part of their legacy is still felt. The Labour Party is heavily influenced by unions, which are at the core of that political organization's origins. The Labour Party put immigration controls on people coming from Commonwealth nations under Tony Blair—a demand that the nationalist right had been insistent upon.

Since at least the 1960s in Britain, a branch of the conservative right, led by Enoch Powell, a torrential speaker and firebrand populist, had been warning of violence if curbs were not placed on foreigners. A phrase from one of his speeches, in which he quoted from the Romans, still echoes today and is often cited by friends and foes alike: "I seem to see the river Tiber foaming with much blood."[2] It is striking that a man such as the late Powell, loathed by the British left and antithetical in almost every regard to the union movement, could in practice have found himself, from the 1970s until quite recently, on the same side as organized labor, albeit with a distinct rhetoric and a focus on specific aspects of the issue he felt strongly about.

In the United States, the split on the issue of immigration has also been visible on the left for quite some time, although it used to be much more acute. Organized labor was traditionally opposed to immigration. The irony is that iconic labor leaders such as César Chávez, a Mexican American, were not so long ago vociferous critics of illegal immigration. They accused big business, and therefore part of the right, of being behind the insufficient and timid efforts by the authorities to stamp out illegal immigration. Today, part of organized labor remains suspicious of immigration, but some union leaders and members who have seen in immigration a way to offset the dwindling membership have grown more amicable to the idea over the years. Non-Hispanic so-called minorities— for instance, important groups in the black community—reflect mixed feelings.

Some see immigrants as competitors, while others consider them allies against discrimination and in favor of multiculturalism. After almost a century of anti-immigration positions, the unions began to shift gradually in the 1970s, when efforts to recruit more Americans began to show clear signs of difficulty. Their increasing support of immigrant rights did not embrace newcomers, whom they continued to see as a threat, but they did support the legalization of those already in the United States, whom they perceived as a potential mine of new members.

Some of the first visible symptoms of the shift in the union position on immigration emerged in the 1980s with the creation of the National Immigration Forum with union backing. The tendency grew; by 2000, the AFL-CIO (American Federation of Labor and Congress of Industrial Organizations) was rescinding its support of the restrictive law of 1996 on the grounds that it forced illegal immigrants to work under exploitative conditions because of their legal status. This move signified a momentous change, given the history of the labor movement.[3]

The gradual change of position in the labor unions has had the unintended effect of aligning organized labor with the business community. Beyond constituting an ideological curiosity, the importance of this goes to the heart of the contemporary debate in American society over what to do with millions of undocumented workers and market necessities that virtually guarantee the arrival of many more in the future. In the context of the deep divide within the political parties and social organizations over ideological issues, the relative coincidence of views between organized labor and business interests on the matter of immigration marks a notable contrast.

The situation on the right in the United States and other parts of the world is equally interesting from an ideological point of view. On paper, immigration ought to be treated by the free-market right at least as being akin to capital, goods, services, and ideas—i.e., as something that should transcend barriers and allow adjustments between the forces of supply and demand among regions and countries. I say "at least" because human beings take precedence, in any humane view of the world, over other subjects of free trade—goods, services, or capital. Furthermore, the evident role played by immigration in the rise of free nations, the close connection between liberal democracy and the notion of refuge or sanctuary, and the treatment given by totalitarian regimes to those wishing to emigrate point almost by default to immigration as a cause close to the free-market right's heart. And yet the free-market right in the United States, Europe, and Latin America is split on this issue, sometimes very bitterly.

An undercurrent of nationalist sentiment, usually, but not always, cloaked under economic, political, or moral arguments, runs within groups and organizations otherwise inclined to free trade and free markets. Such groups and organizations are locked in a tough struggle with the pro-immigration members of their own family, as reflected, for instance, in the divisions within conservative political parties (among them the Republicans in the United States, the Tories in Britain, or the Popular Party in Spain). This struggle also occurs within the business community, which believes in the blessings of foreign labor both skilled and unskilled, and among media networks, often more prone to whip up nativist fear. In Spain, a sector of the Popular Party attacked the Socialists consistently in the first decade of the twenty-first century for being too permissive. But the same Popular Party, under the leadership of Esperanza Aguirre, president of the autonomous community of Madrid, has led a wide-ranging initiative aimed at establishing fruitful exchanges with immigrants and bringing the party closer to foreign residents by offering programs to facilitate assimilation. The Roman Catholic Church is also torn between two strands on both sides of the Atlantic. Catholics in the United States are at the front line of the pro-immigration cause, while right-wing activists who are influential in Protestant denominations are in the opposite camp.

In the 1990s, by far the most ardent pro-immigration forces in the U.S. were agricultural interests, that is, farmers, in the Northwest and Southwest. They valued the economic effect of immigration, particularly cheap labor. Other types of organizations linked to business and the economy were very vocal too. U.S. Chamber of Commerce, the Associated General Contractors of America, the American Retail Federation, and Kmart Corporation raised their voices.[4] Later, emblematic leaders of the high-tech IT revolution, such as Bill Gates, were at the forefront of the pro-immigration camp, making the economic argument for more open policies. The ideological as well as the economic argument on the right came from the *Wall Street Journal,* which has maintained a pro-immigration stance for decades but was especially vocal in the defense of open borders in the 1990s.[5] The newspaper even editorialized in favor of a constitutional amendment that would guarantee free immigration.[6] Emblematic figures of the intellectual right such as Grover Norquist campaigned against a proposal in Congress that would have restricted legal immigration even further in 1996.[7]

Other social forces linked directly or indirectly to the establishment were also highly active in the pro-immigration camp. One notable example is the Catholic Church, which has a large stake in the immigration issue as it affects millions of Catholic Latin American migrants. The Conference of Catholic Bishops took up a very public institutional position. The connections between the Catholic Church and the immigrant community at the grassroots level are well known. Newly arrived immigrants usually come into contact with Catholic networks in order to find access into the new society, including work possibilities. It is not uncommon for immigrants who fear being deported, or who have been advised to leave the country, to seek refuge in Catholic churches around the country, sometimes making the television news, particularly Univision, the most powerful Spanish-language network in the United States.

Some of the most important pieces of legislation regarding immigration have vividly exposed the left-right coalitions on both sides of the political divide. Despite the strong pushback by parts of both the right and the left, Congress passed strongly restrictive measures in the mid-1990s, when Bill Clinton reached a compromise with a Republican-controlled Congress. Title IV of the Personal Responsibility and Work Opportunity Act and the Medicaid Restructuring Act confirmed the ineligibility of undocumented and non-migrant foreigners for most welfare benefits. This measure reflected a growing anti-immigrant sentiment at a time of massive immigration prompted by a growing economy; it was only partially offset by the arguments made by pro-immigration intellectual, political, and business-related organizations and leaders.[8] Most notable was not so much the defeat of the pro-immigration camp, but the fact that the political composition on both sides was very heterodox.

When, in April 2010, the governor of Arizona signed a controversial law (SB 1070) that, in effect, made undocumented immigration a state crime and granted the police authority to request documentation from anyone it deemed suspect, the discomfort among many members of the Republican Party was very telling. That law, approved by the Republican majority in the state legislature and supported by Arizona conservatives, placed many right and center-right politicians who favor a realistic immigration approach in an impossible quandary. Since polls were showing that an overwhelming majority of Arizonians backed the law, Senator John McCain, then locked in a bitter primary battle for the nomination to be reelected, had to twist his thought process and his language painfully and embarrassingly in order to defend what he clearly thought was indefensible. Just as awkwardly, he had to use vague terms hoping that his traditional supporters, and Hispanics in general, could perceive them as a wink signifying his subtle message that he would revert to his traditional position when the campaign was over. Others, such as Republican Senator Lindsey Graham, were much more direct about it and said that the law was unconstitutional.[9]

The tension within each camp was no less intense and public than that between the two parties. One side of the Republican Party—even its conservative community —who were more inclined towards libertarian ideas was incensed with a law that would corner the organization into a nativist position and alienate it from an emerging force in society. But the base of the party and its Southern leadership, disregarding a history of iconic conservatives from Winston Churchill to Ronald Reagan who embraced immigration, seemed intent on forcing the Republicans to adopt a tough anti-immigrant stance. This stood in the face of signals that the Obama administration, which also encountered resistance among conservative Democrats, wanted to combine stricter border security with a path to legalization for foreigners already in the country. In turn, Democrats who tended to be pro-immigration put forward reform proposals that generally sought to emphasize the law enforcement and border security aspects as a precondition for any permissiveness towards undocumented foreigners, even though there had been a 50 percent reduction in the number of illegal entries in previous years. These party divisions reflected, no doubt, the geographical divisions over immigration in the country.

Eventually, the Obama administration filed a lawsuit against the Arizona law claiming that immigration policy is, according to the Constitution, a matter for the federal government, not the state legislatures; the Supremacy Clause was invoked. Many observers saw this suit as a political, rather than legal, statement, considering that there are precedents for immigration policy being conducted by states (many Southern states tied immigration to race and property in the nineteenth century, for example). A District Court judge later blocked the toughest provisions of the law—the opening shots of a prolonged legal battle. On paper, at least, it seems clear that immigration policy is made at the federal level, although the application has varied from state to state based on different criteria and on less than strict adherence to the federal statutes. The Obama administration also filed a suit in August, 2010, against the town of Fremont, Nebraska, seeking to overturn an ordinance banning illegal immigrants from taking jobs or renting homes. In June 2012, the Supreme Court finally struck down three of the four provisions of the Arizona law, including the one that allowed the police to arrest a person purely on the suspicion of being an illegal immigrant. The police can still check the immigrant status of anyone that is stopped or detained for other reasons if they suspect that person is an illegal immigrant.

Generally speaking, it is probably accurate to say that Republicans closely connected to states with large numbers of immigrants have a personal inclination to see them with sympathy. Senator John McCain, from Arizona, has usually been on the side of the immigrants—despite his support, for purely electoral reasons, of the 2010 Arizona law. It is likely that George W. Bush's upbringing in Texas explains part of his pro-immigration positions. At the same time, cultural conservatives, including those in the Republican Party, see immigrants as a threat to the social fabric more than an economic boon or a part of the natural exchanges between nations that share borders. They accuse pro-immigration free-marketeers of aiding the cause of socialism because trade unions, in order to stem the decline in their membership, have been generally supportive of immigration in recent years, at least in times of plenty, when they thought that foreigners could help swell their depleted ranks.[10] Democrats appear to be more unified on immigration, which partly explains, together with historical reasons, the tendency of Hispanics to vote for them. But some Democrats, particularly from the South, view Hispanics with suspicion on grounds of national security, while others, especially in industrial cities, regard them as having an undesirable impact on wages.

The tacit coalition of conservative Democrats and social conservative Republicans against immigration is not new—it has been more or less permanent for a century. The restrictionist policy implemented in the 1920s was imposed by a broad alliance of cultural conservatives that included Republicans and Southern Democrats, who had collaborated to pass Prohibition, demanded a patriotic assertiveness by public institutions, and reinforced racial segregation. Interestingly, this coalition was supported at the time by the labor unions![11]

Missing from the discussion—perhaps because the labyrinthine politics involved did not allow for a clear two-sided debate—was any substantial reference to the practical implications of ideology or prejudicial sentiment. The anti-immigration supporters of the Arizona law did not address the fundamental question of what it would mean to expel all illegal immigrants in the country, that is, a little less than 5 percent of the population—the equivalent of the total population of the state of Illinois. Apart from the obvious factor that the courts would be clogged up and law enforcement agencies overwhelmed beyond imagination, an organization that is not in favor of open borders estimated that it would take 166,666 buses, more than 13 billion gallons of fuel, and 48 million pounds of food just to transport them to the nearest border. In the hypothetical scenario in which all illegal immigrants, who are mixed up with the population at large, were actually rounded up, a civil rights nightmare would ensue. The cost of that nightmare contrasts with the tax revenue that those millions of illegals would bring through federal and income taxes should they become part of the formal system (more than $50 billion a year). Add to this cost the collapse of the numerous industries and areas of the economy in which their participation both as producers and as consumers matters—in 2008, the last year for which data is available, "illegals" accounted for 19 percent of the workforce in building, grounds keeping, and maintenance; 17 percent in construction trades; and 12 percent in food preparation and services.[12] Not to mention the horrific damage to the country's international image by the pictures depicting millions of people being corralled and herded to the border on CNN and Fox News.

Equally absent from the ideological discussion on immigration was basic information about how people on the ground close to the practical implications of the statute were reacting to the Arizona law. For instance, one of the arguments behind the decision by Governor Jan Brewer to sign it was that there was the danger of a spillover effect from Mexico's drug war through unauthorized entries. And yet Roy Bermudez, assistant police chief of the border city of Nogales, told the *Arizona Republic,* "We have not, thank God, witnessed any spillover violence from Mexico." In fact, according to FBI crime reports and local police agencies, crime rates had been essentially flat for the previous decade. Enhanced security along the border probably had to do with this, but the period included a time, before the heavy increase in security, when the border was supposedly much more vulnerable to Mexican crime.

At the end of 2009, I visited Nogales—the principal border town in Arizona—on both sides. I witnessed a colossal amount of security that meant illegal crossings were only possible through remote areas fraught with all sorts of perils. It was clear, by the time the new law was enacted, that security had already greatly improved, even taking into account that the recession had helped to create declining numbers of illegal entries, and that the high-tech virtual fence made of sensors and cameras in some parts of the border was failing to discern people from wildlife.

The aim of "securing the borders," the mantra used by anti-immigrant politicians and by pro-immigrant politicians, who had been intimidated by opponents into adopting it, was already being achieved without the need for new laws.[13] But nobody seemed to notice this in Washington, D.C., where the complexities and ideological contradictions of immigration politics generally meant that the facts and information were lost amid the brouhaha and the posturing.

Notes

1. Zig Layton-Henry, *The Politics of Immigration: Immigration, "Race" and "Race" Relations in Post-War Britain* (Oxford, U.K, and Cambridge, Mass.: Blackwell, 1992), 46–48.

2. Layton-Henry, *The Politics of Immigration*, 80–81.

3. The many historical instances of decisive support for restrictive measures had included the American Federation of Labor's backing of the 1924 immigration law with cultural arguments that echoed those of the right, as well as economic ones (there had also been an element of precaution on the part of the unions, which wanted to distance themselves from the danger of communist infiltration). Only a few unions, particularly the International Ladies Garment Workers Union, which counted among its member many female immigrant workers from Central and Eastern Europe, had taken a different view in previous decades For an account of the International Ladies Garment Workers Union, see Gus Tyler, *Look for the Union Labor: A History of the International Ladies Garment Workers Union* (Armonk, N.Y.: M.E. Sharpe, 1995).

4. Georgie Anne Geyer, *Americans No More* (New York: The Atlantic Press, 1996), 261.

5. Geyer, *Americans No More*, 260.

6. Peter Brimelow, *Alien Nation: Common Sense About America's Immigration Disaster"* (New York: Random House, 1995, 140–141).

7. Samuel T. Francis, *America Extinguished: Mass Immigration and the Disintegration of American Culture* (Monterey, Va.: Americans for Immigration Control, 2002), 25.

8. Aristide R. Zolberg, "Immigration Control Policy: Law and Implementation," in *The New Americans: A Guide to Immigration Since 1965*, eds. Mary C. Waters and Reed Ueda (Cambridge, Mass.: Harvard University Press, 2007), 38.

9. Senator Graham's position was widely reported. See, for instance, this post on the CBS website on April 27, 2010, http://www.cbsnews.com/8301-503544_162-20003549 -503544.html

10. The study, conducted by David Gewirtz and titled "Why Illegal Immigrants Are Here to Stay," is part of the "How To Save Jobs" series and was published by the US Strategic Perspective Institute, Palm Bay, Fla., on April 27, 2010, http://usspi.org/press-releases/ usspi-20100427-immigration.htm

11. Francis, *America Extinguished*, 123.

12. The year 2008 is the last year for which data provided by the Census Bureau is available. See Edward Schumacher-Matos, *The Washington Post*, July 30, 2010.

13. Eugene Robinson, "Border Insecurities," *The Washington Post*, May 4, 2010, A23.

15

Shock and Awe

A SUDDEN INTRUSION by a substantial number of foreigners into any community will produce dislocation and shock. The larger the intrusion and the smaller or the more tightly concentrated the community, the greater the immediate effect. In a large, widely dispersed and complex society, the impact of a mass infusion of outsiders is less traumatic and the ability to quickly absorb it greater than in a smaller, closely knit community. As a general proposition, any group of people suddenly confronted with an alien presence is bound to experience a mixture of fear, threat, and prejudice.

The notion that free immigration and open borders can happen overnight and work out as quickly and smoothly as in the logical argument of a pro-immigration author would seem belied by the way in which communities have traditionally reacted to foreigners, at least at first instance, and especially in times of trouble and uncertainty. A large part of humanity seems instinctively scared of open borders, regardless of how secure they are against criminals. That has been true since before the dawn of civilization and continues to be so in the twenty-first century. Similar attitudes have been registered in under-developed societies and in the most advanced ones. There may come a time, in the evolution of mankind, when deeply ingrained ideas about nationhood and the nation state, as well as the instinctive discomfort that many people feel towards outsiders, will cede their, place to more open, flexible, and globalized ideas of human coexistence, and less defensive attitudes. But in the present world, tribal sentiments are easily aroused even in the most civilized societies.

Nationalist sentiments are easily triggered by any foreign presence, depending on its size or its symbolism. Even in capitalist America in the globalized twenty-first century, there was an outcry when Anheuser-Busch, the owner of the Budweiser brand, America's beloved lager, was bought by InBev, a Belgian-Brazilian concern that was the world's number-one brewing company. The fact that Budweiser had originally been inspired by a similarly named brand from a town in Bohemia (Czech Republic) was irrelevant: This was an American brand being taken over by foreigners who were causing an affront to America. The move by bold Anheuser-Busch in 2008 sparked off commentary in the media, grandstanding by politicians, and soul-searching by those who thought this presaged the end of America's preeminence. There is only a difference of context and degree—not of essence—between this reaction in the media or among politicians, and the cruder, more direct reaction that takes place at the street level against people who look or sound different in a town or city suddenly faced with outsiders. That essence is a tribal, protectionist sentiment against invasion. Its civilized expression is verbal hostility; its extreme expression is violence, verbal, or physical.

There have been periods in contemporary times in which sudden and large inflows of foreigners provoked "shock and awe" on the part of the host society. This sensation was followed by a hardening of the anti-immigrant edge that appeared to have been softening for some time. The 1990s was such a time in the United States and Europe. In the early part of that decade, some 10 million Mexicans migrated to the United States; 3 million people from the Maghreb countries moved to France; and 5 million foreigners, including 2 million Turks, immigrated to Germany. The reception in these countries was not excessively hostile at first. But after the initial uncertainty, the perception emerged that sustained immigration was changing the composition of the nation and threatening a way of life. For years, immigration had been more or less accommodated and tolerated. The changing perception brought about by the growth in numbers translated into much more open hostility towards foreigners.

When, exactly, is an influx of foreigners "too large" in the eyes of the natives? There seems to be no objective or consistent benchmark. It depends on many factors, ranging from mass psychology, to the given context, to triggering events. A large influx obviously enhances that suspicion. Precisely because there is no objective standard, a fall in immigrant numbers may not be enough for hostile feelings to subside. When the Arizona law was passed in 2010, the annual influx of illegal immigrants had been dropping during recent years and stood at about one-third of its most recent peak. For many Americans, then, it might not be any consolation to explain that the Mexican population is aging rapidly because fertility and birth rates have experienced a big drop in the last twenty years or that, by 2015, the pool of potential immigrants will have shrunk automatically since Mexicans over 45 tend not to migrate.[1]

The reaction to immigrants in developed countries may or may not be directly proportional to the increase in the numbers of foreigners. Sometimes the perception, and not necessarily the actual reality, is enough to convince people that something unusual and unprecedented is happening that entails a new kind of threat. France had been receiving immigrants for almost a century in noticeable numbers, and yet it was only at the end of the 1970s and in the early 1980s that, in a context of high unemployment, a reaction began to take place across parts of society. The fact that three and four decades ago, immigrants were mostly from Southern Europe (e.g., Portuguese, Spanish, Italian), rather than North Africa, made no difference. It became a national issue even if the proportion of foreigners in France hovered around no more than 5 percent of the total population.[2] The sensibility to this issue grew subsequently more acute in the face of renewed and diversified immigration, until the tensions associated with the last years of the twentieth century and the beginning of the new one flared up. The growth of immigrant numbers acted much more as an additive to tensions that were already brewing than an outright cause.

Even today, the hostility against use of the Muslim veil in France, which the French Parliament prohibited in 2010, has more to do with fear than reality. It is estimated that no more than 1 percent of immigrant girls and female adults actually wear it, but its visible presence in a few schools is enough to make millions of French people afraid that the trend will eventually grow. Regardless of the fact that many girls are forced to wear it by authoritarian fathers and many women are compelled to cover their faces by husbands who constrain their free will—two very strong reasons to consider that the rights of the women involved are being violated by Muslim families—the fact is that the general perception inspired by foreign communities not yet seen as having assimilated is usually shaped by a sense of menace.

It is one thing to accept and even value that one's country was enriched by immigrants in the past, and it is quite another to tolerate the same phenomenon presently. In the state of mind of a society shocked by the high level of foreigners, any fact that seems to validate the "foreigner phobia" becomes proof of immigrants' guilt. People begin to look with new fearful eyes at the same neighborhoods through which they used to pass without much notice. The boulevards of California packed with Asian signs suddenly feel invaded. Americans who see the names of Asian candidates running for the school board or city council, or who sit behind someone reading on a bus and find themselves staring at a newspaper they cannot read—such as *Sin Tao,* a publication from Hong Kong with more than a million readers in North America—these Americans begin to sense that their country is being taken away from them. It doesn't matter that the Asians suburbs of California mirror unwittingly the suburbs settled by Jews who left the cities on the East Coast after the 1940s. That was then, and now is now. The election of the first mayor of Asian descent in San Francisco in late 2011 can only mean, for those who are shocked by immigration, a confirmation of their worst fears.

Unlike the Jewish suburbanization of the 1950s and 1960s, the Asian "invasion" of the suburbs that started in California in the 1970s and 1980s was made up of settlers who arrived directly from Asia without establishing themselves in cities first. Despite the differences, in both cases the reaction was hostile. Those who dislike the Asian presence in California suburbs seem not to know that Jewish suburbanization was equally resented and that time has demonstrated how unjustified those fears were.[3] The growth of the Asian population over three decades was periodically marked by tension. In the 1960s, Monterey Park was a small village where locals cultivated crops. Attracted by the relatively open space, the Taiwanese began to establish themselves there because of its proximity to the Los Angeles Chinatown. Their presence generated a land boom that benefited the natives, who nonetheless resented them. Various ordinances mandated that signs be posted in English and sought to limit the influx. The change in the composition of the city was gradual. Eventually it built up, and in 1985 Monterey Park elected the first Chinese mayor—Lily Lee Chen. By the 1990s, almost 65 percent of the residents claimed Chinese descent. The native population, angry with the Taiwanese even though many of them were also recent newcomers to the city, was about half its former size, while the number of Hispanics had increased.

By then, the Chinese from the mainland were replacing the Taiwanese as the dominant group. Eventually, many Taiwanese left Monterey Park in what was compared to the "white flight" of the 1970s. However, the schools, the street names, the laws, and the business climate were American in the sense that they did not differ from many other cities and states in the country with much smaller Asian populations.[4] The tension that marked this transformation proved to be entirely prejudicial. The population changed, but not the basic rules and the general environment because every wave that came in settled into traditions, laws, and a general way of life that was already well established, and which connected this part of California to the rest of the country. By the time the next wave came in, the previous one already had a vested interest in abiding by American rules.

The tension that punctuated the Asian expansion in California contains an important message. People approach transformation, especially when it involves a change in the composition of the population, with trepidation. It happens everywhere, as we have seen, not just in America. Eventually, a majority of Americans in California saw that the consequence of this influx of foreigners was not the transformation of the American system, but a successful absorption by American cities of large inflows of foreigners whose economic and cultural contribution was undeniable.

This adaptation would seem to confirm one scholar's observation that "the pattern of civic life remains what it was before a wave of immigration, unless the immigrants are greater in number or riches than the prior residents. The chances that any immigrants into the United States will meet that condition are nil."[5] In the case of Monterey Park, there came a time when the immigrants were greater in number than the natives, but the effect on civic life was not pernicious because the expansion was gradual and the city is part of a larger country with established laws, institutions, and ways of doing things. These laws, institutions, and ways of doing things are not only enforced: they are equally useful to natives and foreigners, who adopt them to their benefit, as the Asians of Monterey Park have proven.

In Europe, the reaction to the perception that there was a sudden and massive influx of foreigners was much worse than in the United States in recent decades. Since 1990, it has been common to read and see in the international media that various groups of xenophobes have attacked immigrants in Europe. On May 29, 1993, a house occupied by Turkish immigrants in Solingen, a town of 170,000 inhabitants and 7,000 Turks, was torched by skinheads. Between February 5 and February 7, 2000, following the killing of a Spaniard by a young North African, a wave of racist violence against immigrants swept El Ejido, in the south of Spain. North African homes and shops were set on fire. During a recent visit to the area, I was struck to find out how vividly these and other such images have stayed in people's minds all these years. A town in Almería, in Spain's Andalusia region, El Ejido is a flashpoint of the confrontational discussion on immigration in that country. Living conditions are tough—a report by *Almería Acoge* indicated at the end of that decade that no more than one-third of the dwellings in which immigrants lived could be considered up to standard—and sentiments run very high on all sides of the issue in the surrounding areas. Any incident can spark off severe violence in that tinderbox of a place.[6]

In subsequent months and years, there were echoes of these tensions in other parts of Spain. Many of them took place in Catalonia, a major recipient of foreign settlers. Conflicts between locals and Moroccans shook such cities as Terrassa or Santa Coloma de Gramenet, mostly inhabited by domestic immigrants, and their descendants, who moved to the North in the 1950s and 1960s from other Spanish regions, particularly Andalusia.

The buildup of Muslim communities in parts of Spain has given rise to tensions over exterior signs of the Muslim religion despite the negligible influence of Islam on the country's spiritual life today. Efforts to establish mosques have triggered periodic protests in parts of the country. In October and November of 2004, there were demonstrations by Spanish neighbors against Moroccans who wanted to set up a mosque in Singerlín, in Barcelona. The authorities finally had to relocate it to the outskirts of the city among complaints from Taoukik Cheddadi, the spokesman for the Singerlín Muslim community, who asked, "Where is integration?"[7]

Today's reactions in Europe echo those of yesteryear. In Britain, as far back as 1919, there were severe race riots in London, Glasgow, Liverpool, Cardiff, and other cities out of a fear of losing jobs to foreigners and, perhaps just as importantly, of having to coexist with people who looked, spoke, and acted differently. *The Times* of London summed it up quite succinctly in May of 1919: "Any colored man who appeared was greeted with abuse and had to be escorted by the police."[8] Two years later, a member of the Motherwell Trades Council, describing Indians as "these aliens," alleged at a meeting that they were "a menace to the social and industrial community."[9] The number of Indians back then, both in absolute terms and as a proportion of the population, was considerably smaller than it would become in later times, with the mass arrival of immigrants from the former colonies. But the perception that alien bodies had infiltrated the sacred space of the nation was enough to trigger these kinds of tribal attitudes among natives. The attitudes were not dissimilar to those that greeted the arrival of Chinese coolies in nineteenth-century America, even though they constituted a tiny percentage of the population of the host country.

Winston Churchill famously praised the hospitality of the British people towards immigrants who had settled in his country. During a speech on the Race Relations Bill, he asked, "Would the Home Secretary at the same time pray tribute to the wonderful way in which the British people have accepted for the greater part the very substantial influx of alien culture and alien race into their midst without open conflict or prejudice?"[10] However, that was an idyllic vision of what had really happened. The foreigners had been welcomed as doctors, nurses, drivers, conductors, cleaners, and carpenters, as well as a wide range of other capacities, in the 1950s and 1960s, when labor was scarce and there was an acute understanding of the necessity of hiring foreign workers. But as *people*—that is, as friends, as neighbors, as fellow church members—foreigners had been received with much less enthusiasm. Even when foreign laborers were recruited to do the work that natives rejected and occupied inner-city accommodation that the natives wished to leave, they were seen by many British citizens as dangerous competitors for jobs, housing, and other scarce resources. Tensions were never very far away, and integration was difficult, even if, as a general statement, it can be said that peaceful coexistence was maintained.[11]

Terrorism

After September 11, 2011, the fear that a large number of immigrants had caused in previous years was fueled by a new kind of perception. The discussion on immigration became entangled with the discussion about terrorism in the wake of the global war on Islamic terrorist organizations unleashed by the attacks. If there is one word that characterizes people's reactions to immigration, that word is insecurity. A traumatic event involving outsiders inevitably deepens the sense of insecurity, as the 2001 attacks did, strengthening the connection between immigration and perceived threats.

Whether it be cultural, economic, or social insecurity, large numbers of citizens fear that which they know little about. The natural uncertainty has been heightened by this transformative global era in which many new political, economic, and social forces are producing dislocations. As more people become incorporated into the marketplace and countries shake off decades of inward-looking policies, the bug of movement seems to have stung everyone and everything. In the disconcerting context of globalization, the insecurity that the flow of people across borders naturally stirs up has been compounded by Islamic terrorism, and, more generally, by the violence directed at Western liberal democracies by organizations that harbor resentment against those governments and institutions.

The circumstances that have given rise to the connection between terror and foreigners in the minds of many people are not just the figment of someone's imagination. These circumstances are real and stem from a persistent attack on Western societies—on their innocent civilians as well as on their armies—by groups that cannot be dismissed as imaginary enemies conjured up by America's heightened state of paranoia. Regardless of the history of humiliation that may be behind this hatred, and of the past mistakes or abuses of foreign policy on the part of Western governments, it cannot be denied that there are militants out there ready to strike at ordinary citizens who have no relation to the causes the attackers may have in mind when targeting prosperous liberal democracies. Moreover, the fact that the attackers of the World Trade Center, the Pentagon, and the airplane flying over Pennsylvania were foreigners who had little trouble penetrating the United States indicates that even with migratory restrictions, enemies of the U.S. government can set up camp inside this territory. These realities would be enough to cause social commotion and deep insecurity in the citizens of any country.

The fact that 9/11 produced thousands of deaths inside the United States, where a large-scale attack on the mainland was unprecedented, had profound psychological implications. If the only superpower was now vulnerable on its mainland, the world order was more fragile than generally thought. The tragedy compounded the fears and insecurity of Americans who were already having difficulty adapting to this highly competitive new phase of globalization, and had been reacting to immigration with hostility for more than a decade. The commotion was not confined to the United States, of course. It also instilled renewed fear of outsiders elsewhere. One does not need to be a professional student of people's psychologies to see how the resulting state of mind hardened prejudices against immigrants on both sides of the Atlantic, debilitating the position of those who see in immigration a source of strength and favor increased communications and exchanges between peoples.

The fear and uncertainty has been compounded by the fact that the locations where terrorism originates continuously shift, as do the various tools with which terrorists exploit the system prevailing in open societies. The 9/11 hijackers came from countries that were not on the official list of terrorist sponsors. That means three things: (1) the list, often the result of political considerations rather than objective data, is part of the problem; (2) terrorism is a moving target; and (3) all countries of the world are potential enemy sources—a labyrinth that points to the futility of basing a security system on migratory considerations, but makes people even more scared of outsiders. One-third of the 48 foreign-born al Qaeda operatives who committed crimes in the United States from 1993 until 2001 were on temporary visas, another third were legal residents or naturalized citizens, one-fourth were undocumented, and the rest were former undocumented foreigners with pending asylum applications.[12] Because of the foreign origin of the 9/11 attackers, some Americans tended to overreact against *all* foreigners and pressure the authorities to do the same.

Those who would like a police state in response to terrorism want to make innocent foreigners pay for the inefficiency of the customs and immigration bureaucracy that is guilty, among other things, of having let Mohamed Atta enter the country through the Miami airport, despite having overstayed his visa during a previous visit. However, except for sealed borders under a perfect police state, migratory restrictions would not have prevented quite a few of these people from penetrating the United States. In the absence of good intelligence on them, the only possibility of preventing their entry would have been to make dozens of millions of innocent people pay the price of closing off the United States impenetrably. The vast majority of the 6 million visas issued by officers to foreigners around the world in a typical year are not awarded to terrorists.[13] Intelligence and a certain degree of efficiency, rather than migratory restrictions, would have been much more useful in the days prior to 9/11. The same can be said of the 2004 bombing in the commuter trains in Madrid that overturned an election that the governing Popular Party seemed set to win, handing victory, a few days later, to the Socialists.

A system that works and makes sense will need to take these lessons to heart. However, in the climate of opinion created by the ongoing war on terrorism, extremist nativists in all countries are able exert considerable pressure on those who make the political decisions. The odds do not look good, in the foreseeable future, of governments being able to expand on the freedoms that have allowed, tolerated, or turned a blind eye to a large numbers of immigrants in the past. If recent years are anything to go by, the trend has moved in the opposite direction. The momentum of sentiment against foreigners is so strong that even the evidence that no new attacks have been committed in the United States since 9/11 has not been enough to quell it, nor has the fact that migratory restrictions have little to do with a state's ability to pursue terrorists who think ahead of the bureaucracy. The fact that the Obama administration was not able to put before Congress an immigration reform bill during his 2009–12 administration is an indication of the environment that the fear of insecurity has generated vis-à-vis newcomers in general. The same can be said to a large extent of many European countries.

The history of the Immigration and Naturalization Service (INS) itself is revealing of the way approaches to immigration have evolved based on fear and security concerns. Until 1940, this service was part of the Labor Department, meaning that migratory flows were mostly seen through the lens of the economy. The INS moved to the Justice Department during the war out of concern that immigration might be a vehicle for spies and saboteurs intent on operating inside the country. In 2003, as a result of the USA Patriot Act signed into law two years earlier, the INS functions were transferred to three different agencies within the newly created Department of Homeland Security—one handles legal status issues, another takes care of investigations and enforcement, and the third deals with border patrols. The budget of the border patrol agents along the Canadian border, for instance, was tripled. In subsequent years, the bureaucracy linked to national security grew exponentially. In July of 2010, a *Washington Post* exposé based on a two-year investigation revealed that 1,271 government organizations and 1,931 private companies work on programs related to counterterrorism, homeland security, and intelligence, in more than 10,000 locations across the United States, and that 854,000 people hold top-secret security clearances.[14]

It would be a mistake to think that only developed liberal democracies have been led by fear and insecurity to overreact in areas where it was not necessarily warranted—and underreact in others. After the second Gulf War, Iraqis and citizens of countries supportive of Iraq, such as the Palestinians, the Yemenis, and the Sudanese, were forced to leave the Arab territories around the Persian Gulf in which they were guest workers. More than 1.5 million people were displaced—up to 1 million Yemenis were expelled from Saudi Arabia, 158,000 Egyptians were kicked out of Kuwait, and some 200,000 Jordanians and 150,000 Palestinians were removed from various places, mainly Kuwait. The deportations were often brutal. The disruption was generally costly for most countries, although the expulsions had some unintended positive consequences. Jordan, for example, experienced healthy economic growth rates when repatriated citizens brought their savings back with them.[15] Even in the case of Jordan, however, the sudden influx of Palestinians returning after many years had shocking effects on society.

Turning prosperous liberal democracies into impoverished dictatorships—which is what the consequence of sealed borders and police states would mean for the United States and Europe—is precisely what the enemies of Western civilization pursue. They maintain that there is no real liberty in these societies, and they do everything in their power to be proven right. All terrorist organizations—from the Baader-Meinhof in Germany in the 1970s to Peru's Shining Path in the 1980s—that combated, or still combat, a liberal democracy understand how vital it is for that system to crumble and be replaced with a Fascist-type regime that legitimizes their revolutionary cause. Turning the United States into a country subjected to domestic imperialism—under a dictatorship—is a major objective of Muslim fanatics who view Western military bases in their own countries as a symbol of imperialism. By playing on the insecurities of Western societies so that fear induces their governments to take illiberal actions and gradually suffocate the citizens' freedoms—Islamic terrorists know exactly what they are doing.

In history, as Enzensberger wrote, a minimum of civilization has been achieved exceptionally and temporarily:

Whoever wants to defend it from external challenges faces a dilemma: The more fiercely civilization defends itself against an external threat and puts up barriers around itself, the less, in the end, it has left to defend. But, as far as the barbarians are concerned, we need not expect them at the gates. They are already within us"[16]

His words seem written yesterday and are clearly aimed at warning liberal democracies against the temptation to defend themselves against threats from outside by renouncing their freedoms. One of those freedoms is immigration.

The issue of security is not the stuff of this book. Suffice it to say that only by sealing the borders of the United States and Europe hermetically would these citizens be relatively immune from the danger of penetration by foreign enemies. I say "relatively" because even with sealed borders, the possibility of naturalized or native citizens acting on behalf of foreign terrorists would still exist—a scenario that only a police state with unprecedented efficiency could counter. Even establishing a perfect police state is a near impossibility if we countenance the fact that totalitarian governments were not able to prevent all sorts of banned conducts—whether political or social. Tsarist Russia was no more able to prevent anarchist terrorism than Soviet Russia was able to stamp out alcoholism. This leads to an obvious conclusion: A country's fight against terrorism cannot hang on its ability to seal off borders and enforce a police state, both because total success would not be guaranteed even under such conditions and because such a scenario would lead to tragic side effects, from the loss of liberty to the destruction of massive amounts of capital. Consider the fate that has befallen the citizens of countries big or small that closed themselves to the outside world. In 1957, Ghana was the richest developing country in the British Empire. Within a decade after Ghana closed its borders to all foreign influence, it was bankrupt (eventually it learned the lesson, which is why things have looked better in recent times). The same happened to Burma, once one of the wealthiest countries in Asia.

Leaving aside commuters from Canada and Mexico, documented foreign entrants to the United States normally number around 60 million, half of whom are covered by the visa waiver program. In order to provide a total guarantee that terrorists and their weapons will be kept out, therefore, border inspectors would have to make millions of correct decisions.[17] No degree of efficiency except totally sealed borders under a police state that was efficient beyond imagination could live up to such a standard.

The process of adaptation to a world dominated by free flows of people will need to be gradually encouraged, persuasively argued, and smoothly facilitated if we want to avoid in the short run worse reactions out of fear and insecurity than those we are trying to correct. The worst way to confront a social phenomenon is not to acknowledge its existence and, if its effect is transformative in any way, not to understand its magnitude and consequences. Pro-immigration advocates need to pay attention to people's anxieties and prejudices when shaping their ideas and communicating them if they aspire to change prevailing attitudes. But the strategy should not shy away from confronting the remnants of tribalism, especially taking into account that migration is a fact that cannot simply be wished away.

Clandestine migration worldwide amounted to between 20 and 30 million people, about one-sixth of total migration, in recent times (half of them, incidentally, were women), and there are 215 million first-generation migrants around the world, about 3 percent of the world population.[18] This is a transformative force that, as is the case with other aspects of globalization, cannot simply be wished away. The process of accommodation is difficult; the effects will include ones that can be anticipated from past experience, as well as unpredictable ones that will emerge from the interactions, the actions and reactions, of millions of people from different backgrounds encountering each other in the global village. It would be infantile to deny that there is something challenging and disruptive, even a bit scary, about this force, especially for people accustomed to the old world, and even for those of us who pay attention to past experience understand how many extraordinary consequences it will bring about. At the same time, to think that the transformative force of migration can be stopped through repression would be self-defeating and naive.

Free countries need to find a way to be secure and implacably efficient against terrorism while maintaining—actually, enhancing—the freedoms enjoyed by their citizens. If the United States and Europe are to avoid falling into the security trap to which terrorists try to lure them by exploiting their fears, taking appropriate measures to preempt the penetration of porous borders by terrorists must go hand in hand with a sensible approach to immigration. In some ways, the enemies of liberty have already obtained a victory in forcing countries to adopt measures against other countries because a small number of terrorists are able to operate from there or hold that citizenship. Since 2001, the Philippines, for instance, has been identified by the United States Department of Justice as an "al Qaeda active nation," which has led to a record number of deportations of Filipinos.[19] One can only imagine what the situation is like for the roughly 350,000 Iranians living in the United States because of daily rhetorical hatred spewed by Iran's lunatic president against the West.

Notes

1. Jorge Castañeda, *Ex Mex: From Migrants to Immigrants* (New York: The New Press, 2007), 111.

2. Yuan Gastaut, *l'Immigration et l'Opinion en France Sous la Veme République* (Paris: Éditions du Seuil, 2000), 9–10.

3. According to the 2000 census, the largest percentage of Asians, between one-quarter and one-third, are in the counties of San Francisco, Santa Clara, Alameda, and San Mateo. In the south of the state, Los Angeles suburbs such as Monterey Park, where Asians comprise 63 percent of the population, or San Marino, where seven out of ten school-age kids are Asian-American, or even Hacienda Heights, with its large Korean community, have been part of the general landscape for awhile. See Alejandra Lopez, *Asians in California: 1990 to 2000* (Stanford, Calif.: Center for Comparative Studies in Race and Ethnicity, Stanford University, April 2002). This is the eighth report in the CCSRE Race and Ethnicity in California: Demographics Report Series, http://ccsre.stanford.edu/reports/report_8.pdf

4. Joel Millman, *The Other Americans* (New York: Viking, 1997), 259–260.

5. Julian Simon, "Why Control the Border—An Immigration Debate," *National Review* 45, no. 2 (February 1, 1993): 27–29.

6. Bullent Kaya, *The Changing Face of Europe—Population Flows in the 20th Century*, (Strasbourg: Council of Europe Publishing, 2002), 45.

7. Two years earlier, in Premià de Mar, another Catalonyan location, a group of neighbors had also protested against plans to open a mosque, while in Almería, at the other end of the country, construction of a Moroccan consulate was stalled three times in 2001—in three different neighborhoods—because of fears that it would attract large numbers of North Africans. See Daniela Flesler, *The Return of the Moor: Spanish Responses to Contemporary Morrocan Immigration* (West Lafayette, Ind.: Purdue University Press, 2008), 35.

8. Rozina Visram, *Asians in Britain: 400 Years of History* (London: Pluto Press, 2002), 198–199.

9. Visram, *Asians in Britain*, 200.

10. Zig Layton-Henry, *The Politics of Immigration: Immigration, "Race" and "Race" Relations in Post-War Britain* (Oxford, U.K, and Cambridge, Mass.: Blackwell, 1992), 36.

11. Layton-Henry, *The Politics of Immigration*, 19.

12. Mark Krikorian, *The New Case Against Immigration: Both Legal and Illegal* (London: Sentinel, 2008), 101.

13. Krikorian, *The New Case Against Immigration*, 103.

14. Dana Priest and William M. Arkin, "A Hidden World, Growing Beyond Control," *Washington Post,* July 19, 2010, http://projects.washingtonpost.com/top-secret-america /articles/a-hidden-world-growing-beyond-control/

15. Andrzej Kapiszewski, "Arab Labor Migration to GCC States," in *Arab Migration in a Globalized World* (Geneva: International Organization for Migration, League of Arab States, 2004), 121–122.

16. Hans Magnus Enzensberger, *Civil War* (London: Granta Books, 1994), 138.

17. Neeraj Kaushal, Cordelia W. Reimers, and David M. Reimers, "Immigrants and the Economy," in *The New Americans: A Guide to Immigration Since 1965*, eds. Mary C. Waters and Reed Ueda (Cambridge, Mass.: Harvard University Press, 2007), 40.

18. "The Magic of Diasporas," *The Economist*, November 19, 2011, 13.

19. Catherine Ceniza Choy, "Philippines," in *The New Americans,* eds. Waters and Ueda, 567.

16

Why Things and Not People?

GLOBALIZATION HAS HAPPENED before, several times in fact, since the Age of Discovery in the fifteenth and sixteenth centuries made the world truly global for most regions. Oceanic trade by Europeans first made it possible for millions of people to move over great distances. For citizens in the nineteenth century, the pace of globalization was nothing short of miraculous, a force that had migration as a driver: More than 50 million Europeans migrated to the Americas, Asia, and Africa. Until the end of the eighteenth century, people spoke of "emigration," not "immigration," but whether the focus was on those who left one country or those who entered another, the movement of capital, goods, and ideas (in the form of technology) was intertwined with the flow of people.[1] Today, many people seem to have little notion of how inseparable these component parts of earlier phases of globalization were. Attitudes prevalent today value the circulation of *things*, but not necessarily of *people*, and stem from the idea, belied by historical precedent, that globalization is possible without a great measure of mobility of human beings across borders.

Some 215 million people live today in a country in which they were not born, of whom close to 16 million are refugees. If we look at single countries, the United States has the largest number of foreign-born people, followed by Russia, Germany, the Ukraine and France—in that order.[2] If we consider intra-European Union migration as domestic flows, Asia was clearly the region with the largest number of international migrants—one in three.[3] Behind the social maelstrom of international migration is a complex mixture of motives, needs, and dreams. But one thing is clear: Things—goods, services, and capital—do not move alone; they do so accompanied by the circulation of people. This has been the case for the last 500 years in the global village, as it was the case in

248

smaller areas long before globalization. We should not be surprised that today the movement of people is also trying to shadow that of things in a world characterized by myriad exchanges.

In order to understand why the movement of people is germane to globalization, it is necessary to understand how ell-encompassing globalization is becoming. Increasingly, it goes well beyond the economy. It encompasses even domains such as justice. In 1980, the Second Circuit Court of Appeals held the *Filartiga v. Peña-Irala* decision that a Paraguayan citizen residing in the United States could bring civil action in American courts against a Paraguayan official accused of murdering a person in his own country.[4] The internationalization of justice has emerged—as signified by the emergence of the International Criminal Court and its high-profile cases relating to genocide. Although in its infancy, this trend is moving in the direction of reinterpreting national sovereignty too. It is a trend that runs contrary to anti-immigration notions of nationhood.

Foreign policy in developed countries is also feeling the impact of internationalization. A few so-called minorities of foreign descent in the United States have periodically influenced policy towards their fatherland, but new countries are being added to the list. In recent decades, diasporas from Greece and Turkey have had a major say on how Foggy Bottom (location of the U.S. Department of State) and Capitol Hill (indeed the White House itself) viewed affairs in those countries. Foreign policy decisions relating to the conflicts in the Caucasus, the recognition of Macedonia, support for Croatia in the Bosnian wars, intervention in Haiti, NATO's expansion, or the conflict in Northern Ireland have experienced strong influence from domestic so-called minorities since the 1980s and 1990s.

It is only a matter of time before Asian Americans, particularly Indians and people of Chinese origin, make their pressure felt in U.S. policy towards that part of the world. Some are already playing a major role in economic relations between the United States and their countries of origin by initiating robust trade via subsidiaries, joint ventures, and subcontracting arrangements that they establish in their home countries. So far, Hispanic groups in the United States have not had great impact on foreign policy vis-à-vis Latin America (with the exception of Cubans), but one can only assume that this will happen sooner or later. Immigration issues are already becoming central in relations between the United States and both Mexico and Central America.

Conversely, many Asian countries have turned emigration into a pillar of their own foreign policies. I am not only referring to cases such as the Philippines, where emigrants are considered heroes who contribute to the development of their people as a whole, but also to a country such as Sri Lanka, which regularly conducts official research on the international labor market in search of potential niches. Authorities do not specifically target women niches, but in practice, demand for women has increased compared to demand for men, and the government has detected opportunities for women migrants.[5]

The fact that some emigrant groups choose to engage themselves in civic and political activities in their fatherland is another potentially beneficial aspect of so-called transnational communities. Colombians in the United States, whose loyalty and contribution to their adopted society is highlighted in their impressive rate of achievement and assimilation, are more likely than other groups to be engaged in politics back in their country of origin once they become naturalized. Against what one might expect, it is only when immigrant take firm roots in the country to which they migrate that they feel comfortable and ready to make a contribution to the country they left behind.[6] For Colombia, the participation of emigrants who are familiar with the workings of liberal democracy and the market economy in the most powerful country on Earth can be a blessing. For the United States, the possibility that its own citizens can become influential in the internal affairs of Colombia without the anti-imperialistic backlash of yesteryear is surely a welcome prospect; the result might one day be more stability and prosperity south of the border.

This transformation brought about by migrants in international relations and the framework in which they take place amounts to the slow, tortuous, and sometimes painful adaptation of policy to a social reality that is proving tough to continue to ignore. International migration is a force so powerful that governments of "receiving" countries and governments of "sending" countries have to factor it into their outlook and actions. International law and international interactions are being forced to follow the massive movement of people.

The recognition of migration by interactions among governments and the international framework in which they take place came on the heels of international exchange and trade. In modern times, people have tended to follow things more often then the other way round, although now both follow each other. The connection between the two is unmistakable.

In the 1960s, Taiwan, Korea, Singapore, and other countries replaced import-substitution with more trade-oriented economies. Their success had a contagion effect on others, such as the Philippines and Sri Lanka,[7] subsequently triggering a flow of people beyond native borders. The connection between migration and the flow of goods and services in Asia points to a similar dynamic in developed countries whose exchanges have increased in the era of free trade agreements, including Latin America. Anti-immigration efforts run contrary to the stated chain of international causes and effects.

The embrace of migratory flows by many Asian countries, coupled with the receptiveness of businesses that have hired their nationals, has had a transformative effect on many fronts. It has contributed, for instance, to liberating women from the taboos and restrictions that held back their massive incorporation into the labor force. "Export-oriented industrialization in Asia has helped create a social environment and social legitimacy conducive to international female migration," Oishi has written.[8] Generally speaking, new global production processes have opened up opportunities for women in many developing countries. Their incorporation into the labor market has brought social change in those countries by expanding the sphere of autonomy of the female population: Many migrate from rural areas to cities within the national boundaries, but also across borders, in part because the domestic migrants' improved access to education has led to a greater acceptance of international migration. The connection between the flow of goods and the flow of people in the Arab world has taken a different form: The movement of things has tended to follow that of people. This constitutes somewhat of an exception worldwide. In terms of human mobility, Arab countries are highly integrated among themselves, even if not with the rest of the world. Because the Arab countries place much greater obstacles to trade in goods than to migration, labor and the other flows that stem from it, particularly monetary remittances, have been the most important mechanism through which the benefits of oil wealth have been spread to non-oil Arab countries. Foreign workers constitute on average 35 percent of the labor force in oil-producing countries, giving the Gulf nations the highest concentration of immigrants in the world.[9]

Thus, while in Asia, trade led to migration, in the Arab world, migration was a more powerful force than trade for awhile. However, trade is catching up, as Arab economies gradually embrace the circulation of things as well as people.

In the West, trade and migration have tended to go hand in hand, although the backlash against immigration at a time when trade is more fluent than ever bodes ill for the anti-immigration cause. In the unlikely case that the opponents of immigration should succeed in stifling the black market of illegal migration, presumably today's developed countries would eventually see a reduction in commerce too. Only if policymakers fail to see the profound connection between trade and migration can the law turn its back on one while purporting to embrace the other.

For all the hostility that immigration generates, the proportion of migrants is still very small if one compares it with the circulation of capital, goods, services, and ideas. The incidence of international migration stands at a small 3 percent of the world's population.[10] Domestic migration is four times larger than international migration. The economic impact of migration remains modest compared with that of the cross-border movement of goods, services, and capital: By the middle of the 2000 decade, trade equaled 27 percent of the world's Gross Domestic Product, while roughly 20 percent of total savings were invested outside of the country of origin.[11] That only one in ten Europeans is born to foreign parents is a fact that seems out of sync with a continent in which the citizens of 27 countries are already free to move about—and more will be when new members are incorporated.[12]

Barring a concerted effort to stem migration by brutal means, it is inconceivable that the number of migrants will remain at present levels for a very extended period of time. In a world in which the mindset of national borders is being traumatically redefined and gradually replaced with the mindset of mobility and transnationality, the continuing growth of exchanges and communication presages a much larger migratory force.

We may not be able to predict the exact trajectory of this flow. In great part it will depend on how much opportunity emerging countries can offer the millions of people aspiring to something better, and on where the center of gravity of economic and cultural development will be in the future. But we do know that it will take more than nativism to stop this force and that countries open to trade will need to accept that migration is part of the global deal. If the number of migrants has more than doubled since 1970—precisely the period in which the circulation of capital, goods, services, and ideas has taken off spectacularly—we can only assume that the trend will be reinforced in years to come. It will perhaps be slowed down now and then by financial and economic disruptions, or interrupted by occasional backlashes due to nativist reactions, but the migratory force is virtually unstoppable.

It is too late to reverse the tide. The economic and social effects of such a reversal would be devastating in the event that it was feasible. How do you undo the fact that 11 percent of the Mexican population lives in the United States, or that one-fifth of Ecuador's population lives in the United States and in Spain?[13] Historically, how do you undo the evolution of Britain from a Celtic to an Anglo-Saxon to a Norman to a multinational society? You don't even try. Instead, you learn and recite Daniel Defoe's famous 1701 poem, *The True-Born Englishman*:

> Dutch, Walloons, Flemings, Irishmen and Scots,/Vaudois, Valtelins and Huguenots . . . /Fate jumbled them together, God knows how,/What'er they were, they're true-born English/now."[14]

How do you undo the African and Roman mix in St. Augustine, a pivotal man in the development of Western Christianity? How do you undo centuries upon centuries of flows between North Africa and the Iberian Peninsula? "Why, if we are Berber," asked Miguel de Unamuno, the famous Spanish philosopher, pointing to the *mélange* of southern Europe's roots, "should we not feel and proclaim ourselves such?"[15]

In this globalized environment, migration signals the power of markets over attempts by governments to stifle them. As David Gregory said in a speech in 1980, "It has been migrants and their employers—not government—that have determined the magnitude and destination of migration flows in most parts of the world. The most that government can really do is to facilitate or impede the population movements, not to stop them."[16]

In the last four decades, Mexico, Bangladesh, the Philippines, Kazakhstan, Vietnam, Sri Lanka, and Colombia have been among the top emigration nations, but the list looks very different from previous migration eras and will change in years to come. Conversely, although it is unlikely that the United States—still a free society compared to most, despite the worrying growth of its government—will not cease to be a magnet for international migration anytime soon. However, it would be in keeping with historical precedent for other countries to displace it eventually as a major destination. The United Arab Emirates, where three-quarters of the population is foreign; Israel and Singapore, whose populations are one-third immigrant; and Estonia, a country in which one out of every four people is from outside, will likely continue to harbor significant numbers of people from other places for many years. But other nations will surely join these nations as immigrant destinations, or surpass them later.

International migration is a flux, a constant movement reacting to information that no one mind can possibly absorb and predict.[17] Its characteristics are always mysterious and temporary even if some of its effects, such as the growth of prosperity resulting from increased exchanges, and perhaps a more peaceful international coexistence, are relatively enduring. People are uncertain as to what this whirlwind means for their future prospects and for the world as they know it. Many communities have been defining themselves in narrower terms than in the past, as if an instinctive reaction told them they will be safer clinging to local connections than to national boundaries that are gradually being shattered. The resurgence of separatism and regional nationalism in some European countries may be an epiphenomenon of the changing environment. But generally speaking the tendency is towards more migration in a world where exchanges continue to increase.

Nothing New, Nothing to Fear

Relations between immigrant communities and the countries of origin are much more complex than critics realize, and these relations constitute another major symptom and consequence of the connection between the movement of people and things. Trade, investment, and communications among nations are vivified by the material and emotional ties of expatriate communities, and their descendants, with the fatherland. As is widely known, Chinese Americans have played a major role in the explosion of exchanges between the United States and China. Since the 1980s, for instance, Chinese, Korean, and Filipino developers have marketed the towns that host big proportions of Asian residents directly to investors in Asia. The effect has been transformative, not only from a demographic and sociological perspective, but also from an economic one.

Because of the emergence of China as a powerhouse in recent decades, immigrants of that origin in Western countries have been taking for some time a keen interest in their homeland or that of their forebears, increasingly interacting with it in ways that were unthinkable before 1978. American companies have heeded that awakening, aggressively recruiting Chinese professionals to run programs in China. A study shows that by 1996, among those who run foreign businesses or manage joint ventures in Beijing, one-half were Chinese transnational immigrants. By the early years of the decade 2000–09, almost one-third of the more than 600,000 Hong Kong residents who had migrated to the West between 1985 and 1997 had moved back to either Hong Kong or mainland China.[18] American companies that employ lots of Chinese people find it much easier to set up in China without a joint venture with a local partner.

A survey conducted in the middle of the decade 2000–09 found that close to one-quarter of Brazilians living in Portugal, the "mother" country, and one in six Brazilians living in Japan aspired to open businesses in their adopted countries. Many of them considered bringing their connections to Brazilian suppliers and clients to bear in their future enterprises. Almost four in ten Brazilians in Portugal expressed the intention to invest at some point in their country of origin. While nine in every ten Brazilians in Portugal were renting, half of them owned a home in Brazil. In other words, Brazil's emigrants do not see mutually exclusive benefits in pursuing business opportunities in Portugal and Brazil. Their ability to do both brings new possibilities for both sides of the pond.[19]

Buying real estate property in their country of origin is very common for migrants no longer based there. It is by no means a purely Brazilian aspiration. Moroccans do it too. Their purchases have a multiplier effect because of the numerous small and even mid-sized businesses connected to that sector of the economy. Investments made by recipients of remittances in Morocco have helped agriculture by expanding the area under cultivation as well as the financial system.

A century of migration has led to the development among Mexicans and Americans of many thousands of binational kinship-employer networks that directly link potential migrants in Mexico to their United States-based relatives and employers. These networks, as Wayne Cornelius has written, operate as a sort of informal employment agency for foreigners.[20] In a world in which the flow of goods, services, capital, ideas, and people is growing—despite nativist backlashes— the advantage of binational and multinational networks arising from foreign communities established in adopted territories is evident.

Several of the most common concerns voiced by detractors of immigration are that (1) people of foreign provenance keep too many attachments and loyalties to their fatherland; (2) that they create self-centered enclaves or closely-knit communities that seek to separate them from the rest, and (3) that they reserve the fruits of their best efforts for their relatives back home. Those Americans who resent what they see as a pattern of deliberate non-assimilation do not believe that an immigrant community can be a sturdy bridge connecting the adopted nation to the outside world. Those who understand that immigrant communities can serve the purpose of bonding countries of origin and host countries still think that the benefits are outweighed by the ills of family reunification, ghetto-like communities, and sending remittances abroad. In sum, critics do not believe that immigrants help to make the adopted country more competitive. They see immigration as sapping the energy of the host society.

At the very least, these objections miss obvious social benefits derived from some of the conducts they decry outright. As mentioned, the participation of women in immigration is one among many. The idea of Penelope waiting while Ulysses travels is no longer valid—women migrants have become a key part of the immigrant mix. One of the avenues for their increased participation has been family reunification, although much less so today.[21] But, more generally, the objections made in the United States and other countries also betray a certain misunderstanding of human nature—they mistake conducts common to most communities for supposedly alien habits. Although the numbers are not as great, Americans abroad have also created communities whose members are closely bonded to each other—including the 1-million-plus Americans living in Mexico. They keep close ties back home. Thanks to dual citizenship, Americans overseas have influenced other countries in direct ways. That was the case of president Valdas Adamkus in Lithuania and of Congressman Andrés Bermúdez in Mexico's national Congress. Both of them were American citizens when they held these posts.

Asian migration to the United Kingdom, the subsisting xenophobia against Indians and Pakistanis in some quarters notwithstanding, is generally seen as having exercised a positive influence on the British economy and society—and is often favorably contrasted with more recent newcomers. And yet Asian arrivals after the war followed a pattern of chain migration of the type that is so feared and criticized today: Early immigrants encouraged their friends and family members to follow them, eventually recruited them in their own businesses, and even channeled them towards native employers desperate for labor. The United Kingdom's post-war recovery owes much to chain migration.[22]

I have seen compact groups of Filipinos loiter in Statue Square in the heart of Downtown Hong Kong, just as I have seen Peruvians, Colombians, and other South Americans linger about in various corners of El Retiro, the well-known park in Madrid. They were not doing anything that Indians did not do in some neighborhoods in London in the 1960s and 1970s or that Peruvians did in Paterson, N.J., decades ago—and still do. Their conduct was— and is—a bridging, connecting, communicating force benefiting the host society's awareness of, and ties to, the outside world.

Among most migratory waves, a gradual adaptation to the host country has traditionally coexisted with the maintenance of some ties to other nationals from the same country and to the fatherland. In many cases, some of the incoming migration was circulatory—migrants saw themselves as transitory sojourners and wished to go back, but because governments placed major impediments to migration, the possibility of return was cut off. The paradoxical effect of increased obstacles aimed at reducing the inflow of foreigners was to "trap" immigrants who had no intention of remaining permanently in the host country. Of the 30 million Indians who left their country between the 1830s and the late 1930s, nearly 24 million returned.[23] That figure speaks both to the attachment that many Indians felt for their home country and to the relative ease with which people were able to come and go before restrictive policies spawned a more static and permanent type of migration.

A summary look at how immigrant communities that are now held in high regard behaved in the past confirms that what anti-immigration critics view as unsavory foreign traits of conduct limiting their nation's energy in today's competitive world differs little from the conduct of previous generations of newcomers in the United States, Europe, Australasia, and other parts of the world. These earlier immigrants also kept ties to the fatherland and to fellow nationals in the adopted countries.

Among Chinese immigrants in the nineteenth century; Italians, and Slavs at the turn of the twentieth century; and West Indians, Mexicans, and Puerto Ricans in the first half of the twentieth century, there were, in the words of a scholar of immigrant flows:

... cohorts that in their individual and collective lives sustained transnational economic, political and cultural connections bridging the
United States and their homeland. At the same time these very groups
participated gradually in the core patterns and institutions of American
life within two or three generations."[24]

As mentioned earlier, for a long time, Central and Eastern European Jews
were employed by German Jews in so-called sweatshops. They saved most of
the money they made in order to bring their families left back in Europe. Thus,
two-thirds of all the Central and Eastern Jewish immigrants who arrived in the
United States in the early twentieth century had their passage paid by family
members[25]—exactly the kind of family reunification attacked as being uneco-
nomic nowadays with regard to Hispanics or Africans on both sides of the Alan-
tic. America's competitiveness was not hurt by immigrant families. The families
added workers to the economy, facilitated economies of scale and, though this is
less easy to quantify, fostered a more stable social environment in communities
of foreign origin.

In Argentina, the mutual aid societies set up by Italians limited admission
policies to those from certain parts of Italy.[26] In American cities, Italians from
certain towns concentrated in particular neighborhoods and even streets.[27]
Neapolitans and Sicilians settled in different parts of New York. Eventually,
second-generation marriages began to occur between Italians and non-Italians,
although in 1920, 97 percent of Italian men still had Italian wives.[28] The current
tendency of first-generation immigrants to marry endogamously is nothing new
or peculiar to certain nationalities, nor is it an a priori burden on the nation's
competitiveness.

In the nineteenth century, the period of the great rise of the United States,
the existence of tight German enclaves meant their members never had "to
venture into the English-speaking world." Places such as Hermann, in Mis-
souri, had street signs in German, and German was spoken in the streets of
Cincinnati; there were German newspapers in some American cities—as there
are Spanish newspapers and TV programs today.[29] Social cohesion among Germans only declined because of hostility to them after World War I.[30] By then,
the United States was a world power. Many Americans of Scandinavian and
German descent still identify themselves as such a century and a half later. Their

contribution continues to be robust and no one accuses them of debilitating the country's standing in the face of competitors. The fact that 70 percent of Chinese immigrants in Los Angeles speak Chinese at home today and that four major Chinese-language dailies circulate in the United States—one of which, the *Chinese Daily News*, prints some 250,000 copies—mirrors what took place among European immigrants in the past.[31]

Is there a fundamental difference between the creation of the first Japanese language daily news outlet in San Francisco in 1892; the first Korean newspaper in Honolulu in 1905; the first form of Latino news, the so-called musical press known as *corridos* that continued the oral tradition of reporting the news through storytelling in the nineteenth century; and the emergence, in 1848, of the first newspaper created by and for Mexican-Americans?[32] There is no fundamental difference. Those did not spell the disintegration of the United States as an economic and cultural power, but rather the strength of its component parts and the country's ability to be in better communication with the rest of the world.

Did the Asian community-oriented patterns of early immigrants from that continent make the United States less strong and competitive in the world in the nineteenth and early twentieth centuries? The answer is obvious. Did the fact that between 1900 and 1906, 5 million letters from migrants in the United States arrived in Russia and Australia in the same way that millions of phone calls or e-mails are exchanged between immigrants in the United States and their families back home today place this country in a position of disadvantage? I would posit that it did not. This communication, and other forms of conduct, had much more to do with clinging to the familiar and easing the transition to the adopted country than with expressing some kind of recalcitrant anti-assimilationist sentiment.[33]

Undeniably, many immigrants look for comfort in communities made up of fellow nationals. Whenever possible, they like to associate with immigrants from the same region, city ward, or district in which they originated. Associations of Mexicans from the same region of origin abound in the United States. There are clubs through which people, connected to each other by place of birth, send money back home, teach English to new arrivals, organize sports events, practice philanthropy, or advise others on matters ranging from legal issues to job hunting. Although most of these clubs are in California, they can be found in others states. By 2003, there were more than 600 such associations.[34] But many other immigrant communities do the same. This is by no means a habit confined to Mexicans in the United States. Most immigrant associations are not enclaves removed from the host society, but actually a vehicle for engagement with, even assimilation into, the adopted country.

Sentimental attachments among expatriates and mutually supportive connections among fellow nationals abroad is by no means incompatible with the function of facilitating an immigrant's sense of belonging in the host country and helping him or her navigate the adopted waters, as many associations do. Similarly, fellow nationals celebrating events relating back to their fatherland can coexist with a firm attachment to the territory in which they have settled and to which they make a daily contribution. The Spanish fans who cheered fervently the victory of their soccer squad in the World Cup in 2001 at *Jaleo*, a famous restaurant in Bethesda, Md., owned by fabled chef José Andrés Puerta, were not perpetrating the Balkanization of the United States. They were simply celebrating a triumph that resonated with them—and then went on with their assimilated lives in this country.

The associations that help fellow nationals stay connected to each other should not be confused with others, much less numerous and with tiny influence in the wider immigrants communities, that smack of ethnic-based militancy and resentment against the adopted country of their forebears. Those groups are less notorious today but gained some attention in their heyday. The word "Chicano," for instance, was revived in the 1960s as a term of social and political awareness for Mexican youths who rejected assimilation. The irony was that those young people were much less Mexican than American—an extreme form of multiculturalism *avant la lettre*. They were never perceived as representative by the wider Mexican community. Their cultural manifestations were not seen in Mexico as native, but rather as a byproduct of migration to America.

Foreign communities go through different phases in their adopted countries. Youngsters of Indian descent are known to go through a cycle of early identification with American culture and only later of identification with Indian culture without renouncing their American belonging. In fact, even when they become more interested in their heritage, they do not necessarily see themselves as part of an organic Indian community of immigrants across the United States.[35]

The evidence suggests that Hispanics and Asians express great optimism about their lives in America. They believe hard work will be rewarded, and they put much faith in the "system."[36] The inference is that their behavior as immigrants when associating with other immigrants or cherishing their roots is not meant as an act of defiance against assimilation, but quite the contrary—as a way of making the transition to the new society smoother. The notion that Hispanics are disproportionately tied to their home country is a myth. Less than 10 percent of all Latino immigrants can be considered highly attached to the fatherland. Those would be the ones who can be said to have engaged in the three main transnational activities: sending remittances, making weekly phone calls, and traveling to the native country in the previous two years. A much larger proportion—28 percent—of foreign-born Latinos do not perform any of these activities. A total of 63 percent show a moderate attachment in general. The longer they have been in the United States, the less connected they are to the fatherland; if they migrated with their children, they are even less connected. Family reunification, seen as highly undesirable by anti-immigrant critics, actually weakens attachments to the home country and accelerates assimilation.

"Immigrants who maintain ties to their country of origin," the study concludes, "also cultivate attitudes that show they are putting down psychological roots in the United States." How much time an immigrant has spent in the host nation evidently is a factor.[37]

One major symptom of the exchanges that flow from relations between emigrants and the fatherland—constituting a strong link between the movement of people and things—is remittances sent back home. They have grown by leaps and bounds. Between 1970 and the first few years of the new millennium, the flow of money sent home by emigrants worldwide increased from $2 billion to more than $110 billion, a sum that surpassed the one for coffee and crude oil trade at the time.[38] Recently, global remittances have hovered around $300 billion per year, a sum not far from total foreign direct investment in developing countries.[39]

Remittances have always been attacked by critics of immigration. Chinese immigrants were traditionally accused of exporting the money out of the country in which they made it either in the form of remittances or savings that they took with them when returning home. Similar charges are made today against

Hispanics in the United States and Spain, and against Africans in France. The accusation absurdly presupposes that immigrants are able to take out of country all the wealth they generate for themselves and for others in the land in which they work and do business. What they send home is only a small percentage of what they generate for themselves and for the economy, and most probably the money represents a sum they would have otherwise spent on themselves.[40]

In some cases, remittances even have a way of returning to the place of origin. I spend some time in Spain every summer, and I am always fascinated by the spectacle, in the expressways of the South, of thousands of Northern Africans, particularly Algerians, driving to their native countries in vans swamped with goods such as appliances, electronic devices, kitchenware, lamps, furniture, and many other items that they sell relatively cheaply, bringing the money back to the European countries upon their return. Petty trade, or "suitcase trade," as this is sometimes called, is occasionally not so petty. Even the cars that crowd the ferries from Southern Spanish ports to Tangier, Melilla, or Ceuta are destined for such sales, as I found out during a trip to Ceuta.

A more legitimate concern regarding financial transfers from migrants to underdeveloped countries has to do with the tendency of those funds to go towards consumption rather than production. Studies have shown that in many countries, a great deal of the money sent by migrant communities is not employed in productive activities. More than 30 million Africans living outside of their country of origin send more than $40 billion every year, but between 30 and 40 percent of those funds are destined to rural areas where subsistence and basic consumption are the obliged use.[41] Less deprived parts of the world also show a pattern of consumption rather than production resulting from remittances. In this, remittances to some extent mirror the use made of transfers by governments in developed countries to poor societies through foreign aid—without the colossal corruption.

Studies conducted by the Community of Madrid's immigration program have concluded that remittances sent to Latin America do not necessarily translate into the creation of businesses and go towards consumption. In the course of a long, Spanish-style lunch in December of 2009, Javier Fernández-Lasquetty, the then Secretary of Immigration and Cooperation at the regional government of the Community of Madrid, confirmed to me that countries such as Mexico, the Dominican Republic, Peru, Ecuador, and others show similar household uses for money received from overseas.

However, he pointed to a few interesting cases of collective remittances sent by migrant organizations to support community projects in Mexico and Central America. In Mexico, the state of Zacatecas offers a "3 for 1" program created with support from the federal government whereby for every dollar sent by migrants, the federal and the state authorities contribute one dollar each. The money goes towards development projects designed and set up by the local population. A similar plan has been implemented in Cuenca, in Ecuador. The Community of Madrid is planning to get involved in these and other such initiatives in order to provide incentives to channel remittances towards production rather than consumption.

Although they are exceptional cases, in some countries remittances have had a more direct effect on production. At the turn of the new century, savings originated by emigrants amounted to 40 percent of term and site deposits in the Moroccan banking system. By the beginning of the new millennium, remittances, which represented 50 percent of export earnings, were estimated to have contributed very substantially to reducing poverty to 19 percent from 23.2 percent.[42]

But even if consumption, rather than investment, is the preferred option, the lost opportunity—if it can be termed a lost opportunity—affects the countries that receive the monies rather than those that send it. However, consumption also helps the economy—both of the country where it takes place and the country from which the consumed exports are sent. Remittances sent by foreigners do not per se make an adopted country less competitive; not to mention, of course, that it is up to the individual and the families, not the authorities, to decide how to spend the money sent by their relatives.

Besides remittances, critics look at immigrants' other types of attachments to their countries of origin or to communities made up of fellow nationals as proof of the dubious loyalty immigrants profess for their adopted countries. It is true, for instance, that many so-called minorities are drawn to what has come to be termed, with much inaccuracy, "ethnic culture." This is behavior expressed, for instance, in reliance on certain types of media. But watching programs or reading newspapers that cater specifically to certain groups is a conduct that straddles all sorts of communities, including native ones. The niche media is a feature of today's fragmented information age with its virtually unlimited supply of cable TV and Internet-based programming. About 45 percent of all African Americans, Hispanics, Asian Americans, Native Americans, and Arab American adults prefer "ethnic" television or newspapers to the mainstream media.[43] But many native youths prefer niche-based media too.

Critics confuse a tendency of immigrant groups to seek each other's vicinity and business with a pattern of hostility to assimilation. There is a substantial difference between South Americans who live in neighborhoods where Hispanics outnumber non-Hispanic whites and, say, African tribes whose culture is more deliberately anti-assimilationist. Some African migrant communities chose to segregate themselves and engage in endogamy because of tradition. A popular Yoruba adage says, *"Didun ajo ni ka ta ka jere ka kere oke dele,"* which translates literally as "The joy of sojourning in a foreign land is to sell, make profit and make remittances home."[44] But there is scant relation between this conduct and the one exhibited by most foreign communities, including those of African descent. The attitude of migrant groups that critics mistake for an attack on the social fabric of their nation is perfectly in keeping with tradition. Japanese farmers tended to concentrate in a few districts in the 1920s and 1930s, making their accomplishments more conspicuous. Latino and Asian neighborhoods in California or New York belong to that kind of tradition rather than the one contained in the Yoruba adage.

The expansion of exchanges and choice will probably diminish the possibility that some foreign communities will entirely control certain industries, as happened in the past. Between World War I and the 1930s, for instance, Chinese migration to Thailand reached a record rate that allowed the Chinese to establish a very powerful, closely knit community. This ability translated into the control of four major exports—rice, timber, tin, and rubber—due in part to their connections with export markets.[45] The much more diversified nature of today's commercial exchanges, while not necessarily precluding dominant positions by foreign communities in some industries in the adopted country, is fostering a more competitive and open economic environment.

The adopted countries of millions of migrants have little to fear. In an era of expanded commerce and communication, it is only natural that more and more people will move from one place to another and look at the world as an open space where free circulation is a necessary corollary of the free exchange of things. Accepting this, as we will see next in this book, will require rethinking some of the received ideas regarding the nation state. But it is ultimately in any country's best interest to do so.

In business, attitudes are perhaps more daring and minds more open than in other areas when it comes to migration, and they should serve as a guide to other parts of society that are less familiar with the positive aspects of migration. In 1996, consumer activist Ralph Nader wrote to the CEOs of the one hundred largest companies in the United States saying that because they were getting subsidies, they should open stockholder meetings with the Pledge of Allegiance. The head of Ford Motor Co. appropriately responded: "As a multinational, Ford in its largest sense is an Australian company in Australia, a British company in the United Kingdom, a German company in Germany."[46]

It is not only companies that are transnational or multinational (horrendous adjectives that enclose wonderful meanings). Executives, academics, civil servants, and others are too. They are estimated to number at least 20 million, of whom 40 percent are American.[47] Not all of them have a vision of the world as a place of free cross-border circulation of goods, services, capital, ideas, and people; many have a penchant for bureaucracy and would like to replace the nation state with a supranational, big-government alternative. But the mindset of many of these international executives is a harbinger of a society that will embrace globalization in its human no less than its economic mobility.

Many industries and other segments of American society have been prescient in this embrace of globalization. Hollywood is an industry that thrives on cross-border movements and multinational exchanges, in which a person's nation of origin does not determine the limits of possibility. For many decades, it has been at the forefront of globalization. Universities, with their substantial foreign student bodies, have also learned the virtues of exchanges between peoples of all origins. Attitudes to immigration among these circles ought to radiate throughout the rest of society more forcefully.

Notes

1. Nancy L. Green, *Repenser Les Migrations* (Paris: Presses Universitaires de France, 2002), 55. Also see Georgie Anne Geyer, *Americans No More* (New York: The Atlantic Press, 1996), 54.

2. Mary C. Waters and Reed Ueda, "Introduction," in *The New Americans: A Guide to Immigration Since 1965*, eds. Mary C. Waters and Reed Ueda (Cambridge, Mass.: Harvard University Press, 2007), 2–3.

3. "Overcoming Barriers: Human Development and Mobility," Human Development Report 2009, United Nations Development Program, October, 2009), 1 and statistical tables at the end, http://hdr.undp.org/en/media/HDR_2009_EN_Complete.pdf

4. http://openjurist.org/630/f2d/876/filartiga-v-pena-irala

5. Nana Oishi, *Women in Motion: Globalization, State Policies, and Labor Migration in Asia*, (Stanford, Calif.: Stanford University Press, 2005), 61.

6. Luis Eduardo Guarnizo and Marilyn Espitia, "Colombia," in *The New Americans*, eds. Waters and Ueda, 383.

7. Oishi, *Women in Motion*, 146.

8. Oishi, *Women in Motion*, 147-8.

9. Abbas Mehdi, "Globalization, Migration and the Arab World," in *Arab Migration in a Globalized World* (Geneva: International Organization for Migration, League of Arab States, 2004), 14–15.

10. "Overcoming Barriers," http://hdr.undp.org/en/media/HDR_2009_EN_Com plete.pdf

11. Giovanni Peri, "America's Stake in Immigration: Why Almost Everybody Wins," *The Milken Institute Review* (3rd qtr. 2007): 42.

12. Maxime Tandonnet, *Le Grand Bazar ou l'Europe Face à l'Immigration* (Paris: l'Harmattan, 2001), 13–14.

13. Jorge Castañeda, *Ex Mex: From Migrants to Immigrants* (New York: The New Press, 2007), xiii.

14. Henry Morley, ed., *The Earlier Life and Chief Earlier Works of Daniel Defoe* (London: George Routledge & Sons, 1899), 175–218.

15. The original quote is, "¿Y por qué, si somos berberiscos, no hemos de sentirnos y proclamarnos tales…?" Miguel de Unamuno, "Sobre la europeización (arbitrariedades)," in *Obras Completas,* vol. 3 (Madrid: Escélicer, 1968), 436.

16. Wayne A. Cornelius, "Mexican Migration to the United States: The Limits of Government Intervention, in *Proceedings of the Academy of Political Science* 34, no. 1 (1981): 1. http://www.jstor.org/stable/1174031

17. Reed Ueda, "Immigration in Global Historical Perspective," in *The New Americans,* eds. Waters and Ueda, 19.

18. Xiao-huang Yin, "China: People's Republic of China," in *The New Americans*, eds. Waters and Ueda, 348–350.

19. The survey was conducted by Bendixen & Associates and sponsored by the Multilateral Investment Fund of the Inter-American Development Bank, September 29, 2005, http://bendixenandassociates.com/studies/miami%20herald%20Americas%20confer ence%202005.pdf

20. Cornelius, "Mexican Migration to the United States," 1–2.

21. For a good account of female immigration in a developed nation see, for instance, Isabel Taboada Leonetti and Florence Levy, *Femmes et Immigrés: L'insertion des Femmes Immigrés en France* (Paris: Documentation Francaise, 1978).

22. Zig Layton-Henry, *The Politics of Immigration: Immigration, "Race" and "Race" Relations in Post-War Britain* (Oxford, U.K. and Cambridge, Mass.: Blackwell, 1992), 12–13.

23. Kingsley Davis, *The Population of India and Pakistan* (Princeton, N.J.: Princeton University Press, 1951), 99. Also see M.C. Madhavan, "Indian Emigrants: Numbers, Characteristics, and Economic Impact," *Population and Development Review* (September 1985), 462, 466.

24. Ueda, "Immigration In Global Historical Perspective," in *The New Americans,* eds. Waters and Ueda, 26.

25. Moses Rischin, *The Promised City: New York's Jews, 1870–1914* (Cambridge, Mass.: Harvard University Press, 1967), 63.

26. Robert F. Foerster, *The Italian Emigration of Our Times* (New York: Arno Press, 1969), 272.

27. Dino Cinel, *From Italy to San Francisco: The Impact Experience* (Stanford, Calif.: Stanford University Press, 1982), 59–65.

28. Cinel, *From Italy to San Francisco,* 177.

29. Thomas Sowell, *Migrations and Cultures* (New York: Basic Books, 1996), 73.

30. Charles H. Anderson, *White Protestant Americans* (Englewood Cliffs, N.J.: Prentice-Hall, 1970), 85.

31. Yin Xiao-huang, "China: People's Republic of China," in *The New Americans* eds. Waters and Ueda, 350.

32. K. Viswanath and Karen Ka-man Lee, "Ethnic Media," in *The New Americans* eds. Waters and Ueda, 204–205.

33. Similar patterns can be seen in other countries. In Brazil, during the period between 1908 and 1947, the rate of marriage beyond the immigrant community among Japanese females never reached 1 percent, while among males it was barely 4 percent. Ukrainians taken to Britain after World War II in order to provide badly needed labor raised their children in Ukrainian and even set up Ukrainian schools. They and other Central and Eastern Europeans refused to adopt British citizenship for a long time. Today, early Central and Eastern Europeans immigrants are perceived as having made a strong contribution to a country that was devastated by the war effort. See Inge Weber-Newth, "Narratives Of Settlement: East European Migrants In Post-War Britain," in *Histories And Memory: Migrants And Their Histories In Britain*, eds. Panikos Panayi and Kathy Burrell (London: I.B. Tauris, 2006), 88.

34. Castañeda, *Ex Mex,* 158.

35. Karen Isaksen Leonard, "India," in *The New Americans,* eds. Waters and Ueda, 467.

36. The survey was ordered by *New America Media* and conducted by Bendixen & Associates, and published under the title of "Deep Divisions, Shared Destiny," on December 12, 2007.

37. Almost one-third of Latinos say they describe themselves as Americans, while among recent arrivals, the proportion who do so is one-sixth. For those who have been in the United States for three decades, the figure who do so surpasses 50 percent. See Roger Waldinger, "Between Here and There: How Attached Are Latino Immigrants to

Their Native Country?" Pew Hispanic Center, Washington, D.C., October 2007, http://www.pewhispanic.org/reports/report.php?ReportID=80

38. "Balance of Payments Statistics," *International Monetary Fund*, Washington, D.C., 2003.

39. Up until the financial crisis of 2007–08, remittances by Mexicans amounted to roughly 2.5 percent of the economy of their country of origin. Surveys by Mexico's Central Bank indicate that six out of every ten senders make more than $1,500 a month, 36 percent more than $2,000 and one-quarter more than $2,500. Six in every ten households that receive money from migrants belong to the lowest 20 percent of the population in terms of income. Remittances represent an even greater proportion of the Central American economies, as well as that of Ecuador—above 10 percent. Central and Eastern European nations, including the Balkans and the Caucasus regions, also benefit from vast remittances from emigrants in Europe and other parts of the world. The proportion of their economies represented by this money oscillates between 5 and 10 percent, depending on the country. In 2001, it is estimated that money sent home by foreign workers in Saudi Arabia amounted to 10 percent of the total economy. See "FFR Update: Financial Facility for Remittances," *IFAD*, Issue 1 (4th qtr. 2009) and "Foreign Direct Investment Rose by 34% in 2006," United Nations Conference on Trade and Development, September 1, 2007, http://www.unctad.org/templates/webflyer.asp?docid=7993&intItemID=4431&lang=1

40. Sowell, *Migrations and Cultures*, 182.

41. "FFR Update: Financial Facility for Remittances." Also see "Foreign Direct Investment Rose by 34% in 2006," *United Nations Conference on Trade and Development*.

42. Mohamed Khachani, "Moroccan Migration to Europe: What Impact On The Economies of Countries of Origin," in *Arab Migration in a Globalized World*, (Geneva: International Organization for Migration, League of Arab States, 2004), 47. Also see Abbas Mehdi, "Globalization, Migration and the Arab World," in *Arab Migration in a Globalized World*, 11.

43. The poll was conducted by Bendixen & Associates and published by the New America Media. See "Ethnic Media in America: the Giant Hidden in Plain Sight," New America Media, New York and Washington, D.C., June 7, 2005, http://news.new americamedia.org/news/view_article.html?article_id=0443821787aco210cbecebe8b1f576a3

44. Isaac Olawale Albert, "Host-Stranger Conflicts in the Context of International Migrations in Africa," in *Etre Etranger et Migrant en Afrique Au XXe Siècle: Enjeux Identitaires et Modes d'Insertion,* vol. 1, Catherine Coquery-Vidrovitch, ed., (Paris: l'Harmattant, 2003), 149.

45. G. William Skinner, *Chinese Society in Thailand: An Analytical History* (Ithaca, N.Y.: Cornell University Press, 1957), 336. Also see Sowell, *Migrations and Cultures*, 188–189.

46. Samuel Huntington, *Who Are We? The Challenges of America's National Identity* (New York: Simon & Schuster, 2004), 7.

47. John Micklethwait and Adrian Woolbridge, *The Future Perfect: The Challenge and Hidden Promise of Globalization* (New York: Crown Business, 2000), 235.

17

Credo or Nationality?

A NEW PARADIGM with strong moral connotations is gradually emerging because of the nature of the world in which we live. It is the idea of transcending borders and nationality. Fiercely resisted by many and still a minority view, the idea of a transnational citizenship is taking shape. I do not refer to supranational bureaucratic structures or a world government embodied in the United Nations or some such entity. I speak of a world in which nationality and nationhood are becoming ever so slowly decoupled from national borders—sometimes in practice and other times in the imagination of some pioneering romantics of a new kind. It is unclear where this trend is leading. Given the powerful reaction to dissolving the nation-state into looser cross-border arrangements that replace old boundaries with novel ways of framing the ties between individuals and communities, it is by no means inconceivable that the transnational trend will come to a stop and be followed by a potent backlash—although if that happens, it is likely to be a temporary or intermittent situation.

Transnationalism (a phenomenon for which a less cacophonic word is urgently needed) is understood by modern scholars as "a shift beyond membership in a territorial state or nation and its accompanying civic and political claims toward more encompassing definitions such as universal humanism, membership in a super-State (European Union) and panreligious solidarity." It refers to economic involvement, social networks, and cultural identities that link people and institutions in two or more nation-states, making them members of plural civic and political entities.[1] Implicit in the trend is also a revolutionary concept: the idea of dispensing, somewhere down the road, with the constraints of the nation-state as we have known it since the end of the sixteenth century and basing political arrangements on a definition of identity that is much more personal, not bound by territorial loyalties or national kinship. To an extent, this was already true in some parts of the world even before the contemporary phase of globalization stretched national boundaries and opened the ongoing discussion on transnationalism. For many Muslim people, for example, loyalty to clan, family, or tribe, and, more broadly, to the Islamic community (*umma*) has been greater than loyalty to the nation-state.[2] Muslims in Western Europe have had less latitude to act upon this type of loyalty than in Muslim countries for obvious reasons, but even the gradual dissolution of national borders into the wider European Union has created new opportunities to do so, just as it has on the other hand encouraged a strong nationalist and even separatist current in some regions of the continent.

Transnationalism manifests itself not only in how individuals perceive their own loyalties, but also in the conduct of governments vis-à-vis their emigrant communities. Governments feel increasingly obliged to support their diasporas—which creates a paradoxical situation: the very incarnation of the nation-state acting as if it had jurisdiction beyond the confines of the nation-state. In 1990, Mexico created a Program for the Mexican Abroad as a subsidiary of the Foreign Ministry. The budgets of the 42 Mexican consulates in the United States were substantially beefed up. Today Mexicans in the United States, regardless of their legal status, are given a *matrícula consular*, a form of identity card that some American institutions accept for various purposes. The government provided support to the National Association of Bilingual Education and through its consulates distributed textbooks among many of its nationals. Mexico now recognizes dual citizenship, prompting many Mexican Americans to clamor for the right to vote in Mexican elections. Other Hispanic communities already have an impact in elections in their home countries. About 15 percent of the funds spent in elections in the Dominican Republic come from Dominicans living abroad, mostly in the United States and, to a much lesser extent, in Spain.[3]

The support given by some governments to their emigrants has led detractors of immigration to decry what they see as an apotheosis of extraterritoriality. Some defenders of the active involvement of governments with their nationals abroad remind us that various governments did the same thing in the distant past, and that migration itself should not be held accountable for the rights or wrongs of a state's foreign policy. What governments do today is "like the role France and Russia asserted," in the view of one defender, "as protectors of the oppressed Christian minorities in the Ottoman Empire." He was evoking the time when the French monarchy established treaties through which it gave protection to Catholic sites and to the clergy in the Holy Land, as well as to the treaty that Russia signed in 1774 making the Tsar the guarantor of commitments by the Turkish sultan to provide safety for Orthodox Christians.[4] Italian foreign policy between the 1900s and the 1930s attempted to support Italians in the United States; among other things, Italy admitted dual citizenship.[5] The practice of extending a state's power beyond a territory because of emigration can be innocuous or, as most things states do when exercising their power, very dangerous.

Regardless of the conduct of the governments of the countries of origin, the authorities of the "receiving" countries face the dilemma of how to treat, from a legal point of view, the immigrants in their midst. In doing so, they are constantly challenged by the institutions of the nation-state and the ideology that supports them. Generally, states define citizenship as *jus sanguinis* (right of blood) or *jus solis* (right of soil). Many countries have a combination of the two. Germany belonged squarely to the *jus sanguinis* for a long time, but Bonn eventually had to make exceptions and introduce some flexibility. In the United States, the children of undocumented immigrants become citizens if they are born in the country. Anti-immigrant groups have lashed out against this right, which is enthroned by the Fourteenth Amendment to the Constitution. But *jus sanguinis* has so far survived the onslaught.

Non-citizen residents of the United States have every right enjoyed by citizens except to participate in politics and government, as well as a few smaller restrictions derived from the post-2001 environment. Until 1920, immigrants were allowed to vote in several states (today non-citizens can vote in local elections only in a few places such as Takoma Park, Barnesville, Martin's Additions, Somerset, and Chevy Chase, all in Maryland). Perhaps the rights that come with residency—coupled with the fear of losing one's original nationality when dual citizenship was not fashionable or possible—had some bearing on the relatively slow pace of naturalization in recent decades.[6]

In theory, when a foreign resident becomes a U.S. citizen, he or she has to renounce the citizenship of origin at the swearing-in ceremony. In practice, that rule is not enforced. Many countries do not allow citizens to renounce their citizenship unless they formally express their determination to do so before their own authorities, which means that a declaration made before an American judge at the swearing-in ceremony is invalid in their eyes. The U.S. government does not ordinarily pursue the issue, allowing many U.S. citizens who hold a second or third citizenship to continue to be citizens of this country.

Tolerance for dual citizenship is a sign of something more than the difficulty of enforcing the renunciation of a naturalized person's original citizenship. In some respect, it is the tacit acceptance of the transnational world of our days. A century ago, Theodore Roosevelt called dual citizenship "a self-evident absurdity."[7] Today that absurdity has become irresistible even for the political heirs of Mr. Roosevelt, who tolerate it without much discussion—Republicans have made no greater effort than Democrats on that front. But Roosevelt was not expressing an isolated point of view. He was speaking for a long tradition. The notion of dual citizenship would have been difficult to conceive for those who passed the first law dealing with naturalization in 1790 (it conferred that privilege only to free white persons). The Founding Fathers saw the immigration process, of which naturalization was a culminating event, as a form of Americanization whereby a value system reflected in a set of institutions became the common heritage of those who lived in the country, assimilated foreigners included. They welcomed and had extensive dealings with foreigners, from the Revolutionary period to the emergence of the United States as a republic, but for them naturalization was a form of Americanization, a transformative event, not simply a concession or an acceptance of transnationality.

The tradition of naturalizing foreigners as a way to Americanize them was largely maintained. In the wake of the 1848 Guadalupe-Hidalgo Treaty that ceded part of Mexico to the United States, people living in the affected territory were granted U.S. citizenship. The intention was evidently to Americanize those new citizens, not to dilute American citizenship by extending it to foreigners. In time, however, the complexities of modern events forced the U.S. government to tinker with the legacy. Puerto Rico is a case in point. Negotiations with the island established a commonwealth whereby Puerto Ricans do not pay federal taxes, are not allowed to vote in national elections, and can conduct affairs of state in Spanish even though they hold a U.S. passport. The transnational trend has reopened a debate about whether being an American relates essentially to a certain credo—a set of values and institutions—or to nationhood—a mystical, sentimental notion derived from an individual's ties to the territory of his or her forebears. Critics of dual citizenship and of interpreting Americanization as the acceptance of a credo rather than the adoption of a "national" character have attacked what they term the "commoditization" of citizenship.[8] In the mind of such critics, the end of the nation-state to which globalization seems to point will create a "bazaar" with private clubs lacking common beliefs and values.[9] For them, having a free trade zone such as that created by the North American Free Trade Act (NAFTA) means there could eventually be mobility of voting rights in local elections; they note with sarcasm that the movement for non-citizen vote is the new suffrage movement.[10] They see with alarm that many Central and Eastern Europeans established in the United States went back to their countries to serve in public office and that many American Jews left to fight for Israel. In their eyes, this is "akin to bigamy."[11] They resent that some cities conduct affairs in English and Spanish, or that the children of immigrants can become citizens simply by being born in the United States under an amendment to the Constitution that was passed after the Civil War in order to confer citizenship to freed slaves.

In Europe, where nationhood is even more powerfully engrained in people's psyche, the debate is also being spurred by the sense that transnational forces continue to dilute national borders. For the French, the defense of nationhood goes back to the times of Vercingétorix, the Gaul who unsuccessfully tried to overthrow the Roman Empire. French national heroes and heroines tend to be those who stopped invasions, and France prides itself on being a unique nation that extended civilization to the rest of the world. Since the French Revolution, this civilizing role that informs the sense of nationhood instilled by official institutions and civil leaders in successive generations has been associated with spreading certain universal rights and principles of government—the credo of *liberté, egalité, fraternité*.

In the 1920s, that very credo led, for instance, the first organization of Algerians that fought for independence from France to invoke the principles and values of 1789 against the very country that exported them to the world.[12] Since the Revolution, more generally, France's idea of integration was theoretically based on *l'égalité républicaine,* that is, a credo rather than ethnicity or social status. But the reality is that the French have interpreted nationhood in such a way that the nation-state as a mystical entity has become intertwined with the credo emanated from the Revolution. To them, being French is not simply being a believer in the principles of the French Revolution, but being a part of the nation. If universal citizenship were ever to become a reality, it would force the French, who arguably contributed to the notion of universal citizenship by exporting the principle of universal human rights derived from their Revolution, to either accept that their credo ultimately overcame their nationhood—or to renounce the principle of universality and negate the revolutionary legacy.

Few passions are more inflammatory when collectively expressed than nationalism, or any other feelings connected to nationhood. Nationalism is both a defensive passion—against perceived threats from outside—and an aggressive passion—in favor of expanding the power of the nation. The idea that a person from a different country can become a citizen of one's nation is instinctively threatening to many people who fear the erosion of nationhood. The prejudice is so potent that, despite the traumatic social consequences of denying a path to citizenship to millions of established foreigners who are excluded by unrealistic laws, nativists and nationalists fiercely oppose granting them such a status. The risk implicit in the nationalist blindness to the consequences of maintaining a two-tier system that excludes millions from a legal status is not small. Some observers go as far as to contend that the growth of Islamic radicalism in Europe is linked to the marginalization of foreigners. The exclusion of immigrants from the realm of full citizenship, it is said, created a vacuum that fanatics tried to fill by providing them with a sense of belonging—or a vehicle to vent their rancor. Those who offer such views maintain that the vacuum left by the unsuccessful *Movement des Beurs* in the 1980s—a movement of North African immigrants seeking citizenship—was ultimately filled by Islamist organizations.[13] The perception that paths to assimilation were definitively truncated may have bred resentment in younger generations of North Africans in France.

Ideology and ignorance make a combustible combination. Nationalism has had a pernicious effect on the discussion about immigration. It is an ideology that seeks to advance a nation at the expense of others, built upon mystical notions of ancient kinship and propped up by the use of symbols and propaganda. By enthroning a narrow and static notion of what a nation is, nativism has pushed many well-meaning but ill-informed people to confuse their love for their country—as well as the respect for their forebears and their cherished traditions—with a fortress view of nationhood conceived as the protection of a purity and singularity achieved through the ages. The idea of America's exceptionalism, whose origin probably and ironically dates back to the Frenchman Alexis de Tocqueville's view of America as unique, has morphed into jingoistic myths seeking to draw inspiration from a past that is highly romanticized. The idea of immutable nationhood runs contrary to the historical reality of nations that have evolved in traumatic and dynamic ways, most often through conquest and dislocation, and whose purity has long been diluted—if it ever existed. The notion of immutable nationhood also tacitly negates the greatest achievement of civilization: the gradual emergence of the individual as a sovereign being, as the depositary of rights and the subject of voluntary exchanges upon which common life thrives. Those for whom the nation is sovereign over individual rights have a poor concept of civilization.

The modern state was born in part from the gradual dislocations forced upon the population by empires. People were transferred to those parts where they were economically necessary for the preservation of the empire. Paradoxically, the authorities that forcibly uprooted communities also would let their members cross borders fairly easily rather than encircle them. This flexibility was probably derived from practical considerations and from the empires' ambitions to grow indefinitely. But the empires were too big and their smaller units gradually became stronger, tearing apart the loosened imperial structure. Between the thirteenth and the fifteenth centuries, the Germanic Holy Roman Empire gave rise to the first manifestations of the modern nation-state, whose centralizing powers were suited for war.[14] Wars made it necessary for the state to generate a national consciousness and create a bureaucratic machinery for it.[15] As Charles Tilly wrote, "War made the state and the state made war."[16] King and state were now separate, and sovereignty came to reside in the state, which the king protected. The obligation to defend the king's state in France became superior to feudal obligations towards the lord. The relationship between kings and subjects was framed by legal codes. The metaphysical notions of "fatherland" and "nation" were eventually enthroned. They became part of the public discourse in the eighteenth century but had been in the air for a long time. The state used these terms to legitimize its rules—and its costly exploits.

This is not to say there were no cultural affinities linking members of various communities and differentiating them from other communities. Clearly, the German peoples that straddled different political units in centuries prior to the unification of Germany had strong cultural bonds that distinguished them from Mediterranean peoples. But nationhood was a political artifice that built a system of symbols and ultimately an ideology upon kinships that sometimes were real and sometimes highly exaggerated. Nationhood served the purpose of sustaining authoritarian monarchs. As has been mentioned, when the French Revolution defeated the monarchy, the republican ideology tried to replace these mystical notions with the Lights of the Enlightenment— freedom, emancipation, and human rights. Unlike the American Revolution, however, which was based on the republican idea of individual rights, the French Revolution did not entirely renounce collectivist notions of fatherland and nationhood inherited from the old regime. The legacy was accommodated to fit their republican project, which turned out to be despotic.

When the royalists reacted against the Revolution, the revolutionaries used the argument that the "fatherland" was in danger. National sovereignty eclipsed popular sovereignty—not to speak of individual sovereignty, which had always been weak as a revolutionary ideal. Citizenship was not voluntary, but an imposition. The nation-state had become what it still is today.[17] Several French thinkers reacted against national sovereignty as superior to individual sovereignty, but French nationalism withstood the attack. Montesquieu's dictum—"I am a man before being French. . . . I am necessarily a man and I am only French by chance"—was to no avail.[18] Nationalist intellectuals pushed back and resonated with societies where collectivist instincts were still strong.

The ideology of nationhood traveled fast. Everywhere it sought to legitimize vertical rule through myths that fed on kinships, real or imagined. Even today one can see how inadequate these imposed structures are in a region like Africa, where no society or community was built around a national idea, but where nation-states established within borders demarcated by European powers replaced colonial rule with often devastating effects. Africans had traditionally been tied together by lineage and clans, but when the nation-state was imposed on them it was cunningly used by politicians to enthrone their own tribe and oppress others.[19]

We think of the nation-state today as an eternal structure, but its existence is a blip in the course of human history and will probably evolve into something else in the future—whether through the definitive erosion of nationhood or its replication in smaller units. The new phase of globalization gives us daily examples of the former. But the latter dynamic is also at work, for instance in the way a construct such as the European Union has reinforced a narrowing of identities, so that Scotts, Catalans, Basques, Corsicans, and others see themselves as such before they see themselves—if at all—as Spanish, British, or French.

No nationality is pure or spontaneous. Ethnic groups, themselves a debatable proposition given the constant mixing of people and communities, may be the products of a semi-spontaneous evolution—if we accept their existence— but the much wider concept of nation is a deliberate creation.[20] The idea that a nation shares common blood or a common race is silly. There are only four blood groups to begin with, and everything else is part of the long evolutionary process according to the geographic location of various groups of people. However, science and common sense have not been able to defeat the appeal of nationalism, whose ideological foundation was definitively consolidated in the nineteenth century. The myth of nationhood gained intellectual respectability thanks to the ideologues of modern nationalism, not all of whom saw themselves as such, and among whom there are many differences—Herder, de Maistre, Hegel, Fichte, Schelling, Maurras, and others.[21] Since then, nationalism has permeated many societies, even the most advanced and scientifically disposed. American nativism is one example.

The birth of nationalism in countries such as the United States, Canada, and Australia is particularly interesting. Their founding myth was the idea of starting from scratch and basing the new community on principles not necessarily beholden to a national mystique.[22] Nationalism came much later. In the United States, nationalism eventually emerged with the increasing consciousness of the country's prosperity and might, and it was fed by the dynamic of the frontier. But the cornerstone of the revolutionary legacy was the credo based on individual rights. This credo was the pillar that upheld the uniqueness of the country that foreign observers so admired. The national mystique was paradoxically born out of the credo of liberty and the blessings this credo brought to the country, not out of ideas of ethnic heritage. In time, pushed by nativist ideology, that national mystique also morphed into a type of nationalism loosely akin to that of European countries—hence the recurring cultural arguments against immigration. But if European nations are complex mixes of peoples from different parts, what can we say about the United States, made up of different European groups to which many others from around the globe were added in the course of its history?

Identity, wrote Lévi-Strauss, is a sort of virtual home to which it is necessary to refer in order to explain a certain number of things.[23] In other words, it is what one wants to make of it. With sufficiently persuasive powers, states and ideologues can sustain the illusion of a national identity that is superior to individual sovereignty and to factual history. Xenophobia and racism are extreme expressions of this superstition. The superstitious idea of national identity has convinced many people of the danger that immigration represents for the receiving country.

French president Nicolas Sarkozy decided, at the end of the decade 2000–09, to sponsor a debate on "national identity." He introduced legislation giving mayors the authority to ban foreign flags in weddings of immigrants. Parliament discussed whether to restrict use of the all-face Muslim veil, a tricky decision given that the French constitution guarantees freedom of religion. In July of 2010, the lower house approved the ban. The French people's response to the debate betrayed strong anti-Muslim sentiments, generating in turn much resentment among Muslims. The fire that was being stoked by some of the more irrational voices was not small considering that there are an estimated 5 million Muslims in France, the largest Muslim community in the European Union.

In an article published in *Le Monde* on December 8, 2009, soon after the Swiss vote of November 29 barring the construction of minarets in mosques, Sarkozy wrote that "in our country, where Christian civilization has left such a deep trace, where republican values are an integral part or our national identity, everything that could be taken as a challenge to this heritage and its values would condemn to failure the necessary inauguration of French Islam." The president was evidently trying to be sympathetic to both sides—the article was titled: "Respecting those who arrive, respecting those who host"—but the point of the quote is to emphasize how the entire debate and Mr. Sarkozy's participation in it revolved around the notion of a French national identity. He contrasted the idea of national identity to tribal and communal identity, rather than to individual identity, revealing the extent to which collectivist notions of identity derived from the ideology of nationhood influence the way citizens relate to foreigners.[24]

The debate over whether the United States is essentially a nation or a credo—and therefore whether immigration is a national threat or a blessing under the common credo—is not purely academic. It goes to the heart of what the United States is and where it wants to go in the future. Several scholars and thinkers have pointed to the distortion of Americas' roots implicit in the idea of national sovereignty as the paramount paradigm. In a famous article published in 1975, legal scholar Alexander Bickel argued that citizens' rights and immigrants' rights were virtually identical; American citizenship, he concluded, "is at best a simple idea for a simple government."[25] Against ideas of national identity espoused by Samuel Huntington, Joel Millman has argued that America is not a nation—not a German Volk or a Russian *narod*, that Latinos are not a single *pueblo*, and that African Americans do not constitute a single race with a common past. "What's common in America is the now," he states. America is not a large tribe ruling over a variety of subtribes—unlike the former Soviet Union or, in democratic form, India and Brazil. Other nations treasure their common past, either as a bulwark against the encroachments of the Über Tribe or as a means to become one. America is the anti-tribe. "Admission here is open to anyone, which is the reason why we are everyone's mother country." Immigrants help renew the values, the credo.[26]

Those who argue that the United States is a credo, a market, a set of institutions under which anyone willing to abide by individual liberty can make a life are often caricatured and misrepresented as inimical to sentimental attachments to their country of birth or their forebears. But in fact, to argue that the common heritage of Americans is a credo, the most appealing and successful one in the course of human history, is to render the United States the greatest of honors. The millions of immigrants who chose America as their adopted country value the enticing possibilities they come here to pursue. Those possibilities are born out of a credo. In that sense, the truly universal citizenship is that of credo.

Georgie Anne Geyer, a brilliant writer and a critic of immigration, has argued that universalism is really protected only by mutual obligations, codified in laws and citizenship, which in turn are only possible under the nation-state system, at least until we became perfect human beings.[27] The first part of her reasoning is a defense of credo as the binding force of civilization; the second, contradicting the first, is an act of faith in the nation-state as we know it. Why, if liberal democracy, private property, and the contract society were the result of a very long evolution, must the nation-state in its current stage be the definitive political structure? There is nothing to suggest that the evolutionary dynamic has to stop. In fact, in today's world, everything seems to point in the direction of an evolving process that makes the traditional nation-state seem to be a rigid, obsolescent structure. The conflict over immigration—a clash between movement and static structures—is good proof.

Many Americans on the right who value their country's heritage would be incensed at the idea that defending the prevalence of credo over other considerations is unpatriotic. A few days before California's Proposition 187 denying public welfare to undocumented immigrants was voted, Jack Kemp and Bill Bennett, two well-known figures of the Republican Party, put out a statement attacking it. They said, "The vast majority of immigrants hold principles which the Republican Party warmly embraces: an entrepreneurial spirit and self-reliance, hostility to government intervention, strong family values, and deeply-rooted religious faith." They went on to state, "The American national identity is not based on ethnicity, or race, or national origin, or religion. . . . [It] is based on a creed, a set of principles and ideas."[28] Other conservatives need to be reminded of these important truths if the United States is going to remain a country of sovereign individuals. Conservatives should be immensely proud of the credo of the United States and feel no need to make nationhood its foundation.

The first systematic codes in the English language were drawn up in Virginia (1606), Bermuda (1612), Plymouth (1636), and Massachusetts Bay (1648). And the first written constitution of modern democracy was the Fundamental Orders of Connecticut, adopted in 1638. With such an extraordinary legacy of credo, why would anyone feel the need to cling to a different idea of America's origin?[29]

Notes

1. Ewa Marawska, "Transnationalism," in *The New Americans: A Guide to Immigration Since 1965*, eds. Mary C. Waters and Reed Ueda (Cambridge, Mass.: Harvard University Press, 2007), 150.

2. Samuel Huntington, *Who Are We? The Challenges of America's National Identity* (New York: Simon & Schuster, 2004), 16.

3. Michael Jones-Correa, "Under Two Flags: Dual Nationality in Latin America and its Consequences for Naturalization in the United States," *International Migration Review* 35 (Winter 2001), 1004, 1008.

4. Mark Krikorian, *The New Case Against Immigration: Both Legal and Illegal*, (London: Sentinel, 2008), 49.

5. John Fonte, "Dual Allegiance: A Challenge to Immigration Reform and Patriotic Assimilation," Center for Immigration Studies, Washington, D.C., November 2005, http://www.cis.org/articles/2005/back1205.html

6. The rate of naturalization dropped from 63.6 percent in 1970 to 37.4 percent in 2000, although the 1986 amnesty gave rise to massive naturalizations for a brief period in the 1990s. The 2001 terrorist attacks against the Twin Towers and the Pentagon also triggered a spike on naturalization probably because of the fear of deportation. Mexican naturalizations are among the lowest and Asian ones among the quickest. In the case of Mexicans, the recent Mexican law allowing dual citizenship could have a major impact in years to come on the number of immigrants willing to acquire U.S. citizenship. See Michael Jones-Correa, *Between Two Nations: The Political Predicament of Latinos in New York* (Ithaca, N.Y.: Cornell University Press, 1998), 200. Also see Joel Millman, *The Other Americans* (New York: Viking, 1997), 256–257.

7. Krikorian, *The New Case Against Immigration*, 33.

8. Georgie Anne Geyer used this term a few years ago. It is widely used by commentators today in print articles and on websites—for instance Michael Vass, author of *Black Entertainment USA*. See Georgie Anne Geyer, *Americans No More* (New York: The Atlantic Press, 1996), 5. Also see Michael Vass, "Illegal Immigration: The Problem and a Potential Solution," January 6, 2009, http://www.mvass.com/2009/01/illegal-immigration-problem-and.html

9. Christopher Lasch, *The Revolt of the Elites and the Betrayal of Democracy* (New York: W. W. Norton & Co., 1995). Quoted in Geyer, *Americans No More*, 28.

10. The idea was expressed by Jamie Ruskin in an interview with Georgie Anne Geyer. See Geyer, *Americans No More*, 61.

11. Geyer, *Americans No More*, 68.

12. Roger Fauroux and Hanifa Chérifi, *Nous Sommes Tous des Immigrés* (Paris: Éditions Robert Lafont, 2003), 57–59.

13. Fauroux and Chérifi, *Nous Sommes Tous des Immigré*, 166-168.

14. For the relationship between war and the rise of the modern state, see for instance Bruce D. Porter, *War and the Rise of the State: The Military Foundations of Modern Politics* (New York: Free Press, 1994).

15. Samuel Huntington, *Who Are We? The Challenges of America's National Identity* (New York: Simon & Schuster, 2004), 16.

16. Charles Tilly, "Reflections on the History of European State-Making," in ed. Charles Tilly, *The Formation of National States in Western Europe* (Princeton, N.J.: Princeton University Press, 1975), 42.

17. Monique Chemillien Gendreau, "La contingence historique de la nation et la nationalité" in *Etre Etranger et Migrant En Afrique Au XXe Siècle: Enjeux Identitaires et*

Modes d'Insertion, vol. 1, ed. Catherine Coquery-Vidrovitch (Paris, l'Harmattant, 2003), 21–22.

18. The French sentence is: *"Déjà que je suis un homme avant d'etre francais, ou bien parceque je suis nécéssairement homme, et ne suis francais que par hazard."* Baron de Montesquieu, "Pensée no. 741," in *Oeuvres Complètes*, vol. 2 (Paris: Nagel, 1950), 221–222.

19. Gendreau, "La contingence historique de la nation et la nationalité" in ed. Vidrovitch, *Etre Etranger et Migrant En Afrique Au XXe Siècle*, 21–22.

20. Hans Magnus Enzensberger, *Civil War* (London: Granta Books, 1994), 107.

21. Alberto Benegas Lynch, *Estados Unidos Contra Estados Unidos* (Guatemala City: Fondo de Cultura Económica, 2008), 262–263.

22. Enzensberger, *Civil War*, 108.

23. Jorge Lozano, "En los límites. Fronteras y confines en la semiótica de la cultura," *Revista de Occidente* no. 316 (September 2007): 63.

24. Nicolas Sarkozy, "Respecter ceux qui arriven, respecter ceux qui acceuillent," *Le Monde*, December 8, 2009, http://www.lemonde.fr/opinions/article/2009/12/08/m-sarkozy-respecter-ceux-qui-arrivent-respecter-ceux-qui-accueillent_1277422_3232.html

25. Alexander Bickel, *The Morality of Consent* (New Haven, Conn., Yale University Press, 1975), 54.

26. Millman, *The Other Americans*, 56–57.

27. Geyer, *Americans No More*, 334.

28. Samuel T. Francis, *America Extinguished: Mass Immigration and the Disintegration of American Culture* (Monterey, Va.: *Americans for Immigration Control*, 2002), 9–10.

29. Huntington, *Who Are We?*, 43.

18

A Path to Citizenship

VISAS ARE TREATED by governments as a matter of national security. And yet, no country in history has lost a war because of visas.¹ Visa policies have little connection to the needs and preferences of those wishing to travel, their host countries, or their potential employers or customers in the countries to which they wish to go. Therefore, visas tend to create more problems than they solve. One need only look at how countries handle tourist visas and work permits to understand how reactive, incoherent, and ad hoc their policies are regarding arrivals from abroad. Visa policies often contradict official discourse and do not seem to leave anyone satisfied—either critics or supporters of foreign arrivals. Although politicians may pay tribute to high-skilled as opposed to low-skilled migration, they still obstruct the arrival of professionals from abroad.

In recent years, the United States quota for high-skilled work permits, i.e., H-1B visas, has been fixed at 85,000 per year, but the arbitrary nature of this number was made manifest in 2008 when the quota was exhausted before the end of the first day! Countless hardworking, loyal American companies that had applied on behalf of their prospective foreign workers were left out in the cold by their own government. The rigidity of the quota was made even more patent when in the first two weeks of 2009, evidently due to the recession, only 42,000 requests were made, while in the same period in 2010 no more than 13,500 were filed.² The government rules (politics) and the market (real life) simply did not match.

A further example of the inadequacy of visa policies is the annual lottery held by the United States worldwide. The idea—a sound one—is to offer participants the possibility to migrate with their families. However, the rules are such that even though millions of aspiring migrants participate, a big proportion of the 50,000 winners are often unable to make use of it. In the first few years of the decade 2000–09, more than 10 million people applied annually, but only half the winners were able to make use of the prize, the coveted *green card*, because they were unable to move immediately, as the rules require.[3]

Every time a country comes up with a visa policy that looks like it may help to separate undesirable migrants from the rest—and usually "undesirable" means low-skilled—other governments begin to imitate it or express the intention of doing something similar. By demanding certain qualifications, Australia's point system, somewhat similar to Canada's policy, supposedly winnows the low-skilled chaff from the educated grain that will contribute to the economy.[4] In reality, the points system, under which one is asked to meet certain educational, linguistic, and professional standards before being issued a permit, is a cloak for a policy that sets out, in terms as arbitrary as those of the United States' H-1B quota, to satisfy a theoretical need that in practice has scant relation to reality. The quota is politically motivated rather than economically or otherwise driven. A prominent anti-immigration leader in the United Kingdom used Australia's example during a speech against allowing Turkish migrants into the European Union to illustrate the hypocrisy of his country's Labour Party, which, wanted to adopt the points system, as did others around the world. "They are bluffing," he said, "because Australia starts by placing number limits and then picks."[5]

Most developed countries that favor high-skilled over low-skilled immigration grant visas to wealthy people in exchange for the commitment to undertake some kind of entrepreneurial activity. A foreigner is eligible to live in Canada, for instance, if he or she brings Can$800,000, legally earned, or produces Can$300,000 and agrees to open a business. The United Kingdom has had a "highly skilled migrant program" since 2001, while Germany grants immigrant status to anyone who invests 500,000 euros in a German business or starts a company employing at least five people. Does it make sense to discriminate between various migratory classes and create incentives based on the idea that a foreigner who wants to open a business in the host country can get a permit when, according to evidence, immigrants of all conditions are inclined to create businesses anyway? The French, for their part, have favored scientists, researchers, and students—a policy that has paid off well in some areas—but disdained entrepreneurs.[6] Does it make sense to favor scientists but disdain businesspeople when basing policy on the contribution that a high-skilled foreigner can make to a country's progress?

Perhaps nothing illustrates the dysfunctional nature of visa policies more than the periodic legalizations in countries with large foreign populations. This ritual amounts to the acceptance by host countries of their failure to match the law with reality, and to establish policies that have long-term horizons and do not need to be constantly overhauled. No wonder citizens are so confused that polls tend to reflect very contradictory sentiments regarding legalization.

The positive experience of legalization in the United States and elsewhere has not been sufficiently understood or effectively communicated. If it had, President George W. Bush, a conservative, would have succeeded in legalizing millions of immigrants, granting them a path to citizenship, when he tried at the beginning of his first term in office. And other conservatives, such as Newt Gingrich, who mildly suggested something similar with various caveats during a debate in the Republican primaries in November of 2011, would not have had to face a political firestorm that forced them to back down every time they dared speak the truth. Yet the many precedents of legalization through amnesty or other mechanisms speak to us, in millions of personal stories, of achievement behind the cohesion and progress of communities and the wealth created by multiple industries.

The amnesty law of 1986 (Immigration Reform and Control Act of 1986) transformed agriculture, a fact seldom mentioned when amnesty is debated. At the beginning, thousands of ex-"wetbacks" looked for better jobs in the cities. But the vacancies in agriculture were very quickly filled by new laborers, who continued to flow into California. These younger arrivals—as well as the opportunity that previous generations of immigrants finally had to operate legally in the country—made it possible for thousands of laborers who had been harvesting crops and fruits in California for years to move up the skill ladder, bringing innovation and entrepreneurship both to agriculture and to other industries. The economy, which hitherto had not been able to display itself beyond manual labor, benefitted greatly from their talent and hard work. There was talk of an agricultural transformation in the mid-1990s. The number of Hispanic farmers grew more than 20 percent across forty states, while that of Asian farmers also experienced a rise.[7]

In the wake of the 1986 amnesty, red herrings and hair-splitting substituted for reason and healthy discussion. Critics complained for years about the "dumbing down" of the citizenship test, claiming that by outsourcing it to private groups, the government was accommodating the immigrants who had been granted amnesty. Critics raised with an alarming tone the danger that the watered-down citizenship process posed to the linguistic and cultural foundations of the nation. These detractors were often the same ones who wagged angry fingers at the low rate of naturalization among members of certain foreign-born communities.[8] By the time the transformation of the 1990s was evident—which many of the recently legalized workers helped bring—not many observers noted its connection to the amnesty of 1986, and myths continued to find their way into the discussion on foreigners.

Critics of legalization and of offering various paths to citizenship to illegal immigrants often miss an important side effect that ought to resonate strongly with them: return migration. I have mentioned before the effects that restrictions have on those who would otherwise return to their countries after a certain period, or the many foreign workers who would only engage in seasonal migration if they could go back and forth. The evidence suggests that return and circular migration shoot up after a process of legalization. That was the case in the 1970s and the 1980s in the United States. Return migration was as high as 15 percent and 25 percent in the 1970–74 and the 1990–94 periods, respectively. Both periods followed a process of legalization or amnesty that brought to the surface millions of human beings who had been trapped in the underground for years.

Between 1970 and 1978, the number of people receiving legal documents rose 108 percent, while it grew by a factor of 14 between 1986 and 1991 as a result of the amnesty law, when almost 2.5 million Mexicans, among other undocumented foreigners, became legal residents. The cause-and-effect relationship between the increase in return and circular migration, on the one hand, and the rise in the number of immigrants who left the shadows to become legal is umbilical.[9] Similar connections can be found in the more distant past. During the Bracero program and the Temporary Worker Program put in place between the 1940s and the 1960s—in effect, a legalization of labor-related immigration—there were four seasonal immigrants for every permanent immigrant.

Even allowing for the benefits of past amnesty laws, it is important, for future purposes, to bear in mind the often inconsistent, contradictory, and ad hoc nature of the legalization process when it does take place. The amnesty law of 1986 included sanctions against employers who gave work to undocumented foreigners, but employers were not asked to verify the authenticity of documents they were obliged to request, a loophole that spawned an entire industry of forged documentation. Of course, transferring the responsibility for such verification to private enterprise would have meant placing a burden on businesses and making a mockery of the federal government's monopoly of immigration policy (the same constitutional principle invoked by the federal government against state laws and municipal ordinances relating to immigration). They closed the loophole in subsequent legislation, but by then the e-verify mechanism enforced by the government, which matches an employee's Employment Eligibility Verification Form I-9 against data from government records, had given rise to new problems. These included raising suspicions on perfectly legitimate employees and creating a legal limbo for dubious cases in which the workers in question were allowed to continue to work while further verification was undertaken, a process that could last long.

In advanced countries, every legalization is followed by new illegal arrivals whose accumulation over time makes it impractical to deport them, giving rise to a new debate in which "amnesty" becomes a dark word that critics hurl at those who argue for a path to citizenship as if exorcising the demon in them. Governments then try to find a way to legalize foreign workers and their families without using the term "amnesty" and seeking to offset the concession with tough measures designed to placate anti-immigrant voters, thus ensuring that the ranks of the underground economy will soon be filled again (the employer sanctions attached to the 1986 amnesty was just that). The United States found itself once again in that kind of situation in 2010.

Amnesties and legalizations are frequent in Europe too. They have had the same positive consequences as those seen in the United States but have eventually also proven to be as temporary or insufficient because of their inability to accommodate the future. Legalization has gradually become an entirely political mechanism removed from juridical, ethical, economic, or social considerations even if the rationale used by the authorities is cloaked in language that may suggest otherwise. Soon after his victory in the 2004 elections in Spain, president José Luis Rodríguez Zapatero undertook a process of legalization that he was forced to defend in Brussels before some of his European critics for a very long time. He made the case that there were "700,000 immigrants who work in the illegal economy, exploited and without paying social security taxes."[10] His arguments were not political, but the decision had been taken in the context of a vicious ideological confrontation in Spain. He was acting no differently than other European governments of the left or the right that in recent decades have succumbed to reality. But the very countries that criticized Zapatero for his amnesty had legalized immigrants themselves, and faced their own detractors with similar justifications. France legalized 100,000 in 1997 and 1998, Belgium pulled 40,000 out of the shadows in 2000, Italy gave legal status to 250,000 at the turn of the millennium, and Greece dignified the status of half of its undocumented foreigners—400,000 of them.[11]

Because immigration and visa policies are inconsistent and reactive, they give rise to problems for which the answer is always temporary solutions that keep recurring. One such solution is the Temporary Protected Status (TPS) created by the U.S. government in 1990 and granted to people of certain nationalities. It was supposed to allow immigrants from places to which it was unsafe to return for reasons of war or natural disaster permission to work here for 18 months, but it has been extended numerous times. Handled by the Department of Homeland Security, the program benefits for instance immigrants from Honduras, El Salvador, and Sudan. The gulf that separates the security scene in Honduras from that of Sudan is very wide. Does no one in the Department of Homeland Security realize that the countries that used to be unsafe many years ago are no longer as unsafe today, and that other parts of the world that were reasonably peaceful are now in turmoil?

Many bureaucrats may actually realize these inconsistencies, but the main reason why in some cases the list is not updated is that politics dictate that the program be extended even if the country in question is no longer as unsafe as it was. One example is El Salvador, where there is a fairly stable democracy and where the natural disaster invoked by the American authorities to justify the latest concession took place seven years before the 2008 extension.[12] Although violence related to gangs and drug trafficking has increased exponentially in recent years, it is not the reason why the country is on the list. The reason has to do with U.S. foreign policy towards Central America.

Following the devastating earthquake that killed an estimated 230,000 people in Haiti on January 12, 2010, the United States government announced that it would grant TPS to Haitians in the United States. In the announcement, the authorities emphasized that this status would be granted to Haitians who were in the United States before January 12 but not to those who arrived after that date—a curious approach since the people most affected by it were not those who lived in the United States before the earthquake, but the estimated 1 million who, having had the fortune to be spared the death suffered by their relatives, friends, and neighbors, were without a home and without basic services![13]

The point here is not that all Haitians should have been made residents of the United States, but that the thinking behind immigration policy is very confused and many steps behind the real world. More generally, the TPS scheme creates scenarios in which people who were illegal citizens before their country was declared eligible for TPS become legal under the program and then go back to being illegal once their country of origin is taken off the list.

This inability of policy to match reality is not new. In the 1970s, when an economic crisis prompted many European countries to ban legal immigration, the British kept a certain amount of labor-related new arrivals going, mostly nationals from Australia, South Africa, and New Zealand, members of the Commonwealth. The other countries soon realized that the market realities were out of sync with their drastic policies and were forced to adopt various programs destined to encourage limited immigration again. By the 1990s, Germany was bringing into the country some 230,000 seasonal workers from Central and Eastern European countries while publicly railing against immigration and either maintaining or creating tough laws against other foreign arrivals.[14]

When I lived in Madrid in the early 1990s, I remember being struck by comments from friends and colleagues who thought that the issue of immigration, about which I wrote frequently in the press with reference to other European countries, was far removed from their country's preoccupations. And yet the authorities were already taking some initiatives in anticipation of the social tension that might occur in the future if the trend that was slowly insinuating itself intensified. One of those initiatives, in 1992, was a cooperative agreement between the government and the Islamic communities in Spain. The argument given was that Islam was "noticeably rooted" in Spanish society. The living conditions of Moroccans and the treatment given to Spain's Islamic past in school textbooks, as one scholar reminds us, was at odds with this historical valuation,[15] but the more interesting aspect of the initiative in question is how little effect it had: Twelve years later, in the wake of al Qaeda's terrorist attacks against commuter trains in Madrid, Zapatero, the new president, launched a "dialogue of civilizations with Islam" aimed at correcting the misunderstandings and prejudices that the agreement of 1992 was supposed to have corrected.

The hardening of European immigration policy in the new millennium was itself an admission of the failure of patchy and spotty initiatives taken in previous years. In 1993, many countries, but especially France, Germany, and the Netherlands, adopted major decisions to combat the abuse of asylum laws. They were so tough that even the *Aussiedler,* the Germans from Central and Eastern Europe that the country had been so proud to integrate back into Germany, suddenly faced restrictions to enter the land of their ancestors. The tough new measures were to no avail. A decade and a half later, the European Union (EU) saw itself in desperate need to adopt new rules in reaction to a social reality— the tidal rise in the number of illegal immigrants—that the previous initiatives had been unable to prevent. For the most part the EU countries resisted further legalization, but in doing so they came up with policies that quickly proved to be inadequate.

Immigration policy has been struggling to catch up with reality for a very long time. It has happened in developing countries too, where for decades governments have periodically signed contracts with poorer nations in order to secure the supply of workers; meanwhile, other aspects of policy kept immigrants away or in the shadows. An oscillating migrating system was instituted in South Africa following the rapid growth of the gold mining industry during the early part of the twentieth century. Mostly low-skilled mining and farm workers were hired to work in South Africa for one or two years and were not allowed either to renew their contracts or to obtain residency. The policy was eventually outdone by reality. In the early 1960s, South Africa signed treaties with Botswana, Lesotho, Swaziland, and Mozambique, expanding the early policy. But again the government soon realized that the policy was too restrictive for the needs of the economy. The result was that in the 1980s, most contracts were "stabilized" to the effect that the hired workers remained in the country with the tacit approval of the government, even though they were not allowed to enjoy the rights of residency. In solving one problem, the government created another by placing these foreigners in a sort of legal limbo.[16]

Although somewhat restrictive, riddled with minor problems, subject to periodic revisions and too attached to government projects, immigration policy in the Gulf countries has been more systematic, consistent, and reflective of a long-term vision than in developed countries. It works on a rotation basis, which means that workers are hired for a certain number of years only. But at all times, policy at least seeks to adjust the number of workers allowed in the Gulf countries to the real needs of the economy, without arbitrary quotas dictated by politics. Foreigners already constituted 31 percent of those countries' population in the 1970s; by 2002, the proportion had grown to 38.5 percent on average, while in Qatar, the United Arab Emirates, and Kuwait, foreign workers were actually the majority.

The first wave of foreign workers was made up of Yemenis and Egyptians, but other groups followed, including the Iraqis who escaped the Baath Party coup of 1968 and the Palestinians fleeing from violence after the Arab-Israeli war of 1973. Eventually, Asians from India and Pakistan, as well as Iranian workers and traders, joined the Arab immigrants as a result of contracts between the respective governments and the authorities of the Gulf states.

The flexible immigration policies adopted by Gulf countries started with the post-1973 boom based on oil revenues, when the authorities undertook development efforts on an unprecedented scale. Investment rose ten times in the 1970s decade. In Saudi Arabia, the growth of capital formation reached 27.8 percent per year in that same decade. Massive Arab labor migration was the natural consequence of an economic dynamic that cried for a supply of labor unavailable at home. Arab foreign workers were openly welcomed; their linguistic and cultural familiarity with the local population made them perfect fits. They helped set up familiar government administration and education facilities, develop health services, build the necessary infrastructure, and run the oil industry. Some problems that I have addressed in previous chapters led to a preference for Asian immigrants later on, but the system both in its Arab and its Asian phases worked reasonably well because of the relative connection between policy and real life.[17]

One element that has been sorely missing in the chaotic realm of immigration policy in the developed world has been the inability of countries to learn from each other's experience. International bodies that aspire to standardize approaches to immigrants have been unable to move governments towards reasonably compatible policies based on the principle that migrants are a global reality that cannot be legislated away. The global governance of international migration—in bureaucratic parlance—is still in rudimentary stage, though some legal instruments exist. International bodies tend to reflect rather than help reformulate policy in the member countries and lack a mechanism for enforcing recommendations or conventions.

The World Trade Organization (WTO) has not been concerned with the flow of people across borders, despite the communicating vessels that connect the circulation of goods, services, and capital, on the one hand, and workers on the other. Meanwhile, the 1990 United Nations International Convention on the Rights of All Migrants, Workers and Members of their Families could not come into force until 2003 because of opposition from the member states that are supposed to apply it. Even now there are questions as to how rigorously the Convention, which includes some healthy principles protecting foreigners from abuse, violence, and state-sponsored discrimination mixed with articles that spell bureaucratic interventionism, is really applied. Some of the mass deportations that I have witnessed along the border between the United States and Mexico appear to contradict the article prohibiting collective punishment.[18] The announcement in mid-2010 that more than 400,000 people had been kicked out of the United States in the previous twelve months does not seem in keeping with this international legal standard.

The International Labor Organization (ILO), for its part, is incapable of enforcing Conventions 97 (which dates back six decades) and 143 (which dates back three decades) because governments do not follow its recommendation to give equal treatment to nationals and foreigners[19] (some of the ILO recommendations are not worthy of adoption, particularly protectionist suggestions in line with the more statist labor policies that body espouses from time to time—but that is another matter).

Meanwhile, developed and underdeveloped countries fail to understand the lesson of past amnesties and other mechanisms geared towards creating a path to citizenship for illegal immigrants. The lesson is that, even though it has proven to be insufficient and has been subsequently overtaken by events (namely, new waves of illegal immigrants), legalization has been by far the most successful way to deal with foreigners who were undocumented at the time when the policy was implemented. The temporary and insufficient nature of the policy lay in its inability to provide a path to citizenship in the future, but at least it was able bring those who were in the shadows out of that condition at the time. Ideally, once legalization was admitted in principle, it should lead to a much broader and more consistent implementation, without the need for the kinds of contradictory measures that, as we saw in the case of the 1986 amnesty, were adopted simply to make legalization more palatable to critics. For that, as we will see next, minds will have to change.

Notes

1. Jim Rogers, "Open the Doors," December 3, 2002. The article is available at http://www.jimrogers.com

2. Sonia Plaza, "No Takers for H-1B Visas?" *World Bank* (blog), April 21, 2010. http://blogs.worldbank.org/peoplemove/no-takers-for-h1-b-visas

3. Lant Princhett, *Let Their People Come* (Washington, D.C.: Center for Global Development, 2006), 71.

4. Lawrence Brunner and Stephen M. Colarelli, "Immigration in the 21st Century," (Working Paper for *The Independent Review*, May 2005).

5. The speech was given by Sir Andrew Green, chairman of Migration Watch U.K., during the forum "Immigration: The Impact of the European Union" organized by the Bruges Group on May 20, 2009, http://www.Brugesgroup.com

6. Maxime Tandonnet, *Le Grand Bazar ou l'Europe Face à l'Immigration* (Paris: l'Harmattan, 2001), 21–22.

7. Joel Millman, *The Other Americans* (New York: Viking, 1997), 103, 114–115.

8. Georgie Anne Geyer, *Americans No More* (New York: The Atlantic Press, 1996), 149–159.

9. Jorge Durand, Douglas S. Massey, and Rene M. Zenteno, "Mexican Immigration to the United States: Continuities and Change," *Latin America Research Review* 36, no. 1 (2001): 122.

10. "Zapatero defiende en Bruselas la regularización de inmigrantes," *Agencia Efe*, March 4, 2008, http://www.parainmigrantes.info/zapatero-defiende-en-bruselas-la-regularizacion-de-inmigrantes/

11. Maxime Tandonnet, *Le Grand Bazar ou l'Europe Face à l'Immigration* (Paris: l'Harmattan, 2001), 46.

12. "Temporary Protected Status Extensions," Leadership Journal Archive, Department of Homeland Security, September 28, 2008, http://www.dhs.gov/journal/leadership/2008/09/temporary-protected-status-extensions.html

13. "Obama Team Grants Special Status to Haitian Nationals in the U.S.," *USA Today*, January 15, 2010.

14. Maxime Tandonnet, *Le Grand Bazar ou l'Europe Face à l'Immigration* (Paris: l'Harmattan, 2001), 19–22.

15. Daniela Flesler, *The Return of the Moor: Spanish Responses to Contemporary Morrocan Immigration* (West Lafayette, Ind.: Purdue University Press, 2008), 1.

16. Lloyd B. Hill, "The Politics of Migrations and Citizenship in South Africa," in *Etre Etranger et Migrant en Afrique au XXe Siècle: Enjeux Identitaires et Modes d'Insertion,* vol. 1, ed. Catherine Coquery-Vidrovitch (Paris: l'Harmattant, 2003). Chapter 3 looks in depth at South Africa's immigration policies.

17. Andrzej Kapizewski, "Arab Labor Migration to GCC States" in *Arab Migration in a Globalized World* (Geneva: International Organization for Migration, 2004), 117–119.

18. The full text of the Convention adopted by the United States is available online. See http://www2.ohchr.org/english/law/cmw.htm

19. Mohamed Mghari, "Exodus Of Skilled Labor: Magnitude, Determinants, And Impacts On Development," in *Arab Migration in a Globalized World*, 80–82.

19

Open Minds

THE DEBATE OVER immigration has obfuscated the real facts, the historical precedents, and the principles of civilization that warrant what I would characterize as an open minds approach. The idea of a policy of open borders under the law and within a reasonable security framework has become so caricatured and ideologically loaded that it has been stripped of its real meaning. It will take a lot of time and adaptation, many comings and goings, and much trial and error to get to a point in which decision makers and the societies that inform those decisions accept that culture, the economy, and security are compatible with the free circulation of people. It will take time to convince them that a system that is open and flexible will not only survive a legal and sustained inflow of foreigners, but will actually be strengthened by it because it will facilitate assimilation. Precedent suggests that, by and large, migrants realize it is in their interest to respect the principles of life, liberty, and private property of the developed nations that welcome them.

It is essential, until we get to that desirable point, that all of us who have the extraordinary privilege of living, working, and raising families in the most developed parts of the world rid ourselves of prejudice and fear, and restore the right course in a discussion that has steered dangerously off it. Migrants are a force so powerful and so germane to the times in which we live that our culture will suffer from serious atrophy, our economies will become less competitive and relevant, and our security will reveal more vulnerability unless we open our minds to the vertiginous cross-fertilization that a world with massive movements of people across continents entails.

Countries can slow down these movements, freeze them temporarily, or do their best to adapt to and embrace them, but they will not be able to reverse them. I do not think the trajectory of history is determined by any ineluctable force or destiny. The future is what we make of it. But there are times when the power of individuals is unleashed in certain directions, and trying to stop them becomes a futile enterprise. It does not mean the energy that flows from that power cannot be altered or that there will not be periods of deviation from the trajectory marked by the simultaneous and vigorous actions of people around the world. It just means that standing in the way of this force made by the voluntary interaction of individuals who understand the creative power with which they are endowed is suicidal. Those who tried to stop the age of discovery in the fifteenth and sixteenth century, or the Industrial Revolution a couple of centuries later, were as reactionary and ultimately self-defeating as the governments and leaders who even today want to prosper by turning their backs on globalization.

By all appearances, opening barriers between nations and making borders flexible in this new phase of globalization will continue to bring choice and opportunity to societies rich and poor, young and old. Those who have not yet accepted this evident fact swim against the current at their peril. Yes, globalization means more competition and the need to adjust, sometimes painfully, as the United States and Europe are having to do in the face of Asia's rise. But it also means, for those who do adjust, that new avenues for progress are constantly opening before their eyes. Trying to decouple the approach to immigration from policy towards the circulation of goods, services, capital, and ideas is to misunderstand markets, globalization, and history. Placing more barriers to stave off the "pernicious" effects of competition, as the reactionaries who decry the free circulation of people, goods, services, capital, or ideas would do, will render a disservice to the very nations seeking to preserve their international leadership. Trying to be open in some areas—the circulation of goods—and protectionist in others will place nations at a disadvantage vis-à-vis those that understand that freedom is indivisible and that breaking it up into compartments severely curtails its blessings.

By delaying their own adaptation to changing circumstances, those who fear migration, commerce, or investment by foreigners will achieve precisely what they would want to prevent—their decline as a society. Unless we remove the barriers that keep millions of people in the shadows and turn human beings into "illegal aliens"—the overwhelming majority of whom have done no harm to anybody—assimilation will continue to face unnecessary hindrances and prejudice will erode the constructive social coexistence on which the most developed countries based their ascent as liberal democracies. The more we put off the day when open minds will lead to some form of open borders under the law and within a reasonable security framework, the more we will miss the chance to fully exploit the possibilities that come attached to free exchange between nations. The result will be less integration, and therefore less peace and prosperity.

I hope I have shared with readers abundant information to allow them to make a more serene judgment about what is at stake here.

One often wonders how sincere the arguments against immigration are when they purport to defend and protect native workers from low-wage competition, native taxpayers from welfare free riders, or the nation's liberties from the illiberal cultural habits of aliens. As one academic has rightly suggested, the burden of proof is on the enemies of immigration to prove their case for restrictions that run contrary to common sense and to a certain sense of morality.[1] Unlike other things that appear to be wrong but are morally justified, such as surgery, he suggests, impeding the free circulation of people and disrupting the lives of immigrants who have made their host country their own even if they are undocumented is something that needs a very powerful moral justification. Critics have simply not made the moral case convincingly.

If all illegal immigrants were expelled from the United States, the economic havoc and social disruption would be colossal, as anyone who looks at the issue with serene eyes realizes. Some prices would collapse (in real estate, for instance, as if those had not dropped enough already!), while others would skyrocket (food, for instance, as if those had not risen enough already!). Assets would have to be expropriated from those who departed because many of them would have been obtained in illegal circumstances. Imagine the judicial nightmare. Entire families would be split apart—another judicial nightmare, not to mention the obvious humanitarian implications.

But taking into account only the economic aspect of the consequences of deporting millions of people, the question obviously arises: Does the temporary and small drop in wages suffered by natives who are at the bottom end of the scale when immigrants come in outweigh the calamity that would be brought on several major industries, such as agriculture and construction, by the mass expulsions? If the answer is "yes," and critics of immigration are honest in their use of the economic argument, then why don't they propose that immigrants coming into the country offset the temporary effect on wages by paying more taxes than natives? The fact that they don't suggest this, or any other solution to accommodate immigrants, would seem to indicate that the economic argument is really a fig leaf behind which other passions hide.

Similarly, it is evident that immigrants contribute more to society than what they take away through the welfare state—as producers, as consumers, as entrepreneurs, and as members of communities that have helped regenerate parts of America that had fallen into decay, or prevented other parts of the country from doing so. They also make it easier, through the taxes they pay, to support the native retirees and the older natives who need health care. But if welfare is the real argument, then conservative critics of immigration, who are also critics of the welfare state, need to make a decision: Is the welfare state right or wrong? If they think it is wrong, then they ought to welcome the effect that their own argument says immigrants have on the welfare state. But if the welfare state is right, immigration critics ought to give up all pretense of really wanting to do away with immigration or substantially reduce it. And they ought to be consistent when arguing against immigration by proposing, for instance, that immigrants be cut off from all types of welfare services obtained through society's taxes. But they don't propose such a thing. What they propose instead is throwing out the millions already here and impeding the arrival of those who would want to come. Again, it looks as if welfare is not the real argument but a smokescreen concealing other reasons.

The same happens with the cultural argument. By most metrics—including marriage, children, social activities, economic activities, and religion—immigrants echo the family values and the hardworking, entrepreneurial, self-sufficient ethos of the American way of life. And while it is true that a majority of new immigrants tend to speak little English, it is also true that their assimilation patterns do not depart in major ways from those of earlier waves of immigrants. The second generation always speaks good English; the third by and large speaks only English, or rudimentary forms of the mother tongue of its grandparents. But if language or other cultural traits were the real problem with immigration, critics would propose solutions that included certain tests to make sure new arrivals comport with mainstream cultural patterns.

Anywhere we look, the consequences of embracing immigration even timidly are the same—innovation, energy, growth. Why has Israel, a country about which we usually get to read only news items related to conflict and war, become the country with the greatest density of start-ups per capita and with the largest number of companies listed on NASDAQ—after the United States? It was in large part because of immigration. And when I say immigration, I do not mean arrivals from one or two countries in particular—I mean people from Western Europe, Central and Eastern Europe, Africa, Latin America, and Asia who were able to settle there, often unable to speak Hebrew. I had a chance to see this dynamic first-hand during a trip to Israel in May of 2010. The effects of innovation as it relates to both processes and products by Israeli companies and research centers filled with immigrants from all over the world are breathtaking. One feels it in conversation, in everyday life, in media articles, in the presence of foreign companies everywhere. Even in the dangerous environment of the Middle East, multinational high-tech companies such as Microsoft and Intel have major research centers and affiliates in Israel because of the irresistible attraction of immigrant-driven innovation.

In 2008, seed capital investment per person in Israel was 2.5 times greater than in the United States, 30 times greater than in Europe, 80 times greater than in China, and 350 times greater than in India or Brazil. In the last couple of decades, an estimated 240 private equity and venture capital funds were created in Israel for the purposes of helping companies grow into economic powerhouses. With no natural resources, a serious scarcity of water, a geographic location that is a constant source of conflict, and just 7 million people, Israel is a veritable success story despite having an interventionist government that meddles more than necessary.[2] As Dan Senor and Saul Singer have explained in *Start-Up Nation: The Story of Israel's Miracle*, the Israeli diaspora and the inviting immigration policy were crucial factors in engendering this extraordinary achievement.[3]

Everywhere, open minds, or at least minds more open than in competing countries of the same area, have created similar effects, allowing peoples to prosper. Botswana, the small African country whose success in the last quarter of the twentieth century stands in stark contrast with that of neighboring territories such as Zimbabwe, is a case in point. After one of his motorcycle tours of the world, during which he faced grueling challenges in attempting to traverse African borders, Jim Rogers said this about Botswana:

> Crossing into Botswana by motorcycle, there was no hassle from guards at the border. It was perfectly efficient and straightforward. I filled out forms and nobody asked me for bribes. In the country there is no black market for the local currency. There were real traffic lights and office buildings. I did more homework and found that Botswana had a huge trade surplus and a balanced budget, compared to many other countries. There was a democracy where they had elections and a stock market. It's been one of the greatest stock markets in the world for the last 20 years.[4]

Rogers' impression was similar to mine after visiting Botswana a decade ago. Open minds seemed to rule that country's borders, unlike what happened elsewhere in southern Africa. I quickly realized that open minds at the border went a long way towards explaining why people, goods, capital, and ideas had helped Botswana prosper despite its small territory, limited conditions, and periodic setbacks.

No country has become culturally inferior because of its exchanges with the outside world and the infusion of migrants. Culture is not something that is engraved on some people forever. It is not something one can or should place fences around, as a well-known Argentinean economist and writer, has said.[5] Culture is a malleable, protean matter that needs permanent contact with outsiders in order to improve itself and renew its vitality and energy. Cosmopolitan Vienna at the end of the nineteenth and the beginning of the twentieth centuries produced some of the most extraordinary cultural achievements mankind has ever known when an explosion of talent took place across all the art forms and fields of intellectual endeavor, from music to law, from literature to economics, from philosophy to psychoanalysis. Why was that possible? It was so because of Vienna's open mind, its willingness and ability to attract and absorb what all kinds of outsiders had to offer without fear that new blood would contaminate the old. As Stefan Zweig, the famous novelist and essayist, and a superb son of Vienna himself, wrote:

> The German was related in blood to the Slavic, the Hungarian, the Spanish, the Italian, the French, the Flemish: and it was the particular genius

of this city that dissolved all the contrasts harmoniously into a new and unique thing, the Austrian, the Viennese.[6]

Could something very similar not be said about the United States at different periods of its fabulously successful life as a republic? Is it not a country of countries, a universal home in which all of us, no matter what background we have, feel a part of something harmonious and cogent, and yet pluralistic? It is because the United States had a relatively open mind for long stretches of its existence vis-à-vis the outside world, with the horrific exceptions I have discussed, that its culture was vibrant and open to constant improvement, and that it was able to innovate and create new things in so many domains. Why are American universities so popular with foreigners? Because, despite the deterioration that certain intellectual fads have brought about in not a few of them, they continue to churn out knowledge and foster an environment of free inquiry that attracts people from everywhere. And why are they able do to this? In part because they know that the outstanding output they produce is heavily dependent on the outstanding input they receive, much of which comes from people who originate in other countries and do not necessarily find the same opportunity to cultivate their minds at home. American universities have maintained an open mind even as the skewed immigration discussion was closing the minds of so many other Americans who lost sight of the truth about their own ancestry and history. The microcosm that is the American university largely accounts for its supremacy even in these times when other areas of American life are no longer supreme in the world or will cease to be soon.

Jim Rogers, who as a citizen of the world has denounced the closing of minds to the truth about the vivifying power of migration, said eight years ago:

> [O]pening our borders to the free movement of labor may be the only way the United States is going to remain competitive in the coming century. Tightening our borders is already hurting various sectors of our economy. Some of our best sources of foreign earnings are education, tourism and medical care. U.S. schools and universities have attracted tens of thousands of students annually, but the influx has been cut severely. Foreign tourists are skipping the U.S. now since it is so hard to get in. The Mayo Clinic and others are suffering since many high-paying foreigners are not allowed for treatment."[7]

Something similar can be said of Europe, where the welfare state, even more intrusive and expensive than that of the United States, is aging as fast as the population and where many people are unaware of the fact that immigrants are a major reason why it has not yet collapsed. The circulation of workers from one country to the other within the European Union has belied every catastrophic prediction that was made by those who feared workers from one European country "invading" the labor market of a neighboring European country. Were it not for the invigorating effect the presence of people from certain places within the union has had on other parts, much like the constant flow of persons from one state to another within the United States of America, the crisis of the European model would be infinitely worse. Unfortunately, the free circulation of workers within the union stands in marked contrast with the growing fortress mentality that is keeping outsiders from other parts at bay with arguments that echo those offered on the other side of the Atlantic—or indeed in developing countries that also "protect" their economies and culture from citizens from poorer places.

The battle for the free movement of goods, services, capital, and ideas has been won in principle. There are still numerous barriers to their free circulation, but almost everywhere progress has been significant, even in communist China and Vietnam, to name two ideological transvestites of our time. Countries that still erect barriers are careful to cloak their decisions in language that does not appear to be protectionist. But human beings, who have clearly lost their preeminence over things in the estimation of the detractors of immigration, are considered less worthy of such treatment. Calling for the expulsion of one's neighbors or fellow workers because they came in from another country is respectable, whereas arguing for tariffs against competition for the sake of protecting an industry has lost its prestige and comes at a price for those who dare speak openly in such terms.

Governments, activists, and everyday critics do not feel in the least bit ashamed of justifying barriers against immigration in the language of police states. They have lost sight of both the humane issue at heart—a person's freedom to move as long as that person does not harm another's life or property—and of the dire consequences that the closing of minds to the advantages of migration will have for peaceful coexistence. They are oblivious to the obvious fact that when a citizen advocates the expulsion of a foreigner who works for—or rents a room from, or buys products sold by—another fellow citizen, he or she is going against the principle of equality before the law. Why should an anti-immigration citizen enjoy the support of the state against another citizen who wants to bring an immigrant into his home or business?

On May 19, 2010, during a visit by First Lady Michelle Obama and First Lady of Mexico Margarita Zavala to a school in Silver Spring, Maryland, a poignant scene took place, shaking consciences across the country. With television cameras rolling, a seven-year-old girl asked Mrs. Obama why the president was "taking everybody away that doesn't have papers." The First Lady responded, "That is something that we have to work on, right?" The girl, however, insisted, "But my mom doesn't have any papers."[8]

There is no dearth of sound proposals in developing countries for bringing into the light the millions who are trapped in the shadows and to create sensible rules that will enhance the culture, the economy and, yes, the security of nations by fostering exchange and movement rather than isolation and sclerosis. Some of them are imaginative, innovative, and interesting—including, for example, the one by economist Gary Becker, the 1992 Nobel Prize winner, who has suggested that immigrants who are already in the United States or wish to move here pay for that right. Becker argued that such a payment would reduce taxes, negate the charge that immigrants seek mostly welfare benefits, attract many high-skilled people, and bring illegal entries down very substantially.[9] I am not necessarily endorsing this particular proposal, but raising the basic point that anything that moves the debate forward in the direction of freedom of circulation within the rule of law and a reasonable security arrangement will be a drastic improvement on systems that generate such tension and a second-tier society. But the ultimate goal should be to remove all the barriers that currently separate the law from reality.

Legalizing those undocumented immigrants who are already here and making the law flexible enough to absorb future waves will not result in "all of Mexico" moving to the United States—experience teaches us that migration can be self-regulating, as are other parts of human society, as long as there is not undue interference. The reasonably efficient way in which illegal migration functions despite the monumental obstacles is good indication in and of itself.

Some in Europe have compared the migration issue to a lifeboat packed with survivors from a shipwreck in which the occupants confront the dilemma of rescuing swimmers who want to cling to their boat thus ensuring that everybody dies, or pushing them away and therefore committing murder. Noted German writer Hans Magnus Enzensberger rightly responded that such images were used to justify behavior conceivable only in extreme circumstances and that it was invalid with regard to situations that are not extreme.[10] Immigration is not a dilemma between suicide and murder.

It does not help the cause of open minds that many people who defend immigrants do so from a perspective that departs from principles of freedom and individual rights. The use of collectivist ideas, including the multicultural fallacy, provides nativists and xenophobes with plenty of ammunition to shoot at a cause that should have nothing to do with undermining the pillars of the free society—the ones that attracted the "refuse" of the world in the first place.

Javier Fernández-Lasquetty, who has worked hard to persuade his party, the *Partido Popular*, in Spain to embrace immigration and, together with Mauricio Rojas, has tried to help Spaniards and immigrants integrate into a pluralistic community in Madrid, has proposed a vision that other conservatives ought to embrace, and that left-leaning minds should heed too. The six fundamental principles he laid out in a document were these:

1. The immigrant is a person, not a member of a collective entity or an ethnic group.
2. The immigrant is a free and responsible individual.
3. The immigrant is not a victim but a person capable of achieving more prosperity with his or her own effort.
4. The immigrant also prefers freedom and democracy.
5. There are no collective guilts.
6. Integration, proximity, cordiality: a pluralist society.[11]

These principles, or any other combination of principles along these lines, strike me as the right approach to one of the least understood and more combustible themes of our time. It cuts to the core of what immigration is about—freedom—while stripping the debate of the many collectivist subterfuges that, on the left or on the right, point to the closing of minds.

Immigration is not a threat to culture, the economy, or security. And it is not a welfare program, a corporatist entity, a collectivist ideal, a historical indemnity, or an ethnic claim. It is, pure and simple, the right to move, live, work, and die in a different place to that in which one was born—the victory of choice over chance.

Notes

1. Bryan Caplan, "Immigration Restrictions: A Solution in Search of a Problem," a Power Point presentation available online. The presentation was prepared for the Economic Liberty Lecture Series organized by the Future of Freedom Foundation and George Mason University Economics Society that took place in September 2010. http://www.fff.org/comment/com1009f.asp

2. Javier Santiso, "Israel, Ejemplo de Innovación Económica," *El Universal*, May 19, 2010.

3. Dan Senor and Saul Singer, *Start-Up Nation: The Story of Israel's Economic Miracle* (Paris: Hachette Book Group, 2009). Quoted by Javier Santiso, "Israel, Ejemplo de Innovación Económica," *El Universal*, May 19, 2010.

4. Interview with Jim Rogers by David Bogoslow, "Jim Rogers: How He's Investing After the Crisis," *Business Week*, April 14, 2009, http://www.businessweek.com/investor/content/apr2009/pi20090414_131044.htm?chan=rss_topEmailedStories_ssi_5

5. Alberto Benegas Lynch, *Estados Unidos Contra Estados Unidos* (Guatemala City, Fondo de Cultura Económica, 2008), 261.

6. Stefan Zweig, *The World of Yesterday* (London: Cassel and Co., 1947), 21–22.

7. Jim Rogers, "Open the Doors," December 3, 2002. The article is available at http://www.jimrogers.com

8. Michael D. Shear and Michael Birnbaum, "First Ladies Get a Firsthand Lesson About Immigration," *The Washington Post*, May, 20, 2010, A1.

9. Gary Becker, "Pay to Stay," *Becker-Posner Blog*, February 3, 2008, http://www.becker-posner-blog.com/archives/2008/03

10. Hans Magnus Enzensberger, *Civil War* (London: Granta Books, 1994), 113–114.

11. The author handed me the document in typed, unpublished form, under the title "Una visión liberal de la política de inmigración" in Madrid during a luncheon in which we discussed these matters in some depth. The text is dated July, 15, 2007.

Appendix

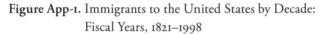

Figure App-1. Immigrants to the United States by Decade:
Fiscal Years, 1821–1998

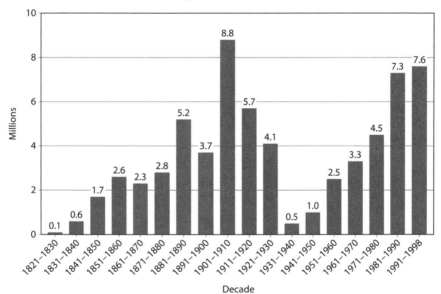

Source: U.S Immigration and Naturalization Service, Table 1.

Table App-1. Leading Countries of Birth of the Foreign-Born Population: Selected Years, 1850 to 1990 (Resident population)

Subject	1850	1880	1900	1930	1960	1970	1980	1990
Number of 10 Leading Countries by Region								
Total	10	10	10	10	10	10	10	10
Europe	8	8	9	8	8	7	5	3
Northern America	1	1	1	1	1	1	1	1
Latin America	1	—	—	1	1	2	2	2
Asia	—	1	—	—	—	—	2	4
10 Leading Countries by Rank¹ (foreign-born population in thousands)								
1	Ireland 962	Germany 1,967	Germany 2,663	Italy 1,790	Italy 1,257	Italy 1,009	Mexico 2,199	Mexico 4,298
2	Germany 584	Ireland 1,855	Ireland 1,65	Germany 1,609	Germany 990	Germany 833	Germany 849	China 921
3	Great Britain 379	Great Britain 918	Canada 1180	United Kingdom 1,403	Canada 953	Canada 812	Canada 843	Philippines 913
4	Canada 148	Canada 717	Great Britain 1,68	Canada 1,310	United Kingdom 833	Mexico 760	Italy 832	Canada 745
5	France 54	Sweden 194	Sweden 582	Poland 1,269	Holland 748	United Kingdom 686	Cuba 669	Cuba 737
6	Switzerland 13	Norway 182	Italy 484	Soviet Union 1,154	Soviet Union 691	Poland 548	United Kingdom 608	Germany 712
7	Mexico 13	France 107	Russia 424	Ireland 745	Mexico 576	Soviet Union 463	Philippines 501	United Kingdom 640
8	Norway 13	China 104	Poland 383	Mexico 641	Ireland 339	Cuba 439	Poland 48	Italy 581
9	Holland 10	Switzerland 89	Norway 336	Sweden 595	Austria 305	Ireland 251	Soviet Union 406	Korea 568
10	Italy 4	Bohemia 85	Austria 276	Czechoslovakia 492	Hungary 245	Austria 214	Korea 290	Vietnam 543

— Represents zero. ¹In general, countries as reported at each census. Data are not totally comparable over time due to changes in boundaries for some countries. Great Britain excludes Ireland. United Kingdom includes Northern Ireland. China in 1990 includes Hong Kong and Taiwan. *Source:* U.S. Census Bureau.2001, Tables 3 and 4.

Figure App-2. A Population of Changing Dimensions

In 25 years, non-Hispanic whites will not be a majority in four states, including the two most populous ones, and in 50 years, they will make up barely half the U.S. population.

Source: The Washington Post

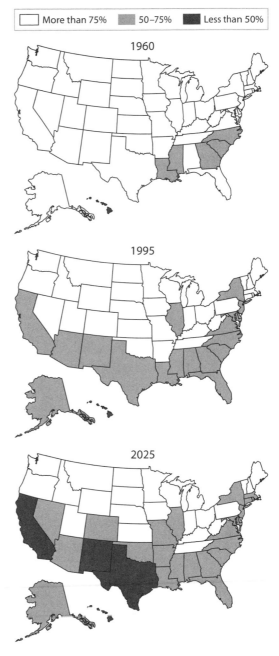

Non-Hispanic Whites as Percentage of State Population

☐ More than 75%　　▨ 50–75%　　■ Less than 50%

1960

1995

2025

Table App-2. Legal Permanent Resident Flow by Region and Country of Birth: Fiscal Years 2007 to 2009

	2009		2008		2007	
	Number	Percent	Number	Percent	Number	Percent
Total	1,130,818	100.0	1,107,126	100.00	1,052,415	100.0
REGION						
Africa	127,050	11.2	105,915	9.6	94,711	9.0
Asia	413,312	36.5	399,027	36.0	397,834	37.8
Europe	105,398	9.3	103,719	9.4	106,495	10.1
North America	375,236	33.2	395,253	35.5	339,355	32.2
Caribbean	146,127	12.9	137,098	12.4	119,123	11.3
Central America	47,868	4.2	50,840	4.6	55,296	5.3
Other North America	181,241	16.0	205,315	18.5	164,306	15.6
Oceania	5,578	0.5	5,263	0.5	6,101	0.6
South America	102,878	9.1	98,555	8.9	106,525	10.1
Unknown	1,366	0.1	1,394	0.1	1,394	0.1
COUNTRY						
Mexico	164,920	14.6	189,989	17.2	148,640	14.1
China	64,238	5.7	80,271	7.3	76,655	7.3
Philippines	60,029	5.3	54,030	4.9	72,596	6.9
India	57,304	5.1	63,352	5.7	65,353	6.2
Dominican Republic	49,414	4.4	31,879	2.9	28,024	2.7
Cuba	38,954	3.4	49,500	4.5	29,104	2.8
Vietnam	29,234	2.6	31,497	2.8	28,691	2.7
Columbia	27,849	2.5	30,213	2.7	33,187	3.2
South Korea*	25,859	2.3	22,405	2.0	26,666	2.5
Haiti	24,280	2.1	26,007	2.3	30,405	2.9
Jamaica	21,783	1.9	18,477	1.7	19,375	1.8
Pakistan	21,555	1.9	19,719	1.8	13,492	1.3
El Salvador	19,909	1.8	19,659	1.8	21,127	2.0
Iran	18,553	1.6	13,852	1.3	10,460	1.0
Peru	16,957	1.5	15,184	1.4	17,699	1.7
Bangladesh	16,651	1.5	11,753	1.1	12,074	1.1
Canada	16,140	1.4	15,109	1.4	15,495	1.5
United Kingdom	15,748	1.4	14,348	1.3	14,545	1.4
Ethiopia	15,462	1.4	12,917	1.2	12,786	1.2
Nigeria	15,253	1.3	12,475	1.1	12,448	1.2
All Other Countries	410,726	36.3	374,490	33.8	363,593	34.5

(Countries ranked by 2009 LPR flow)

NA: Not Available

*Data for South Korea prior to Fiscal Year 2009 include a small number of cases from North Korea.

Source: U.S. Department of Homeland Security. Computer Linked Applicant Information Management System (CLAIMS), Legal Immigrant Data, Fiscal Years 2007 to 2009.

Figure App-3. Unauthorized Immigrant Population: 2000–2009

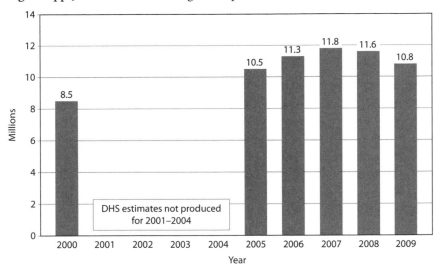

Source: U.S Department of Homeland Security.

Figure App-4. Age and Gender of the Unauthorized Immigrant Population:
January 2009

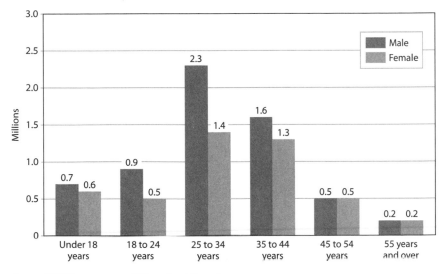

Source: U.S Department of Homeland Security.

Table App-3. Country of Birth and State of Residence of the Unauthorized Immigrant Population: January 2000 and 2005–2009

Country of Birth	Estimated Population in January					
	2000	2005	2006	2007	2008	2009
All countries	8,460,000	10,490,000	11,310,000	11,780,000	11,600,000	10,750,000
Mexico	4,680,000	5,970,000	6,570,000	6,980,000	7,030,000	6,650,000
El Salvador	430,000	470,000	510,000	540,000	570,000	530,000
Guatemala	290,000	370,000	430,000	500,000	430,000	480,000
Honduras	160,000	180,000	280,000	280,000	300,000	320,000
Philippines	200,000	210,000	280,000	290,000	300,000	270,000
India	120,000	280,000	210,000	220,000	160,000	200,000
Korea	180,000	210,000	230,000	230,000	240,000	200,000
Ecuador	110,000	120,000	150,000	160,000	170,000	170,000
Brazil	100,000	170,000	210,000	190,000	180,000	1 50,000
China	190,000	230,000	170,000	290,000	220,000	1 20,000
Other countries	2,000,000	2,280,000	2,290,000	2,100,000	2,000,000	1,650,000

State of Residence	Estimated Population in January					
	2000	2005	2006	2007	2008	2009
All states	8,460,000	10,490,000	11,310,000	11,780,000	11,600,000	10,750,000
California	2,510,000	2,890,000	2,790,000	2,840,000	2,850,000	2,600,000
Texas	1,090,000	1,670,000	1,620,000	1,710,000	1 ,680,000	1,680,000
Florida	800,000	970,000	960,000	960,000	840,000	720,000
New York	540,000	5-60,000	510,000	640,000	640,000	550,000
Illinois	440,000	550,000	530,000	560,000	550,000	540,000
Georgia	220,000	490,000	490,000	490,000	460,000	480,000
Arizona	330,000	510,000	490,000	530,000	560,000	460,000
North Carolina	260,000	370,000	360,000	380,000	380,000	370,000
New Jersey	350,000	440,000	420,000	470,000	400,000	360,000
Nevada	170,000	230,000	230,000	260,000	280,000	260,000
Other states	1,760,000	1,800,000	2,900,000	2,950,000	2,950,000	2,730,000

Detail may not sum to totals because of founding,

*Revised as noted in the 1/1/2007 unauthorized estimates report published in September 2008.

Source: U.S. Department of Homeland Security,

Table App-4. Modes of Entry for the Unauthorized Migrant Population

Entered Legally with Inspection	Non-Immigrant Visa Over-stayers	4 to 5.5 Million
	Border Crossing Card Violators	250,000 to 500,000
	Sub-total Legal Entries	*4.5 to 6 Million*
Entered Illegally without Inspection	Evaded the Immigration Inspectors and Border Patrol	6 to 7 Million
Estimated Total Unauthorized Population in 2006		11.5 to 12 Million

Source: Pew Hispanic Center Estimates based on the March 2005 Current Population Survey and Department of Homeland Security reports.

Figure App-5. Mexican-Born Population in the United States, 1850–2008

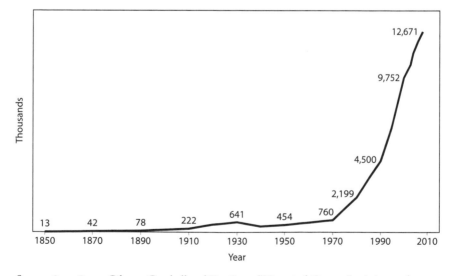

Source: 1850–1890—Gibson, Cambell and Kay Jung, "Historical Census Statistics on the Foreign-Born Population of the United States: 1850–2000," U.S. Census Bureau, Population Division, Working Paper No. 81, 2006; 1995–2008—Pew Hispanic Center tabulations from augmented March Current Population Surveys adjusted for undercount.

Figure App-6. Mexican-Born Population in the U.S. as Share of Mexicans
in the U.S. and Mexico, 1950–2008

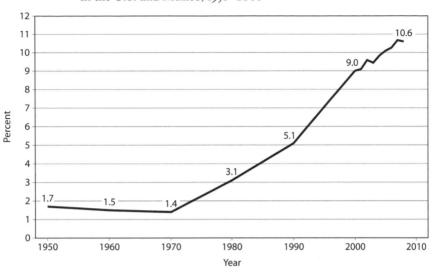

Source: Mexican data from CONAPO (National Population Council of mexico), United
Nations Population Division, and U.S. Census International Programs; for source
of U.S. data, see Figure 1.

Figure App-7. Mexican-born Population as Share of U.S. Foreign-born
Population, 1950–2008

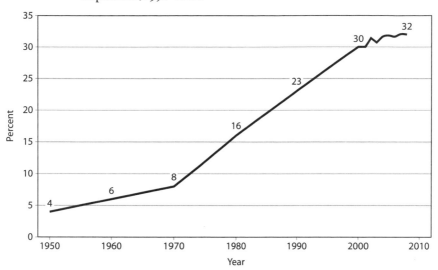

Source: 1850–1890—Gibson, Cambell and Kay Jung, "Historical Census Statistics on the
Foreign-Born Population of the United States: 1850–2000," U.S. Census Bureau,
Population Division, Working Paper No. 81, 2006; 1995–2008—Pew Hispanic
Center tabulations from augmented March Current Population Surveys adjusted
for undercount.

Table App-5. Hispanic or Latino Population for the United States, Regions, and States, and for Puerto Rico: 2000 and 2010

(For information on confidentiality protection, nonsampling error and definitions, see *www.census.gov/prod/cen2010/doc/sf1.pdf*)

Area	2000 Total	2000 Hispanic or Latino Number	2000 Hispanic or Latino Percent of total population	2010 Total	2010 Hispanic or Latino Number	2010 Hispanic or Latino Percent of total population	Population Change, 2000 to 2010 Total Number	Total Percent	Hispanic or Latino Number	Hispanic or Latino Percent
United States	281,421,906	35,305,818	12.5	308,745,538	50,477,594	16.3	27,323,632	9.7	15,171,776	43.0
REGION										
Northeast	53,594,378	5,254,087	9.8	55,317,240	6,991,969	12.6	1,722,862	3.2	1,737,882	33.1
Midwest	64,392,776	3,124,532	4.9	66,927,001	4,661,678	7.0	2,534,225	3.9	1,537,146	49.2
South	100,236,820	11,586,696	11.6	114,555,744	18,227,508	15.9	14,318,924	14.3	6,640,812	57.3
West	63,197,932	15,340,503	24.3	71,945,553	20,596,439	28.6	8,747,621	13.8	5,255,936	34.3
STATE										
Alabama	4,447,100	75,830	1.7	4,779,736	185,602	3.9	332,636	7.5	109,772	144.8
Alaska	626,932	25,852	4.1	710,231	39,249	5.5	83,299	13.3	13,397	51.8
Arizona	5,130,632	1,295,617	25.3	6,392,017	1,895,149	29.6	1,261,385	24.6	599,532	46.3
Arkansas	2,673,400	86,866	3.2	2,915,918	186,050	6.4	242,518	9.1	99,184	114.2
California	33,871,648	10,966,556	32.4	37,253,956	14,013,719	37.6	3,382,308	10.0	3,047,163	27.8
Colorado	4,301,261	735,601	17.1	5,029,196	1,038,687	20.7	727,935	16.9	303,086	41.2
Connecticut	3,405,565	320,323	9.4	3,574,097	479,087	13.4	168,532	4.9	158,764	49.6
Delaware	783,600	37,277	4.8	897,934	73,221	8.2	114,334	14.6	35,944	96.4
District of Columbia	572,059	44,953	7.9	601,723	54,749	9.1	29,664	5.2	9,796	21.8
Florida	15,982,378	2,682,715	16.8	18,801,310	4,223,806	22.5	2,818,932	17.6	1,541,091	57.4
Georgia	8,186,453	435,227	5.3	9,687,653	853,689	8.8	1,501,200	18.3	418,462	96.1
Hawaii	1,211,537	87,699	7.2	1,360,301	120,842	8.9	148,764	12.3	33,143	37.8
Idaho	1,293,953	101,690	7.9	1,567,582	175,901	11.2	273,629	21.1	74,211	73.0
Illinois	12,419,293	1,530,262	12.3	12,830,632	2,027,578	15.8	411,339	3.3	497,316	32.5
Indiana	6,080,485	214,536	3.5	6,483,802	389,707	6.0	403,317	6.6	175,171	81.7
Iowa	2,926,324	82,473	2.8	3,046,355	151,544	5.0	120,031	4.1	69,071	83.7
Kansas	2,688,418	188,252	7.0	2,853,118	300,042	10.5	164,700	6.1	111,790	59.4
Kentucky	4,041,769	59,939	1.5	4,339,367	132,836	3.1	297,598	7.4	72,897	121.6
Louisiana	4,468,976	107,738	2.4	4,533,372	192,560	4.2	64,396	1.4	84,822	78.7

Maine	1,274,923	9,360	0.7	1,328,361	16,935	1.3	53,438	4.2	7,575	80.9
Maryland	5,296,486	227,916	4.3	5,773,552	470,632	8.2	477,066	9.0	242,716	106.5
Massachusetts	6,349,097	428,729	6.8	6,547,629	627,654	9.6	198,532	3.1	198,925	46.4
Michigan	9,938,444	323,877	3.3	9,883,640	436,358	4.4	-54,804	-0.6	112,481	34.7
Minnesota	4,919,479	143,382	2.9	5,303,925	250,258	4.7	384,446	7.8	106,876	74.5
Mississippi	2,844,658	39,569	1.4	2,967,297	81,481	2.7	122,639	4.3	41,912	105.9
Missouri	5,595,211	118,592	2.1	5,988,927	212,470	3.5	393,716	7.0	93,878	79.2
Montana	902,195	18,081	2.0	989,415	28,565	2.9	87,220	9.7	10,484	58.0
Nebraska	1,711,263	94,425	5.5	1,826,341	167,405	9.2	115,078	6.7	72,980	77.3
Nevada	1,998,257	393,970	19.7	2,700,551	716,501	26.5	702,294	35.1	322,531	81.9
New Hampshire	1,235,786	20,489	1.7	1,316,470	36,704	2.8	80,684	6.5	16,215	79.1
New Jersey	8,414,350	1,117,191	13.3	8,791,894	1,555,144	17.7	377,544	4.5	437,953	39.2
New Mexico	1,819,046	765,386	42.1	2,059,179	953,403	46.3	240,133	13.2	188,017	24.6
New York	18,976,457	2,867,583	15.1	19,378,102	3,416,922	17.6	401,645	2.1	549,339	19.2
North Carolina	8,049,313	378,963	4.7	9,535,483	800,120	8.4	1,486,170	18.5	421,157	111.1
North Dakota	642,200	7,786	1.2	672,591	13,467	2.0	30,391	4.7	5,681	73.0
Ohio	11,353,140	217,123	1.9	11,536,504	354,674	3.1	183,364	1.6	137,551	63.4
Oklahoma	3,450,654	179,304	5.2	3,751,351	332,007	8.9	300,697	8.7	152,703	85.2
Oregon	3,421,399	275,314	8.0	3,831,074	450,062	11.7	409,675	12.0	174,748	63.5
Pennsylvania	12,281,054	394,088	3.2	12,702,379	719,660	5.7	421,325	3.4	325,572	82.6
Rhode Island	1,048,319	90,820	8.7	1,052,567	130,655	12.4	4,248	0.4	39,835	43.9
South Carolina	4,012,012	95,076	2.4	4,625,364	235,682	5.1	613,352	15.3	140,606	147.9
South Dakota	754,844	10,903	1.4	814,180	22,119	2.7	59,336	7.9	11,216	102.9
Tennessee	5,689,283	123,838	2.2	6,346,105	290,059	4.6	656,822	11.5	166,221	134.2
Texas	20,851,820	6,669,666	32.0	25,145,561	9,460,921	37.6	4,293,741	20.6	2,791,255	41.8
Utah	2,233,169	201,559	9.0	2,763,885	358,340	13.0	530,716	23.8	156,781	77.8
Vermont	608,827	5,504	0.9	625,741	9,208	1.5	16,914	2.8	3,704	67.3
Virginia	7,078,515	329,540	4.7	8,001,024	631,825	7.9	922,509	13.0	302,285	91.7
Washington	5,894,121	441,509	7.5	6,724,540	755,790	11.2	830,419	14.1	314,281	71.2
West Virginia	1,808,344	12,279	0.7	1,852,994	22,268	1.2	44,650	2.5	9,989	81.4
Wisconsin	5,363,675	192,921	3.6	5,686,986	336,056	5.9	323,311	6.0	143,135	74.2
Wyoming	493,782	31,669	6.4	563,626	50,231	8.9	69,844	14.1	18,562	58.6
Puerto Rico	**3,808,610**	**3,762,746**	**98.8**	**3,725,789**	**3,688,455**	**99.0**	**-82,821**	**-2.2**	**-74,291**	**-2.0**

Source: U.S. Census Bureau, *Census 2000 Summary File 1 and 2010 Summary File 1.*

Table App-6. Selected Characteristics of Immigrants and Natives[1]

	Natives (percent)	All Immigrants (percent)	Arrived 2000–2007 (percent)
Less than high school	7.5	29.0	35.5
High school only	30.9	24.8	24.6
Some College	30.7	17.7	13.9
Bachelor's	20.8	17.4	16.0
Graduate or Professional	10.1	11.0	10.0
Median Annual Earnings[3]	$40,344	$31,074	$24,712
Median Household Income[4]	$49,201	$43,933	$39,691
Average Household size[4]	2.43	3.11	3.06
Average Age[5]	35.9	40.5	29.4

Source: Center for Immigration Studies analysis of March 2007 Current Population Survey.

[1]Education figures are for persons 18 and older in the labor force

[2]Indicates the year that immigrants said they came to the United States

[3]Earnings are for full-time year-round workers

[4]Immigrant and native households based on nativity of household head.
 Income is from all sources.

[5]All persons

Table App-7. Educational Attainment, Ages 25–64

	Percent Less Than High School	Percent College or More
Guatemala	64.4	4.0
Mexico	60.0	5.8
El Salvador	54.7	7.2
Honduras	53.8	7.1
Dominican Republic	30.0	10.0
Brazil	26.9	31.4
Ecuador	26.7	15.8
Vietnam	21.3	31.7
Italy	19.7	20.2
Cuba	19.0	21.8
Haiti	17.6	23.8
Jamaica	16.0	28.1
China	15.8	54.8
Columbia	11.9	37.4
Iran	11.9	54.2
Poland	7.7	26.3
Peru	7.7	28.3
USSR	4.9	59.6
India	3.6	80.6
Korea	2.9	57.8
Philippines	2.7	51.7
Germany	2.6	50.0
United Kingdom	2.3	55.7
Canada	2.3	54.4
Japan	1.1	63.6
Immigrants	**30.6**	**29.1**
Hispanic Immigrants	50.8	9.8
Natives	**8.4**	**31.1**
Hispanic Natives	18.7	17.9
Non-Hispanic Natives	6.6	34.4
Non-Hispanic Black Natives	13.1	18.7

Source: Center for Immigration Studies analysis of March 2007 Current Population Survey. Figures for white and black natives are for those who chose only one race.

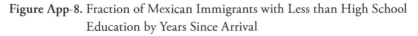

Figure App-8. Fraction of Mexican Immigrants with Less than High School Education by Years Since Arrival

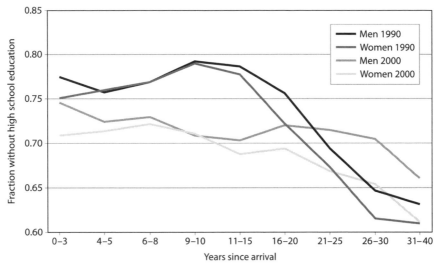

Figure App-9. Married-Couple Families by Nativity of Spouses and Nativity and Age of Related Household Members: 2000

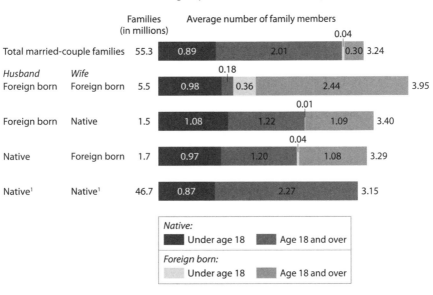

(Civilian noninstitutional population plus Armed Forces living off post or with their families on post)

1. The proportion of foreign-born family members in married couple households where both spouses are native appears to be negligible. Due to sample size the number cannot be determined.

Source: U.S. Census Bureau, 2000b, Table 12-4.

Table App-8. The Activities and Attitudes of Latino Immigrants

Transnational Activities with Native Country	Share of Hispanic Foreign-Born (percent)
Has made at least one trip back	65
Has traveled backj in the past two years	29
Sends remittances	51
Phones at least weekly	41
Never phones home	24
Sends email	15
Owns property	27
Belongs to Immigrant civic organization	9
National Identity and Attachment—U.S. vs. Native Country	
Plans to stay in U.S.	66
More concerned about politics in U.S.	60
Native country is "real homeland"	49
Ever describes self as an American	33
Identifies self first as national of native country	62
U.S. Compared to Native Country	
Racial/ethnic relations better in U.S.	30
Morals better in U.S.	28
Political traditions better in U.S.	55
Expectations of Latino Children's Future	
Children will have better income and jobs	80
Children will stay close to family	68
Expects own children to stay	56
How Much Transnationalism?	
Sends remittances, phones weekly and has traveled in past two years	9
Does not send remittances, phone weekly and \has not traveled back in past two years	28

Source: Pew Hispanic Center, 2006 National Survey of Latinos

Figure App-10. Communication and the Impact of Years in the U.S.

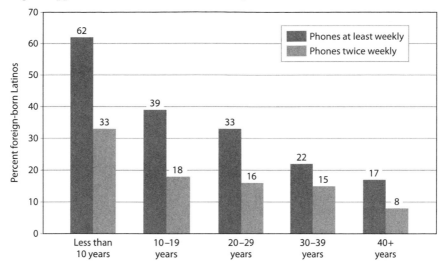

Source: Pew Hispanic Center, 2006 National Survey of Latinos

Figure App-11. Identity and Time in Country

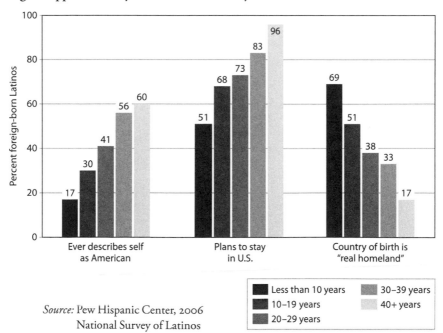

Source: Pew Hispanic Center, 2006
National Survey of Latinos

Figure App-12. Citizenship and Transnational Activities

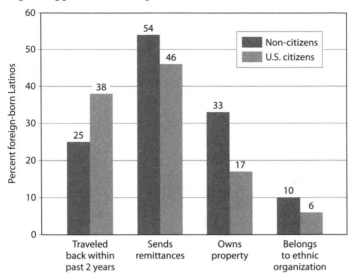

Source: Pew Hispanic Center, 2006 National Survey of Latinos

Figure App-13. Identity and Citizenship Status

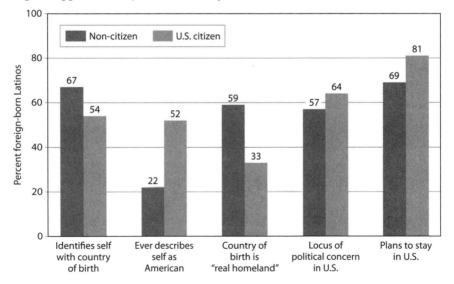

Source: Pew Hispanic Center, 2006 National Survey of Latinos

Figure App-14. Fluency in Spoken English Rises Across Hispanic Generations

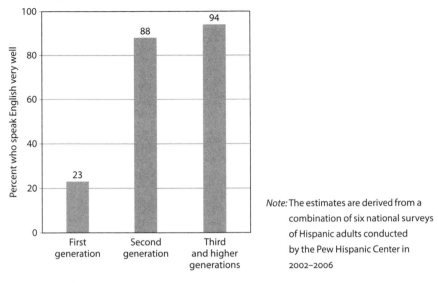

Note: The estimates are derived from a combination of six national surveys of Hispanic adults conducted by the Pew Hispanic Center in 2002–2006

Source: Pew Hispanic center

Figure App-15. English-Speaking Ability by Hispanic Generation

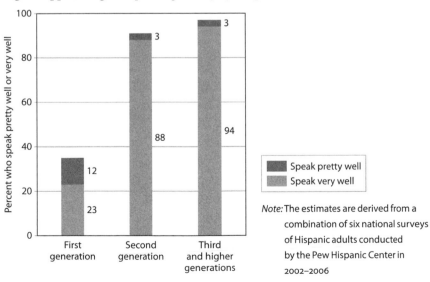

Note: The estimates are derived from a combination of six national surveys of Hispanic adults conducted by the Pew Hispanic Center in 2002–2006

Source: Pew Hispanic center

Table App-9. Statistical Portrait of the Foreign-Born Population in the United States, 2007.

Marital Status, by Region of Birth: 2007
Universe: 2007 resident population ages 18 and older

	Now Married	Separated	Divorced	Widowed	Never Married	Total
All native born	99,359,755	4,122,791	22,786,104	13,275,601	53,073,038	192,617,289
All foreign born	21,482,868	1,140,975	2,498,395	1,839,025	8,129,683	35,090,946
Mexico	6,512,471	443,640	523,937	315,982	2,840,296	10,636,326
South and East Asia	5,717,666	119,086	415,905	442,281	1,650,492	8,345,430
Caribbean	1,595,190	181,118	397,706	200,735	801,320	3,176,069
Central America	1,273,401	131,410	185,050	85,017	856,688	2,531,566
South America	1,373,630	105,717	241,098	92,335	556,436	2,369,216
Middle East	801,312	20,355	93,005	66,705	245,732	1,227,109
All Other	4,209,198	139,649	641,694	635,970	1,178,719	6,805,230
Percent Distribution						
All native born	51.6	2.1	11.8	6.9	27.6	100.0
All foreign born	61.2	3.3	7.1	5.2	23.2	100.0
Mexico	61.2	4.2	4.9	3.0	26.7	100.0
South and East Asia	68.5	1.4	5.0	5.3	19.8	100.0
Caribbean	50.2	5.7	12.5	6.3	25.2	100.0
Central America	50.3	5.2	7.3	3.4	33.8	100.0
South America	58.0	4.5	10.2	3.9	23.5	100.0
Middle East	65.3	1.7	7.6	5.4	20.0	100.0
All Other	61.9	2.1	9.4	9.3	17.3	100.0

Note: Middle East consists of Afghanistan, Iran, Iraq, Israel/Palestine, Jordan, Kuwait, Lebanon, Saudi Arabia, Syria, Turkey, Yemen, Algeria, Egypt, Morocco and Sudan.
Source: Pew Hispanic Center tabula lions of 2007 American Community Survey (1% IPUMS)

Table App-10A. Statistical Portrait of the Foreign-Born Population
in the United States, 2007

Full-time, Year-round Workers, by Personal Earnings and Region of Birth: 2007
Universe: 2007 resident population defined for persons who worked
at least 35 hours per week and at least 48 weeks in the past year

	Now Married	Separated	Divorced	Widowed	Never Married	Total
All native born	99,359,755	4,122,791	22,786,104	13,275,601	53,073,038	192,617,289
All foreign born	21,482,868	1,140,975	2,498,395	1,839,025	8,129,683	35,090,946
Mexico	6,512,471	443,640	523,937	315,982	2,840,296	10,636,326
South and East Asia	5,717,666	119,086	415,905	442,281	1,650,492	8,345,430
Caribbean	1,595,190	181,118	397,706	200,735	801,320	3,176,069
Central America	1,273,401	131,410	185,050	85,017	856,688	2,531,566
South America	1,373,630	105,717	241,098	92,335	556,436	2,369,216
Middle East	801,312	20,355	93,005	66,705	245,732	1,227,109
All Other	4,209,198	139,649	641,694	635,970	1,178,719	6,805,230
Percent Distribution						
All native born	51.6	2.1	11.8	6.9	27.6	100.0
All foreign born	61.2	3.3	7.1	5.2	23.2	100.0
Mexico	61.2	4.2	4.9	3.0	26.7	100.0
South and East Asia	68.5	1.4	5.0	5.3	19.8	100.0
Caribbean	50.2	5.7	12.5	6.3	25.2	100.0
Central America	50.3	5.2	7.3	3.4	33.8	100.0
South America	58.0	4.5	10.2	3.9	23.5	100.0
Middle East	65.3	1.7	7.6	5.4	20.0	100.0
All Other	61.9	2.1	9.4	9.3	17.3	100.0

Note: Middle East consists of Afghanistan, Iran, Iraq, Israel/Palestine, Jordan, Kuwait, Lebanon, Saudi
Arabia, Syria, Turkey, Yemen, Algeria, Egypt, Morocco and Sudan.
Source: Pew Hispanic Center tabula lions of 2007 American Community Survey (1% IPUMS)

Table App-10B. Statistical Portrait of the Foreign-Born Population
in the United States, 2007

Full-time, Year-round Workers, by Personal Earnings and Region of Birth: 2007
Universe: 2007 resident population defined for persons who worked
at least 35 hours per week and at least 48 weeks in the past year

	less than $20,000	$20,000 to $49,999	$50,000 or more	Total
All native born	10,462,509	41,332,275	32,112, 797	83,907,581
All foreign born	3,922,860	8,163.642	4, 745,274	16,831,776
Mexico	1,989,292	2,825,629	527,972	5,342,893
South and East Asia	521,850	1,662,605	1,812,591	3,997,046
Caribbean	324,377	833,795	382 639	1,540,811
Central America	461,494	740,883	179,174	1,381,551
South America	255,317	652,735	304,702	1,212,754
Middle East	66,244	202,244	269,521	538,009
All other	304,286	1,245,751	1,268,675	2,818,712
Percent Distribution				
All native born	12.5	49.3	38.3	100.0
All foreign born	23.3	48.5	28.2	100.0
Mexico	37.2	52.9	9.9	100.0
South and East Asia	13.1	41.6	45.3	100.0
Carribean	21.1	54.1	24.8	100.0
Central America	33.4	53.6	13.0	100.0
South America	21.1	53.8	25.1	100.0
Middle East	12.3	37.6	50.1	100.0
All other	10.8	44.2	45.0	100.0

Notes: Due to the way in which IPUMS adjusts annual incomes, these data will differ from those that
might be provided by the U.S. Census Bureau. Middle East consists of Afghanistan, Iran, Iraq,
Israel/Palestine, Jordan, Kuwait, Lebanon, Saudi Arabia, Syria, Turkey, Yemen, Algeria, Egypt,
Morocco and Sudan.

Source: Pew Hispanic Center tabulations of 2007 American Community Survey (1% IPUMS)

Table App-11. Poverty, Near Poverty and Income Based on Length of Time in U.S.

Number of Years in the United States[1]	Poverty (percent)	In or Near Poverty[2] (percent)	Average Age for Poverty Figures	Median Earnings Full-Time, Year-Round Workers	Average Age for Full-Time, Year-Round Workers
>57	15.9	47.49	77	$50,056	67
48-57	11.7	48.0	69	$46,188	59
43-47	9.9	29.2	63	$46,223	57
38-42	10.6	29.5	59	$45,060	53
33-37	10.0	30.3	54	$38,272	50
28-32	9.8	30.0	51	$40,412	47
26-27	11.3	35.5	48	$35,603	45
24-25	12.8	31.3	45	$36,081	43
22-23	12.4	36.3	44	$32,363	43
20-21	15.1	33.4	42	$32,191	42
18-19	13.1	40.1	41	$31,691	40
16-17	13.2	39.5	39	$31,886	40
14-15	16.1	41.1	37	$31,590	38
12-13	14.9	42.1	37	$26,831	38
10-11	15.6	40.7	35	$28,081	38
8-9	17.2	45.0	32	$27,092	36
6-7	18.3	47.2	31	$25,614	35
4-5	18.9	50.6	29	$23,631	35
<4	24.3	49.4	28	$24,032	33
All Immigrants	15.2	40.1	41	$31,074	41
Natives[3]	11.4	28.0	37	$40,344	42

[1] Based on the year that immigrants said they came to the United States to stay.

[2] In or near-poverty defined as income under 200 percent of the poverty threshold.

[3] Poverty and age figures to native exclude the U.S.-born children (under 18) of immigrant fathers.

Source: Center for Immigration Studies analysis of March 2007 Current Population Survey.

Table App-12. Household Income and Size by State

	Median Household Income		Number of Persons Per Household		Per-Person Median Household Income		Percent Native Per-Person Income is Higher than Immigrant
	Immigrant	Native	Immigrant	Native	Immigrant	Native	Immigrant
Arizona	$30,590	$51,087	3.2	2.5	$9,559	$20,435	114
Colorado	$35,430	$57,891	3.2	2.5	$11,072	$23,156	109
Texas	$32,988	$46,332	3.3	2.5	$9,996	$18,533	85
California	$47,292	$60,011	3.4	2.5	$13,909	$24,004	73
L.A. County	$43,618	$55,087	3.3	2.4	$13,218	$22,953	74
Massachusetts	$41,634	$59,446	2.9	2.5	$14,357	$23,778	66
Florida	$41,301	$47,050	3.2	2.3	$12,907	$20,457	58
Nevada	$46,863	$54,766	3.1	2.4	$15,117	$22,819	51
Georgia	$49,115	$50,758	3.4	2.4	$14,446	$21,149	46
New York	$41,212	$51,052	2.8	2.4	$14,719	$21,272	45
New York City	$38,116	$41,688	2.8	2.2	$13,613	$18,949	39
Illinois	$48,965	$48,866	3.2	2.4	$15,302	$20,361	33
North Carolina	$41,230	$39,750	3.3	2.4	$12,494	$16,563	33
New Jersey	$66,170	$68,988	3.1	2.5	$21,345	$27,595	29
Maryland	$64,160	$64,273	3.2	2.5	$20,050	$25,709	28
Virginia	$56,605	$57,536	3.1	2.5	$18,260	$23,014	26
Nation	$43,933	$49,201	3.1	2.4	$14,172	$20,500	45

Source: Center for Immigration Studies analysis of the March 2007 Current Population Survey.

Figure App-16. Increase in the Supply of Workers Caused by
Post-2000 Immigration[1]

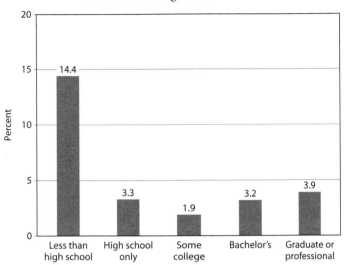

1. Figures are for persons 18 and older in the labor force who are immigrants who arrived
in 2000 or later relative to natives and pre-2000 immigrants in the labor force.

Source: Center for Immigration Studies analysis of March 2007 Current Population Survey

Table App-13. Immigrants and Natives by Occupation in 2007,
Ranked by Native Unemployment Rate of Occupation (thousands)

	Native Unemployment Rate (percent)	Share of Occupation Comprised of Immigrants (percent)	Number of Natives Employed	Number of Unemployed Natives	Number of Recently Arrived Immigrants (2000–07) Employed[1]
Total	4.8	15.7	122,347	6,130	5,569
Farming, Fishing & Forestry	10.9	36.3	580	71	95
Building Cleaning & Maintenance	10.8	36.0	3,276	396	532
Construction & Extraction	10.6	30.0	6,581	778	1,142
Construction Only	10.7	29.6	6,383	764	1,139
Food Service & Preparation	7.9	22.5	6,067	518	569
Waiters/Waitresses	6.4	14.7	1,669	114	93
Transportation & Moving	7.4	17.8	7,058	566	362
Production	6.1	21.6	7,394	484	513
Meat/Poultry/Fish Processing	7.9	33.9	363	31	66
Sales	4.6	12.0	14,661	699	371
Personal Care & Service	4.3	18.9	3,811	172	194
Arts, Entertainment & Media	4.3	11.9	2,462	111	54
Protective Service	4.2	5.8	2,770	120	32
Healthcare Support	4.0	17.9	2,676	112	107
Office & Administrative Support	3.8	9.7	17,621	705	305
Installation and Repair	3.8	13.7	4,338	171	135
Business and Financial	2.5	11.4	5,517	144	110
Legal Occupation	2.3	5.9	1,566	37	14
Life, Physical & Social Science	2.2	20.8	1,140	26	109
Management Occupations	1.8	10.6	13,552	252	230
Computer/Mathematical	1.7	21.8	2,563	45	230
Community & Social Service	1.7	9.2	2,093	36	29
Architecture & Engineering	1.6	16.2	2,447	39	103
Education, Training	1.4	8.9	7,976	112	182
Healthcare Practitioner	1.0	13.7	6,198	64	151

[1]Indicates the year that immigrants said they came to the United States.

Source: Center for Immigration Studies analysis of March 2007 Current Population Survey.
Figures are for persons 16 and older in the civil labor force. Totals include figures for persons who did not report and occupation

Table App-14: Self-Employment For Employed Persons 25 and Older (percent)

Korea	30.8
Iran	27.5
Italy	25.2
Vietnam	19.5
Canada	18.4
Poland	17.5
Peru	16.1
Germany	15.2
Cuba	14.5
Brazil	13.9
Former USSR	12.7
Columbia	11.9
United Kingdom	11.6
India	11.1
China	11.1
Japan	10.9
Honduras	10.2
Jamaica	9.1
El Salvador	7.9
Guatemala	7.8
Mexico	7.8
Ecuador	7.3
Philippines	5.8
Haiti	5.5
Dominican Republic	5.1
All Immigrants	**11.3**
Hispanics	7.5
All Natives	**12.6**
Hispanic Natives	8.8
Non-Hispanic White Natives	17.2
Non-Hispanic Black Natives	7.0
Immigrant Average Self-Employment Income	$24,737
Native Average Self-Employment Income	$25,269

Source: Center for Immigration Studies analysis of March 2007 Current Population Survey. Figures for white and black natives are for those who chose only one race.

Figure App-17. Labor Force Participation Rates of the Foreign-Born Population 25 to 54 Years Old by Region of Birth and Sex: 2000

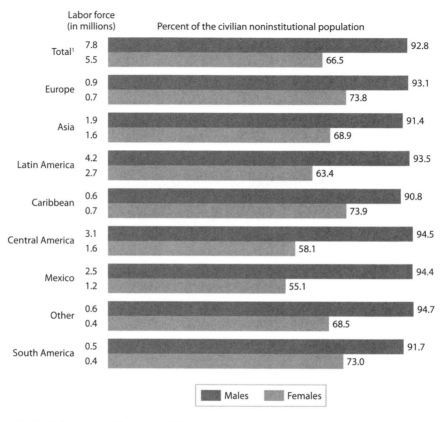

1. Total includes areas not shown separately

Source: U.S. Census Bureau, 2001, Table 15-3D

Figure App-18. Immigration and the Rate of Employment, 1990–2005

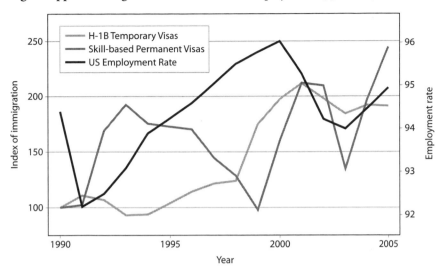

Sources: DHS, "2005 Yearbook"; B. Lindsay Lowell, "H-1B Temporary Workers: Estimating the Population" (mimeo, Institute for the Study of International Migration, George-town University, 2000); and the U.S. Department of State Office of Visa Statistics (http://travel.state.gov/visa/frvi/statistics/). For further information on calculations of values, see footnote 31.

Figure App-19. Households Receiving Selected Means-Tested Noncash or Cash
Benefits by Nativity, Length of Residence in the United States,
and Citizenship Status of the Householder: 1999

(Households as of march 2000. Civilian noninstitutional population
plus Armed Forces living off post or with their families on post)

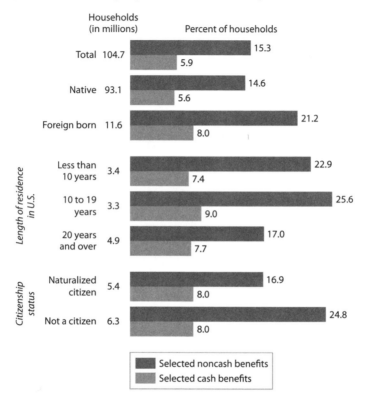

Source: U.S Census Bureau, 2001, Tables 20-1A, 20-1B, 20-1C, 20-2A, 20-2B, and 20-2C.

Index

About the Author

ALVARO VARGAS LLOSA is Senior
Fellow at the Independent Institute. He was named
Young Global Leader by the World Economic Forum
in Davos, Switzerland, and he has been a nationally
syndicated columnist for the *Washington Post Writers
Group*. Among his books, *Liberty for Latin America*
received the Sir Anthony Fisher International Me-
morial Award and *Lessons from the Poor: Triumph
of the Entrepreneurial Spirit* received the Templeton
Freedom Award. His other books include *Guide to
the Perfect Latin American Idiot* (with Carlos Alberto Montaner and Plinio
Apuleyo Mendoza), *The Che Guevara Myth and the Future of Liberty, Riding the
Tiger, El Exilio Indomable, Cuando Hablaba Dormido, El Diablo en Campaña,
En el Reino del Espanto, Tiempos de Resistencia*, and *La Contenta Barbarie*.

Mr. Vargas Llosa wrote and hosted the National Geographic, four-part
television documentary series on contemporary Latin American history, *Consequences*. He has also been a member of board of the Miami Herald Publishing
Company and op-ed page editor and columnist at the *Miami Herald,* and a
contributor to the *Wall Street Journal, New York Times, Los Angeles Times,* BBC
World Service, *Time Magazine, Granta* magazine, *El País, International Herald
Tribune*, and many other media.

He is also the recipient of the Juan Bautista Alberdi Award for his defense of
freedom across the western hemisphere and the Freedom of Expression Award
from the Association of Ibero-American Journalists. He received his B.Sc. in
international history and M.A. from the London School of Economics.

Independent Studies in Political Economy